"The narrative moves like the best Nirvana anthems. Smells like the real deal." —*Time*

"Until someone writes a book that is more daring in its psychological and social analysis—and as thorough in its reporting—*Heavier Than Heaven* will be the place to start the dark journey into Cobain's claustrophobic inner world." —*Rolling Stone*

"What emerges . . . is the life story of someone who never grew up, someone whose maturation was half done before he was twenty-one, someone who extracted art from a perpetual adolescence that was over much too soon." —*The New Yorker*

"The results of Cross' assiduous reporting show through in every chapter. A remarkable portrait." —*Entertainment Weekly*

"One of the most moving and revealing books ever written about a rock star. An invaluable look at the life of a troubled artist." —*Los Angeles Times*

"In his early teens, Cobain told a friend, 'I'm going to be a superstar musician, kill myself and go out in a flame of glory.' This well-reported book . . . provides the most grounded account of how Cobain, not too many years later, did just that." —*The New York Times Book Review*

"The biography that the most important rocker of his generation has always deserved: exhaustively researched, full of insight into the 'real' Cobain as opposed to the manipulated media image, and written in a clear and compelling . . . voice." —*Chicago Sun-Times*

"A cautionary tale of a talented, lucky musician who became fatally confused about whether fame was a reward or a death sentence." —*People*

HEAVIER THAN HEAVEN

heavier than heaven

A BIOGRAPHY OF
KURT COBAIN

CHARLES R. CROSS

HYPERION
NEW YORK

Library of Congress Cataloging-in-Publication Data

Cross, Charles R.
    Heavier than heaven : a biography of Kurt Cobain / by Charles R. Cross.—1st ed.
      p.   cm.
    ISBN 0-7868-6505-9
    1. Cobain, Kurt, 1967-1994. 2. Rock musicians—United States—Biography. I. Title.
    ML420.C59 C76   2001
    782.42166'092—dc21
    [B]   2001024187

Paperback ISBN 0-7868-8402-9
ISBN-13: 978-0-7868-8402-5

Book design by Casey Hampton

FIRST PAPERBACK EDITION

20 19 18 17 16 15 14 13 12 11

FOR MY FAMILY, FOR CHRISTINA,
AND FOR ASHLAND

CONTENTS

AUTHOR'S NOTE

Less than a mile from my home sits a building that can send a graveyard chill up my spine as easily as an Alfred Hitchcock film. The gray one-story structure is surrounded by a tall chain link fence, unusual security in a middle-class neighborhood of sandwich shops and apartments. Three businesses are behind the fencing: a hair salon; a State Farm Insurance office, and "Stan Baker, Shooting Sports." It was in this third business where on March 30, 1994, Kurt Cobain and a friend purchased a Remington shotgun. The owner later told a newspaper he was unsure why anyone would be buying such a gun when it wasn't "hunting season."

Every time I drive by Stan Baker's I feel as if I've witnessed a particularly horrific roadside accident, and in a way I have. The events that followed Kurt's gun shop purchase leave me with both a deep unease and the desire to make inquiries that I know by their very nature are unknowable. They are questions concerning spirituality, the role of madness in artistic genius, the ravages of drug abuse on a soul, and the desire to understand the chasm between the inner and outer man. These questions are all too real to any family touched by addiction, depression, or suicide. For families enshrouded by such darkness—which includes mine—this need to ask questions that can't be answered is its own kind of haunting.

Those mysteries fueled this book but in a way its genesis began years before during my youth in a small Washington town where monthly packages from the Columbia Record and Tape Club offered me rock 'n' roll salvation from circumstance. Inspired in part by those mail-order albums, I left that rural landscape to become a writer and magazine editor in Seattle. Across the state and a few years later, Kurt Cobain found a similar transcendence through the same record club and he turned that interest into a career as a musician. Our paths would intersect in 1989 when my magazine did the first cover story on Nirvana.

It was easy to love Nirvana because no matter how great their fame and glory they always seemed like underdogs, and the same could be said for Kurt. He began his artistic life in a double-wide trailer copying Norman Rockwell illustrations and went on to develop a story-telling gift that would infuse his music with a special beauty. As a rock star, he always seemed a misfit, but I cherished the way he combined adolescent humor with old man crustiness. Seeing him around Seattle—impossible to miss with his ridiculous cap with flaps over his ears—he was a character in an industry with few true characters.

There were many times writing this book when that humor seemed the only beacon of light in a Sisyphean task. *Heavier Than Heaven* encompassed four years of research, 400 interviews, numerous file cabinets of documents, hundreds of musical recordings, many sleepless nights, and miles and miles driving between Seattle and Aberdeen. The research took me places—both emotional and physical—that I thought I'd never go. There were moments of great elation, as when I first heard the unreleased "You Know You're Right," a song I'd argue ranks with Kurt's best. Yet for every joyful discovery, there were times of almost unbearable grief, as when I held Kurt's suicide note in my hand, observing it was stored in a heart-shaped box next to a keepsake lock of his blond hair.

My goal with *Heavier Than Heaven* was to honor Kurt Cobain by telling the story of his life—of that hair and that note—without judgment. That approach was only possible because of the generous assistance of Kurt's closest friends, his family, and his bandmates. Nearly everyone I desired to interview eventually shared their memories—the only exceptions were a few individuals with plans to write their own histories, and I wish them the best in those efforts. Kurt's life was a complicated puzzle, all the more complex because he kept so many parts hidden, and that compartmentalization was both an end result of addiction, and a breeding ground for it.

At times I imagined I was studying a spy, a skilled double agent, who had mastered the art of making sure that no one person knew all the details of his life.

A friend of mine, herself a recovering drug addict, once described what she called the "no talk" rule of families like hers. "We grew up in households," she said, "where we were told: 'don't ask, don't talk, and don't tell.' It was a code of secrecy, and out of those secrets and lies a powerful shame overtook me." This book is for all those with the courage to tell the truth, to ask painful questions, and to break free of the shadows of the past.

—*Charles R. Cross*
Seattle, Washington,
April 2001

HEAVIER THAN HEAVEN

NEW YORK, NEW YORK
JANUARY 12, 1992

Heavier Than Heaven
—A slogan used by British concert promoters to describe
Nirvana's 1989 tour with the band Tad. It summed up both
Nirvana's "heavy" sound and the heft of 300-pound Tad
Doyle.

The first time he saw heaven came exactly six hours
and fifty-seven minutes after the very moment an entire generation fell
in love with him. It was, remarkably, his first death, and only the earliest
of many little deaths that would follow. For the generation smitten with
him, it was an impassioned, powerful, and binding devotion—the kind
of love that even as it begins you know is preordained to break your
heart and to end like a Greek tragedy.

It was January 12, 1992, a clear but chilly Sunday morning. The
temperature in New York City would eventually rise to 44 degrees,
but at 7 a.m., in a small suite of the Omni Hotel, it was near freezing.
A window had been left open to air out the stench of cigarettes, and
the Manhattan morning had stolen all warmth. The room itself looked
like a tempest had engulfed it: Scattered on the floor, with the random-
ness of a blind man's rummage sale, were clumps of dresses, shirts, and
shoes. Toward the suite's double doors stood a half dozen serving trays
covered with the remnants of several days of room service meals. Half-
eaten rolls and rancid slices of cheese littered the tray tops, and a handful
of fruit flies hovered over some wilted lettuce. This was not the typical
condition of a four-star hotel room—it was the consequence of someone warning housekeeping to stay out of the room. They had altered a

"Do Not Disturb" sign to read, "Do Not EVER Disturb! We're Fuck-ing!"

There was no intercourse this morning. Asleep in the king-size bed was 26-year-old Courtney Love. She was wearing an antique Victorian slip, and her long blond hair spread out over the sheet like the tresses of a character in a fairy tale. Next to her was a deep impression in the bedding, where a person had recently lain. Like the opening scene of a film noir, there was a dead body in the room.

"I woke up at 7 a.m. and he wasn't in the bed," remembered Love. "I've never been so scared."

Missing from the bed was 24-year-old Kurt Cobain. Less than seven hours earlier, Kurt and his band Nirvana had been the musical act on "Saturday Night Live." Their appearance on the program would prove to be a watershed moment in the history of rock 'n' roll: the first time a grunge band had received live national television exposure. It was the same weekend that Nirvana's major label debut, *Nevermind*, knocked Michael Jackson out of the No. 1 spot on the *Billboard* charts, becoming the best-selling album in the nation. While it wasn't exactly overnight success—the band had been together four years—the manner in which Nirvana had taken the music industry by surprise was unparalleled. Vir-tually unknown a year before, Nirvana stormed the charts with their "Smells Like Teen Spirit," which became 1991's most recognizable song, its opening guitar riff signifying the true beginning of nineties rock.

And there had never quite been a rock star like Kurt Cobain. He was more an anti-star than a celebrity, refusing to take a limo to NBC and bringing a thrift-store sensibility to everything he did. For "Saturday Night Live" he wore the same clothes from the previous two days: a pair of Converse tennis shoes, jeans with big holes in the knees, a T-shirt advertising an obscure band, and a Mister Rogers–style cardigan sweater. He hadn't washed his hair for a week, but had dyed it with strawberry Kool-Aid, which made his blond locks look like they'd been matted with dried blood. Never before in the history of live television had a performer put so little care into his appearance or hygiene, or so it seemed.

Kurt was a complicated, contradictory misanthrope, and what at times appeared to be an accidental revolution showed hints of careful orchestration. He professed in many interviews to detest the exposure he'd gotten on MTV, yet he repeatedly called his managers to complain that the network didn't play his videos nearly enough. He obsessively—and compulsively—planned every musical or career direction, writing ideas out in his journals years before he executed them, yet when he was bestowed the honors he had sought, he acted as if it were an inconvenience to get out of bed. He was a man of imposing will, yet equally driven by a powerful self-hatred. Even those who knew him best felt they knew him hardly at all—the happenings of that Sunday morning would attest to that.

After finishing "Saturday Night Live" and skipping the cast party, explaining it was "not his style," Kurt had given a two-hour interview to a radio journalist, which finished at four in the morning. His working day was finally over, and by any standard it had been exceptionally successful: He'd headlined "Saturday Night Live," had seen his album hit No. 1, and "Weird Al" Yankovic had asked permission to do a parody of "Teen Spirit." These events, taken together, surely marked the apogee of his short career, the kind of recognition most performers only dream of, and that Kurt himself had fantasized about as a teenager.

Growing up in a small town in southwestern Washington state, Kurt had never missed an episode of "Saturday Night Live," and had bragged to his friends in junior high school that one day he'd be a star. A decade later, he was the most celebrated figure in music. After just his second album he was being hailed as the greatest songwriter of his generation; only two years before, he had been turned down for a job cleaning dog kennels.

But in the predawn hours, Kurt felt neither vindication nor an urge to celebrate; if anything, the attention had increased his usual malaise. He felt physically ill, suffering from what he described as "recurrent burning nauseous pain" in his stomach, made worse by stress. Fame and success only seemed to make him feel worse. Kurt and his fiancée, Courtney Love, were the most talked-about couple in rock 'n' roll, though some of that talk was about drug abuse. Kurt had always believed that recognition for his talent would cure the many emotional pains that marked his early life; becoming successful had proven the folly of this and increased the shame he felt that his booming popularity coincided with an escalating drug habit.

In his hotel room, in the early hours of the morning, Kurt had taken a small plastic baggie of China white heroin, prepared it for a syringe, and injected it into his arm. This in itself was not unusual, since Kurt had been doing heroin regularly for several months, with Love joining him in the two months they'd been a couple. But this particular night, as Courtney slept, Kurt had recklessly—or intentionally—used far more heroin than was safe. The overdose turned his skin an aqua-green hue, stopped his breathing, and made his muscles as stiff as coaxial cable. He slipped off the bed and landed facedown in a pile of clothes, looking like a corpse haphazardly discarded by a serial killer.

"It wasn't that he OD'd," Love recalled. "It was that he was DEAD. If I hadn't woken up at seven . . . I don't know, maybe I sensed it. It was so fucked. It was sick and psycho." Love frantically began a resuscitation effort that would eventually become commonplace for her: She threw cold water on her fiancé and punched him in the solar plexus so as to make his lungs begin to move air. When her first actions didn't get a response, she went through the cycle again like a determined paramedic working on a heart-attack victim. Finally, after several minutes of effort, Courtney heard a gasp, signifying Kurt was breathing once again. She continued to revive him by splashing water on his face and moving his limbs. Within a few minutes, he was sitting up, talking, and though still very stoned, wearing a self-possessed smirk, almost as if he were proud of his feat. It was his first near-death overdose. It had come on the very day he had become a star.

In the course of one singular day, Kurt had been born in the public eye, died in the privacy of his own darkness, and was resurrected by a force of love. It was an extraordinary feat, implausible, and almost impossible, but the same could be said for so much of his outsized life, beginning with where he'd come from.

1 YELLING LOUDLY AT FIRST

> *He makes his wants known by yelling loudly at first, then crying if*
> *the first technique doesn't work.*
> —Excerpt from a report by his aunt on the eighteen-month-old
> Kurt Cobain.

Kurt Donald Cobain was born on the twentieth of February, 1967, in a hospital on a hill overlooking Aberdeen, Washington. His parents lived in neighboring Hoquiam, but it was appropriate that Aberdeen stand as Kurt's birthplace—he would spend three quarters of his life within ten miles of the hospital and would be forever profoundly connected to this landscape.

Anyone looking out from Grays Harbor Community Hospital that rainy Monday would have seen a land of harsh beauty, where forests, mountains, rivers, and a mighty ocean intersected in a magnificent vista. Tree-covered hills surrounded the intersection of three rivers, which fed into the nearby Pacific Ocean. In the center of it all was Aberdeen, the largest city in Grays Harbor County, with a population of 19,000. Immediately to the west was smaller Hoquiam, where Kurt's parents, Don and Wendy, lived in a tiny bungalow. And south across the Chehalis River was Cosmopolis, where his mother's family, the Fradenburgs, were from. On a day when it wasn't raining—which was a rare day in a region that got over 80 inches of precipitation a year—one could see the nine miles to Montesano, where Kurt's grandfather Leland Cobain grew up. It was a small enough world, with so few degrees of separation that Kurt would eventually become Aberdeen's most famous product.

The view from the three-story hospital was dominated by the sixth busiest working harbor on the West Coast. There were so many pieces of timber floating in the Chehalis that you could imagine using them to walk across the two-mile mouth. To the east was Aberdeen's downtown, where merchants complained that the constant rumbling of logging trucks scared away shoppers. It was a city at work, and that work almost entirely depended on turning Douglas fir trees from the surrounding hills into commerce. Aberdeen was home to 37 different lumber, pulp, shingle, or saw mills—their smokestacks dwarfed the town's tallest building, which had only seven stories. Directly down the hill from the hospital was the gigantic Rayonier Mill smokestack, the biggest tower of all, which stretched 150 feet toward the heavens and spewed forth an unending celestial cloud of wood-pulp effluence.

Yet as Aberdeen buzzed with motion, at the time of Kurt's birth its economy was slowly contracting. The county was one of the few in the state with a declining population, as the unemployed tried their luck elsewhere. The timber industry had begun to suffer the consequences of offshore competition and over-logging. The landscape already showed marked signs of such overuse: There were swaths of clear-cut forests outside of town, now simply a reminder of early settlers who had "tried to cut it all," as per the title of a local history book. Unemployment exacted a darker social price on the community in the form of increasing alcoholism, domestic violence, and suicide. There were 27 taverns in 1967, and the downtown core included many abandoned buildings, some of which had been brothels before they were closed in the late fifties. The city was so infamous for whorehouses that in 1952 *Look* magazine called it "one of the hot spots in America's battle against sin."

Yet the urban blight of downtown Aberdeen was paired with a close-knit social community where neighbors helped neighbors, parents were involved in schools, and family ties remained strong among a diverse immigrant population. Churches outnumbered taverns, and it was a place, like much of small-town America in the mid-sixties, where kids on bikes were given free rein in their neighborhoods. The entire city would become Kurt's backyard as he grew up.

Like most first births, Kurt's was a celebrated arrival, both for his parents and for the larger family. He had six aunts and uncles on his mother's side; two uncles on his father's side; and he was the first grandchild for both family trees. These were large families, and when his mother went to print up birth announcements, she used up 50 before she was through the immediate relations. A line in the *Aberdeen Daily World*'s birth column on February 23 noted Kurt's arrival to the rest of the world: "To Mr. and Mrs. Donald Cobain, 2830½ Aberdeen Avenue, Hoquiam, February 20, at Community Hospital, a son."

Kurt weighed seven pounds, seven and one-half ounces at birth, and his hair and complexion were dark. Within five months, his baby hair would turn blond, and his coloring would turn fair. His father's family had French and Irish roots—they had immigrated from Skey Townland in County Tyrone, Ireland, in 1875—and Kurt inherited his angular chin from this side. From the Fradenburgs on his mother's side—who were German, Irish, and English—Kurt gained rosy cheeks and blond locks. But by far his most striking feature was his remarkable azure eyes; even nurses in the hospital commented on their beauty.

It was the sixties, with a war raging in Vietnam, but apart from the occasional news dispatch, Aberdeen felt more like 1950s America. The day Kurt was born, the *Aberdeen Daily World* contrasted the big news of an American victory at Quang Ngai City with local reports on the size of the timber harvest and ads from JCPenney, where a Washington's Birthday sale featured $2.48 flannel shirts. *Who's Afraid of Virginia Woolf?* had received thirteen Academy Award nominations in Los Angeles that afternoon, but the Aberdeen drive-in was playing *Girls on the Beach*.

Kurt's 21-year-old father, Don, worked at the Chevron station in Hoquiam as a mechanic. Don was handsome and athletic, but with his flattop haircut and Buddy Holly–style glasses he had a geekiness about him. Kurt's 19-year-old mother, Wendy, in contrast, was a classic beauty who looked and dressed a bit like Marcia Brady. They had met in high school, where Wendy had the nickname "Breeze." The previous June, just weeks after her high-school graduation, Wendy had become pregnant. Don borrowed his father's sedan and invented an excuse so the two could travel to Idaho and marry without parental consent.

At the time of Kurt's birth the young couple were living in a tiny house in the backyard of another home in Hoquiam. Don worked long hours at the service station while Wendy took care of the baby. Kurt slept in a white wicker bassinet with a bright yellow bow on top. Money was tight, but a few weeks after the birth they managed to scrape up enough to leave the tiny house and move into a larger one at 2830 Aberdeen Avenue. "The rent," remembered Don, "was only an extra five dollars a month, but in those times, five dollars was a lot of money."

If there was a portent of trouble in the household, it began over finances. Though Don had been appointed "lead man" at the Chevron in early 1968, his salary was only $6,000 a year. Most of their neighbors and friends worked in the timber industry, where jobs were physically demanding—one study described the profession as "more deadly than war"—but with higher wages in return. The Cobains struggled to stay within a budget, yet when it came to Kurt, they made sure he was well-dressed, and even sprang for professional photos. In one series of pictures from this era, Kurt is wearing a white dress shirt, black tie, and a gray suit, looking like Little Lord Fauntleroy—he still has his baby fat and chubby, full cheeks. In another, he wears a matching blue vest and suit top, and a hat more suited to Phillip Marlowe than a year-and-a-half-old boy.

In May 1968, when Kurt was fifteen months old, Wendy's fourteen-year-old sister Mari wrote a paper about her nephew for her home economics class. "His mother takes care of him most of the time," Mari wrote. "[She] shows her affection by holding him, giving him praise when he deserves it, and by taking part in many of his activities. He responds to his father in that when he sees his father, he smiles, and he likes his dad to hold him. He makes his wants known by yelling loudly at first, then crying if the first technique doesn't work." Mari recorded that his favorite game was peekaboo, his first tooth appeared at eight months, and his first dozen words were, "coco, momma, dadda, ball, toast, bye-bye, hi, baby, me, love, hot dog, and kittie."

Mari listed his favorite toys as a harmonica, a drum, a basketball, cars, trucks, blocks, a pounding block, a toy TV, and a telephone. Of Kurt's daily routine, she wrote that "his reaction to sleep is that he cries when he is laid down to do so. He is so interested in the family that he doesn't want to leave them." His aunt concluded: "He is a happy, smiling baby and his personality is developing as it is because of the attention and love he is receiving."

Wendy was a mindful mother, reading books on learning, buying flash cards, and, aided by her brothers and sisters, making sure Kurt got proper care. The entire extended family joined in the celebration of this child, and Kurt flourished with the attention. "I can't even put into words the joy and the life that Kurt brought into our family," remembered Mari. "He was this little human being who was so bubbly. He had charisma even as a baby. He was funny, and he was bright." Kurt was smart enough that when his aunt couldn't figure out how to lower his crib, the one-and-a-half-year-old simply did it himself. Wendy was so enamored of her son's antics, she rented a Super-8 camera and shot movies of him—an expense the family could ill afford. One film shows a happy, smiling little boy cutting his second-year birthday cake and looking like the center of his parents' universe.

By his second Christmas, Kurt was already showing an interest in music. The Fradenburgs were a musical family—Wendy's older brother Chuck was in a band called the Beachcombers; Mari played guitar; and great-uncle Delbert had a career as an Irish tenor, even appearing in the movie *The King of Jazz*. When the Cobains visited Cosmopolis, Kurt was fascinated by the family jam sessions. His aunts and uncles recorded him singing the Beatles' "Hey Jude," Arlo Guthrie's "Motorcycle Song," and the theme to "The Monkees" television show. Kurt enjoyed making up his own lyrics, even as a toddler. When he was four, upon his return from a trip to the park with Mari, he sat down at the piano and crafted a crude song about their adventure. "We went to the park, we got candy," went the lyrics. "I was just amazed," recalled Mari. "I should have plugged in the tape recorder—it was probably his first song."

Not long after he turned two, Kurt created an imaginary friend he called Boddah. His parents eventually became concerned about his attachment to this phantom pal, so when an uncle was sent to Vietnam,

Kurt was told that Boddah too had been drafted. But Kurt didn't completely buy this story. When he was three, he was playing with his aunt's tape machine, which had been set to "echo." Kurt heard the echo and asked, "Is that voice talking to me? Boddah? Boddah?"

In September 1969, when Kurt was two and a half, Don and Wendy bought their first home at 1210 East First Street in Aberdeen. It was a two-story, 1,000-square-foot house with a yard and a garage. They paid $7,950 for it. The 1923-era dwelling was located in a neighborhood occasionally given the derogatory nickname "felony flats." North of the Cobain house was the Wishkah River, which frequently flooded, and to the southeast was the wooded bluff locals called "Think of Me Hill"—at the turn of the century it had sported an advertisement for Think of Me cigars.

It was a middle-class house in a middle-class neighborhood, which Kurt would later describe as "white trash posing as middle-class." The first floor contained the living room, dining room, kitchen, and Wendy and Don's bedroom. The upstairs had three rooms: a small playroom and two bedrooms, one of which became Kurt's. The other was planned for Kurt's sibling—that month Wendy had learned she was pregnant again.

Kurt was three when his sister Kimberly was born. She looked, even as an infant, remarkably like her brother, with the same mesmerizing blue eyes and light blond hair. When Kimberly was brought home from the hospital, Kurt insisted on carrying her into the house. "He loved her so much," remembered his father. "And at first they were darling together." Their three-year age difference was ideal because her care became one of his main topics of conversation. This marked the beginning of a personality trait that would stick with Kurt for the rest of his life—he was sensitive to the needs and pains of others, at times overly so.

Having two children changed the dynamic of the Cobain household, and what little leisure time they had was taken up by visits with family or Don's interest in intramural sports. Don was in a basketball league in winter and played on a baseball team in summer, and much of their social life involved going to games or post-game events. Through sports, the Cobains met and befriended Rod and Dres Herling. "They were good family people, and they did lots of things with their kids," Rod Herling recalled. Compared with other Americans going through the sixties, they were also notably square: At the time no one in their social circle smoked pot, and Don and Wendy rarely drank.

One summer evening the Herlings were at the Cobains' playing cards, when Don came into the living room and announced, "I have a rat." Rats were common in Aberdeen because of the low elevation and abundance of water. Don began to fashion a crude spear by attaching a butcher knife to a broom handle. This drew the interest of five-year-old Kurt, who followed his father to the garage, where the rodent was in a trash can. Don told Kurt to stand back, but this was impossible for such a curious child and the boy kept inching closer until he was holding his father's pant leg. The plan was for Rod Herling to lift the lid of the can, whereupon Don would use his spear to stab the rat. Herling lifted, Don threw the broomstick but missed the rat, and the spear stuck into the floor. As Don tried in vain to pull the broom out, the rat—at a calm and bemused pace—crawled up the broomstick, scurried over Don's shoulder and down to the ground, and ran over Kurt's feet as he exited the garage. It happened in a split second, but the combination of the look on Don's face and the size of Kurt's eyes made everyone howl with laughter. They laughed for hours over this incident, and it would become a piece of family folklore: "Hey, do you remember that time Dad tried to spear the rat?" No one laughed harder than Kurt, but as a five-year-old he laughed at everything. It was a beautiful laugh, like the sound of a baby being tickled, and it was a constant refrain.

In September 1972, Kurt began kindergarten at Robert Gray Elementary, three blocks north of his house. Wendy walked him to school the first day, but after that he was on his own; the neighborhood around First Street had become his turf. He was well-known to his teachers as a precocious, inquisitive pupil with a Snoopy lunchbox. On his report card that year his teacher wrote "real good student." He was not shy. When a bear cub was brought in for show-and-tell, Kurt was one of the only kids who posed with it for photos.

The subject he excelled in the most was art. At the age of five it was already clear he had exceptional artistic skills: He was creating paintings that looked realistic. Tony Hirschman met Kurt in kindergarten and was impressed by his classmate's ability: "He could draw anything. Once we were looking at pictures of werewolves, and he drew one that looked just like the photo." A series Kurt did that year depicted Aquaman, the Creature From the Black Lagoon, Mickey Mouse, and Pluto. Every holiday or birthday his family gave him supplies, and his room began to take on the appearance of an art studio.

Kurt was encouraged in art by his paternal grandmother, Iris Cobain. She was a collector of Norman Rockwell memorabilia in the form of Franklin Mint plates with *Saturday Evening Post* illustrations on them. She herself recreated many of Rockwell's images in needlepoint—and his most famous painting, "Freedom From Want," showing the quintessential American Thanksgiving dinner, hung on the wall of her doublewide trailer in Montesano. Iris even convinced Kurt to join her in a favorite craft: using toothpicks to carve crude reproductions of Rockwell's images onto the tops of freshly picked fungi. When these oversized mushrooms would dry, the toothpick scratchings would remain, like backwoods scrimshaw.

Iris's husband and Kurt's grandfather, Leland Cobain, wasn't himself artistic—he had driven an asphalt roller, which had cost him much of his hearing—but he did teach Kurt woodworking. Leland was a gruff and crusty character, and when his grandson showed off a picture of Mickey Mouse that he'd drawn (Kurt loved Disney characters), Leland accused him of tracing it. "I did not," Kurt said. "You did, too," Leland responded. Leland gave Kurt a new piece of paper and a pencil and challenged him: "Here, you draw me another one and show me how you did it." The six-year-old sat down, and without a model drew a near-perfect illustration of Donald Duck and another of Goofy. He looked up from the paper with a huge grin, just as pleased at showing up his grandfather as in creating his beloved duck.

His creativity increasingly extended to music. Though he never took formal piano lessons, he could pound out a simple melody by ear. "Even when he was a little kid," remembered his sister Kim, "he could sit down and just play something he'd heard on the radio. He was able to artistically put whatever he thought onto paper or into music." To encourage him, Don and Wendy bought a Mickey Mouse drum set, which Kurt vigorously pounded every day after school. Though he loved the plastic drums, he liked the real drums at his Uncle Chuck's house better, since he could make more noise with them. He also enjoyed strapping on Aunt Mari's guitar, even though it was so heavy it made his knees buckle. He'd strum it while inventing songs. That year he bought his first record, a syrupy single by Terry Jacks called "Seasons in the Sun."

He also loved looking through his aunts' and uncles' albums. One time, when he was six, he visited Aunt Mari and was digging through her record collection, looking for a Beatles album—they were one of his favorites. Kurt suddenly cried out and ran toward his aunt in a panic. He was holding a copy of the Beatles' *Yesterday and Today*, with the infamous "Butcher cover," with artwork showing the band with pieces of meat on them. "It made me realize how impressionable he was at that age," Mari remembered.

He was also sensitive to the increasing strain he saw between his parents. For the first few years of Kurt's life, there wasn't much fighting in the home, but there also hadn't been evidence of a great love affair. Like many couples who married young, Don and Wendy were two people overwhelmed by circumstance. Their children became the center of their lives, and what little romance had existed in the short time they'd had prior to their kids was hard to rekindle. The financial pressures daunted Don; Wendy was consumed by caring for two children. They began to argue more and to yell at each other in front of the children. "You have no idea how hard I work," Don screamed at Wendy, who echoed her husband's complaint.

Still, for Kurt, there was much joy in his early childhood. In the summer they'd vacation at a Fradenburg family cabin at Washaway Beach on the Washington coast. In winter they'd go sledding. It rarely snowed in Aberdeen, so they would drive east into the small hills past the logging town of Porter, and to Fuzzy Top Mountain. Their sledding trips always followed a similar pattern: They'd park, pull out a toboggan for Don and Wendy, a silver saucer for Kim, and Kurt's Flexible Flyer, and prepare to slide down the hill. Kurt would grab his sled, get a running start, and hurl himself down the hill the way an athlete would commence the long jump. Once he reached the bottom he would wave at his parents, the signal he had survived the trip. The rest of the family would follow, and they would walk back up the hill together. They'd repeat the cycle again and again for hours, until darkness fell or Kurt dropped from exhaustion. As they headed toward the car Kurt would make them promise to return the next weekend. Later, Kurt would recall these times as the fondest memories of his youth.

When Kurt was six, the family went to a downtown photo studio and sat for a formal Christmas portrait. In the photo, Wendy sits in the center of the frame with a spotlight behind her head creating a halo; she rests on an oversized, wooden high-backed chair, wearing a long white-and-pink-striped Victorian dress with ruffled cuffs. Around her neck is a black choker, and her shoulder-length strawberry blond hair is parted in the middle, not a single strand out of place. With her perfect posture and the manner in which her wrists hang over the arms of the chair, she looks like a queen.

Three-year-old Kim sits on her mom's lap. Dressed in a long, white dress with black patent leather shoes, she appears as a miniature version of her mother. She is staring directly at the camera and has the appearance of a child who might start crying at any moment.

Don stands behind the chair, close enough to be in the picture but distracted. His shoulders are slightly stooped and he wears more of a bemused look than a legitimate smile. He is wearing a light purple long-sleeved shirt with a four-inch collar and a gray vest—it's an outfit that one could imagine Steve Martin or Dan Aykroyd donning for their "wild and crazy guys" skit on "Saturday Night Live." He has a far-off look in his eyes, as if he is wondering just why he has been dragged down to the photo studio when he could be playing ball.

Kurt stands off to the left, in front of his father, a foot or two away from the chair. He's wearing two-tone, striped blue pants with a matching vest and a fire-truck red long-sleeved shirt a bit too big for him, the sleeves partially covering his hands. As the true entertainer in the family, he is not only smiling, but he's laughing. He looks notably happy—a little boy having fun on a Saturday with his family.

It is a remarkably good-looking family, and the outward appearances suggest an all-American pedigree—clean hair, white teeth, and well-pressed clothes so stylized they could have been ripped out of an early seventies Sears catalog. Yet a closer look reveals a dynamic that even to the photographer must have been painfully obvious: It's a picture of a family, but not a picture of a marriage. Don and Wendy aren't touching, and there is no suggestion of affection between them; it is as if they're not even in the same frame. With Kurt standing in front of Don, and Kim sitting on Wendy's lap, one could easily take a pair of scissors and sever the photograph—and the family—down the middle. You'd be left with two separate families, each with one adult and one child, each gender specific—the Victorian dresses on one side, and the boys with wide collars on the other.

2 | I HATE MOM, I HATE DAD

I hate Mom, I hate Dad.
—From a poem on Kurt's bedroom wall.

The stress on the family increased in 1974, when Don Cobain decided to change jobs and enter the timber industry. Don wasn't a large man, and he didn't have much interest in cutting down 200-foot trees, so he took an office position at Mayr Brothers. He knew eventually he could make more money in timber than working at the service station; unfortunately, his first job was entry level, paying $4.10 an hour, even less than he'd made as a mechanic. He picked up extra money doing inventory at the mill on weekends, and he'd frequently take Kurt with him. "He'd ride his little bike around the yard," Don recalled. Kurt later would mock his father's job, and claim it was hell to accompany Don to work, but at the time he reveled in being included. Though he spent all of his adult life trying to argue otherwise, acknowledgment and attention from his father was critically important for Kurt, and he desired more of it, not less. He would later admit that his early years within his nuclear family were joyful memories. "I had a really good childhood," he told *Spin* magazine in 1992, but not without adding, "up until I was nine."

Don and Wendy frequently had to borrow money to pay their bills, one of the main sources of their arguments. Leland and Iris kept a $20 bill in their kitchen—they joked that it was a bouncing twenty because each month they'd loan it to their son for groceries, and immediately after repaying them Don would borrow it again. "He'd go all around, pay all his bills, and then he'd come to our house," remembered Leland. "He'd pay us our $20, and then he'd say, 'Hell, I done pretty good this week. I got 35 or 40 cents left.'" Leland, who never liked Wendy because he perceived her as acting "better than the Cobains," remembered the young family would then head off to the Blue Beacon Drive-In on Boone Street to spend the change on hamburgers. Though Don got along well with his father-in-law, Charles Fradenburg—who drove a road grader for the county—Leland and Wendy never connected.

Tension between the two came to a head when Leland helped remodel the house on First Street. He built Don and Wendy a fake fireplace in the living room and put in new countertops, but in the process he and Wendy battled increasingly. Leland finally told his son to make Wendy stop nagging him or he'd exit and leave the job half finished. "It was the first time I ever heard Donnie talk back to her," Leland recalled. "She was bitching about this and that, and finally he said, 'Keep your god damn mouth shut or he'll take his tools and go home.' And she shut her mouth for once."

Like his father before him, Don was strict with children. One of Wendy's complaints was that her husband expected the kids to always behave—an impossible standard—and required Kurt to act like a "little adult." At times, like all children, Kurt was a terror. Most of his acting out incidents were minor at the time—he'd write on the walls or slam the door or tease his sister. These behaviors frequently elicited a spanking, but Don's more common—and almost daily—physical punishment was to take two fingers and thump Kurt on the temple or the chest. It only hurt a little, but the psychological damage was deep—it made his son fear greater physical harm and it served to reinforce Don's dominance. Kurt began to retreat into the closet in his room. The kind of enclosed, confined spaces that would give others panic attacks were the very places he sought out as sanctuary.

And there were things worth hiding from: Both parents could be sarcastic and mocking. When Kurt was immature enough to believe them, Don and Wendy warned him he'd get a lump of coal for Christmas if he wasn't good, particularly if he fought with his sister. As a prank, they left him pieces of coal in his stocking. "It was just a joke,"

Don remembered. "We did it every year. He got presents and all that—we never didn't give him presents." The humor, however, was lost on Kurt, at least as he told the story later in life. He claimed one year he had been promised a Starsky and Hutch toy gun, a gift that never came. Instead, he maintained he only received a lump of neatly wrapped coal. Kurt's telling was an exaggeration, but in his inner imagination, he had begun to put his own spin on the family.

Occasionally, Kim and Kurt got along, and at times they'd play together. Though Kim never had the artistic talent of Kurt—and she forever felt the rivalry of having the rest of the family pay him so much attention—she developed a skill for imitating voices. She was particularly good at Mickey Mouse and Donald Duck, and these performances amused Kurt to no end. Her vocal abilities even gave birth to a new fantasy for Wendy. "It was my mom's big dream," declared Kim, "that Kurt and I would end up at Disneyland, both of us working there, with him drawing and me doing voices."

March of 1975 was filled with much joy for eight-year-old Kurt: He finally visited Disneyland, and he took his first airplane ride. Leland had retired in 1974, and he and Iris wintered that year in Arizona. Don and Wendy drove Kurt to Seattle, put him on a plane, and Leland met the boy in Yuma, before they headed for Southern California. In a mad two-day period, they visited Disneyland, Knotts Berry Farm, and Universal Studios. Kurt was enthralled and insisted they go through Disneyland's "Pirates of the Caribbean" ride three times. At Knotts Berry Farm, he braved the giant roller coaster, but when he departed the ride, his face was white as a ghost. When Leland said, "Had enough?" the color rushed back and he rode the coaster yet again. On the tour of Universal Studios, Kurt leaned out of the train in front of the *Jaws* shark, spurring a guard to yell at his grandparents, "You better pull that little towheaded boy back or his head will get bitten off." Kurt defied the order and snapped a picture of the mouth of the shark as it came inches away from his camera. Later that day, driving on the freeway, Kurt fell asleep in the backseat, which was the only reason his grandparents were able to sneak by Magic Mountain without him insisting they visit that as well.

Of all his relatives, Kurt was closest to his grandmother Iris; they shared both an interest in art and, at times, a certain sadness. "They adored each other," remembered Kim. "I think he intuitively knew the hell she'd been through." Both Iris and Leland had difficult upbringings, each scarred by poverty and the early deaths of their fathers on the job. Iris's father had been killed by poisonous fumes at the Rayonier Pulp Mill; Leland's dad, who was a county sheriff, died when his gun accidentally discharged. Leland was fifteen at the time of his father's death. He joined the Marines and was sent to Guadalcanal, but after he beat up an officer he was committed to the hospital for a psychiatric evaluation. He married Iris after his discharge, but struggled with drink and anger, especially after their third son, Michael, was born retarded and died in an institution at age six. "On Friday night he'd get paid and come home drunk," recalled Don. "He used to beat my mom. He'd beat me. He beat my grandma, and he beat Grandma's boyfriend. But that's the way it was in those days." By the time of Kurt's youth, Leland had softened and his most serious weapon was foul language.

When Leland and Iris weren't available, one of the various Fradenburg siblings would baby-sit—three of Kurt's aunts lived within four blocks. Don's younger brother Gary was also given child care duties a few times, and one occasion marked Kurt's first trip back to the hospital. "I broke his right arm," Gary recalled. "I was on my back and he was on my feet, and I was shooting him up in the air with my feet." Kurt was a very active child, and with all the running around he did, relatives were surprised he didn't break more limbs.

Kurt's broken arm healed and the injury didn't seem to stop him from playing sports. Don encouraged his son to play baseball almost as soon as he could walk, and provided him with all the balls, bats, and mitts that a young boy needed. As a toddler, Kurt found the bats more useful as percussion instruments, but eventually he began to participate in athletics, beginning in the neighborhood, and then in organized play. At seven, he was on his first Little League team. His dad was the coach. "He wasn't the best player on the team, but he wasn't bad," Gary

Cobain recalled. "He didn't really want to play, I thought, mentally. I think he did it because of his dad."

Baseball was an example of Kurt seeking Don's approval. "Kurt and my dad got along well when he was young," remembered Kim, "but Kurt wasn't anything like how Dad was planning on Kurt turning out."

Both Don and Wendy were facing the conflict between the idealized child and the real child. Since both had unmet needs left from their own early years, Kurt's birth brought out all their personal expectations. Don wanted the father/son relationship he never had with Leland, and he thought participating in sports together would provide that bond. And though Kurt liked sports, particularly when his father wasn't around, he intuitively connected his father's love with this activity, something that would mark him for life. His reaction was to participate, but to do so under protest.

When Kurt was in second grade, his parents and teacher decided his endless energy might have a larger medical root. Kurt's pediatrician was consulted and Red Dye Number Two was removed from his diet. When there was no improvement, his parents limited Kurt's sugar intake. Finally, his doctor prescribed Ritalin, which Kurt took for a period of three months. "He was hyperactive," Kim recalled. "He was bouncing off the walls, particularly if you got any sugar in him."

Other relatives suggest Kurt may have suffered from attention deficit hyperactivity disorder (ADHD). Mari remembered visiting the Cobain house and finding Kurt running around the neighborhood, banging on a marching drum and yelling at the top of his lungs. Mari went inside and asked her sister, "Just what on earth is he doing?" "I don't know," was Wendy's reply. "I don't know what to do to get him to stop—I've tried everything." At the time, Wendy presumed it was Kurt's way of burning off his excess of boyish energy.

The decision to give Kurt Ritalin was, even in 1974, a controversial one, with some scientists arguing it creates a Pavlovian response in children and increases the likelihood of addictive behavior later in life; others believe that if children aren't treated for hyperactivity, they may later self-medicate with illegal drugs. Each member of the Cobain family had a different opinion on Kurt's diagnosis and whether the short course of treatment helped or harmed him, but Kurt's own opinion, as he later told Courtney Love, was that the drug was significant. Love, who her-self was prescribed Ritalin as a child, said the two discussed this issue frequently. "When you're a kid and you get this drug that makes you feel that feeling, where else are you going to turn when you're an adult?" Love asked. "It was euphoric when you were a child—isn't that memory going to stick with you?"

In February 1976, just a week after Kurt's ninth birthday, Wendy in-formed Don she wanted a divorce. She announced this one weekday night and stormed off in her Camaro, leaving Don to do the explaining to the children, something at which he didn't excel. Though Don and Wendy's marital conflicts had increased during the last half of 1974, her declaration took Don by surprise, as it did the rest of the family. Don went into a state of denial and moved inward, a behavior that would be mirrored years later by his son in times of crisis. Wendy had always been a strong personality and prone to occasional bouts of rage, yet Don was shocked she wanted to break up the family unit. Her main com-plaint was that he was unceasingly involved in sports—he was a referee and a coach, in addition to playing on a couple of teams. "In my mind, I didn't believe it was going to happen," Don recalled. "Divorce wasn't so common then. I didn't want it to happen, either. She just wanted out."

On March 1 it was Don who moved out and took a room in Ho-quiam. He expected Wendy's anger would subside and their marriage would survive, so he rented by the week. To Don, the family repre-sented a huge part of his identity, and his role as a dad marked one of the first times in his life he felt needed. "He was crushed by the idea of divorce," remembered Stan Targus, Don's best friend. The split was complicated because Wendy's family adored Don, particularly her sister Janis and husband Clark, who lived near the Cobains. A few of Wendy's siblings quietly wondered how she would survive financially without Don.

On March 29 Don was served with a summons and a "Petition for Dissolution of Marriage." A slew of legal documents would follow; Don would frequently fail to respond, hoping against hope Wendy would change her mind. On July 9 he was held in default for not responding to Wendy's petitions. On that same day, a final settlement was granted awarding the house to Wendy but giving Don a lien of $6,500, due whenever the home was sold, Wendy remarried, or Kim turned eighteen. Don was granted his 1965 Ford half-ton pickup truck; Wendy was allowed to keep the family 1968 Camaro.

Custody of the children was awarded to Wendy, but Don was charged with paying $150 a month per child in support, plus their medical and dental expenses, and given "reasonable visitation" rights. This being a small-town court in the seventies, the specifics of visitation weren't spelled out and the arrangement was informal. Don moved in with his parents in their Montesano trailer. He remained hopeful that Wendy would change her mind, even after the final papers were signed.

Wendy would have nothing of it. When she was done with something, she was over it, and she couldn't have been more over Don. She quickly became involved with Frank Franich, a handsome longshoreman who made twice as much money as Don. Franich was also prone to violence and anger, and Wendy loved nothing better than to see that venom projected toward Don. When a new driver's license of Don's was accidentally mailed to Wendy's house, someone opened the envelope, rubbed feces on the picture of Don, resealed it, and forwarded it to Don. This wasn't a divorce—it was a war, filled with the hatred, spite, and revenge of a blood feud.

To Kurt, it was an emotional holocaust—no other single event in his life had more of an effect on the shaping of his personality. He internalized the divorce, as many children do. The depth of his parents' conflicts had been primarily hidden from him, and he couldn't understand the reason for the split. "He thought it was his fault, and he shouldered much of the blame," observed Mari. "It was traumatic for Kurt, as he saw everything he trusted in—his security, family, and his own maintenance—unravel in front of his eyes." Rather than outwardly express his anguish and grief, Kurt turned inward. That June, Kurt wrote on his bedroom wall: "I hate Mom, I hate Dad. Dad hates Mom, Mom hates Dad. It simply makes you want to be so sad." This was a boy who as an infant was so bonded to his family that he fought sleep, as Mari had written in her home economics report seven years previously, because "he doesn't want to leave them." Now, through no fault of his own, he had been left. Iris Cobain once described 1976 as "Kurt's year in purgatory."

It was hard on Kurt physically as well. Mari recalled Kurt in the hospital during this time; she'd heard from her mother he was there as a result of not eating enough. "I remember Kurt being in the hospital because of malnutrition when he was ten," she said. Kurt told his friends he had to drink barium and get his stomach X-rayed. It's possible that what was thought to be malnutrition was the first symptom of a stomach disorder that would plague him later in life. His mother had suffered a stomach condition in her early twenties, not long after his birth, and when Kurt first started having stomachaches, it was assumed he had the same irritable condition as Wendy. Around the time of the divorce, Kurt also had an involuntary twitching in his eyes. The family assumed it was stress related, which it probably was.

While his parents were divorcing, his life as a pre-adolescent boy, with all its internal challenges, was continuing. About to enter fourth grade, he began to notice girls as sexual beings and to be concerned with social status. That July he got his picture in the *Aberdeen Daily World* when his baseball team won first place in the Aberdeen Timber League after compiling a record of fourteen wins and one loss. The other highlight of the summer was his adoption of a black kitten that had been wandering around the neighborhood. It was his first pet, and he named it Puff.

Three months after the divorce was final, Kurt expressed an interest in living with his father. He moved into the trailer with Don, Leland, and Iris, but by early fall, father and son rented their own single-wide trailer across the street. Kurt visited Wendy, Kim, and Puff on weekends.

Living with his father solved some of Kurt's emotional needs—once again he was the center of attention, an only child. Don felt bad enough about the divorce that he overcompensated with material gifts, buying Kurt a Yamaha Enduro-80 mini-bike, which became a neighborhood attraction. Lisa Rock, who lived a few blocks away, first met Kurt that fall: "He was a quiet, very likeable kid. Always with a smile. He was a little shy. There was this field where he'd ride his mini-bike, and I'd ride alongside him with my bicycle."

Rock's observation of the nine-year-old Kurt as being "quiet" echoed a word that would be used repeatedly to describe him in adulthood. He was able to sit in silence for long stretches without feeling a need to make small talk. Kurt and Lisa had the same birthday, and when they both turned ten, they celebrated with a party at her house. Kurt was glad to be included, yet he was tentative and uncomfortable with the attention. He'd been fearless as a four-year-old; as a ten-year-old he was surprisingly fearful. Post-divorce, he held himself with reserve, always waiting for the other person to make the first move.

After the divorce, and with the onset of Kurt's puberty, his father took on a role of heightened proportions. After school Kurt would stay at his grandparents', but as soon as Don returned from work, they were together the rest of the day and Kurt was happy to do whatever Don wanted, even if that meant sports. After baseball games the two Cobain males occasionally ate dinner together at the local malt shop. It was a bonding that both savored, but each of them couldn't help but feel the loss of family—it was as if a limb had been severed, and though they got through the day without it, it was never far from their thoughts. Their love for each other that year was stronger than it was before or after, but both father and son were still profoundly lonely. Afraid he might lose his dad, Kurt asked Don to promise not to remarry. Don gave his son this assurance and said the two of them would always be together.

During the winter of 1976, Kurt transferred to Beacon Elementary School in Montesano. Montesano's schools were smaller than Aberdeen's and within weeks of transferring, he found a popularity that had escaped him previously and his fearlessness seemed to return. Despite his outward confidence, he held on to a bitterness about his circumstances: "You could tell he was tormented by his parents' divorce," recalled classmate Darrin Neathery.

By the time he began fifth grade, in the fall of 1977, Kurt was a fixture in "Monte," the name locals used for the town—every student in the small school knew him, and most liked him. "He was a good-looking kid," remembered John Fields. "He was smart, and he had everything going for him." With his blond hair and blue eyes, Kurt became a favorite of the girls. "It was no exaggeration to say that he was one of the most popular kids," observed Roni Toyra. "There was a group of about fifteen kids who would hang out together, and he was an important part of that group. He was really cute, with his blond hair, big blue eyes, and freckles on his nose."

That outward attractiveness hid a struggle for identity that hit a new plateau when, in October 1977, Don began to date. Kurt disliked the first woman Don met, so his father dropped her. With his ten-year-old's narcissism, Kurt didn't understand his father's desire for adult companionship or why Don wasn't happy with just the two of them. In late fall, Don met a woman named Jenny Westby, who herself was divorced with two kids: Mindy, a year younger than Kurt, and James, five years younger. From the very beginning, the courtship was a family affair, and their first date was a hike with all their kids around Lake Sylvia. Kurt was friendly to Jenny and her children, and Don thought he had a match. He and Jenny married.

At first Kurt liked Jenny—she provided him with female attention he was lacking—but his positive feelings about his new stepmother were canceled out by an internal conflict: If he cared for her, he would be betraying his love for his mother and his "real" family. Like his father, Kurt had held on to a hope that the divorce was just a temporary setback, a dream that would pass. His father's remarriage, and the now severely cramped trailer, destroyed that illusion. Don was not a man of many words, and his own background made expressing feelings difficult. "You told me you weren't going to get married again," Kurt complained to Don. "Well, you know, Kurt, things change," his father replied.

Jenny tried to reach out to him, without success. "At the beginning, he had a lot of affection toward everybody," Jenny recalled. Later, Kurt continually referred to Don's promise not to remarry, and kept withdrawing. Don and Jenny attempted to compensate by making Kurt the center of attention around the house—he got to open presents first, and he was given leeway on chores—but these small sacrifices only served to increase his emotional withdrawal. He enjoyed his step-siblings as occasional playmates, but he also teased them and was merciless to Mindy about her overbite, cruelly imitating her voice in front of her.

Things temporarily improved when the family moved into a home of their own at 413 Fleet Street South in Montesano. Kurt had his own room, which had been fashioned with round windows to look like a ship. Not long after the move, Jenny gave birth to another son, Chad Cobain, in January 1979. Now two other children, a step-mom, and a baby were all competing for the attention that had once been Kurt's alone.

Kurt had free rein in Monte's parks, alleyways, and fields. It was a town so small transportation was hardly required; the baseball field was four blocks away, school was just up the road, and all his friends were within walking distance. In contrast to Aberdeen, Monte seemed like something from a Thornton Wilder play, a simpler and friendlier America. Every Wednesday was designated family night at the Cobain house. Activities included board games like Parcheesi or Monopoly, and Kurt was as excited about these evenings as anyone.

Money was tight, so most vacations entailed camping trips, but Kurt was the first person in the car when they were getting ready. His sister Kim went on their trips until Don and Wendy had a battle about whether vacations meant less child support; after that, Kim saw less of her father and brother. Kurt continued to visit his mother on weekends, but rather than warm reunions, these times would usually just irritate the old wound of the divorce; Wendy and Don were hardly civil, so trips to Aberdeen meant having to watch his two parents battle over the visitation schedule. Another sadness befell him one weekend: Puff, his beloved cat, ran away and was never seen again.

Like all children, Kurt was a creature of routine and he enjoyed the structure of things like family night. But even this small comfort left him conflicted: He yearned for closeness while fearing being close would result in abandonment down the road. He had hit the stage of puberty where most adolescent males begin to differentiate themselves from their parents, to find their own identity. Yet Kurt still mourned the loss of the original family nest, so breaking away was fraught with both necessity and dread. He dealt with these many conflicting feelings by disassociating himself emotionally from Don and Wendy. He told himself and his friends that he hated them, and in this vitriol he was able to justify his own remoteness. But after an afternoon of hanging with his buddies and talking about what rotten parents he had, he would find himself yet again participating in family night and being the only one in the house who didn't want the evening's festivities to end.

Holidays were always a problem. Thanksgiving and Christmas of 1978 meant Kurt was shuttled around to a half dozen different households. If his feelings for Jenny were a mixture of affection, jealousy, and betrayal, his feelings for Wendy's boyfriend, Frank Franich, were pure anger. Wendy also began to drink heavily, and intoxication made her more acerbic. One night Franich broke Wendy's arm—Kim was in the house and witnessed the incident—and Wendy was hospitalized. When she recovered, she refused to press charges. Her brother Chuck threatened Franich, but there was little anyone could do to change Wendy's commitment to him. At the time, many thought Wendy stayed with Franich because of the financial support he provided. She'd begun working after the divorce as a clerk at Pearson's, an Aberdeen department store, but it was Franich's longshoreman's salary that afforded them luxuries like cable television. Before Franich came along, Wendy had been so in arrears on paying her bills that her electricity was about to be turned off.

Kurt was eleven that year, and small and scrawny, but he never felt as impotent or weak as when he was around Franich. He was helpless to protect his mother, and the stress of watching these fights made him fear for her life and perhaps for his. He both pitied his mother and hated her for having to pity her. His parents had been his gods when he was younger—now they were fallen idols, false gods, and not to be trusted.

These internal conflicts began to exhibit themselves in Kurt's behavior. He talked back to adults, refused to do chores, and despite his small size, began to bully another boy with such force that the victim refused to go to class. Teachers and parents became involved, and everyone wondered why such a sweet boy had turned so rancid. At the end of their ropes, Don and Jenny finally took Kurt to counseling. There was an attempt at family therapy, but Don and Wendy never could manage to arrive at the same appointment. The therapist, however, spent a couple of sessions talking with Kurt. His conclusions were that

Kurt needed a single family. "We were told if he was going to be with us, we needed to get legal custody of him, so that he knew we were accepting of him as part of our family," Jenny recalled. "Unfortunately, all this did was to cause problems between Don and Wendy, as they debated it."

Don and Wendy had been divorced for several years, yet their anger with each other continued, and in fact escalated through their children. It had been a difficult spring for Wendy—her father, Charles Fradenburg, had died of a sudden heart attack ten days after his 61st birthday. Wendy's mother, Peggy, had always been a recluse, and Wendy worried that this would increase her mother's isolation. Peggy's strange behavior may have resulted from a grisly childhood incident: When she was ten years old, Peggy's father stabbed himself in the abdomen in front of his family. James Irving survived the suicide attempt, and was committed to the same Washington mental hospital that later would give shock therapy to actress Frances Farmer. He died from his original injury two months later; when hospital staff weren't watching, he ripped open his stab wounds. Like many of the family's tragedies, Kurt's great-grandfather's mental illness was discussed only in a whisper.

But even the travails of the Fradenburg family failed to bring Don and Wendy together in shared grief. Their discussions about Kurt ended, as all their conversations did, with an argument. Wendy finally signed a document that read: "Donald Leland Cobain shall be solely responsible for the care, support and maintenance of said child." On June 18, 1979, three weeks short of three years after the date of Don and Wendy's divorce, Don was granted legal custody of Kurt.

3 | MEATBALL OF THE MONTH

His favorite food and drink are pizza and coke. His favorite saying is "excuse you."
—From a *Puppy Press* profile.

In September 1979, Kurt began seventh grade at Montesano Junior High School. It was an important milestone, and school began to take on a bigger role in his life. He had begun music classes in fifth grade, and by seventh grade he was playing drums with the school band, an accomplishment he sought to downplay to his friends while also savoring it. Most of what he studied and practiced was marching band or small ensemble drums, learning snare and bass drum for songs like "Louie, Louie" and "Tequila." The Monte band rarely marched—mostly they played for assemblies or basketball games—but Kurt was a fixture at any event where they appeared.

His band director, Tim Nelson, remembered him as "a regular, run-of-the-mill music student. He was not extraordinary, but he also wasn't awful." Kurt was pictured that year in the Montesano "Sylvan" yearbook, playing snare drum at an assembly. He had a pageboy haircut and looked a bit like a young Brad Pitt. His clothing tended toward preppy—a typical outfit included Hash bellbottom jeans, a striped Izod rugby shirt, and Nike athletic sneakers. He dressed like every other twelve-year-old, though he was slightly short and small for his age.

As one of the more popular kids in school, he was selected to be profiled in the October 26, 1979, edition of the mimeographed student newspaper, the *Puppy Press*. The article ran under the heading "Meatball of the Month" and read:

> Kurt is a seventh grader at our school. He has blonde hair and blue eyes. He thinks school is alright. Kurt's favorite class is band and his favorite teacher is Mr. Hepp. His favorite food and drink are pizza and coke. His favorite saying is "excuse you." His favorite song is "Don't Bring Me Down," by E.L.O. and his favorite rock group is Meatloaf. His favorite TV show is "Taxi" and his favorite actor is Burt Reynolds.

The "excuse you" saying was Kurt's twist on Steve Martin's "excuse me." This was consistent with his wry, sarcastic sense of humor, which involved transposing phrases or asking absurd rhetorical questions—imagine an adolescent Andy Rooney. Typical of these jokes was when he shouted out at a bonfire, "How can you ruin a perfectly good fire by making smoke?" Being a small boy his method of surviving within the adolescent male culture was to joke his way out of conflicts and belittle any tormenters with his superior intellect.

Kurt watched countless hours of television. This was a running battle with Don and Jenny; they wished to limit his hours in front of the tube, but he begged and screamed for more. When he was denied this freedom, he'd simply visit his best friend, Rod Marsh, who lived a block away, and watch television there. Though "Saturday Night Live" was past his bedtime, he rarely missed a week, and the next Monday at school he'd be imitating all the best skits. He also did a wicked impression of Latka, the Andy Kaufman character on "Taxi."

The previous summer Kurt had dropped out of Little League, but when winter came, he joined the junior varsity wrestling squad, which pleased his father. Don attended every match and endlessly quizzed Kurt on his progress. The coach was Kinichi Kanno, the Monte art teacher, and Kurt joined the team as much to spend more time with Kanno as to wrestle. In Kanno, Kurt found a male role model who encouraged his creativity, and he became Kanno's favorite student. One of Kurt's drawings was featured on the cover of the *Puppy Press* that Halloween: It showed a bulldog, Montesano's mascot, emptying a trick-or-treat bag on a doghouse. In a typical Cobain touch, he hid a can of beer among the candy. For a Christmas card that year, Kurt drew a pen-and-ink portrait of a small boy who was attempting to fish but had cast the hook into his back—it was as good as most Hallmark cards. As classmate Nikki Clark remembered it, Kurt's artwork was "always very good. Kanno never had to help him since he seemed like an advanced student." Even when he wasn't in art class, Clark recalled, Kurt was never far from a pen: "He doodled constantly in every class."

His doodles mostly were of cars, trucks, and guitars, but he also began to craft his own crude pornography. "He once showed me this sketch that he'd drawn," said classmate Bill Burghardt, "and it was a totally realistic picture of a vagina. I asked him, 'What's that?' and he laughed." At the time, Kurt had never seen a vagina up close, except in books or the adult magazines the boys traded. Another specialty of his was Satan, a figure he sketched in his notebook during every class.

Roni Toyra was Kurt's girlfriend in seventh grade, but it was an innocent first crush that never got serious. He gave her a piece of his art to tie their union. "There were kids in school that clearly were troubled or were outcasts, but he wasn't one of them," she said. "About the only thing that was different was that he was quieter than most kids. He wasn't unsociable, just quiet."

At home, he was anything but quiet, complaining vociferously over what he felt was unfair treatment from Don or Jenny. Few second marriages with children ever meld perfectly, but this one was always on delicate ground, and issues of favoritism and fairness would haunt the family. Kurt's complaints usually led to arguments between Don and Jenny or increased his parents' rancor, which continued to simmer over issues of visitation and child support. Don complained that Wendy made Kim phone if his support check was late by a day.

Toward the end of seventh grade, the school nurse called and said Kurt's proportions were what they considered borderline for scoliosis, or curvature of the spine. Don and Jenny took Kurt to a doctor, and after a thorough examination, the physician determined that Kurt didn't suffer from the syndrome—he simply had longer arms than most kids his size, which made the original measurements seem askew. But this didn't reassure Wendy. Through the family system of communication—

which resembled a bad version of the children's game of telephone—
she had heard Kurt had scoliosis. She was shocked Don wasn't alarmed
and that Kurt wasn't in a full-body cast. Kurt decided to believe his
mother's diagnosis, and in later years claimed he had "minor scoliosis
in junior high." Though his assertion is at odds with the facts, Kurt used
it as one more example of how his father had failed him.

Like many children of divorce, Kurt masterfully played each parent
off the other. In 1980, Wendy was working in Monte at the County
Commissioner's Office, and Kurt frequently visited her after school, if
only to report on some new torture put upon him by Don or Jenny.
As things became worse for Kurt in Monte, he hoped Wendy would
take him back. But his mother had her own problems at the time with
Frank Franich. She told Kim she feared that if Kurt witnessed the dysfunction in her home he would turn gay. Years later, when Kurt
brought up the topic with Wendy and Kim, his mom told him: "Kurt,
you don't even know what it was like. You would have ended up in
juvie or jail."

One of Kurt's repeated laments to Wendy was that Jenny's children
were favored in the household. When Jenny's ex-husband would give
Mindy and James gifts, Kurt felt jealous. Kurt assumed any discipline
meted out to him was because he wasn't Jenny's biological child. He
told his friends he hated Jenny, complained about her cooking, and
claimed she rationed how much soda he was allowed to drink. He
asserted Jenny could "hear a Pepsi can open from three rooms away,"
and for lunch he was allowed "only two slices of Carl Buddig ham per
sandwich, and two Grandma's Cookies."

Leland Cobain would lecture Don about what he also thought was
a prejudice against Kurt: "There could be fruit sitting on the table, and
Mindy or James could go up and take an apple and start eating it. Kurt
would go get one like that, and Donnie would give him hell for it."
Leland speculated Don was so afraid Jenny would leave him, like
Wendy had, that he sided with Jenny and her children. Don admitted
discipline was more a problem with Kurt than with Jenny's kids, but
argued it was because of Kurt's personality, not favoritism. But Don did
worry that Jenny would leave him if Kurt became too much trouble:

"I was afraid that it was going to get to the point of 'either he goes or she goes,' and I didn't want to lose her."

Kurt's relationship with his siblings and step-siblings became more balanced as he grew older. He adored his half-brother Chad because he loved babies. He'd punch Mindy, but on occasions when there was no school, he'd spend the day playing with her. Yet when Kurt's schoolmates would mention his family—several of his buddies thought Mindy was cute—he was quick to correct them if they called her his "sister." He described Mindy to his friends as, "*not* my sister—my dad's new wife's daughter," speaking the words as if she were some torture he was forced to endure.

He and James got along better, perhaps because Kurt was never overshadowed by the younger boy. When another boy slugged James, who was the bat-boy on one of Kurt's baseball teams, Kurt stepped in and threatened the attacker. They also shared an interest in movies. In the summer, the family would go to a two-screen drive-in. Don and Jenny would each take a car, then park one with the kids in front of a PG-rated movie, while they'd watch a more adult film on the other screen. Kurt taught James that rather than having to sit through another Don Knotts comedy, they could walk to the bathroom and view more adult fare—like *Heavy Metal*, which Kurt loved—by standing just outside the lot. Kurt enjoyed describing films he had already seen to his younger stepbrother. He had watched *Close Encounters of the Third Kind* the previous year and could recite all the dialogue from the film. "He used to play with his mashed potatoes at dinner and make them into the shape of the mountain from that movie," James recalled.

In 1981, at fourteen, Kurt began to make his own short films, using his parents' Super-8 camera. One of his first productions was an elaborate Orson Welles' *War of the Worlds* rip-off that showed aliens—played by figures Kurt sculpted with clay—landing in the Cobain backyard. He showed the alien film to James in a successful attempt to convince the younger boy that their house had been invaded. Another film he made in 1982 shows a far darker side of his psyche: He titled it *Kurt Commits Bloody Suicide,* and in it, Kurt, playing to a camera held by James, pretends to cut his wrists with the edge of a torn-in-half pop can. The film is complete with special effects, fake blood, and Kurt dramatically playing out his own final death scene in a manner he must have seen in silent pictures.

This gruesome film simply added ammunition to concerns his parents already had about a darkness they saw inside him. "There was something *wrong*," Jenny argued, "something wrong with his thought process even from the beginning, something unbalanced." He was able to calmly discuss the kinds of events that would give most young boys nightmares: murder, rape, suicide. He wasn't the only teenage boy in history to bring up self-slaughter, but the offhanded way he joked about it struck his friends as odd. One day he and John Fields were walking home from school when Fields told Kurt he should be an artist, but Kurt casually announced he had other plans: "I'm going to be a superstar musician, kill myself, and go out in a flame of glory," he said. "Kurt, that's the stupidest thing I ever heard—don't talk that way," Fields replied. But Kurt was steadfast: "No, I want to be rich and famous and kill myself like Jimi Hendrix." Neither boy was aware at the time that Hendrix's death wasn't suicide. Fields was not the only friend of Kurt's from Monte who reported such a story—a half dozen other acquaintances tell similar versions of the same conversation, always with the same dark outcome.

That Kurt would be talking indifferently about suicide at age fourteen didn't surprise anyone in the family. Two years earlier, Kurt's great-uncle, 66-year-old Burle Cobain, Leland's oldest brother, had used a snubbed-nose .38 pistol to shoot himself in both the stomach and head. Leland had discovered the body. There were allegations that Burle was about to be charged with sexual molestation. Burle hadn't been as close to the family as Kurt's other uncles, but Kurt talked about it incessantly with his friends. He would casually joke that his uncle had "killed himself over the death of Jim Morrison," though Morrison had passed away a decade before.

What had been a joke to Kurt was a devastating blow to Leland. The year prior to Burle's suicide, in 1978, Leland's brother Ernest had died of a cerebral hemorrhage. While Ernest's death, at 57, was not officially ruled a suicide, it came after he'd been warned he would die if he continued drinking. He persisted, and eventually fell down the stairs, causing the aneurysm that killed him.

These weren't the only deaths that affected Kurt. When Kurt was in eighth grade, a Montesano boy hanged himself outside one of the elementary schools. Kurt knew the boy; it was Bill Burghardt's brother. Kurt, Burghardt, and Rod Marsh discovered the corpse hanging from a tree as they were walking to school and they stared at it for half an hour before school officials finally shooed them away. "It was the most grotesque thing I ever saw in my life," recalled Marsh. From Kurt's own family history, and from this incident, suicide became a concept and a word that was no longer unmentionable. It was, instead, simply part of his milieu, just like alcoholism, poverty, or drugs. Kurt told Marsh he had "suicide genes."

Kurt's experimentation with drugs commenced in the eighth grade when he started smoking marijuana and using LSD. He began smoking pot at parties, then with his friends, and, finally, smoking daily by himself. By ninth grade, he was a full-on pothead. Marijuana was cheap and plentiful in Monte—most of it homegrown—and it helped Kurt forget his home life. What began as a social ritual became his chosen anesthetic.

At the time he began using drugs, he also started cutting class regularly. When he skipped school with his friends, they would buy weed or steal booze from someone's parents' liquor cabinet. But Kurt started skipping school by himself, or going to school but leaving after the first period. He saw less of his friends and appeared alienated from everything except his own anger. Trevor Briggs ran into Kurt on New Year's Eve 1980 sitting in a park in Monte by himself, swinging on a swing and whistling. Trevor invited Kurt to his parents' house, and the two got high while watching Dick Clark on television. The year ended with both of them throwing up from smoking an excessive amount of homegrown.

What just a couple of years earlier had seemed like an idyllic place to go to school soon became Kurt's own kind of prison. In conversations with his friends, he now slammed Monte along with his parents. Having just read Harper Lee's "To Kill a Mockingbird," he declared the book a perfect description of the town. By the beginning of 1981, a different

Kurt had begun to emerge, or *not* emerge, as was more often the case: He spent increasing amounts of time in isolation. In the Fleet Street house, he had moved to a remodeled basement bedroom. Kurt told his friends that he felt the shift was a banishment. In his basement room, Kurt spent his time with a Montgomery Ward's pinball machine he'd gotten for Christmas, a stereo Don and Jenny had handed down to him, and a stack of albums. The record collection included Elton John, Grand Funk Railroad, and Boston. Kurt's favorite album that year was Journey's *Evolution*.

His conflicts with Don and Jenny had reached a breaking point. All their attempts to get him involved with the family failed. He had begun to boycott family night and, feeling internally abandoned himself, decided to outwardly abandon his family. "We had chores for him, just typical stuff, but he wouldn't do them," Don remembered. "We began trying to bribe him with an allowance, but if he didn't do certain chores, we'd subtract from the allowance. But he refused to do anything. It ended up with him owing us money. He'd get violent, slam doors, and storm downstairs." He also seemed to have fewer friends. "I noticed that some of his friends were dropping off," said Jenny. "He was home a lot more, but he wasn't with us even when he was home. He seemed to become a lot more introverted. He was quiet and sullen." Rod Marsh recalled that Kurt killed a neighbor's cat that year. In this incident of teenage sadism—that would be in striking contrast to his adult life—he trapped the still-alive animal in his parents' chimney and laughed when it died and stunk up the house.

In September 1981, Kurt began his freshman year of high school in Montesano. That fall, in an attempt to fit in, he turned out for the football team. He made the first cut, despite his small stature—an indication, more than anything else, of how tiny a school Montesano was. He practiced for two weeks, but then dropped out, complaining that it was too much work. That year he also joined the track team. He threw the discus—an amazing feat considering his frame—and ran the 200-yard dash. He was by no means the best athlete on the squad—he missed many practices—but he was one of the faster boys. He was pictured in the yearbook photo of the squad, squinting into the sun.

. . .

In February of that year, in a moment of serendipity, Uncle Chuck told Kurt he could have either a bicycle or an electric guitar for his fourteenth birthday. To a boy who drew pictures of rock stars in his notebook, it was no choice at all. Kurt had already destroyed a Hawaiian lap guitar of Don's; he had taken it apart to study the internal workings. The guitar Chuck bought him wasn't much better: It was a cheap, second hand Japanese model. It often broke, but to Kurt it was the air that he breathed. Not knowing how to put the strings on it, he called up Aunt Mari and asked her if it was strung alphabetically. Once he got it working, he played it constantly and carried it to school to show it off. "Everyone asked him about it," remembered Trevor Briggs. "I saw him with it on the street, and he told me, 'Don't ask me to play any songs on this; it's broken.' " That didn't matter—it wasn't as much an instrument as it was an identity.

Athletics were also part of his identity; he had continued with wrestling, moving up, as a freshman, to the varsity squad. The Montesano Bulldogs won the league championship that year, with a record of twelve wins and three losses, though Kurt wasn't a significant part of the effort. He'd begun to skip more practices and matches, and on the varsity team his size was a huge disadvantage. The attitude on the JV team two years earlier was that wrestling was a fun way to roughhouse; the varsity team, in contrast, was deadly serious, and practices required him to wrestle boys who instantly pinned him. At the end of the season, Kurt sat for the team picture wearing knee-high striped socks—among the behemoths of the team, he looked more like the trainer than a member of the squad.

It was on the varsity wrestling mat that Kurt staged one of his greatest battles with his father. On the day of a championship match, as Kurt told it, he went out into the ring intending to send a message to Don in the bleachers. As Kurt later described it to Michael Azerrad, "I waited for the whistle to blow, just staring straight into [Don's] face, and then I instantly clammed up—I put my arms together, and let the guy pin me." Kurt claimed he did this four times in a row, was pinned instantly every time, and Don walked out in disgust. Don Cobain asserted the story was false; Kurt's classmates don't recall it and argue that anyone who intentionally lost would have been shunned, if not pummeled, by their teammates. But Leland Cobain remembered Don telling him the story after the match, saying, "That little shit just laid there. He wouldn't fight back."

Kurt was a master at exaggerating a yarn so as to tell an emotional truth rather than an actual one. What most likely happened was that Kurt had a match against a better opponent and decided not to fight back, which was enough to anger his perfectionist father. But Kurt's telling of the tale, and his description of the look that flashed between him and his father, is evidence of just how much their relationship had deteriorated in the six years since the divorce. They had once spent every spare hour together, and on the day Don bought the mini-bike, Kurt had never loved anyone more. Just down the street from Montesano High was a restaurant where they used to sit—the two of them alone, a singular entity, a family—and eat a quiet dinner together, joined in their loneliness; a little boy who wanted nothing more than to spend the rest of his life with his dad, and a father who only wanted someone to love him with a love that would not fade. But six years later, father and son were locked in a wrestling match of wills, and like all great tragedies, neither combatant felt he could afford to lose. Kurt desperately needed a father, and Don needed to be wanted by his son, but neither could admit this.

It was a tragedy of Shakespearean proportions; no matter how far Kurt moved away from that wrestling mat, in the corner of his eye, he was always looking directly at his father, or—to be more accurate, since his relationship with his father was virtually dead to him after this point—looking at his father's ghost. Almost a decade after his freshman wrestling defeat, Kurt would fire off a bitter lyric in a song titled "Serve the Servants," the words yet another move in his never-ending bout with his greatest opponent: "I tried hard to have a father, but instead I had a dad."

4 PRAIRIE BELT SAUSAGE BOY

ABERDEEN, WASHINGTON
MARCH 1982–MARCH 1983

Don't be afraid to chop hard, put some elbow grease in it.
—From the cartoon "Meet Jimmy, the Prairie Belt Sausage Boy."

It was at his own insistence that in March 1982, Kurt left 413 Fleet Street and his father and stepmother's care. Kurt would spend the next few years bouncing around the metaphorical wilderness of Grays Harbor. Though he'd make two stops that were a year in length, over the next four years he would live in ten different houses, with ten different families. Not one of them would feel like home.

His first stop was the familiar turf of his paternal grandparents' trailer outside Montesano. From there he could take the bus into Monte each morning, which allowed him to stay in the same school and class, but even his classmates knew the transition was hard. At his grandparents', he had the sympathetic ear of his beloved Iris, and there were moments when he and Leland shared closeness, but he spent much of his time by himself. It was yet another step toward a larger, profound loneliness.

One day he helped his grandfather construct a dollhouse for Iris's birthday. Kurt assisted by methodically stapling miniature cedar shingles on the roof of the structure. With wood that was left over, Kurt built a crude chess set. He began by drawing the shapes of the pieces on the wood, and then laboriously whittling them with a knife. Halfway through this process, his grandfather showed Kurt how to operate the jigsaw, then left the fifteen-year-old to his own devices, while watching from the door. The boy would look up at his grandfather for approval, and Leland would tell him, "Kurt, you're doing good."

But Leland was not always so kind with his words, and Kurt found himself back in the same father/son dynamic he'd experienced with Don. Leland was quick to pepper his decrees to Kurt with criticism. In Leland's defense, Kurt could truly be a pain. As his teenage years began, he constantly tested his limits, and with so many different parental figures—and none with ultimate authority over him—he eventually wore out his elders. His family painted a picture of a stubborn and obstinate boy who wasn't interested in listening to any adults or working. Petulance appeared to be an essential part of his nature, as did laziness, in contrast to everyone else in his family—even his younger sister Kim had helped pay the bills with her paper route. "Kurt *was* lazy," recalled his uncle Jim Cobain. "Whether it was simply because he was a typical teenager or because he was depressed, no one knew."

By summer 1982, Kurt left Montesano to live with Uncle Jim in South Aberdeen. His uncle was surprised to be given the responsibility. "I was shocked they would let him live with me," Jim Cobain remembered. "I was smoking pot at the time. I was oblivious to his needs, let alone to what the hell I was doing." At least, with his inexperience, Jim was not a heavy-handed disciplinarian. He was two years younger than his brother Don but far hipper, with a large record collection: "I had a really nice stereo system and lots of records by the Grateful Dead, Led Zeppelin, and the Beatles. And I'd crank that baby up loud." Kurt's biggest joy during his months with Jim was rebuilding an amplifier.

Jim and his wife had an infant daughter and, for space reasons, soon asked Kurt to leave. From there Kurt stayed with Wendy's brothers and sisters. "Kurt was handed down from relative to relative," recalled Jim. He was the quintessential latchkey kid. He got along better with his uncles and aunts than he did with his parents, yet authority issues followed him. His uncles and aunts were less strict, yet in the more laid-back households there was less of an attempt at structured family togetherness. His relatives had problems and struggles of their own—

there wasn't anyone with the space for him, both physically and emotionally, and Kurt knew it.

Kurt spent several months with his Uncle Chuck, where he began to take guitar lessons. Chuck was in a band with a fellow named Warren Mason, one of the hottest guitar players on the harbor. Whenever they rehearsed at Chuck's house—rehearsals that always included pot and a bottle of Jack Daniel's—Kurt would watch from the corner, eyeing Warren like a starving man looking at a meatball sandwich. One day Chuck asked Warren if he'd instruct the boy, and so began Kurt's formal training in music.

As Kurt told the story, he only took one or two lessons, and in that short period he learned everything he needed to know. But Warren remembered the instruction stretching on for months, and Kurt being a serious student who spent hours trying to apply himself. The first thing Warren had to deal with was Kurt's guitar—it was more suited for showing off at school than playing. Warren found Kurt an Ibanez, for $125. Lessons themselves were $5 per half hour. Warren asked Kurt the question he asked all his young students: "What are some of the songs you want to learn?" "Stairway to Heaven," was Kurt's reply. Kurt already knew how to play a crude version of "Louie, Louie." They worked on "Stairway" and then progressed to AC/DC's "Back in Black." The lessons ended when Kurt's poor grades made his uncle reconsider this choice of afternoon recreation.

Kurt continued to go to school in Monte through the second month of his sophomore year, but then transferred to Aberdeen's Weatherwax High. It was the same school his mother and father had graduated from, but despite the family roots and the proximity to his mother's home—it was ten blocks away—he was an outsider there. Built in 1906, Weatherwax stretched over three city blocks, with five separate buildings, and Kurt's class had 300 students—three times as large as Monte. In Aberdeen, Kurt found himself in a school with four factions—stoners, jocks, preppies, and nerds—and he initially fit into none of them. "Aberdeen was full of cliques," observed Rick Miller, another Monte boy who transferred to Weatherwax. "Neither one of us really knew anybody. Even though Aberdeen was Hicksville compared to Seattle, it was still a major step up from Monte. We never could figure out where we fit in." Changing schools as a sophomore would have been difficult for most well-adjusted teenagers; it was torturous for Kurt.

While he'd been popular in Monte—a preppy in his Izod shirts, a jock because of his involvement in sports—in Aberdeen he was an outsider. He kept up with his friends in Monte, but despite the fact that he saw his buddies nearly every weekend, his sense of loneliness increased. His athletic skills weren't sufficient to gain him notoriety in a large school, so he dropped out of sports. Combined with his own self-doubt from his fractured family and nomadic lifestyle, his retreat from the world continued. Later, Kurt would tell repeated tales of being beaten up in Aberdeen, and of the constant abuse he suffered at the hands of redneck high-school kids. Yet his classmates at Weatherwax don't remember any such incidents—he exaggerated the emotional isolation he felt into phantom tales of physical violence.

There was at least one redeeming grace to his studies: Weatherwax had an excellent art program, and in this one class Kurt continued to excel. His teacher, Bob Hunter, found him an extraordinary student: "He had both the ability to draw, coupled with a great imagination." Hunter allowed his students to listen to the radio while they worked— he was an artist and musician himself—and encouraged them to be creative. To Kurt, he was the ideal teacher, and like Mr. Kanno before him, he proved to be one of the few adult role models the boy could look up to.

That first year at Weatherwax, Kurt took commercial art and basic art, fifth and sixth periods. These two 50-minute classes—scheduled right after lunch—were the one time when he was certain to be in school each day. His skill impressed Hunter and at times shocked his classmates. For a caricature assignment, Kurt drew Michael Jackson, with one gloved hand in the air and the other holding his crotch. During another lesson the class was asked to show an object as it developed: Kurt depicted a sperm turning into an embryo. His drawing skills were exemplary, but his twisted mind was what drew the attention of his classmates. "That sperm was a shock to all of us," recalled classmate

Theresa Van Camp. "It was such a different mental attitude. People began to talk about him, wondering, 'What does he think of?' " When Hunter told Kurt the Michael Jackson illustration might not be appropriate to display in the school halls, he instead drew an unflattering illustration of Ronald Reagan with a raisin-like face.

Kurt had always drawn obsessively, but now, with the encouragement of Hunter, he began to imagine himself an artist. His scribbles became part of his education. He was adept at cartooning, and in this way he first began to learn the art of storytelling. One recurrent cartoon from this period was the adventures of "Jimmy, the Prairie Belt Sausage Boy," named after a canned meat product. These tales documented the painful childhood of Jimmy—a thinly veiled Kurt—who was forced to endure strict parents. One full-color, multi-panel edition not so subtly told the story of Kurt's conflicts with his father. In the first panel, the father figure lectures Jimmy: "This oil is dirty. I can smell the gas in it. Get me a 9-mm wrench, you lousy little creep. If you're gonna live here, you're gonna live by my rules and they are as serious as my moustache: honesty, loyalty, dedication, honor, valor, strict discipline, God and country, that's what makes America No. One." Another panel shows a mother shouting, "I'm giving birth to your son and aborting your daughter. PTA meeting at seven, pottery class 2:30, beef stroganoff, dog to vet 3:30, laundry, yes, yes, mmm honey, it feels good in the ass, mmm, I love you."

It's unclear whether the mother in the cartoon is meant to be Jenny or Wendy, but the decision to attend Weatherwax had also entailed moving back in with his mother at 1210 East First Street. This was as close to a permanent home as Kurt had, since his upstairs room had remained untouched, a shrine to earlier days within the nuclear family. He'd spent weekends here on and off, continuing to decorate the walls with band posters, many of them now hand drawn. Of course, the best part of his room, and his life, was his guitar. Wendy's house was emptier than his other stops during these years, allowing him to practice without distraction. But the domestic front was only slightly improved; his mom had finally freed herself of Frank Franich, yet Kurt and Wendy were still fighting.

Wendy was a very different mom from the one Kurt had left six years previously. She was now 35 years old, but she was dating younger men and going through a stage that can only be described as the kind of mid-life crisis typically associated with recently divorced men. She was drinking a lot and had become a regular at Aberdeen's many taverns—one of the main reasons Kurt wasn't immediately deposited back in her care after he left Don. That year she began casually dating 22-year-old Mike Medak. During the first few months they saw each other, Wendy didn't even mention to Medak she had kids; mostly she stayed at his house, and he didn't see her children until several months into their relationship. "It was like she was a single woman," he recalled. "It wasn't like we were waiting around Friday night for the baby-sitter—it was as if there was no kids." Dating Wendy wasn't all that different from dating a 22-year-old. "We'd go out to the nearest tavern or dance hall. And we'd party." Wendy complained how Franich had broken her arm, how she struggled financially, and about Don's distance. One of the few stories she told about Kurt was how at five he had walked into the living room sporting a hard-on in front of Don and a bunch of his friends. Don was embarrassed and carried his son out of the room. The incident would become family legend; it still gave Wendy a chuckle to tell it.

As a 22-year-old dating a 35-year-old, Medak was in the relationship mostly for physical reasons; to him Wendy was an attractive older woman, an ideal date if you weren't looking for commitment. Even fifteen-year-old Kurt could sense this, and he was quick to judge. Kurt discussed his mom's dates with his friends, and his words were harsh, though they didn't touch upon the psychological conflict he must have felt at seeing his mother take a lover who was only seven years older than he. "He said he hated his mom, that he thought she was a slut," remembered John Fields. "He didn't agree with her lifestyle. He didn't like her at all, and he'd talk about running away. Kurt would vacate the house if she was there, since she'd yell at him a lot."

Wendy's siblings remember being concerned about her drinking, but because their family communication style was non-confrontational, it was rarely discussed.

His mother's attractiveness also proved to be an embarrassment for Kurt. All his friends had crushes on her, and Wendy's habit of sunbathing in a bikini in the backyard had them peeking through the fence. When friends would spend the night, they would joke how if there wasn't enough room they would gladly agree to sleep with Wendy. Kurt would punch anyone who made this joke, and he did a lot of punching. Wendy also seemed attractive to these young boys because she would occasionally purchase alcohol for them. "Kurt's mom bought us booze a couple of times," remembered Mike Bartlett. "It was with the understanding that we would drink it at the house." Once Wendy paid for beer for the kids and let them watch a video of Pink Floyd's *The Wall*. "One time a few of us were spending the night there," said Trevor Briggs, "and we talked his mom into buying us a fifth of tequila. We got drunk and went out walking. And when we came back, his mom was on the couch making out with a guy." Kurt's drunken, fifteen-year-old response was to yell at his mom's paramour, "Give it up dude! You ain't going to get none. Go home!" It was a joke, but there was nothing comical about his desire for a more traditional family.

That Christmas, Kurt's main request was the Oingo Boingo album *Nothing to Fear*. At the Fradenburg Christmas celebration his aunt took a photo of him holding it. With his still-short hair and boyish looks, he appears much younger than fifteen. Aunt Mari gave him the album *Tadpoles* from the Bonzo Dog Band, containing the novelty tune "Hunting Tigers Out in Indiah." It was Kurt's favorite song that winter and he learned to play it on guitar. Right before Christmas, he'd visited Mari, who'd moved to Seattle, to search record stores. One of the items on Kurt's wish list was a soundtrack album to the "H. R. Pufnstuf" television show, which he adored. Another album he sought, his aunt had never heard of: REO Speedwagon's *Hi Infidelity*.

He turned sixteen that February and passed his driver's test. But the biggest event that spring was something far more important to him than his learner's permit—it was a milestone he talked about constantly through adolescence, though never in adulthood. On March 29, 1983, Kurt journeyed to the Seattle Center Coliseum to see Sammy Hagar and Quarterflash, his first concert. Being big fans of Seattle radio station KISW—the signal would come in clear at night—Kurt loved Hagar's "butt rock" and he also had a fondness for Quarterflash's hit "Harden My Heart." He went with Darrin Neathery, whose older sister drove them. "It was a big deal because it was the first concert we both saw," Neathery said. "Somehow we got a six-pack of Schmidt. Kurt and I sat in the backseat on the way up and had a hell of a good time. When we got to the show, I remember standing on the floor down by the back, where they did the lights, after Quarterflash had played. We were just in awe of it all: the lights and the production. Then a whiskey bottle came flying from the very top stands and smashed right by us. We about crapped our pants. So we hauled out of there and found a place in the upper rafters to watch Sammy. I bought a T-shirt and Kurt did too." Kurt would later rewrite history and claim that the punk band Black Flag was his first concert. Yet what every one of his classmates in Weatherwax remembered was the sixteen-year-old Kurt coming to school the next day, wearing an oversized Sammy Hagar T-shirt, and talking like a pilgrim who had just returned from the holy land.

As the 1983 school year ended, Kurt discovered punk rock, and the Sammy Hagar T-shirt was stuck in a bottom drawer, never to return. That summer he saw the Melvins, and it was an event that would change his life. He wrote in his journal:

> In the summer of 1983 . . . I remember hanging out at a Montesano, Washington Thriftway when this short-haired employee box-boy, who kind [of] looked like the guy in Air Supply, handed me a flyer that read: "The Them Festival. Tomorrow night in the parking lot behind Thriftway. Free live rock music." Monte was a place not accustomed to having live rock acts in their little village, a population of a few thousand loggers and their subservient wives. I showed up with stoner friends in a van. And there stood the Air Supply box-boy holding a Les Paul with a picture from a magazine of Kool Cigarettes on it. They played faster than I ever imagined music could be played and with more energy than my Iron Maiden records could provide. *This was what I was looking for.* Ah, punk rock. The other stoners were bored and kept shouting, "Play some Def Leppard." God, I hated those fucks more than ever. I came to

the promised land of a grocery store parking lot and I found my special purpose.

He had twice underlined "This was what I was looking for."

It was his epiphany—the moment when his small world suddenly became a larger one. The "Air Supply box-boy" was Roger "Buzz" Osborne, who Kurt had known as an aloof older kid at Montesano High. When Kurt complimented Buzz after the show, he played to Osborne's vanity, and Buzz was soon playing mentor, passing along punk rock records, a book on the Sex Pistols, and dog-eared copies of *Creem* magazines. Despite his journal entry, it was not a complete transformation—Kurt still saw Judas Priest play at the Tacoma Dome that summer. Like other kids in Aberdeen, he mixed his punk with loads of heavy metal, though he didn't brag about this in front of Buzz, and he now favored punk T-shirts.

The Melvins had started a year before, naming themselves, mockingly, after another employee at the Thriftway. Buzz claimed to have taught himself to play guitar by listening to the first two Clash records. In 1983, the Melvins had no real fan base—they were heckled and ridiculed by most of the metal-heads in Grays Harbor. Yet a dozen impressionable boys would gather around their practice space behind drummer Dale Crover's house at 609 West Second in Aberdeen. This motley crew of fans were called "Cling-Ons," a name coined by Buzz to describe both their "Star Trek"-like geekiness and habit of clinging to every word he uttered. Buzz himself looked more like Richard Simmons, with his white-man's afro, than the fellow in Air Supply.

Buzz dispensed advice to the "Cling-Ons," made them tapes, and acted as the Socrates of Montesano, an elder statesman spouting off his views on all things worldly to his band of followers. He decided who was allowed at practices and who was banned, and he made up nicknames for all accepted. Greg Hokanson became "Cokenson." Jesse Reed, who Kurt had met in class at Weatherwax and quickly befriended, became "Black Reed" after the band Black Flag, though like all of the crew, he was Caucasian. Kurt never had a nickname that stuck. His friends from this time period always called him "Cobain." His lack of a nickname wasn't a sign he was afforded any special status. In fact, it was the opposite—he didn't have a nickname because he was thought of as this runt who didn't deserve the recognition.

Like Kurt, the Melvins stretched geographically from Monte (where Buzz lived with his parents) to Aberdeen (Crover's practice space). The Melvins' bass player was Matt Lukin, also from Monte, whom Kurt had known from wrestling and Little League, and he soon became a friend. Anytime Kurt traveled to Monte, he was more likely to look up Buzz or Lukin than visit his father.

One particular trip to Monte that summer was fueled by something other than his new love for punk rock—it was motivated by a girl. Andrea Vance was the younger sister of Kurt's friend Darrin Neathery, and she was baby-sitting in Monte one afternoon when Kurt unexpectedly appeared. "He was darling," she recalled. "He had really great blue eyes and a killer smile. His hair was really pretty and soft. He wore it medium length. He didn't talk a lot, and when he did, he was soft-spoken." They watched "The Brady Bunch," and Kurt played Sock-and-Bots with the kids. Like clockwork, he returned the next afternoon, and Vance rewarded him with a kiss. He returned every day for a week, but the romance never progressed beyond necking. "He was very sweet and really respectful," Vance remembered. "I didn't feel like he was a walking hormone."

But underneath the surface, his hormones were raging. That same summer Kurt had what he'd later describe as his "first sexual encounter," with a developmentally disabled girl. As he reported in his journal, he pursued her only after becoming so depressed about the state of his life that he planned suicide. "That month happened to be the epitome of my mental abuse from my mother," he wrote. "It turned out that pot didn't help me escape my troubles too well anymore, and I was actually enjoying doing rebellious things like stealing booze and busting store windows. . . . I decided within the next month that I'll not sit on my roof and *think* about jumping, but I'll *actually* kill myself. And I wasn't going out of this world without actually knowing what it is like to get laid."

His only avenue seemed this "half-retarded girl." One day Trevor

Briggs, John Fields, and Kurt followed her home and stole her father's liquor. They had done this numerous times, but this time Kurt stayed after his friends departed. He sat on the girl's lap and touched her breasts. She went into her bedroom and got undressed in front of him, but he found himself disgusted both with himself and with her. "I tried to fuck her, but I didn't know how," he wrote. "I got grossed out very heavily with how her vagina smelled and her sweat reeked, so I left." Though Kurt retreated, the shame would stick with him for the rest of his life. He hated himself for taking advantage of her, yet he also hated himself for not seeing the scenario through to intercourse, an almost greater shame to a virginal boy of sixteen. The girl's father protested to the school that his daughter had been molested, and Kurt was mentioned as a suspect. He wrote in his journal that only a bit of serendipity saved him from prosecution: "They came with a yearbook and were going to have her pick me out, but she couldn't because I didn't show up for pictures that year." He claimed he was taken to the Montesano Police station and interrogated but escaped conviction because the girl was over eighteen, and "not mentally retarded" by legal statutes.

Back in Aberdeen, Kurt began his junior year at Weatherwax by starting up a romantic relationship with fifteen-year-old Jackie Hagara. She lived two blocks from his house, and he timed it so they would walk to school together. He was so behind in math, he'd been forced to take a freshman math class, where they'd met. Though many of the kids in the class thought Kurt was weird for being kept behind, Jackie liked his smile. After school one day, he showed her a drawing he'd made of a rock star on a desert island. The man was holding a Les Paul guitar with a Marshall stack plugged into a palm tree. For sixteen-year-old Kurt, it was his vision of paradise.

Jackie said she liked the drawing. Two days later he approached her with a gift; he had redrawn the same image but in poster size, complete with airbrushing. "It's for you," he said, looking at the floor as he spoke. "For me?" she asked. "I'd like to go out with you sometime," he explained. Kurt was only slightly disenchanted when Jackie told him she already had a boyfriend. They continued to walk to school together, occasionally holding hands, and one afternoon in front of her house, he pulled her close and kissed her. "I thought he was so cute," she said.

During his pivotal junior year even his appearance began to transform from what had universally been described as "cute" to what some of his Weatherwax classmates would call "scary." He grew his hair long and it was rarely washed. His Izod shirts and rugby pullovers were gone; now he sported homemade T-shirts with the names of punk bands. One he wore frequently read "Organized Confusion," a slogan he fantasized would be the name of his first band. For outerwear, he always had a trench coat—he wore it year round, whether it was raining outside or a 90-degree summer day. That fall, Andrea Vance, his Monte girlfriend from that summer, ran into Kurt at a party and didn't even recognize him. "He had on his black trench coat, hi-top tennis shoes, and his hair was dyed dark red," she recalled. "He didn't look like the same boy."

His circle of friends slowly shifted from his Monte pals to Aberdeen buddies, but with both groups their main activity was getting intoxicated in one way or another. When they were unable to raid a parental liquor stock, they would take advantage of one of Aberdeen's many street people to help buy them beer. Kurt, Jesse Reed, Greg Hokanson, and Eric and Steve Shillinger developed a regular commerce with a colorful character they dubbed "The Fat Man," a hopeless alcoholic who lived in the run-down Morck Hotel with his retarded son, Bobby. The Fat Man was willing to buy them alcohol as long as they paid and helped him get to the store. This was a laborious process that in practice looked a bit like a Buster Keaton skit and could take all day: "First," said Jesse Reed, "we had to push a shopping cart to the Morck. Then we'd go up to his room, and we'd get him up. He'd be in his crusty underwear, and it stank and there were flies and it was awful. We'd have to help him put on these tent pants. Then we'd have to help him downstairs, and he weighed about 500 pounds. He was too fat to walk all the way to the liquor store, so we'd put him in the cart and push him. If we just wanted to drink beer, we'd push him to the grocery store, which, thankfully, was closer. And all we had to do for him was buy a quart of the cheapest malt liquor."

The Fat Man and Bobby, an odd couple if there ever was one, unknowingly became the first subjects of some of Kurt's storytelling. He wrote short stories about them, crafted imaginary songs about their adventures, and sketched them in his journal. His pencil drawing of the Fat Man looked like Ignatius J. Reilly, the anti-hero of John Kennedy Toole's "A Confederacy of Dunces." Kurt loved nothing more than to imitate Bobby's squeaky voice, eliciting fits of cackling laughter from his friends. His relationship with the Fat Man and Bobby wasn't completely without affection; there was a level of empathy Kurt felt for their seemingly hopeless situation. That year for Christmas, Kurt bought the Fat Man a toaster and a John Denver album at Goodwill. Upon grasping these presents in his giant mitt-hands, the Fat Man asked in disbelief: "These are for me?" He started to cry. The Fat Man spent the next few years telling everyone in Aberdeen what a swell fellow Kurt Cobain was. It was a small example of how at times, even in Kurt's shadow world, a sweetness would emerge.

With a regular supply of booze from the Fat Man, Kurt continued to abuse alcohol that spring, and his conflicts with his mother increased as a result. The arguments were worse when Kurt was stoned or frying on acid, which became a regular occurrence. Greg Hokanson recalled going to Kurt's house with Jesse Reed and hearing Wendy yell at Kurt for an hour, as Kurt tripped on LSD, completely unresponsive to her shouts. "Wendy was awful to him," Hokanson said. "He hated her." As soon as they could escape, the trio left the house and went to climb the water tower on "Think of Me Hill." Jesse and Hokanson made it to the top, but Kurt froze halfway up the ladder. "He was too afraid," Hokanson remembered. Kurt never managed to climb the tower.

Trevor Briggs recalled one evening at the Cobains when the battle between Kurt and Wendy went on all evening: "I think she was a little intoxicated, and she came upstairs into his room. She was trying to party and get loose with us. He got pissed off at her about it. And she said, 'Kurt if you don't watch it, I'm going to say in front of your friends what you told me.' And he loudly yelled, 'What are you talking about?' She eventually left. So I asked him what was she going to say. He said, 'Well, I made a comment to her once about how just because a guy gets hair on his balls, doesn't mean he's a grown man or mature.' " This singular issue—having hair on your testicles—was a monumental point of embarrassment for Kurt. His pubic hair arrived later than most boys', and he obsessively inspected his testicles daily, repeatedly watching his friends cross this threshold before him. "Pubes," as he called them, were a frequent topic in his journal. "Not enough pubes yet," he wrote. "Lost years. Gained ideals. Not yet developed. Much past the time in which our pubes fail to grow." In gym class he would dress in a bathroom stall rather than open himself up to the inspection of the boys' locker room. When he was sixteen pubes finally appeared, though since his coloring was light, even these weren't as obvious as those of other boys.

Around the time Kurt turned seventeen, Wendy became involved with Pat O'Connor. O'Connor was Wendy's age and earned $52,000 as a longshoreman. His salary was a matter of public record because soon after he and Wendy became involved, Pat was the subject of one of Washington's first palimony lawsuits. It was filed by his ex-girlfriend, who charged he'd convinced her to quit her job at the local nuclear power plant and then dumped her for Wendy. It was a nasty case, stretching on for the next two years. In court documents, Pat listed his assets as a small house, a few thousand dollars in savings, and a gun rack with three guns—these guns were, oddly, to play a role in Kurt's career. Pat's ex prevailed, winning $2500 in cash, a car, and her attorney's fees.

Pat moved into Wendy's house that winter. Neither of Wendy's children liked O'Connor, and Kurt grew to hate him. Just as he had with his biological father and Franich, Kurt made Pat the ridiculed subject of many of his songs and cartoons. And almost from day one, Pat and Wendy had arguments that made the battles between Don and Wendy look mild in comparison.

One particular blowout served to provide one of the cornerstones of Kurt's own musical mythology. After a big fight, Wendy went out looking for Pat and found him, according to Kim, "cheating on her. He was drunk, as usual." Wendy stormed home in a fit of rage, mumbling about how she might kill Pat. In a panic, she had Kim gather Pat's guns in a big plastic bag. When Pat returned, Wendy declared she was going to murder him. Kurt claimed, in telling this story himself, that Wendy tried to shoot Pat but couldn't figure out how to load the gun; his sister doesn't recall that twist. Upon Pat's exit, Wendy and Kim dragged a bag of guns two blocks from their house to the banks of the Wishkah River. As they pulled the guns along the ground, Wendy kept repeating to herself, "Got to get rid of these or I'm going to end up killing him." She tossed them into the water.

While Pat and Wendy reconciled the next morning, Kurt quizzed Kim on the location of the guns. With his thirteen-year-old sister pointing the way, Kurt and two of his friends fished the rifles out. When Kurt would later tell this story, he'd say he traded the guns for his first guitar, though he actually had owned a guitar since he was fourteen. Kurt was never one to let the truth get in the way of a good story; the tale that he'd pawned his stepfather's guns for his first guitar was simply too good for the storyteller in him to resist. In this one story were all the elements of how he wished to be perceived as an artist—someone who turned redneck swords into punk rock plowshares. In truth, he did pawn the guns but used the proceeds to acquire a Fender Deluxe amp.

The "guns in the river" incident was just one of many of Wendy and Pat's blowouts. Kurt's technique to avoid these fights—or to avoid becoming the subject of them, since Pat loved nothing better than to lecture Wendy on what should be done with her errant son—was to beat a quick path from the front door to his room. In this way, he was typical of most teenagers, though his entrances and exits came at a furious pace. When he needed to surface for some household task—like using the phone or raiding the kitchen—he tried to time his excursions to avoid Pat. His room became his sanctuary, and his description a few years later in his journal about a trip back home was as much emotional as it was physical:

> Every time I come back, it's the same déjà vu memories that send a chill up my spine, total depression, total hatred, and grudges that would last months at a time, old Pee Chees with contents of drawings of rocker dudes playing guitar, monsters, and sayings on the cover like, "This Bud's for you," or, "Get high," intricate sketchings of bongs, alterations of sexual puns on the happy tennis-playing girl. Look around and see the Iron Maiden posters with ripped and hole-filled corners, nails in the walls where tractor hats are still displayed

today. Dents in the table from five years worth of playing a beer game called quarter bounce. The stained rug from snoose spittoon spills, I look around and see all this fucking shit and the thing that reminds me the most about my worthless adolescence is, every time I enter the room I run my finger across the ceiling and feel the sticky residue from a collection of pot and cigarette smoke.

During the spring of 1984, his conflicts with the adults in the house grew to a boiling point. He loathed Wendy for her weakness when it came to men, just as he had found issue with his father's desire to remarry. He hated Pat even more, since the older man provided advice in a manner designed to point out Kurt's inadequacies. The two males in the household also differed on how they thought women should be treated. "Pat was a womanizer," Kim said, "and Kurt wasn't. Kurt was very respectful of women, even if he didn't have a lot of girlfriends. He was looking for someone to fall in love with." Pat's lectures on how "a man needs to be a man and act like a man" were unending. When Kurt repeatedly failed to live up to Pat's standards, he'd be called "a faggot." One Sunday in April 1984, Pat's epithets were particularly vehement: "Why don't you ever bring any girls home?" he asked Kurt. "When I was your age, there were girls in and out of my bed all the time."

With this nugget of manly advice, Kurt went to a party. There he ran into Jackie Hagara. When she and a girlfriend wanted to leave, Kurt suggested they retreat to his house—perhaps he saw an opportunity to illustrate a point to Pat. Still, he snuck them upstairs without disturbing the adults. The girlfriend was quite drunk and proceeded to pass out on the twin bed in the playroom outside of Kurt's bedroom. With her friend incapacitated and unable to walk, Kurt told Jackie, "You can crash here."

Suddenly the moment Kurt had been waiting for arrived. He had long yearned to leave behind his adolescent sexual fantasies and to honestly declare to his high-school classmates that he was no longer a virgin (in fact, like most boys his age, he had been lying about the matter for several years). Growing up in a world where men were rarely touched except with the occasional slap on the back, he was starved for the feel of skin on skin. In Jackie, he had picked a more-than-willing compatriot. Though only fifteen, she was already experienced and on the night she found herself in Kurt's bedroom, her steady boyfriend happened to be in jail. She knew what was going to happen next as they moved into Kurt's room. There was, as Jackie remembered, a moment when they looked at each other and lust filled the room with all the power of an internal combustion engine revving up.

Kurt turned off the lights, the pair pulled off their clothes, and they excitedly jumped into bed and held each other. It would be Kurt's first embrace of a fully naked female, a moment he had long dreamt about, a moment that in many nights of adolescent masturbation, on this very bed, he had imagined. Jackie began to kiss him. At the moment their tongues touched, the door flew open, and in walked Kurt's mother.

Wendy was not, by any stretch of the imagination, happy to see her son in bed with a naked girl. She was also not pleased to see another girl passed out in the hallway. "Get the hell out!" she yelled. She had come upstairs to show Kurt the lightning outside—the fact that a major storm was raging had been lost on the young lovers—only to discover her son in bed with a girl. As she marched down the stairs, Wendy yelled, "Get the fuck out of my house!" Pat, for his part, was completely silent on the matter, knowing any comments from him would further enrage Wendy. Hearing a commotion, Kurt's sister Kim ran in from the next room. She observed Kurt and Jackie putting shoes on a girl, who was passed out. "What the hell?" Kim inquired. "We're leaving," Kurt told his sister. He and Jackie dragged the other girl down the stairs and they went outside into one of the biggest storms of the year.

As Kurt and his two cohorts began walking down First Street—the fresh air had revived the drunk friend—it began to rain, and though that seemed like an ominous sign, before the sun would rise Kurt would lose his virginity. Already he was visibly shaking, his raging hormones mixing with anger, shame, and fear. It had been humiliating to dress in front of Jackie, still sporting an erection. As in his encounter with the retarded girl, lust and shame were equally strong drives within him, hopelessly intertwined and confused.

They headed to Jackie's friend's house. But as soon as they walked in, so did Jackie's boyfriend, just sprung from jail. Jackie had warned Kurt about the violent nature of her paramour, and to avoid a confrontation, Kurt pretended he was the other girl's date. When Hagara and her boyfriend left, Kurt and the girl ended up spending the night together. It wasn't the greatest sex, or so she would later tell Jackie, but it was intercourse, which was all that mattered to Kurt. He had finally walked through that door, the great vaginal divide, and he was no longer leading a life that was a sexual lie.

Kurt left early in the morning to walk around Aberdeen in the pale light of dawn. The storm had passed, birds were chirping, and everything in the world seemed more alive. He walked around for hours thinking about it all, waiting for school to begin, watching the sun come up, and wondering where his life was heading.

5 THE WILL OF INSTINCT

ABERDEEN, WASHINGTON
APRIL 1984–SEPTEMBER 1986

It amazes me, the will of instinct.
—Lyrics from "Polly," 1990.

Early that Monday morning Kurt walked the streets of Aberdeen sniffing her sex on his fingers. For a person who was obsessed with smell it was an intoxicating experience. To relive the act, all he need do was rub his fingers in his own crotch, and when he sniffed them, her scent was still there. Already his mind was forgetting the fact that his sexual initiation was a near catastrophe, and instead he was turning it into triumph in his memory. The actual circumstances didn't matter—crummy sex or not, he was no longer a virgin. Being a romantic at heart, he also assumed this first sexual encounter was just the beginning of many pleasant romps with this girl; that it was the start of his adult sexual experience; a balm that he could count on, like beer or pot, to help him escape his lot. On the walk toward Weatherwax, he stole a flower from a yard. Jackie saw Kurt sheepishly heading toward the smoker's shack outside the high school with this one red rose in his hand—she thought it was for her, but Kurt delivered it to the girl he had slept with, who was unimpressed. What Kurt failed to understand was that it was Jackie who had the crush on him. The other girl, in contrast, was embarrassed by her indiscretion, and further embarrassed by the flower. It was a painful lesson, and for someone as sensitive as Kurt, it further confused his need for love with the complications of adult sexuality.

After school, there were more immediate concerns, the first being finding a place to live. Buzz drove with him to get his stuff. As Kurt had correctly surmised, this tiff with his mother was different from the others; they arrived to find her still in a rage. "His mom was just freaking out the entire time, telling him what a total fucking loser he was," Osborne recalled. "He just kept saying, 'Okay, Mom. *Okay.*' She made it clear she didn't even want him in the house." As he gathered his precious guitar and amp, putting his clothes in a series of Hefty garbage bags, Kurt began his final emotional and physical flight from his family. There had been other flights, and his retreating as a habit began soon after the divorce, but most of those moves were his. This time he was powerless with a very real fear over how he might care for himself. He was seventeen years old, a junior in high school, but failing most of his classes. He had never had a job, he had no money, and all his stuff was in four Hefty bags. He was sure he was leaving, but he had no idea where he was going.

If the divorce had been his first betrayal, and his father's remarriage the second, this third abandonment would be equally significant. Wendy was done with him. She complained to her sisters that she "didn't know what to do with Kurt anymore." Their battles were exacerbating her conflicts with Pat, whom she was planning to marry, and she could ill afford to lose that relationship, if only for economic reasons. Kurt felt, perhaps correctly, that yet again one of his parents was choosing a new partner over him. It was a marginalization that would stick with him: Combined with his earlier emotional wounds, the experience of being kicked out would be something he would return to repeatedly, never able to completely free himself from the trauma. It would lie there just under the surface, a pain that would enshroud the rest of his life with a fear of scarcity. There could never be enough money, enough attention, or—most important—enough love, because he knew how quickly it could all vanish.

Seven years later he would write a song about this period and title it "Something in the Way." The "something" was unexplained by the oblique lyrics, but there was little doubt that *he* was what was in the way. The song implies that the singer is living under a bridge. When asked to clarify it, Kurt always told a story of getting kicked out of the house, dropping out of school, and living under the Young Street Bridge. It would eventually become one of the touchstones of his cultural biography, one of his single most powerful pieces of myth-making, the one piece of Kurt's history certain to appear in any one-paragraph description of his life: This kid was so unwanted he lived under a bridge. It was a potent and dark image, made all the more resonant when Nirvana became famous and pictures began to appear in magazines of the underside of the Young Street Bridge, its rank fetid nature apparent even in photographs. It looked like something a troll would live under, not a child. The bridge was only two blocks from his mother's house, a distance, as Kurt told it, that no amount of love could cross.

The "living under the bridge" story, however, just like the "guns for guitars" story before it, was greatly embellished by Kurt in the telling. "He never lived under that bridge," insisted Krist Novoselic, who met Kurt in school that year. "He hung out there, but you couldn't live on those muddy banks, with the tides coming up and down. That was his own revisionism." His sister echoed the same belief: "He did not *ever* live under the bridge. It was a hangout where all the neighborhood kids would go to smoke pot, but that's all." And if Kurt ever spent a single night under *any* Aberdeen bridge, locals argue it would have been the Sixth Street Bridge, a much bigger span a half mile away, stretching over a small canyon and favored by Aberdeen's homeless. Even this setting is hard to imagine because Kurt was a world-class whiner; few whiners could survive an Aberdeen spring outdoors, where the weather is something just short of a daily monsoon. There is significance, though, to the bridge story, if only because Kurt emphatically told the tale so many times. At a point, he must have begun to believe it himself.

The true tale of where he spent his days and nights during this period is more poignant than even Kurt's rendition of events. His journey began on Dale Crover's porch, where he slept in a cardboard refrigerator box, curled up like a kitten. When his welcome ran out there, his ingenuity and wiliness did not fail him: There were many old apartment buildings in Aberdeen with central heating in the hallways, and this is where he would retreat most nights. He'd sneak in late, find a wide hallway, unscrew the overhead light, spread out his bedroll, go to sleep, and make sure to get up before the residents began their day. It was a life summed up best by a line he'd write a few years later in a song: "It amazes me, the will of instinct." His instinctual survival skills served him well, and his will was strong.

When all else failed, Kurt and another kid named Paul White would walk up the hill to Grays Harbor Community Hospital. There they would sleep in the waiting room. Kurt, the more daring of the two, or maybe the more desperate, would brazenly go through the hospital cafeteria line and charge food to made-up room numbers. "There was a television in the waiting room, and we could watch that all day," remembered White. "People always thought we were waiting for a patient who was ill or dying, and they'd never question you when it concerned that." This was the real story behind the emotional truth captured in "Something in the Way," and perhaps the greatest irony in his life—Kurt had ended up back where he began, back in the hospital with the territorial view of the harbor, back where he was born seventeen years previously. Here he was, sleeping in the waiting room like a fugitive, sneaking rolls out of the cafeteria, pretending to look like a bereaved relative of someone who was ill, but the only real illness was the loneliness he felt in his heart.

After about four months of living on the street, Kurt finally returned to live with his father. It wasn't easy for Kurt, and that he'd even consider moving back in with a parent shows his level of desperation. Don and Jenny heard Kurt was homeless and found him sleeping on an old sofa in a garage just across the alley from Wendy's house. "He was very angry at everybody at that time, and he wanted everyone to think that nobody would take him, which was pretty much what was true," Jenny remembered.

Back in Montesano, Kurt returned to his basement room in the Fleet Street house. His authority struggles with his father escalated—it was as if the time away from Don had only made his resolve stronger. All parties knew Kurt's presence there wasn't a permanent arrangement—they had mutually outgrown their need or want for each other. Kurt's guitar made life tolerable, and he practiced for hours. His friends and family began to notice he was becoming skilled at playing it. "He could play any song after listening to it just once, anything from Air Supply to John Cougar Mellencamp," recalled his stepbrother James. The family rented *This Is Spinal Tap* and Kurt and James watched it five times in a row—soon he began to recite dialogue from the film and play the band's songs.

While Kurt was back with Don and Jenny, there was yet another suicide in the family. Kenneth Cobain, Leland's only remaining brother, grew despondent over the death of his wife and shot himself in the forehead with a .22 caliber pistol. The loss was almost too much for Leland to bear: The cumulative effect of the tragic deaths of his father, his son Michael, and his three brothers tempered his bluster with severe melancholy. If you consider Ernest's death a suicide by alcohol, all three of Leland's brothers had died by their own hand, two by shooting themselves.

Kurt wasn't close to these uncles, but there was a mournful pall over the house; it seemed as if the family was cursed on all fronts. His stepmother made efforts to find Kurt a job doing lawn work, since that was the only work that could be found in Monte other than logging. Kurt mowed a few lawns, but quickly became bored. He looked in the want ads once or twice, but there weren't many jobs to be had in Montesano. The county's biggest economic enterprise—the Satsop Nuclear Power Plant had gone bust before being fully constructed, leaving unemployment at fifteen percent, twice as high as the rest of the state. Things came to a head when Don announced that if Kurt wasn't going to go to school, or work, he had to join the service. The next night, Don invited a Navy recruiter to talk to his son.

Instead of a strong, willful man—who later in his life might have grabbed the Navy man by his collar and thrown him headfirst out the door—the recruiter found a sad and broken boy. Kurt, to everyone's surprise, listened to the pitch. At the end of the evening, much to his father's relief, Kurt said he'd consider it. To Kurt, the service sounded like a hell, but it was a hell with a different zip code. As Kurt told Jesse Reed, "At least the Navy could give you three hots and a cot." To a kid who had been living on the street and sleeping in hospital waiting rooms, the security of shelter and food without a parental price to pay appeared tempting. But when Don tried to convince him to let the recruiter return the next night, Kurt said to forget it.

Desperate for something, he found religion. He and Jesse had become inseparable during 1984, and this extended to going to church together. Jesse's parents, Ethel and Dave Reed, were born-again Christians, and the family went to the Central Park Baptist Church, halfway between Monte and Aberdeen. Kurt began to attend Sunday service regularly, and even made appearances at the Wednesday night Christian Youth Group. He was baptized in the church that October, though none of his family members were present. Jesse even remembered Kurt going through a born-again conversion experience: "One night we were walking over the Chehalis River bridge and he stopped, and said he accepted Jesus Christ into his life. He asked God to 'come into his life.' I remember him distinctly talking about the revelations and the calmness that everybody talks about when they accept Christ." In the next couple of weeks, Kurt displayed the tone of an evangelical born-again Christian. He began to chastise Jesse for smoking pot, disregarding the Bible, and being a poor Christian. Kurt's religious conversion coincided with one of his many sober periods; his history with drugs and alcohol would always consist of a binge, followed by a fast. He wrote a letter to his Aunt Mari that month espousing his views on marijuana:

> I just got done watching *Reefer Madness* on MTV . . . It was made in the thirties and if people took one toke of the devil drug, marijuana, they spaced-out big time, killed each other, had affairs, ran over innocent victims in cars. They sent this teenager, who looked like the Beaver, on a murder rap. Wow, that's more excitement than I can handle. It was like a big over-exaggeration. But I accept the whole idea behind it. Pot sucks. I know that from personal experience, because for a while there I became almost as lethargic as a moldy piece of cheese. I think that was a big problem with my mom and I.

Yet almost as soon as he mailed the letter and found himself settling into the pattern of church life, Kurt discarded his faith like a pair of pants he'd outgrown. "He was hungry for it," Jesse said, "but it was a transitory moment out of fear." When fear subsided, Kurt started smoking pot again. He attended Central Park Baptist for another three months, but his talk, as Jesse remembered, "was more moving against God. After that he was on an anti-God thing."

Jesse's parents had grown attached to Kurt, and since he was at their house so often, they suggested he move in. They lived in North River, a rural area fourteen miles outside of Aberdeen. At the time the two boys seemed to provide something to each other that was missing in their individual lives. The Reeds discussed the possibility of Kurt moving to North River, and Wendy, Don, and Jenny all agreed it was worth a try. Wendy told the Reeds she was "at her wit's end," a point echoed by Don and Jenny. "Dave Reed came to us," recalled Jenny, "and said he thought he could do something for him. They were a religious family, and Dave felt he could discipline him when no one else could." "We really loved Kurt," explained Ethel Reed. "He was such a sweet kid; he just seemed lost." In September, Kurt packed his belongings once again—this time he had a duffel bag—and moved to North River.

The Reeds lived in a 4,000-square-foot home and the boys had the run of a huge upstairs. Perhaps the best thing about the house was that it was so remote, they could crank their electric guitars as loud as they wanted. They would play all day. Though Dave Reed was a Christian Youth counselor—he resembled Ned Flanders from "The Simpsons," with his short hair and mustache—he wasn't a square. Reed had been playing rock 'n' roll for twenty years, and had been in the Beachcombers with Kurt's Uncle Chuck, so he was known to the family. The house was stocked with amps, guitars, and albums. The Reeds were also less strict than Don: They let Kurt travel to Seattle with Buzz and Lukin to see the seminal punk band Black Flag. *The Rocket* called the show the second best of 1984, but to Kurt it was second only to the Melvins' parking lot show. In every interview he did later in his life, he claimed that this was the first concert he ever saw.

It was here at the Reeds' house where Kurt first jammed with Krist Novoselic. Novoselic was two years older than Kurt, but he was impossible to miss around Grays Harbor: At six-foot seven, he resembled a young Abraham Lincoln. Krist was of Croatian heritage, and came from a family marked by divorce that could compete against Kurt's for dysfunction (Krist had been known as "Chris" in Aberdeen; he changed the spelling of his name back to his original Croatian birth name in 1992).

Kurt had met Krist in high school and at the Melvins' practice space, but their lives had also intersected in one place neither of them would ever mention again—the Central Park Baptist Church. Krist had been attending the church, but even the elders like Mr. Reed knew he was there "just for the girls." Jesse invited Krist to his house one afternoon, and the three jammed. Krist was playing guitar at this point, as were Jesse and Kurt, so the session sounded like a "Wayne's World" taping as they ran through the usual Jimmy Page imitations. Krist and Jesse switched guitars for a while; left-handed Kurt just stuck with his own. They did play a few of Kurt's original songs with the three-guitar assault.

Once Kurt moved in with the Reeds, he made several short attempts to return to school at Weatherwax. He was already so behind in his classes it was inevitable he wouldn't graduate with his class. Kurt told his friends he might pretend to be retarded to get into special-ed classes. Jesse would tease Kurt and call him "Slow Brain" because of his poor grades. His only real participation in school was art class, the one place he didn't feel incompetent. He entered one of his class projects in the 1985 Regional High School Art Show, and his work was put into the permanent collection of the Superintendent of Public Instruction. Mr. Hunter told Kurt that if he applied himself he might be able to get a scholarship to an art school. A scholarship, and college, would have required graduating from Weatherwax, something Kurt didn't see as a possibility unless he was held over an extra year (later in his life, he claimed falsely to have been offered several scholarships). Eventually Kurt dropped out completely, but not before first enrolling in Aberdeen's alternative Continuation High School. The curriculum was similar to Weatherwax's, but there were no formal classes: Students worked with teachers on a one-on-one basis. Mike Poitras tutored Kurt for about a week, but the boy didn't stick with it long enough to complete the orientation. Two weeks later, Kurt dropped out of the school for dropouts.

Once Kurt stopped going to school altogether, Dave Reed found him a job at the Lamplighter Restaurant in Grayland. It paid $4.25 an hour, and he worked as dishwasher, prep assistant, relief cook, and busboy. It was the winter season and the restaurant was usually deserted, which suited Kurt fine.

It was through exposure to Dave Reed, along with his Uncle Chuck and Aunt Mari, that Kurt first began to imagine that one day he might have a future in the music business. Dave and Chuck had recorded a single with the Beachcombers in their early days—"Purple Peanuts," backed with "The Wheelie"—and it was a prized possession in the Reeds' home. Kurt and Jesse played the record constantly, mimicking it on their guitars. Kurt himself was writing songs faithfully—he had several Pee Chees stuffed with sheets of lyrics. Some of the titles were "Wattage in the Cottage," "Samurai Sabotage," and a tune about Mr. Reed called "Diamond Dave." Kurt even wrote a song mocking a fellow Aberdeen classmate who had committed suicide. The boy's name was Beau; the song was called "Ode to Beau" and was sung in a country and western style.

A former member of the Beachcombers had gone on to become a Capitol Records promotion person in Seattle. The instant Kurt found this fact out, he clung on to it for dear life. He hounded Dave to introduce him, not knowing at the time that a promotion person was not a talent scout. "He always wanted to meet him because he thought it would catapult his career," recalled Jesse. This was the nascent beginning of Kurt Cobain, the professional musician, and his constant pleading for this introduction—which never came—is evidence that, at seventeen, he was imagining a career in music. If Kurt had admitted his major label ambitions around the Melvins' rehearsal shack, he would have been treated as a heretic. He kept his ambition to himself, but he never stopped looking at ways to move beyond his circumstances.

Life with the Reeds came close to recreating the family he'd lost in the divorce. The Reeds ate dinner together, attended church as a group, and the boys' musical talents were encouraged. A real affection and love was obvious and tangible among all members of the household, Kurt included. When Kurt turned eighteen in February 1985, the Reeds held a birthday celebration for him. His Aunt Mari sent him two books:

Hammer of the Gods, the Led Zeppelin biography, and a collection of Norman Rockwell illustrations. In a thank-you note Kurt wrote his aunt, he described his birthday party: "All the kids from the church Youth Group came over, brought cake for me and Jesse, then we played stupid games and Pastor Lloyd sang some songs (he looks exactly like Mr. Rogers). But it was nice to know people care about ya."

Yet even with a church youth group, Pastor Lloyd, and the surrogate family of the Reeds, Kurt could not psychologically escape the abandonment he felt from his own fractured family of origin. "He was hard on himself," Dave Reed observed. Though Kurt had little contact with his mother, Dave Reed would update Wendy monthly. In August 1984 she had married Pat O'Connor, and by the next spring she was pregnant. During her pregnancy Kurt stopped by the house once, and when Wendy saw how lost he looked, she broke down crying. Kurt got down on his knees, embraced his mother, and told her he was fine.

And he was, at least for the moment, but then crisis returned. In March 1985, Kurt cut his finger washing dishes at work and quit in a fit of panic. "He had to get stitches," remembered Jesse, "and he told me that if he lost his finger and couldn't play guitar, he'd kill himself." With no job and an injury that kept him from the guitar, Kurt hibernated in the house. He convinced Jesse to skip school, and the two of them would spend all day drinking or doing drugs. "He withdrew more and more," remembered Ethel Reed. "We tried to draw Kurt out, but we just couldn't. As time progressed we decided that we weren't helping him, and that all we were doing was providing a place for him to withdraw further from people."

Kurt's dissociation came to a head in April, when he forgot his key one afternoon and kicked in a window to get in. That was the last straw for the Reeds, and they told Kurt he had to find another place to live. It was a rainy April that year in Grays Harbor, and while most kids his age were concerned with going to the prom or preparing for graduation, Kurt was once again looking for shelter.

Back on the streets, Kurt resumed the endless cycle of crashing in friends' garages or sleeping in hallways. Desperate, he finally turned to the mercy of the government, and began receiving $40 a month in food stamps. Through the local unemployment office, he found a job working at the YMCA beginning May 1. It was part-time and administered by a local "Youth Work" grant, but he would describe this brief employment as his favorite day job. The job was a glorified janitorial position, but if other employees were sick, he was the substitute lifeguard or activity instructor. Kurt loved the work, particularly working with kids. Though Kurt wasn't a particularly strong swimmer himself, he enjoyed filling in as a lifeguard. Kevin Shillinger, who lived a block away from the YMCA, observed Kurt teaching five- and six-year-olds to play T-ball—during the entire lesson there was a huge smile on Kurt's face. Working with children, he could find the self-esteem he lacked in the other areas of his life: He was good with them, and they were non-judgmental.

He also took a second part-time job, though this one he rarely discussed. It was a position as a janitor at Weatherwax High School. Each evening he would don a brown jumpsuit and push a mop through the hallways of the school he had dropped out of. Though the school year was almost over by the time he began, the contrast between his peers' preparing for college and his own particulars left him feeling as diminished as he ever did in his life. He lasted two months before quitting.

Once Kurt left the Reeds' household, Jesse followed. For a while the pair stayed at Jesse's grandparents' house in Aberdeen. Then, on June 1, 1985, they moved into an apartment at 404 North Michigan Street. By any standards this tiny $100-a-month studio—the walls of which were painted pink and thus earned it the name "the pink apartment"—was a dump, but it was their dump. The apartment came with some modest furnishings, which they supplemented with lawn ornaments, Big Wheel tricycles, and backyard recliners stolen from the neighborhood. A picture window faced the street and Kurt took this to be his public easel, writing "666" and "Satan Rules" on the glass with soap. A blow-up doll hung from a noose and was covered in shaving gel. Edge Shaving Gel was everywhere in the apartment; samples had been given away in the neighborhood and Kurt and Jesse discovered they could suck the fumes from the cans and get high. One night they had taken a couple of hits of acid when a Grays Harbor County sheriff knocked at the door and told them to remove the doll. Luckily, the officer didn't enter their apartment: He would have observed three weeks of dishes stacked in the sink, numerous pieces of stolen lawn furniture, Edge Shaving Gel wiped on all the walls, and the booty from their latest prank—stealing crosses from headstones at the graveyard and painting them with polka dots.

This would not be Kurt's only run-in with the law during the summer of 1985. Kurt, Jesse, and their buddies would wait like werewolves for nightfall and then go forth to terrorize the neighborhood by stealing lawn furniture or spray-painting buildings. Though Kurt would later claim that his graffiti messages were political ("God is Gay," "Abort Christ," he listed as a few of his slogans), in fact, most of what he wrote was nonsensical. He enraged a neighbor with a boat by painting "Boat Ack" in red letters on the ship's hull; on the other side he lettered, "Boat people go home." One night he painted graffiti on the wall of the YMCA; in no small stroke of poetic justice, the next day he was assigned the job of cleaning it off.

On the night of July 23, 1985, Detective Michael Bens was patrolling Market Street—just a block from the Aberdeen Police Station—when he observed three men and a blond-haired boy in an alley. The men fled as Bens's car approached, but the blond kid stood frozen, looking like a deer in the headlights, and Bens saw him drop a graffiti marker. On the wall behind him was the prophetic statement: "Ain't got no how watchamacallit." Typographically, it was a work of art, as the letters were in random upper and lower case, and every "T" was four times larger than the other characters.

Suddenly, the boy bolted and ran two blocks before the patrol car caught up with him. Once it did, he stopped and was handcuffed. He gave his name as "Kurt Donald Cobain," and was a picture of politeness. At the station, he wrote and signed a statement, which read in full:

> Tonight, while standing behind SeaFirst Bank in the alley by the library talking to three other people, I wrote on the SeaFirst building. I don't know why I did it, but I did. What I put on the wall was, "Ain't got no how watchamacallit." Now I see how silly it

was for me to have done this, and I'm sorry that I did. When the police car came into the alley I saw him, and I dropped the red marker that I had used.

He was fingerprinted, had mug shots taken, and was then released but required to show up in court for a hearing a few weeks later. He received a $180 fine, a suspended 30-day sentence, and was warned not to get into any more trouble.

For eighteen-year-old Kurt, that was easier said than done. One night when Jesse was at work, the usual "Cling-Ons" came over and everyone jammed with their guitars. One of the neighbors, a large man with a mustache, pounded on the wall and told them to be quiet. In Kurt's later telling of this story, he said the neighbor mercilessly beat him for hours. It was one of the many tales Kurt told about his constant abuse at the hands of Aberdeen's rednecks. "It wasn't like that," recalled Steve Shillinger. "The guy did come over, told him to be quiet, and when Kurt wised off, the fellow punched him a couple of times and told him to 'shut the fuck up.' " Jesse wasn't there that night, but in the entire time he knew Kurt he recalled only one fight: "He was usually too busy making people laugh. I was always around to protect him." Jesse was short like Kurt, but he had lifted weights and was heavily built.

During the pink apartment period, Jesse probably would have killed for Kurt, a fact Kurt took full advantage of. One day, Kurt announced they were both getting Mohawks. They marched down to the Shillingers, hair clippers were produced, and Jesse soon had a Mohawk. When it came time for Kurt's shave, he declared it was a dumb idea. "One time, Kurt said if he could write something on my forehead, I could write something on his," remembered Jesse. "He took permanent ink and wrote '666' on me, and then he took off running. I was always the nitwit who everyone used to experiment on. If there was a chemical or a drink, they'd always want me to try it first." There was a dark side to Kurt's torment of his best friend. Despite all his goofing off, Jesse had managed to graduate that spring. One night when Jesse was at work at Burger King, Kurt ripped the pictures out of Jesse's yearbook, pasted them to the wall, and marked red crosses through them. It was more of a display of his own self-hatred than it was a reflection of his feelings for Jesse. Perhaps in a fit of shame over his rage, Kurt decided to kick Jesse out of the apartment. Never mind that Jesse had been the one who had put down the deposit. Soon Jesse was living with his grandmother, and Kurt was on his own. Jesse had plans to join the Navy anyway, and Kurt felt threatened by this. It was a pattern he would play out his entire life: Rather than lose someone he cared for, he would withdraw first, usually by creating some mock conflict as a way of lessening the abandonment he felt was inevitable.

Kurt continued to write songs while living in the pink apartment, and though most were still thinly disguised stories of the characters and events around him, many were humorous. That summer he wrote a song called "Spam," about the meat product, and another called "The Class of 85," which was an attack on Jesse and the graduating class he missed. It went: "We are all the same, just flies on a turd." Though his songs were about an insular world, even at this stage Kurt was thinking big. "I'm going to make a record that's going to be even bigger than U2 or R.E.M.," he bragged to Steve Shillinger. Kurt loved both these bands, and he talked unceasingly of how great the Smithereens were, though these were influences he was careful not to mention around Buzz for fear of breaking the punk code that no popular music mattered. He read every fanzine or music magazine he could find, which in Aberdeen wasn't many; he even wrote out lengthy imaginary interviews with himself for nonexistent publications. Kurt and Steve talked about starting their own fanzine, going so far as to draft up a sample issue; Steve bailed on the project when he realized that Kurt was writing positive reviews of records he had never listened to. Kurt also talked about starting his own record label, and one night he and Steve recorded a friend named Scotty Karate doing a spoken word monologue. Like so many of his ideas at the time, nothing ever came of it.

There wasn't money for fanzine publishing or record labels, and even paying the rent was hard. Two months after Jesse's departure, Kurt was evicted. His landlord came to the apartment when Kurt wasn't home, boxed up the few belongings he had, including the stolen crosses and Big Wheels, and left them on the street.

. . .

For the third time in two years, Kurt was without a home. Once again, he considered the Navy. Trevor Briggs was signing up for the service, and he urged Kurt to take advantage of the Navy's buddy system, where they could be placed at boot camp together. Unemployment had grown even higher in Grays Harbor, and options for an eighteen-year-old dropout were limited. Kurt went to the Navy recruiting office on State Street and spent three hours taking the ASVAB vocational aptitude test. He passed, and the Navy was willing to take him; later Kurt claimed he received the highest score ever registered on the test, but this could hardly be believed since the test included math. At the last minute, as he had before, Kurt balked when it came time to join.

Most nights Kurt would sleep in the backseat of Greg Hokanson's mother's beat-up Volvo sedan, jokingly called "the vulva." By the time October rolled around, and the weather turned bad, nights were miserable in the car seat. Kurt soon found a new benefactor in the Shillinger family, who, after intense lobbying from Kurt, agreed to take him in.

Lamont Shillinger was an English teacher at Weatherwax, and like Dave Reed, he came from a religious background. Though he'd left the Mormon church years before, Lamont still attempted to be, as he described it, "a freelance decent human being." There were other similarities to life at the Reeds': The Shillingers ate dinner together, spent time as a family, and their sons were encouraged to play music. Kurt was accepted like family and put into the rotation of chores, which he did without complaint, grateful for being included. Room was a bit short in the Shillinger household—they had six kids of their own—so Kurt slept on a sofa in the living room, storing his sleeping bag behind it during the day. He spent Thanksgiving and Christmas morning of 1985 with the Shillingers. Lamont bought Kurt a much-needed new pair of Levi's. Later on Christmas Day, Kurt visited Wendy's house— she had just given birth to his half-sister Brianne. The new baby made the O'Connor home a happier place, though there was no talk of Kurt moving back in.

In December 1985, Kurt began to rehearse some of the songs he'd written with Dale Crover on bass and Greg Hokanson on drums. He called this grouping Fecal Matter, and it was his first real band. He convinced Crover to accompany him on a trip to Aunt Mari's to tape

some of the songs. "He arrived," Mari remembered, "with a huge notebook full of lyrics. I showed him how to adjust a few things, how to
record with the reel-to-reel, and he went right at it." Kurt recorded his
voice first, and then he and Crover would track the guitar, bass, and
drum parts over the vocals. Mari was troubled by the lyrics to "Suicide
Samurai," but wrote it off as typical teenage behavior. The boys also
cut "Bambi Slaughter" (the story of how a boy pawned his parents'
wedding rings), "Buffy's Pregnant" (Buffy from the "Family Affair"
television show), "Downer," "Laminated Effect," "Spank Thru," and
"Sound of Dentage." When Kurt got back to Aberdeen, he used the
Shillingers' tape deck to dub off copies. Having the actual tape in his
hand was tangible proof to him that he had talent—it was the first
physical manifestation of the self-esteem he found through music.
Nonetheless, Fecal Matter broke up without ever playing a single gig.

Despite his external circumstances, Kurt's inner artistic life was
growing by leaps and bounds. He continued making movies using the
Super-8 camera. One short silent film from this period has Kurt walking
through an abandoned building wearing a KISW "Seattle's Best Rock"
T-shirt and trying to look like Jean-Paul Belmondo in *Breathless*, with
his wraparound sunglasses. In another he puts on a Mr. T mask and
pretends to snort a huge quantity of what looks like cocaine, a special
effect he created with flour and a vacuum cleaner. Without exception,
these films were inventive and—as with everything Kurt created—disturbing. That spring he attempted to start a business decorating skate-
boards with graffiti. He went so far as to put up flyers around town, but
only one teenager ever hired him, asking for an exploding head. Kurt
gladly drew this—it was his specialty—but the customer never paid and
the business failed.

On May 18, 1986, Kurt again fell under the care and supervision of
the Aberdeen Police Department. At 12:30 in the morning, police were
called to an abandoned building at 618 West Market, and Officer John
Green found Kurt climbing around on a roof, seemingly intoxicated.
Green remembered Kurt being a "nice kid, if a little scared." Kurt was
charged with trespassing and being a minor in possession of alcohol by
consumption. When the cops found that he had an outstanding warrant
for malicious mischief (he had failed to pay the fine for the graffiti arrest),

plus an earlier alcohol arrest from Seattle, and he couldn't come up with bail, they put him in jail. The cell he stayed in was straight out of an old gangster movie: iron bars, concrete floor, no ventilation. On his statement, Kurt listed a "bad back" under "medical conditions," and described himself as "19 years old, 135 pounds, five-foot nine inches, brown hair, and blue eyes." He exaggerated in describing both his height and weight.

Kurt used his one phone call to dial Lamont Shillinger and beg him to bail him out. Lamont decided his parenting of Kurt Cobain had gone far enough, and that Kurt would have to get out of this jam by himself. Lamont did visit the next day, and even though it was against Lamont's religion, he brought Kurt a carton of cigarettes. Unable to raise bail, Kurt stayed eight days.

Several years later Kurt used this experience to create folklore that accentuated his wit and adaptability. He alleged that during his jail time he drew pornography for the other prisoners to masturbate to. His home-drawn porn was in such demand, as he told it, he traded for cigarettes, and soon he had collected all the cigarettes in the jail. At this point he became, the story went, "the man" who "ran the jail." He only dared tell this fictional tale to people who didn't know him—his Aberdeen friends remember him being so scared from all the images of prison films he'd seen over the years that he didn't say a single word to another inmate during his entire stay.

Life at the Shillingers was soon to end for Kurt. He'd been there a year and, at nineteen—well past the age of emancipation—he was neither their blood relative nor official foster child. He'd also begun to quarrel with Eric Shillinger, who thought Kurt had overstayed his welcome. One weekend the Shillinger family went on vacation without Kurt and upon their return discovered he had coerced their two dogs to defecate on Eric's bed. But even this slight wasn't the final straw; it came one night in August 1986, when Eric and Kurt got in a fight over a Totino's mini pizza. By all reports it was the most serious fight Kurt was ever in and Kurt tried to hit Eric with a two-by-four. "I saw Eric the next day," remembered Kevin Shillinger, "and he had a black eye. I saw Kurt, and he had two black eyes." Kurt left that night, nursing a swollen face, and retreated to the Melvins' band room. The next day he paid Steve $10 to haul all his remaining stuff down to Crover's. His life had been reduced to an all-too-familiar pattern of intimacy, conflict, and banishment, followed by isolation.

One of the only bright spots came when Krist Novoselic seemed interested in forming a band. Krist was one of the first people upon whom Kurt had bestowed his Fecal Matter tape. "He had this little demo tape and it had 'Spank Thru' on it," Krist recalled. "I thought it was a really good song." Shelli Dilly, Krist's girlfriend, had been friends with Kurt since high school, and they began to let him crash behind their house, sleeping in Krist's Volkswagen van. "I always made sure he had enough blankets so he didn't freeze to death," said Shelli. She also gave him free food whenever he came into the McDonald's where she worked.

In early September 1986, Hilary Richrod, a librarian at the Aberdeen Timberland Library, heard a knock on the door of her home late one afternoon. She looked through the keyhole and saw a tall boy with red eyes and Kurt, who she recognized: He would frequently spend his afternoons in the library reading or sleeping. Seeing these two motley characters on her doorstep—in a town where burglary and robbery were a part of life—she felt a twinge of alarm as she opened the door. Her alarm was increased when Kurt reached under his coat. But what he pulled out was a tiny pigeon with a broken wing. "It's hurt and can't fly," Kurt said. Richrod was momentarily taken aback. "You're the bird lady, aren't you?" Kurt inquired, sounding almost annoyed. She was indeed the bird lady, running the Aberdeen wild bird rescue organization, but usually people telephoned her when a bird was injured. No one had ever just shown up on her door before, certainly not two stoned-looking teenagers.

Kurt told her he'd found the pigeon under the Young Street Bridge, and they had walked the fifteen minutes to her house as soon as they saw it. How they knew she was the bird lady was never explained. But they watched intently as she began to care for the animal. Walking through the house, they spotted a guitar that belonged to Richrod's husband, and Kurt immediately sized it up: "It's an old Les Paul. It's a copy, but a very early copy." He offered to buy it, but Richrod said it wasn't for sale. She momentarily wondered if they might steal it.

Yet their only concern was the care and comfort of the tiny pigeon. Back in the kitchen, the two men observed while Richrod slowly moved the bird's wing to try to determine how badly it was broken. "He's hurt, isn't he?" Kurt asked. Richrod had two nighthawks in her kitchen, two of the only birds of this species in captivity, and she told them the birds had even been featured in a story on the front page of the *Aberdeen Daily World*.

"I'm in a band," Kurt replied, announcing this fact as if it should have been common knowledge. "But even I'll never get on the front page of the *Daily World*. Those birds have me beat by a mile."

6 DIDN'T LOVE HIM ENOUGH

ABERDEEN, WASHINGTON
SEPTEMBER 1986–MARCH 1987

I obviously didn't love him enough, as I do now.
—A 1987 journal entry.

On September 1, 1986, Wendy loaned Kurt $200—enough for a deposit and first month's rent—and Kurt moved into his first "house." That legal description of the structure at 1000½ East Second Street in Aberdeen was far too generous; it was a shack that in many other municipalities might have been condemned as uninhabitable under any reasonable building code. The roof was rotting, the boards on the front porch had fallen to the ground, and there was no refrigerator or stove. The floor plan was bizarrely broken up into five tiny rooms: two living rooms, two bedrooms, and a single bathroom. It sat behind another house, which was the reason for the strange address.

Still, the location—two blocks from his mother's house—was ideal for a nineteen-year-old who wasn't completely free of Wendy's psychic control. Their relationship had improved in the past year. With Kurt out of the house, they drew closer emotionally; he still very much needed Wendy's approval and attention, even while hiding this vulnerability. She would occasionally bring him food, and he could go to her house to do laundry, use the phone, or raid the refrigerator, all provided that his stepfather wasn't around. The shack was near the Salvation Army and behind a grocery store. Since the house didn't have a refrigerator, Kurt stored beer in an icebox on the back porch until the neighbor kids discovered this.

For a roommate, Kurt chose Matt Lukin from the Melvins. Kurt had always wanted to be in the Melvins; living with Lukin was as close as he got. Kurt's main contribution to the house was sticking a bathtub full of turtles in the middle of the living room and drilling a hole in the floor so the turtle effluence would run under the floorboards. Lukin, at least, used his construction skills to try to rearrange the walls. As an added bonus, Lukin was 21, so he could buy beer. The Fat Man would soon become a distant memory.

It was both a party house and, eventually, a band house. With Lukin as a roommate, Buzz Osborne and Dale Crover visited frequently, and since the living room was filled with band gear, there were impromptu jams. A motley crew of Melvins' "Cling-Ons" came to inhabit the shack. Though much of the bonding was centered around the goal of inebriation, this halcyon time in 1000½ East Second was the most social of Kurt's life. Kurt even became friendly with the neighbors, or at least their teenage kids, who were victims of fetal alcohol syndrome—that didn't stop him from giving them beer. Another neighbor, a senile senior citizen nicknamed "Lynyrd Skynyrd hippie," would visit every day to listen to Kurt's copy of Lynyrd Skynyrd's *Greatest Hits* as he drummed along.

To pay the rent, Kurt got a job as a maintenance man at the Polynesian Condominium Resort in nearby Ocean Shores. He would take the bus for the 25-mile trip to the coastal resort. It was an easy job, since his main responsibility was to repair things, and the 66-room resort wasn't in need of repair. When a job as a maid came up, he recommended Krist's girlfriend, Shelli. "He used to sleep on the bus," she remembered. "It was funny because he wasn't really a maintenance man at all. He'd sleep in the motel rooms or go and raid the refrigerators in the rooms after people left." One benefit of the job, other than the $4-an-hour starting pay, was that he only had to wear a brown work shirt, and not a dreaded uniform.

He bragged about how easy the job was to his friends—describing it as "maintenance butt-boy"—and how he was able to pass most of his days sneaking into rooms and watching television, but what he didn't tell anyone was that he also had to occasionally clean rooms. Kurt Cobain, who was such a bad housekeeper that he should make some kind of hall of fame, had to work as a maid. On the bus to the resort each morning, usually hung over, Kurt would dream of a future that did not include scrubbing toilets and making beds.

What he did think of, all the time, was the idea of forming a band. It was a constant refrain in his head, and he spent endless hours trying to figure out how it could be done. Buzz had done it—and if Buzz had figured it out, he was sure he could too. On a dozen occasions during 1987, he had traveled as a roadie with the Melvins to gigs in Olympia, a college town an hour east, where he'd observed an enthusiastic audience for punk rock, albeit a small one. Once he'd made it all the way to Seattle with the band, and though that meant he had to schlep equipment and go to work with no sleep the next morning, it was a taste of a larger world. Being a Melvins' roadie was not a glamorous job: There was no money or groupies to speak of, and Buzz was infamous for treating everyone like a servant. But it was an abuse Kurt gladly withstood, as there was little that escaped his study. Kurt had pride developing, particularly when it came to his guitar playing; as he carried Buzz's amp, he imagined the roles reversed. He practiced every moment he could, and the fact he was getting better was one of the only avenues to self-confidence he found. His hopes were rewarded when Buzz and Dale asked him to jam with them in Olympia, at the closing night of a club called Gessco. Though only about twenty people witnessed the show—the poster had billed them as Brown Towel, but their name was supposed to be Brown Cow—the night would mark his debut performance in front of a paying audience. Yet rather than playing guitar, Kurt read poetry while Buzz and Dale thrashed at their instruments.

Many of the self-destructive habits he had indulged in at the pink apartment were still evident at the shack. Tracy Marander, who met him during this period, said the amount of LSD he ingested was notable. "Kurt was doing a lot of acid, sometimes five times a week," she recalled. At least part of the reason for his increased drug usage was, strangely, union loyalty; an Aberdeen grocery strike at the time meant you had to either drive to Olympia to buy beer or cross a picket line, and Kurt's usual choice was to take acid instead. When he did buy beer, usually it was "Animal Beer," so called because the Schmidt cans featured wildlife images. When he had more money, Kurt would splurge for Rolling Rock because, he told his friends, "it's almost like 'rock 'n' roll' spelled backwards."

The shack year was one of Kurt's longest and most extreme periods of drug abuse. Previously his pattern had been one of bingeing and then drying out, but living in the shack, he embraced getting messed up like he embraced little else. "He always was pushing it," remembered Steve Shillinger, "using just a little bit more than anyone else, and taking more as soon as he was no longer high." When he was out of money for pot, acid, or beer, he'd go back to huffing aerosol cans. "He was really into getting fucked up; drugs, acid, any kind of drug," Novoselic observed. "He'd get hammered in the middle of the day. He was a mess."

He also continued to talk of suicide and early death. Ryan Aigner lived one block away and from the moment he met Kurt, he remembered daily conversations about death. Once Ryan asked Kurt, "What are you going to do when you're thirty?" "I'm not worried about what's going to happen when I'm thirty," Kurt replied in the same tone he would use to discuss a broken spark plug, "because I'm never going to make it to thirty. You know what life is like after thirty—I don't want that." The concept was so foreign to Ryan, who viewed the world with a young man's sense of possibility, he was momentarily speechless. Ryan could recognize a torment inside Kurt: "He was the shape of suicide. He looked like suicide, he walked like suicide, and he talked about suicide."

By late spring, Kurt had left the resort job. Desperate for money, he would occasionally work as a carpet installer alongside Ryan. The supervisors of the carpet company liked Kurt, and Ryan let him know that a full-time job was possible. But Kurt balked at this prospect because the idea of serious work to him was anathema, and he was afraid of injuring his guitar-playing hand on the double-edged knives used to cut the carpet. "These hands are too important to me," Kurt argued. "I could mess up my guitar-playing career." He said if he cut his hands and was unable to play, it would end his life.

The very fact that Kurt would even use the word "career" to describe his music shows the one place where optimism existed. Those incessant hours practicing were beginning to pay off. He was writing songs at a prodigious rate, crudely scratching out the lyrics on pages in his notebook. He was learning so fast and absorbing so much from the shows he saw and the records he listened to, you could almost see his brain piecing together a plan. There wasn't much focus on "the band," since no single unit existed at the time; instead, caught up in his exuberance to make music, he arranged three or four groups simultaneously. One of the first groupings to practice in the shack featured Kurt on guitar, Krist on bass, and a local drummer named Bob McFadden. Another had Kurt playing drums, Krist on guitar, and Steve "Instant" Newman on bass. To even call these groups, as Kurt did later, was a bit of an exaggeration: They were only real in Kurt's mind, and he would put them together in the way someone might plot the ideal fantasy baseball team. Observing that the Melvins had been paid $60 one night for a gig, Kurt and Krist formed a band called the Sellouts, which only rehearsed Creedence Clearwater Revival songs, knowing these would go over big in Aberdeen taverns. Kurt discussed these bands as if they had lengthy careers, when most just played rehearsal. Only an outfit they called the Stiff Woodies was put on public display, at a kegger of high-school kids who ignored them.

While the jam sessions and parties kept Kurt occupied, by the beginning of 1987 he was already developing a restlessness with Aberdeen. His friends observed that while they were content to use music as a fun way to pass a Friday night, Kurt was practicing a guitar riff or writing a song on Saturday morning. All he lacked was a vehicle for his creative vision, but that was about to change. He and Krist began to play with a neighborhood drummer named Aaron Burckhard in an unnamed group; Krist played bass, Burckhard drummed, and Kurt played guitar and sang. It was the incubation of Nirvana, and Kurt's first exploration of being a musical alpha male. They would practice almost every night during the first few months of 1986, until Kurt thought they had done enough for the evening. After rehearsal they would drive to Kentucky Fried Chicken. "Kurt loved Chicken Littles from KFC," recalled Burckhard. "Once Kurt took electrical tape with him and made an inverted cross on the speaker of the drive-thru. We watched from the van laughing our asses off while the employees had to come outside to peel it off."

In early spring, Buzz announced he was moving to California and the Melvins were breaking up. It was an important point in Aberdeen band history, and watching it, Kurt must have thought that he was seeing a Judas in his midst. "What happened," remembered Lukin, "was that I got left behind. The band was supposedly broken up, which was just a way to get me out. Buzz said, 'Oh, no, I'm not even going to be in a band. I'm just moving to California.' But then a month after they moved, they were playing as the Melvins again. It was hard, since it was exactly the same way Buzz had me kick out our previous drummer."

The severing of his roommate from the Melvins would mark a major milestone in Kurt's own development: Everyone took sides in this spat, and Kurt, for the first time, dared challenge Buzz. "Kurt moved away from the Melvins artistically and emotionally that day," Ryan remembered. Kurt could already see that his own pop-influenced music was never going to live up to Buzz's expectations. Though he would continue to talk about his love for the Melvins, he had begun to outgrow Buzz as a role model. It was a step that had to happen if he was going to develop his own voice, and though it was painful, it freed him creatively and gave him artistic space.

Kurt and Lukin had also grown on each other's nerves—Kurt didn't like a few of Lukin's friends. In a move straight out of an "I Love Lucy" episode, he took masking tape and ran it down the center of the house and told Lukin and his friends they had to stay on their side. When one of Lukin's buddies complained he needed to cross the tape to go to the bathroom, Kurt's reply was, "Go to the bathroom out in the yard, because the bathroom is on my side." Lukin moved out. Kurt lived for a while without a roommate, until a friend from Olympia, Dylan Carlson, moved in. With long, brown hair and a scruffy beard, Dylan looked a bit like Brian Wilson of the Beach Boys during his lost years, but what came out of his mouth were outrageous views on religion, race, and politics. Dylan was a character, but he was bright, talented, and friendly—all qualities Kurt admired. They had met at the Brown Cow show and a friendship was formed.

Dylan moved to Aberdeen, ostensibly to work with Kurt laying carpet. The jobs left something to be desired: "Our boss was this total drunk," Dylan recalled. "We'd show up for work in the morning, and he'd be passed out on the floor in the office. One time, he was passed out in front of the door, and we couldn't get it open to get in to get him up." The jobs fell apart but the friendship between Dylan and Kurt would stick. With a band, a new best friend, and some great songs, it was a more positive Kurt that greeted 1987 and his twentieth year. And soon, surprisingly, even his sexual life would blossom, when Tracy Marander became his girlfriend.

They bonded over rodents—both Kurt and Tracy had pet rats. He had first met her two years earlier outside a punk club in Seattle—it was the location of one of his alcohol arrests. He and Buzz were drinking in a car when Tracy came by to say hi, and Kurt was so enraptured he failed to notice a police car pulling up. They ran into each other over the next year, and in early 1987 they cemented a relationship. "I had been flirting with him for quite a while," Tracy said. "I think he had a hard time believing a girl actually liked him."

Tracy was the ideal girlfriend for the twenty-year-old Kurt, and she would signify a major marker in his path toward adulthood. She was a year older than he was, had been to hundreds of punk rock shows, and knew lots about music, a huge sexual turn-on to Kurt. With dark hair, a curvy body, and large eyes that were as strikingly brown as his were blue, she was a homespun beauty with a down-to-earth attitude. Everyone she met turned into a friend; in this way, and in many others, she couldn't have been more different from him. He was instantly taken with her, though from the beginning he never felt like he deserved her. Even early in their relationship, these inner wounds and his pattern of withdrawal exhibited themselves. One of the first times they went to bed together, they lay in the afterglow of sex, when she commented, seeing him naked, "God, you are so skinny." Though she didn't know it, Tracy couldn't have said anything more hurtful. Kurt's response was to throw on his clothes and storm outside. He came back, though.

Tracy decided she would love him enough so his fear would disappear; she'd love him so much he might even be able to love himself. But for Kurt this was treacherous ground, and at every corner sat an excuse for self-doubt and fear.

The only thing he loved more that spring than Tracy was his pet rat Kitty. He had raised the male rodent from birth, feeding him with an eyedropper the first few weeks. The rat usually stayed in his cage, but on special occasions, Kurt would let it run around the house, since a few rat turds weren't going to spoil the filthy carpet. One day, while Kitty was running around the shack, Kurt found a spider on the ceiling and urged Kitty to get it. "I said, 'See that fucker, Kitty? Get him, kill him, get him, kill him,' " Kurt wrote in his journal. But Kitty failed to attack the spider, and when Kurt returned with a can of Brut deodorant spray in an attempt to kill the spider, he heard a heartbreaking noise and looked down to see:

> My left foot . . . on top of my rat's head. He jumped around squealing and bleeding. I screamed, "I'm sorry," about 30 times. Picked him up in a pair of dirty underwear. Put him in a sack, found a piece of two by four wood, took him outside and clubbed, and laid it on its side, and stepped all over the sack. I felt his bones and guts crush. It took about two minutes to put him out of his misery and then I went into misery for the rest of the night. I obviously didn't love him enough, as I do now. I went back into the bedroom, and observed the blood stains and the spider. I screamed, "Fuck you," to him and thought about killing him, but left him there to eventually crawl across my face as I lie awake all night.

SOUPY SALES IN MY FLY

RAYMOND, WASHINGTON
MARCH 1987

There's a Soupy Sales in my fly.
—Kurt to a crowd of fifteen at the first Nirvana concert.

Kurt Cobain's career as a bandleader was almost over before it even began. On a rainy night in early March 1987, the band finally drove out of Aberdeen in a panel van packed with gear, headed toward their first show. The band still didn't have a name, though Kurt had spent countless hours considering many options, including Poo Poo Box, Designer Drugs, Whisker Biscuit, Spina Biffida, Gut Bomb, Egg Flog, Pukeaharrea, Puking Worms, Fish Food, Bat Guana, and the Imcompotent Fools (intentionally misspelled), among many others. But as of March 1987, he had yet to settle on one.

They were headed for Raymond, a half hour south of Aberdeen but more like Aberdeen than Aberdeen itself; it was truly a town of loggers and rednecks, since nearly every job was timber related. Choosing Raymond for their debut show was like a Broadway production opening in the Catskills—it was a chance to try things out on an audience perceived as not very discerning or sophisticated.

Ryan Aigner, who with his gregarious nature had become their manager for a brief moment, had set up the gig. He nagged Kurt to perform in public, and when his friend was noncommittal, Ryan scheduled a gig at a party without Kurt's prior permission. Ryan borrowed a carpet van from his job, loaded up their equipment, and gathered Kurt, Krist, Burckhard, Shelli, and Tracy, who had to sit among rolls of carpet. During the drive Kurt complained incessantly that the band—which had yet to play anywhere other than in his tiny shack—deserved something better than this gig, for which they would not be paid. "We're playing in *Raymond*," he said, stating the name of the town as if it were a slur. "At someone's *house*, to boot. They don't even know what radio is yet. They're going to *hate* us." "Kurt's theory," observed Ryan, "was that either the crowd would hate them, which they would embrace, or the audience would love them, which would also be fine. He was ready for either." This was a classic example of a device Kurt would apply throughout the rest of his career: By downplaying success, and in fact pronouncing the worst possible scenario, he imagined he could protect himself from true failure. If the actual event he dreaded was anything short of a complete disaster, he could declare some degree of triumph that he had outwitted fate again. This one time, however, his foreshadowing would prove accurate.

The house was located at 17 Nussbaum Road, up a gravel road seven miles outside Raymond in the middle of a field. When they arrived, at 9:30 p.m., Kurt immediately became fearful, seeing an audience of youths he didn't know. "When I saw what the band looked like," remembered Vail Stephens, who was at the party, "I said, 'Uh oh.' They looked very different than the crowd we hung out with." That was exactly the same thought Kurt had as he surveyed the dozen teenagers with Led Zeppelin T-shirts and mullet haircuts. In contrast, Krist was barefoot, while Kurt was wearing a Munsters' T-shirt and a metal stud bracelet with prongs on it that could have come straight from London's King's Road in 1978.

They walked into a house decorated with an "Ernest" poster, a Metallica album flat, and a poster for Def Leppard's latest album. Nailed to a beam were several stolen street signs including a "Mile 69" highway marker. A Tama drum kit was permanently set up in one corner of the small living room, as was a Marshall stack, and there was a keg outside the kitchen.

It took a while for the band to arrange their gear, and in that time the newcomers didn't exactly ingratiate themselves to their hosts. "He didn't speak one word," said Kim Maden of Kurt. "He had his hair down, it was kind of greasy, and it was in his face." At least, in his standoffishness, Kurt was unlike Krist, who marched into the bathroom and started to pee, despite the fact that it was already occupied by a girl. Krist opened the medicine cabinet, discovered a vial of fake Halloween blood, which he used to cover his naked chest, located some duct tape to put on his nipples, and began rifling through the prescription medicine. He left the bathroom, ignored the keg, went for the refrigerator, and, finding Michelob Light, screamed, "Hey, there's good beer!" At that point Kurt had begun to play and Krist had to run and grab his bass because Nirvana's very first concert had started.

They began with "Downer," one of the first songs Kurt ever wrote. It listed classic Cobain laments on the pitiful state of human existence. "Hand out lobotomies / To save little families," Kurt sang. The dark lyrics were completely lost on the Raymond crowd, who could hear nothing more than the chunky guitar and bass riffs. Kurt rushed through it, though the song, and the others that followed, was surprisingly professional. By their very first public show, it was all there, every bit of the Nirvana that would conquer the world in the years to come: the tone, the attitude, the frenzy, the slightly-off-kilter rhythms, the remarkably melodic guitar chords, the driving bass lines that were guaranteed to move your body, and, most important, the hypnotizing focus of Kurt. He was not yet a fully realized performer—and in fact those at the party don't remember him ever raising his head or pushing the hair out of his face—but all the raw, essential building blocks were in place. He was worth watching, if only because he seemed so intense.

Not that the audience noticed, because they were doing what every crowd of teenagers does at a party—drinking and socializing. By far the most remarkable thing about the show was that the crowd didn't clap when they ended their first song. The only person who seemed excited was Krist, who announced, "That sounds pretty good from here," perhaps to keep Kurt's edgy ego from fracturing. Ryan, who was intoxicated, replied, "It sounds a hell of a lot better than usual." "I think you guys might buy a decent P.A.," was Kurt's only comment after finishing his first original song in front of an audience. "We do have a decent P.A.," argued Tony Poukkula, who lived in the house, "it just keeps blowing up." Shelli yelled at Krist to keep his pants on—they were the only clothes he still was wearing—while Kurt joked, "There's a Soupy

Sales in my fly." "Beastie Boys," one woman shouted out. "Bestiality Boys," Kurt answered.

As they tuned between songs, Kurt saw Poukkula, who had a reputation as a hot guitar player in the area, putting his Fender on and approaching the band. What Ryan hadn't told Kurt was that the evening had been described to Poukkula as a jam session. Kurt's expression was one of horror, since, even at this early stage in his career, he did not want to share the spotlight. "That'd be cool to jam," Kurt tactfully lied to Tony, "but do you mind if we play through our set? I really don't know any poppy songs at all, and it's cool to improvise, but I only like to improvise when I'm drunk—that way I don't care." Poukkula was amenable and sat down. The moment was then on Kurt to entertain the crowd and neither Burckhard nor Krist, now lying on top of the console television, seemed to be ready. "Let's just hit this one," Kurt ordered impatiently. "Let's just figure out how we are going to play it." And with that he began the opening guitar solo to "Aero Zeppelin," assuming his bandmates would join in, which they did. Once the song got going, it sounded as finished as it would a year later when they would record it.

As "Aero Zeppelin" ended, the natives began to get restless. There was once again no applause, and this time Kurt was heckled, though to be fair, much of the heckling was coming from Krist and Ryan, both so seriously drunk they were barely standing. The band had managed, as they would at many of their early shows, to subdue the crowd through volume during the songs; they would not be so lucky during these song breaks.

"Hey, who's got all the pot?" yelled Krist.

"Acid. I want acid!" shouted Shelli.

"You should just drink alcohol," said a Raymond woman.

"All I want is some good pot," replied Krist.

"I'm going to pot you in about five minutes," threatened Ryan. "Play some covers. Play anything. I'm sick of you guys acting dumb, so fucking retarded. You are dumb."

"Let's play 'Heartbreaker,' " yelled Krist as he hit the opening bass riff.

"Are you guys drunk?" asked a man.

"Play it like Zeppelin did," another man shouted.

"Play it like Tony Iommi," yelled another man.

"Do some Black Sabbath," someone screamed from the kitchen.

And with that it almost fell apart; Kurt was teetering on the edge of breaking. Krist kept yelling, "play 'Heartbreaker,' " to which Kurt, in a voice that sounded very young, yelled back, "I don't know it." But they nonetheless launched into the Zeppelin song, and Kurt's guitar playing was fine. The rendition crumbled halfway when Kurt forgot the lyrics, but the instant he stopped, the audience edged him back, yelling "Solo." He did his best Jimmy Page imitation on "Heartbreaker," and included bits of "How Many More Times," but as it ended there still was no applause. Kurt wisely called out " 'Mexican Seafood,' everybody," and they started into this original.

They followed that with "Pen Cap Chew," and then "Hairspray Queen." By the end of this number, Krist was standing on top of the television doing a Kiss imitation with his tongue. While Kurt and Aaron continued to play, Krist jumped out a window of the house. Looking like a three-year-old running through a sprinkler on a summer day, he came back in the house, and then did it all again. "It was wild," Krist remembered. "Instead of just playing the show, we thought, why not have an event? It was an *event*."

What happened next guaranteed it would be a party to be remembered. Shelli and Tracy decided to add to the freak show by rubbing their hands on Krist's chest and kissing each other. Kurt quickly introduced the next song: "This one's called 'Breaking the Law.' " They played what would later be titled "Spank Thru," a song about masturbation. The Raymond crowd may have not been the most sophisticated audience, but they began to get the sense that they were the butt of some kind of joke.

Shelli, trying to crib some of the precious Michelob, had the misfortune of catching her necklace on the refrigerator door. When Vail Stephens closed the door and broke the necklace, a fight ensued. "You fat, fucking cunt," Shelli yelled as she and Vail slugged it out in the driveway. "We were just being obnoxious on purpose," remembered Shelli. "To us they were rednecks, and we didn't want to be rednecks."

Kurt, seeing his first show turn into chaos, put his guitar down and walked outside, with equal parts amusement and disgust. Outside the house, an attractive young woman came up to Kurt and as she approached he must have felt that his youthful dreams of being a rock star and attracting groupies were finally coming true. But instead of being an adoring fan, this big-haired blond woman wanted to know the lyrics to "Hairspray Queen." Apparently, she thought the song had been written about *her*, perhaps on the spot. It would only be the first of many instances of Kurt's lyrics being misinterpreted. Even at this first gig, Kurt did not take kindly to an audience misreading his true intent. "I'll tell ya the lyrics," he told her, sounding like he'd been insulted. "They are, 'fuck, cunt, cocksucker, asshole, shit-eating, son-of-a-bitch, anal prober, mother fucker. . . .' " The girl stormed away.

Kurt went to look for Krist and found him atop the panel van, urinating on the cars of the other guests. Seeing this display, and always smartly concerned with his own self-preservation, Kurt told everyone it was time to go. They packed up their gear and left, expecting to have their retreat thwarted by the fists and feet of their hosts. But the Raymond crowd, despite all the craziness and insults they had endured, and despite being imagined as rednecks, had actually turned out to be more accepting than many of the audiences that would pay to see Nirvana over the next several years. A few had even offered up the comment, "you guys aren't half bad." Hearing those words was an elixir to Kurt. Seeing his reflection in an audience, even one that wasn't fully enthusiastic, was far more attractive than his own self-criticism, which was unceasingly brutal. If the crowd had done anything less than hang him from the nearest lightpost, it would have been a triumph. The audience—distracted as they were by cat-fights, beer brawls, and a half-naked man jumping out of windows—had offered him a small taste of something he craved more than anything else in life: the narcotic of attention.

As they all scrunched into the van, there was some argument about who in the group was the least drunk, and though Kurt was the most sober, no one trusted him to drive. He sat in the back while Burckhard took the wheel. "Everybody went out to the driveway to watch them drive away," remembered Jeff Franks, who lived in the house. "They all sat in the back of the van, with the rear door still open, sitting on the rolls of carpet. We could see them pull the slider down as they sped away with gravel spitting out from their tires."

Inside the van there were no windows, and with the sliding door down, it was pitch black. It would be several months before they would again play in front of an audience, but they were already looking out toward their future, with a small piece of their legend already formed.

8 IN HIGH SCHOOL AGAIN

OLYMPIA, WASHINGTON
APRIL 1987–MAY 1988

Fuck, I'm in high school again! I want to move back to Aberdeen.
—Excerpt from a letter to Dale Crover.

Two months after the show in Raymond, Kurt took another significant journey: He once and forever left Aberdeen. He had spent the first twenty years of his life there, but having left he would rarely go back. He packed up his stuff, which at the time consisted of little more than a Hefty bag of clothes, a crate of albums, and his now-empty rat cage, and loaded it into Tracy's car for the 65-mile drive to Olympia. Though Olympia was only slightly bigger than Aberdeen, it was a college town, the state capital, and one of the freakiest places west of the East Village, with an odd collection of punk rockers, artists, would-be-revolutionaries, feminists, and just plain weirdos. Students at Evergreen State College—universally called "Greeners"—created their own curriculum. Kurt wasn't planning on college, but he was at least the right age to fit in. He was to have a conflicted relationship with the town's artsy crowd—he yearned for their acceptance, yet he frequently felt inadequate. It was a recurrent theme in his life.

Kurt moved to Olympia to live with Tracy in a studio apartment in an old house converted to a three-plex at 114½ Pear Street. It was tiny, but the rent was only $137.50 a month, including utilities. And the location, just a few blocks from downtown, was ideal for Kurt, who rarely had access to an operable vehicle. For the first month he looked for jobs without much success, while Tracy supported him working in the cafeteria of the Boeing airplane plant in Seattle. She pulled a grave-yard shift, and the long commute meant she left for work at ten in the evening and didn't arrive home until nine in the morning. The job did provide a steady income—something they both knew couldn't be expected of Kurt—and she could steal food to supplement her salary. Because of her unusual hours, Tracy began leaving Kurt "to do" lists, and this form of communication would turn into a ritual of their relationship. One such list she wrote in late 1987 read: "Kurt: sweep kitchen, behind cat litter box, garbage can, under cat food. Shake mats, put dirty dishes in sink, clean up corner, sweep up floor, shake mats, Vacuum and clean up front room. Please, please, please." The note was signed with a heart and a smiley face. Kurt's note back: "Please set alarm for 11. I will do the dishes then. Okay?"

At first Kurt helped with the housework, doing the dishes and even mopping the floor occasionally. Though the apartment was tiny, it needed constant cleaning due to their menagerie of pets. While the actual inventory would vary over the next two years depending on life span, they had five cats, four rats, a cockatiel, two rabbits, and Kurt's turtles. The apartment had a smell that visitors would often compare unfavorably to a pet shop, but it was a home of sorts. Kurt named their rabbit Stew.

He also painted the bathroom blood red, and wrote "REDRUM" on the wall, a reference to Stephen King's "The Shining." Since Kurt had a tendency to write on walls, they wisely covered most with rock posters, many turned reverse side out, so he would have more space to create. The few posters displayed face side up were all altered in some way as it was. A huge poster of the Beatles now sported an afro and glasses on Paul McCartney. Above the bed was a Led Zeppelin poster to which Kurt had added the following prose: "Loser, wino, alcoholic, scum, trash, degenerate, head lice, scabs, infections, pneumonia, diarrhea, vomits blood, urine, malfunctioning bowel muscle, arthritis, gangrene, psychotic mental illness, unable to form sentences, expected to fend for himself in a box in the snow." Next to this screed was a drawing of a bottle of Thunderbird fortified wine and a caricature of Iggy Pop. The refrigerator sported a photo collage he created of images of meat mixed with old medical illustrations of diseased vaginas. "He was fascinated by things that were gross," Tracy recalled. And though Kurt himself rarely talked about religion—"I think he believed in God, but more in the devil than actually in God," Tracy said—there were crosses and other religious artifacts on the walls. Kurt enjoyed stealing sculptures of the Virgin Mary from the cemetery and painting blood tears under her eyes. Tracy was brought up Lutheran, and most of their religious discussions concerned whether God could exist in a world filled with such horror, with Kurt taking the position that Satan was stronger.

After a couple of months of being a house-husband, Kurt took a short-lived $4.75-an-hour job at Lemons Janitorial Service, a small family-run cleaning business. He claimed to his friends that he cleaned doctors' and dentists' offices and used the occasion to steal drugs. But according to the owner of the business, the route Kurt worked was mostly industrial buildings with few chances to steal anything. He used some of what he earned to buy a rusty old Datsun. One thing was certain about this janitorial service: In ways both physical and emotional it left Kurt with little energy to apply to cleaning his own apartment anymore, which created the first tension between him and Tracy. Even after he quit the job, he apparently felt like no more cleaning was required of him in his lifetime.

In Olympia, his inner artistic life was developing in ways that it never had before. Being unemployed, Kurt set in motion a routine that he would follow for the rest of his life. He would rise at around noon and eat a brunch of sorts. Kraft Macaroni and Cheese was his favorite food. Having tried other brands, his delicate palate had determined that when it came to processed cheese and pasta, Kraft had earned its role as the market leader. After eating, he would spend the rest of the day doing one of three things: watching television, which he did unceasingly; practicing his guitar, which he did for hours a day, usually while watching TV; or creating some kind of art project, be it a painting, collage, or three-dimensional installation. This last activity was never formal— he rarely identified himself as an artist—yet he spent hours in this manner.

He also wrote in his journals, though the inner dialogue he kept was not as much a play-by-play of his day as it was a therapeutic obsessive/compulsive device wherein he let loose his innermost thoughts. The writing was imaginative and many times disturbing. His songs and his journal entries fused together at times, but both were obsessed with human bodily functions: Birth, urination, defecation, and sexuality were topics he was accomplished in. One small segment illustrates the familiar themes that he would revisit again and again:

Chef Boyardee is meaner stronger less susceptible to disease and more dominant than a male gorilla. He comes to me at night. Willfully opening the locks and bending the bars on my window. Costing me horrendous amounts of money in home burglary devices. He comes to me in my bedroom. Naked, shaved and oiled. Goosebumped thick black arm hairs risen off his skin. Standing in a pool of pizza grease. Barfing up flour. It enters my lungs. I cough. He laughs. He mounts me. I'd like to kick his hot-stinking, macho fuckin' ass.

These inner thoughts, many times full of violence, were in marked contrast to Kurt's external world. For the first time in his life he had a steady girlfriend who doted on him and saw to his every need. At times the attention Tracy paid him bordered on mothering, and in a way he needed mothering. He remarked to his friends that she was "the best girlfriend in the world."

As a couple, they exhibited signs of domestic tranquility. They'd walk to the Laundromat together, and when they could afford it, they'd get take-out pizza from the Fourth Avenue Tavern (they lived next door to a different pizza joint but Kurt insisted it sucked). Kurt enjoyed cooking, and he frequently made Tracy his signature entree, "vanilla chicken," or fettuccine Alfredo. "He'd eat the kind of stuff that would make other people gain weight, but he never gained any weight," Tracy observed. His size had always been a matter of concern, and he'd write away to ads in the backs of magazines for weight-gain powders but they had little effect. "His hip bones stuck out and he had knobby knees," Tracy recalled. "He didn't wear shorts unless it got really hot because he was so self-conscious about how skinny his legs were." For one trip to the beach, Kurt came dressed in long johns, a pair of Levi's, a second pair of Levi's worn over the first pair, a long-sleeved shirt, a T-shirt, and two sweatshirts. "He wanted to make himself look bigger," Tracy said.

The one thing in his life that successfully made him feel bigger was his music, and by the summer of 1987 the band was going strong. They still hadn't settled on a permanent name, calling themselves everything from "Throat Oyster" to "Ted, Ed, Fred," after the boyfriend of Greg Hokanson's mom. They played a couple of parties in early 1987, and in April they'd even performed on the college radio station KAOS in Olympia. Tracy gave a tape of the radio show to Jim May at Tacoma's Community World Theater (CWT) and urged Jim to book them. Tracy and Shelli contributed to the band in those early days in ways that cannot be underestimated: They played the informal roles of press agents, managers, bookers, and merchandise-salespeople, in addition to their job of making sure their men were fed, dressed, and rehearsed.

May gave the band their first non-party gig, for which they played under the name Skid Row—at the time, Kurt was not aware that a lite-metal band from New York had the same moniker. It didn't matter; they would change names for every early show, the way a socialite might try on hats. This performance, though not long after the Raymond party, showed the band growing by leaps and bounds. Even Tracy, who was biased since she was in love with the singer, was impressed by how much they'd developed: "When they started to play, my mouth dropped open. I said, 'These guys were good.' "

They may have sounded good, but they certainly looked strange. For this gig, Kurt had attempted to be glam. He wore, as he did at many shows this year, flare pants, a silk Hawaiian shirt, and four-inch platform shoes to look taller. Musician John Purkey happened into the CWT that night and, despite their strange attire, recalled "being blown away. I heard this person's voice singing and it completely impressed me. I never heard a voice like his before. It was very distinct. There was one song, 'Love Buzz,' that definitely stuck out."

"Love Buzz" had been one of the missing pieces the band needed. Krist had discovered the song on an album by a Dutch band called the Shocking Blue, and Kurt embraced it immediately and made it their signature tune. It began with a mid-tempo drum beat, but quickly transitioned into a whirling guitar riff. Their performance of the song mixed equal parts psychedelic-trance with a thudding, slowed-down heaviness from Krist's bass part. Kurt would play the guitar solo on his back on the floor.

They began to play regularly at the CWT, though to suggest that they built an audience there would be an exaggeration. The theater itself was a former porno movie house, and the only source of heat was a propane blower that ran loudly even during the band's sets. Kurt commented that there was the "ever-present smell of urine" in the place. Most in the crowd at their early shows came to see other groups— the night before Kurt played, the lineup was Bleeder, Panic, and Lethal Dose. "Jim May booked those guys when nobody else would touch them," explained Buzz Osborne. "It was where they cut their milk teeth." Kurt, always learning from Buzz, realized that even a gig in front of their friends was a chance to grow. "I could count on them to play anytime," remembered May. "Kurt would never take any money, which was also good for me because I was only doing about twelve shows a month, and only two would make money." Kurt had wisely sized up his situation and realized the band would get more gigs, and more experience, if they played for free. What did they need money for anyway? They had Tracy and Shelli.

Shelli had taken a job alongside Tracy at the Boeing cafeteria. She and Krist had moved to an apartment in Tacoma, 30 miles north of Olympia. With the move, the band briefly fell apart. Previously, with Krist and Aaron both living in the Aberdeen area, Kurt would take the bus back for rehearsals. But with Krist in Tacoma, and working two jobs (at Sears and as an industrial painter), the only one who seemed to have time for the band was Kurt. He wrote Krist a letter to talk him back into the group. "It was funny; it was like a commercial," Krist remembered. "It said, 'Come, join the band. No commitment. No obligation (well some).' So I called him, and said, 'Yeah, let's do it again.' What we did was we built a rehearsal space down in the basement of our house. We cruised construction sites and we took scraps, and built it with old two-by-fours and old carpet." Kurt and Krist had been friends for some time, but this second forming of the band would cement their relationship in deeper ways. Though neither was particularly good at talking about their emotions, they forged a brotherly bond that seemed stronger than all the other relationships in their lives.

But even with a Tacoma rehearsal spot, as 1987 wound down they again faced the drummer problem, which would plague them for the next four years. Burckhard still lived in Grays Harbor, and with a new job as the assistant manager at the Aberdeen Burger King, he couldn't play with them anymore. In response, Kurt placed a "Musicians Wanted" ad in the October 1987 issue of *The Rocket*: "SERIOUS DRUMMER WANTED. Underground attitude, Black Flag, Melvins, Zeppelin, Scratch Acid, Ethel Merman. Versatile as heck. Kurdt 352-0992." They found no serious takers, so by December, Kurt and Krist began to practice with Dale Crover, who was back from California, and they began to talk about making a demo. During 1987 Kurt had dozens of songs, and he had a yearning to record them. He saw an ad for Reciprocal, a studio that charged only $20 an hour for recording, and booked a January session with up-and-coming producer Jack Endino. Endino had no idea who Kurt was and he wrote "Kurt Covain" down in the schedule.

On January 23, 1988, a friend of Novoselic's drove the band and all their gear up to Seattle in a shingle-covered camper heated by a woodstove. It looked like a backwoods shack deposited on a pickup, which it was. Driving into the big city they looked like the Beverly Hillbillies with wood smoke coming out of the back of the camper; their truck was so overweight it scraped against rises in the road.

Reciprocal was run by Chris Hanszek with Endino. Mudhoney, Soundgarden, and Mother Love Bone had all worked there, and it was already legendary by 1988. The studio itself was only 900 square feet, with a control room so tiny three people could not comfortably stand in it at once. "The carpets were worn, the door frames all were coming apart and tacked back a few times, and it showed its age," recalled Hanszek. "You could see that the place had the signs of 10,000 musicians who had rubbed their elbows against the place." Yet to Kurt and Krist, this was exactly what they were seeking: As much as wanting a demo tape, they sought to be in the same league with these other bands. They quickly dispensed with introductions and went into recording almost immediately. In less than six hours, they recorded and mixed nine and a half songs. The last tune, "Pen Cap Chew," was incomplete, as the reel of tape ran out during the recording and the band didn't want to front the additional $30 for another tape reel. Endino was impressed by the band, but not overly so. At the end of the day, Kurt paid the $152.44 bill with cash, money he said he'd saved working at his janitor job.

The camper then was reloaded with equipment and the band headed south—on this day they also had a show scheduled at Tacoma's Community World Theater. During the hour's drive, they listened to the demos twice. The ten songs were, in order, "If You Must," "Downer," "Floyd the Barber," "Paper Cuts," "Spank Thru," "Hairspray Queen," "Aero Zeppelin," "Beeswax," "Mexican Seafood," and the half of "Pen Cap Chew." When the time came for their set, they played the same ten songs in order. It was a day of triumphs for Kurt, his first day as a "real" musician. He'd been to a studio in Seattle, and he'd played another show in front of an adoring crowd of twenty. Dave Foster was in another band on the bill that night, and recalled the performance as particularly inspired: "They were great. Crover was killer, though you had a hard time hearing him above the propane blower, since it was a really cold night."

Backstage, an incident came up that would mark the night in ways Kurt might not have anticipated. Compared to Krist and Kurt, Crover was a veteran, and he and the Melvins had played the CWT several times. He asked Kurt how much they were making for the gig, and when Kurt told him they were doing it for nothing, Crover protested. May explained he'd tried to pay the band for their last few gigs—the club was finally doing a little better—but that Kurt continued to refuse to take any money. Crover started yelling, until Kurt finally announced, "We're *not* taking any money." Crover argued that even if the pay was only a paltry $20, there was a principle at stake: "You should never do this, Kurt. These guys are just screwing you. You'll always get screwed. You've gotta get your money." But Kurt and Krist saw the reality of May's situation. May finally came up with a compromise that would let Kurt keep his integrity and make Crover happy: He convinced the band to take $10 for gas. Kurt put the $10 bill in his pocket and said,

"Thanks." He left the club that night for the first time in his life a professional musician, fingering the bill all the way home.

A month later Kurt celebrated his 21st birthday, finally experiencing the American rite of passage that meant he could legally buy liquor. He and Tracy got drunk—this one time, Kurt bought—and had pizza. Kurt's relationship with alcohol was an on-again/off-again flirtation. Being with Tracy, he was drinking less and doing fewer drugs than in his Aberdeen shack days. None of his friends remember him being the most intoxicated of their group—that distinction usually fell to Krist or Dylan Carlson, who by then was living next door to Kurt on Pear Street—and at times Kurt seemed downright temperate. Their other neighbor, Matthew "Slim" Moon, had stopped drinking two years previously, so there were examples of sobriety around. Kurt's poverty during 1988 meant he could barely afford food, so a luxury like alcohol was saved for celebrations or when he could raid someone else's fridge.

At the time he turned 21, Kurt had temporarily quit smoking, and was adamant about people not lighting up around him (he signed a note to a friend that year as "the stuck-up rock star who bitches about exhaust fumes"). He felt smoking harmed his singing voice and his health. Kurt was always a strange mixture of self-preservation and self-destruction, and meeting him one night, you might hardly imagine he was the same person if you encountered him two weeks later. "We once went to a party in Tacoma," Tracy remembered, "and the next morning he was asking me what he did, because he was really drunk. And I told him he smoked a cigarette. He was shocked!"

His sister Kim visited around the time Kurt turned 21, and they bonded in ways they hadn't done for years, recounting their shared childhood trauma. "He got me ripped on Long Island Iced Teas at his house," Kim recalled. "I got sick, but it was a fun time." By 1988, Kurt stopped drinking before shows—his focus was always on the band, to the exclusion of everything else. At 21, he was as serious about music as he would ever be. He lived, slept, and breathed the band.

Even before the band had a permanent name, Kurt was convinced that getting a video on MTV was their ticket to fame. To this end, Kurt convinced the band to play at the Aberdeen RadioShack while a friend shot the performance on a low-rent video camera, using multiple special effects. When Kurt watched the completed tape, even he realized that it looked more like amateurs pretending to be rock stars than professional musicians.

Soon after their RadioShack appearance, Crover left the band's employ to go back to California with the Melvins. They'd always known Crover was only a temporary solution to their drummer problem. The Melvins' exodus was indicative of what many Northwest bands at the time believed: It had been so long since any Northwest group had broken through—Heart had been the last big success—that a move to a more populous center seemed the only road to fame. Losing Crover added to Kurt's frustration, but it also helped him find an identity of his own, and his group could be thought of as something other than a Melvins offshoot. As late as mid-1988, more people in Olympia knew Kurt as a roadie for the Melvins than as a leader of his own band.

That was about to change. Crover had recommended Dave Foster, a hard-pounding, and hard-living, Aberdeen drummer. Though having a drummer back in Grays Harbor remained a logistical problem, by this time Kurt had his Datsun to help. When it was running, which was infrequently, he would drive to Aberdeen, pick Foster up, take him to Tacoma for practice, and then reverse the whole route later that night or morning, putting in hours of driving.

Their first show with Foster was a party at an Olympia house nicknamed the Caddyshack. One of Olympia's eccentricities was that every student household in the eighties had some kind of nickname—the Caddyshack was near a golf course. Other than their radio show on KAOS and the Brown Cow show at Gessco, this was Kurt's first public performance in Olympia, and it would be part of a painful growth curve. Playing to a living room full of college students, it was culture shock. Kurt had attempted to dress the part—he wore his ripped-up jean jacket with a tapestry of "The Last Supper" sewed on the back and a plastic monkey, Chim Chim, from the "Speed Racer" cartoon, glued to the epaulet. Foster wore a T-shirt, stone-washed jeans, and a mustache. Before the band even had a chance to begin, a kid with a Mohawk haircut grabbed the microphone and yelled, "Drummers from Aberdeen sure look weird." Though it was Foster the kid was criticizing, the comment cut into Kurt as well: He wanted nothing more than to be thought of as an Olympia sophisticate, not an Aberdeen hick. Classism would be a fight he would struggle with his entire life, because no matter how far away he got from Grays Harbor, he felt branded as a hillbilly. Most of the Greeners were from big cities—like many privileged college kids, their prejudice toward people from rural communities was in marked contrast to the liberalism that they professed toward different races. The Caddyshack gig was almost one year to the day after the Raymond party, and it found Kurt in a paradigm he hadn't expected: His band was too hip for Raymond, but here in Olympia, they weren't hip enough.

He discussed this with his bandmates, hoping that if they looked more sophisticated, they would be taken more seriously. Kurt ordered Foster to cut his drum kit down from twelve pieces to six, and then he started on Foster's appearance: "You've got to get with it Dave." Foster angrily replied: "It's not fair to make fun of me as the short-haired guy— I've got a job. We could have green hair and we'd still look like hicks." Despite the fact that he'd say the exact opposite in interviews, Kurt cared very much what people thought of him. If that meant getting rid of his stone-washed jean jacket with the white fleece collar, which now sat in the closet of his apartment, so be it. Foster's dress, other than the mustache, was no different from Kurt's two years before, which may be why Kurt took the criticism so personally. Kurt had discovered that punk rock, despite being billed as a liberating genre of music, came with its own social mores and styles and that these were many times more constricting than the conventions they were supposedly in rebellion against. There *was* a dress code.

Perhaps in some small attempt to leave behind his past and the associations the band had with Aberdeen, Kurt came up with one final name for the group. Foster first heard about the new name when he saw a flyer at Kurt's house for "Nirvana." "Who's that?" he asked. "That's us," replied Kurt. "It means attainment of perfection." In Buddhism, nirvana is the place reached when one transcends the endless cycle of rebirth and human suffering. By renouncing desire, following the Eight-fold Path and through meditation and spiritual practice, worshippers work to achieve nirvana and thus gain release from the pain of life. Kurt considered himself a Buddhist at the time, though his only practice of this faith was having watched a late-night television program.

It would be under the name Nirvana that the band would first gain attention in Seattle, a city with a population of a half million, where Kurt was convinced his Last Supper jacket would fit right in. Jack Endino had remixed the January 23 session on a cassette that he'd passed on to a few of his friends. One went to Dawn Anderson, who wrote for *The Rocket* and ran the fanzine *Backlash*; another to Shirley Carlson, who was a volunteer DJ on KCMU, the University of Washington radio station; and a third he passed on to Jonathan Poneman, co-owner of Sub Pop, a Northwest independent record label. All three cassettes would impact Nirvana's future. Anderson liked the cassette enough that she planned an article; Carlson aired "Floyd the Barber" on KCMU, their first airplay; and Poneman got Kurt's number from Endino. When he phoned, Kurt was there with a visiting Dale Crover.

It was a conversation Kurt had been waiting for his whole life. Later he would recast these events to suggest that fame came without any prodding on his part, but this couldn't be further from the truth. The instant he received the demo, he began dubbing off copies and mailing them to record labels around the country, shopping for a deal. He sent long, handwritten letters to every label he could think of; the fact that he hadn't thought of Sub Pop was only an indication of the label's lowly status. Kurt was most interested in being on SST or Touch and Go. Greg Ginn, one of the owners of SST and a member of the band Black Flag, remembered getting that early demo tape in the mail: "My opinion on them was that they were not that original, that they were by-the-numbers alternative. It wasn't bad, but it wasn't great either." Though Kurt sent dozens of demos to Touch and Go during 1988, and he'd even gone as far as to title these songs "The Touch and Go Demos" in his notebook, the tape made so little impression that no one at the label remembered receiving them.

The tape made a bigger splash with Poneman, who took the cassette to his partner Bruce Pavitt at his day job—at the Muzak Corporation, the elevator music company. The Muzak tape-duplicating room was, strangely, the day job of choice for many of the members of the Seattle rock elite, and Poneman auditioned the tape for those present, including Mark Arm of Mudhoney. They gave it the thumbs down, with Arm dismissing it as "similar to Skin Yard but not as good." Still, Poneman was able to schedule Nirvana on the bottom of a bill at a small Seattle club called the Vogue for one of the label's monthly "Sub Pop Sunday" showcases. These $2-cover showcases featured three bands, though the beer specials were as big a part of the draw as the music. Poneman asked if Nirvana could play the Vogue on the last Sunday of April. Kurt, trying not to sound too enthusiastic, quickly said yes.

The Vogue was a tiny club on Seattle's First Avenue, best known for its transvestite bartender. In a previous life, it had briefly been a new wave club, and before that a gay biker bar. In 1988 the biggest draw was disco night and the lure of beer specials like three bottles of "Beer Beer" for three dollars. In this regard, the Vogue was reflective of the generally poor state of the Seattle club scene at the time, where there were few places for original bands to play. As Pavitt wrote in *The Rocket* in December 1987: "Despite the desperate lack of a good club, Seattle has rarely seen so many bands." The Vogue didn't have as strong a pee-smell as the Community World, but it did have a faint odor of vanilla, a remnant from the many amyl nitrite poppers smashed on the floor during dance night.

Nonetheless, Kurt Cobain couldn't wait to get on that stage. Like senior citizens going to a dentist's appointment, the band made sure they were early for this all-important show—arriving four hours before showtime. Having nothing to do and knowing few people in the city, they drove around aimlessly. Before soundcheck, Kurt puked in the parking lot next to the venue. "It was only because he was nervous," remembered Foster. "He wasn't drinking." Before their call they had to wait in their van, since Foster was underage.

When it came time for them to play, Kurt had become, by Foster's description, "pretty uptight." When they got onstage, they were surprised to see an audience just as small as their usual CWT shows. "There was hardly anyone there," remembered DJ Shirley Carlson. "The few people there all knew Tracy or Kurt from parties, or had heard the tape. We didn't even know who sang."

At best, it was a lackluster performance. "We didn't really fuck up," Foster recalled, "like, we didn't have to stop in the middle of the song. But it was very intimidating, because we knew it was for getting a record deal." They played fourteen songs with no encore, beginning with "Love Buzz," which was unusual at the time. Kurt thought it wise to put their best material first, in case people left.

Some of the audience did leave, and Carlson was one of the few who had anything good to say about the band, comparing them to Cheap Trick: "I remember thinking that not only could Kurt sing and play guitar, though together not very well, but he had a remarkably Robin Zander–like voice." Most of the members of the Seattle rock establishment thought the band stank. Photographer Charles Peterson was so unimpressed he didn't waste any film on them and questioned Poneman about the wisdom of signing the group.

Perhaps the harshest critic of the band's performance, as always, was Kurt himself. When photographer Rich Hansen photographed the band after the show, Kurt, now nursing a drink, shouted, "We sucked!" "They were very self-critical of their set," Hansen recalled. "There seemed to be some discussion of them missing some chords. I was struck by how very green they were. There was an absolute naiveness about them."

Hansen's pictures from that night give much insight into the freak-show appearance of the group. Krist, at six-foot seven, appears as a giant next to Kurt and Foster; he has long sideburns and curly, medium-length hair. Foster, at only five-foot five, reaches to Krist's breast and wears the kind of outfit you can imagine Kurt lecturing him on: stone-washed jeans, a white T-shirt with a mountain silhouette silkscreen, and a backward baseball cap with a Corona Beer logo. He is looking off into the distance, perhaps remembering that he has to be at work by seven that morning. Kurt, who Hansen convinced to sit on Krist's knee for some frames, wears jeans, a gray sweatshirt turned inside out, and a dark sweater. His blond hair had grown to a length three inches below his shoulder. With his five-day beard growth, he bears a striking resemblance to some portrayals of Jesus Christ. Even Kurt's expression in one of the photos—a pained and faraway look, as if he is marking this moment in time—is similar to the image of Christ in Leonardo da Vinci's "The Last Supper."

On the ride home, Kurt discussed the show as their first real setback and vowed they'd never be so embarrassed again. It was four in the morning before they would reach their homes, and on the long drive Kurt pledged to his bandmates, and himself, that he would practice more, write new songs, and they'd no longer suck. But when Poneman called him a couple of days later and suggested they do a record together, suddenly Kurt's own recollections of the show shifted. Two weeks later, Kurt wrote a letter to Dale Crover, titling it, "Oh, and our final name is Nirvana." The purpose of the letter was both to brag and to seek advice. It was one of many letters he wrote but never sent, and its contents describe in detail the parts of the night he was choosing to remember and the parts he had chosen to forget or reconstruct to his own liking. He wrote in full:

So within the last couple of months our demo has been pirated, recorded, and discussed between all the Seattle Scene luminaries. And the Dude, Jonathan Poneman (remember the guy who called me when you were over the last day?) Mr. Big money inheritance, right hand man of Bruce Pavitt, and also Sub Pop Records financial investor, got us a show at the Vogue on a Sub Pop Sunday. Big Deal. But I guess hype and regularly being played on KCMU probably helped. The amount of people who came to JUDGE us, not be at a bar, get drunk, watch some bands and have fun, but just watch the showcase event. 1 hr. There was a representative from every Seattle band there just watching, we felt like they should have had score cards. And so after the set, Bruce excitedly shakes our hands and says, "wow good job, let's do a record" then flashes of cameras go off and this girl from *Backlash* says "gee can we do an interview," yeah sure why not. And then people say good job, you guys are great and now we're expected to be total socialites, meeting people, introducing etc. FUCK, I'M IN HIGH SCHOOL AGAIN! I want to move back to Aberdeen. Nah, Olympia is just as boring and I can proudly say I've only been in the Smithfield [Café] about 5 times this year. And so because of this zoo-event we've at least gotten a contract for a 3-song single to be put out by the end of August and an EP out in Sept. or Oct. We're gonna try to talk them into an LP. Now Jonathan is our manager, he gets us shows remotely in Oregon and Vancouver. He's paying for all recording and distribution costs and now we don't have to have outrageous phone bills. Dave is working out okay. Sometime next year, Sub Pop is going to have a caravan of 2 or 3 Seattle bands go on a tour. Yeah we'll see. Thru your past experiences do you think it would be wise to demand receipts for recording, pressing costs? Enough about records. Oh except this one night last month, Chris and I dropped acid and we were watching the late show (rip off of Johnny Carson) and Paul Revere and the Raiders were on there. They were so fucking stupid! Dancing around with moustaches trying to act comical and goofy. It really pissed us off and I asked Chris, Do you have any Paul Revere and the Raiders albums?

Even in this early stage of his career, Kurt had already begun the process of retelling his own story in a manner that formed a separate self. He was commencing the creation of his greatest character, the mythical "Kurdt Kobain," as he had begun to misspell his name. He would bring out this carefully refined phantom when he needed to distance himself from his own actions or circumstances. He exaggerated every aspect of a show that by his own admission sucked: The crowd was too small for "a representative from every Seattle band" to be there; the camera flashes were mostly metaphorical, since Hansen only shot a couple of frames. In describing the Sub Pop honchos coming up to him, Kurt even attempts to portray himself as an unwilling participant in his own success. But he was a novice actor at this point, and he admits that he planned "to talk [Sub Pop] into" a full-length record. It is worth noting that virtually every business expectation Kurt had of Sub Pop, at least in the short term, went unfulfilled.

TOO MANY HUMANS

OLYMPIA, WASHINGTON
MAY 1988–FEBRUARY 1989

Too Many Humans
—The original title of *Bleach*.

Sub Pop Records had begun in the fall of 1987, issuing records from Green River and Soundgarden among their first releases. Twenty-eight-year-old co-owner Jonathan Poneman looked like
a younger and more heavy-lidded version of Reuben Kincaid, the manager on "The Partridge Family" TV show, and his promotional schemes
sounded straight out of Kincaid's business plan, particularly his idea to
send out groups in a Sub Pop van. Most bands on the label noted his
shifty nature, and he was widely mistrusted. He had used a small inheritance to start the label, fantasizing it would be the Northwest equivalent of Stax or Motown. He had many strengths as a promoter—
thinking small and operating within a budget were not among them.

Poneman's partner, Bruce Pavitt, was a long-time fixture in the
Northwest scene who had gone to Evergreen. In Olympia, Pavitt befriended many bands, started a fanzine called *Subterranean Pop* (later
shortened to *Sub Pop*), and began to release cassette compilations. He
discontinued the fanzine but between 1983 and 1988 wrote a widely
read column in *The Rocket*, which Kurt studied with the rapt attention
most boys only gave to the baseball box scores. Pavitt was the artistic
visionary of Sub Pop, and he looked the part: With his crazy-man eyes,
spooked expression, and penchant for unusual beards, he bore more
than a passing resemblance to the mad Russian monk, Grigori Rasputin.

By 1988 Sub Pop was issuing a handful of singles and EPs every quarter, mostly by Northwest bands. These projects made little business sense, since the production costs of a single were almost as high as a full-length album, yet they retailed for much less. Sub Pop had little choice with a number of their bands—many were so green they hadn't written enough material to fill a full-length album. From their inception the label was burning through their capital like an Internet startup, yet they had stumbled onto a small market niche: Indie singles appealed to record-collecting elitists, and in punk rock these connoisseurs were the taste-makers. By developing a cachet to their label—and by coming up with a consistent design identity for all their releases—they had bands clamoring to be on Sub Pop, if only to impress their friends. Like hundreds of other young musicians who were bad at math, Kurt had a grandly romantic concept of what it meant to record for the label.

Kurt's youthful illusions were quickly dashed. The band's first face-to-face business meeting with Poneman—at the Café Roma in Seattle—was just short of disastrous. Krist showed up swigging from a bottle of wine he hid under the table; Kurt started off shy, but became angry when he realized Poneman was offering them far less than the band wanted. It wasn't so much a question of money—everyone knew there was little of that—but Kurt hoped to jumpstart the band by issuing a slew of albums, EPs, and singles. Poneman suggested they begin with a single of "Love Buzz" and see how it went from there. Kurt admitted "Love Buzz" was their strongest live song, but as a songwriter he felt it disingenuous for a cover to be his initial release. Nevertheless, at the end of the meeting, all parties agreed Nirvana would record a single with Endino producing and Sub Pop picking up the recording costs. To Kurt, the idea of having his own single out was the fulfillment of a dream.

Back in Grays Harbor, events transpired that threatened to derail that dream. Not long after the Vogue show, Dave Foster had the misfortune to beat up the son of the mayor of Cosmopolis. He spent two weeks in jail, lost his driver's license, and had to pay thousands of dollars in medical bills. It couldn't have come at a worse time for Nirvana, who were rehearsing for the upcoming recording session, so Kurt decided to fire Foster. How he handled this dismissal says much about how he dealt with conflict, which is to say he didn't. Kurt had always been a bit afraid of Foster, who was shorter than Kurt but muscled like Popeye. Initially, the band brought back Aaron Burckhard, but when he ended up with a DWI in Kurt's car, they again advertised for drummers. When they found one, Kurt wrote a letter to Foster: "A band needs to practice, in our opinion, at least five times a week if the band ever expects to accomplish anything. . . . Instead of lying to you by saying we're breaking up, or letting this go any further, we have to admit that we've got another drummer. His name is Chad . . . and he can make it to practice every night. Most importantly, we can relate to him. Let's face it, you are from a totally different culture. And we feel really shitty that we don't have the guts to tell you in person, but we don't know how mad you'd get." Apparently, Kurt didn't have the guts to mail the letter: It went unsent. Foster, of course, wasn't from a "totally different culture" from Kurt's—he was from the same culture, though it was a past Kurt sought to escape. Foster found out he was canned when he saw an ad in *The Rocket* for an upcoming Nirvana gig.

Kurt and Krist found Chad Channing at a show at the Community World Theater. "Kurt was wearing these big high-heel shoes, and wide, blue sparkle flare pants," Chad recalled. What Kurt and Krist noticed about Chad was his gigantic North drums—the kit was the biggest drum set they'd ever seen, dwarfing Chad, who at five-foot six, with long hair, already looked a bit like an elf. Directness was not Kurt's forte: Rather than ask Chad to join the band, he simply kept inviting the drummer to practices until it became obvious he was in the group.

After one of those practices, now scheduled back in Aberdeen above Krist's mother's hair salon so they could play all night, the Nirvana veterans decided to show their new drummer the local sites. Chad was from Bainbridge Island and, prior to joining Nirvana, had never been to Aberdeen. The tour was a shock, particularly the neighborhood Kurt grew up in. "It was like stepping into the south side of the Bronx," Chad recalled. "I thought to myself, 'holy crap.' It was really bad. It's probably the poorest section in all of Washington. All of a sudden you have this instant slum."

Chad was more impressed when they drove by the gothic-looking Weatherwax High School. They also showed the drummer the five-story abandoned Finch Building; Kurt said he'd taken acid there as a teenager, though that could have been said for many of the sites in Aberdeen. They pointed out Dils Old Second Hand Store, where a 25-cent album bin stood next to a twenty-foot chainsaw. They went for a beer in the Poorhouse Tavern, where Krist seemed to know every other person. "It was redneck city," observed Chad. "It was tons of dudes with Skoal behind their lips, and with Skoal caps on and neon pink T-shirts, and vans with mud flaps, and mustaches."

When they left the tavern, the two natives planned to take Chad to a haunted house in the hills above the town. Krist pointed the van north and headed into what accounts for Aberdeen's ritzy neighborhood: a hillside of majestic Victorian homes constructed by pioneer lumber barons. But at the top of the hill, Krist headed the van into the woods, and Kurt began to tell the story of Aberdeen's haunted house, a place the locals called "the Castle." He said people had gone in and never come out; one room had pictures of clowns painted on the walls in blood. As he talked, the hillside became heavily forested with trees overhanging the narrow road.

When they arrived at the Castle, Krist pulled into the driveway and killed the lights, but kept the engine running. In front of them was a structure that had been a three-story house before decay had caused it to crumble upon itself. There was moss on the roof, the porch had caved in, and whole rooms appeared to have been eaten away, most likely by small fires. In the darkness, and shrouded by tree limbs, it really did look like the ruins of a crumbled castle in some distant Transylvanian backcountry.

As the van idled, Chad wondered why neither Krist nor Kurt made a move to get out. They just sat there, staring at the house as they might look at an apparition. Finally Kurt turned to Krist and said, "Do you really want to go in?" Krist replied, "Nah, fuck it. I'm not going in there."

As Chad recalled later, he urged them to venture in, since Kurt's stories had made him curious: "I was all excited to check it out and see what was so scary. But when we got there, they just sat in the driveway, staring at the house, unable to move." Chad thought it a dare for him, part of an elaborate hazing rite to test his courage. He had decided that no matter how frightening the house was—and it was plenty scary— he was not going to be too scared to go in. But when he looked at Kurt's face, he saw real fear. "Well, people have died in there," Kurt explained. In the fifteen minutes it had taken to drive from the tavern to the house, Kurt had told such convincing stories of the horror, he had begun to believe his own hyperbole. They turned around and headed back to town, and Chad's tour of Aberdeen was over. Krist took Kurt's dualism at its face value, but for Chad the fear in Kurt's face was one of the first pieces of evidence he had that the bandleader was more complicated than he appeared.

With the new recording session scheduled for the second week of June, Kurt was filled with anticipation and excitement. He could talk about virtually nothing else during May, announcing the upcoming date to everyone he knew, and some he didn't—like a new father over- whelmed with pride, he'd tell the mailman or the grocery store clerk. The band played a couple of gigs that month to get their sea legs with Chad, including a return visit to the Vogue and a party at the "Witch House" for Olympia musician Gilly Hanner. Hanner turned 21 on May 14, 1988, and a friend invited them as entertainment. "They were not like any Evergreen band," she remembered. "Their sound *hit* you. You'd think, 'I've heard this before,' but you hadn't. It was more rock 'n' roll than most stuff of that era, without any noodling." At the party, Kurt joined Gilly to sing a version of Scratch Acid's "The Greatest Gift," and Kurt played a version of "Love Buzz" on his back on the floor. At the time, "Love Buzz" was the best thing about their shows—Kurt was still struggling to settle into an original sound that was raw enough to appeal to his punk sensibilities and still displayed his increasingly com- plicated lyrics. Far too often the band's shows turned into loud feedback sessions where virtually none of Kurt's words could be heard above the din.

While Kurt's expectations for the single grew, financial problems within Sub Pop almost doomed the project. One May afternoon Kurt picked up the phone, only to hear Pavitt asking to borrow $200. It was so laughable, it didn't anger Kurt, though it incensed Krist, Chad, and Tracy. "We were shocked," remembered Chad. "At that point we began to have our suspicions about those guys." Kurt would have been more upset had he known Sub Pop had second thoughts about the band creatively. The label wanted one more look, so Poneman hastily arranged a show at the Central Tavern on June 5, a Sunday night. Jan Gregor, who booked the club, put Nirvana into the middle slot on a three-band evening. The night before the date, Poneman called Gregor and asked if Nirvana could be moved down in the line-up and go on first. Poneman's explanation: "It's a Sunday night—we don't want to stay out that late." When the band went on, there were six people in the audience. Chris Knab of KCMU was one of them: "Bruce and Jon were at the front of the stage, shaking their heads up and down. They must have seen something no one else could, because I thought they sucked." This particular gig—and many to follow—was plagued by sound problems, which put Kurt in a bad mood and compromised his performance. Despite the crummy sound and the lackluster live show, Poneman and Pavitt decided to proceed with the single.

On June 11 Nirvana returned to Reciprocal for the session. This time producer Endino knew how to spell Kurt's name, but the quick and easy studio experience of their first demo was not to be repeated. In five hours they finished only one song. Part of the problem came because Kurt had brought along a cassette of a sound collage he wanted on the single. The only way for this to happen, with the studio's crude gear, was to hit the "play" button on the cassette deck at the correct point during the mixing.

The band returned on June 30 for five more hours, and did a final session on July 16 that consisted of three hours of mixing. In the end, the thirteen-hour stint produced four tracks: "Love Buzz"; a new version of "Spank Thru"; and two Cobain originals, "Big Cheese"—which was to be the B-side—and "Blandest."

Sub Pop hired Alice Wheeler to photograph the band for the sleeve, and during the last week of August they drove to Seattle in Krist's van to pick her up. Their first official photo session was so anticipated, they all took the day off work. Krist returned everyone to Tacoma, where they shot in several locations, including "Never-Never Land" at Point Defiance Park, and the foot of the Tacoma Narrows Bridge. Krist wore a short-sleeved dress shirt and towered over his two tiny bandmates in all the pictures. Chad wore a Germs T-shirt, a beret, and round sunglasses, which gave him the appearance of being the leader of the band. Kurt was in a light-hearted mood, smiling in most of the photos. With his long, girlish hair and a Harley-Davidson T-shirt reading "Live to Ride," he looks too young to drive, much less be in a rock band. He had an outbreak of acne the week before, something he'd struggled with since high school and which gave him fits of self-consciousness. Wheeler told him she was using infra-red film, so his zits weren't going to show. By the time the band drove back to Seattle, they had spent as much time on the photo session as they had in the studio.

In late August Kurt received another unusual phone call from Poneman, and like his previous conversations, he couldn't help but feel he was being conned. Poneman informed Kurt that Sub Pop was starting a new subscription-only singles service, and they planned to use "Love Buzz" as the debut release in their "Singles Club." Kurt could hardly believe his ears; discussing it later with his bandmates, he was outraged. Not only had the single taken months longer than planned, but now it wasn't even going to be for sale in stores. It hardly seemed worth the effort. As a collector, Kurt appreciated the club idea, but he wasn't interested in seeing his band be the test case. But since he didn't have a contract and Sub Pop had paid for the recording, he also didn't have much choice.

Not long after the April show at the Vogue, Kurt had gotten a phone call from Dawn Anderson wanting to interview the band for her *Backlash* fanzine. Rather than conduct the interview over the phone, Kurt offered to drive up to Seattle, making it seem as if he already had business there, which he didn't. Though Kurt had waited for this moment for years—and had prepared for it with the fake interviews with himself he'd written as a youth—in his first press interaction, he became nervous and shy. Most of the hour interview ended up being about the Melvins, a subject Kurt seemed more comfortable with than his own band. Reading a transcript one could almost think he was a member of the Melvins, not Nirvana. "He idolized the Melvins," observed Anderson, something that had been obvious in Grays Harbor for years.

But like the Sub Pop single, which again had been delayed in late August, the article sat on hold for a few months. With so many delays that he couldn't control, Kurt felt like he was the only one in the world ready for his musical career. The *Backlash* article finally ran in September, and even Kurt was surprised to see that in Anderson's 500-word story the Melvins' name appeared twice as many times as Nirvana's. "I've seen hundreds of Melvins' practices," Kurt said. "I drove their van on tour. Everybody hated them, by the way." The piece was flattering, and it was helpful in plugging the upcoming "Love Buzz" single, yet when Kurt said, "Our biggest fear at the beginning was that people might think we were a Melvins rip-off," a casual reader might have had a similar concern. Kurt explained their Vogue debut: "We were uptight. . . . We felt like we were being judged; it was like everyone should've had score cards."

The "score card" line in this first press interview reprised the imagery Kurt had put forth in his letter to Crover; he also used it in later interviews. It came from his divided self, the same self who said his name was spelled "Kurdt Kobain." What his interviewers—and the fans who read these stories—never knew was that almost every word he uttered had been rehearsed: in his head with the band driving around in the van or, in many instances, actually written out in his journals. This wasn't simply craftiness on his part or a desire to put forth the most marketable and attractive image—though despite all the punk ideals he spouted, he, like any other human being, was intrinsically guilty of this—but much of his forethought occurred instinctually. He had imagined these moments since he began retreating from the outside world after his parents' divorce, spending all that time in his room writing in Pee Chee notebooks. When the world tapped him on the shoulder and said, "Mr. Cobain, we are ready for your closeup," he had planned how he'd walk toward the cameras, going so far as to even rehearse the way he would shrug his shoulders, as if to give the impression he had only grudgingly acquiesced.

Nowhere was Kurt's forethought more apparent than in a band bio he wrote that summer to send out with the Endino demo tape. He'd given the tape many titles, but the one used most often was "Safer Than Heaven"—what that meant, only Kurt knew. He wrote dozens of drafts of the bio, and each revision became more exaggerated. One of many examples read like this:

> Nirvana is from Olympia, WA, 60 miles from Seattle. Nirvana's guitar/vocalist Kurdt Kobain and bass[ist] Chris Novoselic lived in Aberdeen 150 miles from Seattle. Aberdeen's population consists of highly bigoted redneck snoose-chewing deer-shooting faggot-killing logger types who "ain't too partial to weirdo new wavers." Chad Channing [drummer], is from an island of rich kid LSD abusers. Nirvana is a trio who play heavy rock with punk overtones. They usually don't have jobs. So they can tour anytime. Nirvana has never jammed on "Gloria" or "Louie, Louie." Nor have they ever had to rewrite these songs and call them their own.

Another, only slightly different, version sent to Touch and Go added the following downcast plea: "We are willing to *pay* for the majority of pressing of 1000 copies of our LP, and all of the recording costs. We basically just want to be on your label. Do you think you could PLEASE send us a reply of 'fuck off,' or, 'not interested,' so we don't have to waste more money sending more tapes?" On the flip side of the tape, he recorded a collage that included snippets of songs from Cher, the Partridge Family, Led Zeppelin, Frank Zappa, Dean Martin, and another dozen disparate artists.

Kurt's offer to pay a label to put out his record shows his increasing level of desperation. He drafted a letter to Mark Lanegan of the Screaming Trees asking for help (Lanegan was one of a number of his idols Kurt regularly wrote to in his journal, rarely mailing this correspondence). He wrote, "We feel like we're not accomplishing anything. . . . It turns out our single will be out in October, but there isn't much hope for an EP within the near future because Sub Pop is having financial problems, and the promise of an EP or LP within the year was just a bullshit excuse for Poneman to keep us from scouting other labels." Kurt also wrote to his friend Jesse Reed, declaring the band was going to self-release their LP since they were so sick of Sub Pop.

Despite Kurt's frustrations, things were actually going better with the band than they had in some time—though it could never be fast enough for Kurt. Shelli had broken up with Krist, which resulted in Krist having more time to practice. Kurt was happy to finally have two other bandmates who were as into the band as he was. On October 28 they landed their most prestigious gig yet, opening for the Butthole Surfers at Seattle's Union Station. Kurt had idolized Gibby Haynes, lead singer of the Surfers, so the show was very important to him. Sound problems again derailed Nirvana from putting on their best performance, but the very fact that Kurt could now announce to his friends, "My band opened for Gibby Haynes," was another piece of evidence to boost his self-esteem.

Two days later they played one of their most infamous shows, and one that turned Olympia's heart. It was a party in Evergreen's K-Dorm on the day before Halloween, and Kurt and Krist had made themselves up for the occasion by pouring fake blood on their necks. There were three bands who played before Nirvana: Ryan Aigner's band the Cyclods, Dave Foster's latest group Helltrout, and a new band fronted by Kurt's neighbor Slim Moon called Nisqually Delta Podunk Nightmare. In the middle of Nisqually's set the drummer punched Slim in the face and a fight ensued. It was such a wild rumble that Kurt wondered what Nirvana could possibly do to upstage such an event. He almost didn't get the chance, as campus police showed up and shut the party down. Ryan Aigner stepped forward and convinced the officers to let Nirvana play, but they were told to be quick.

When Nirvana finally took the stage, or more accurately moved to the corner of the room acting as a stage, they played only a 25-minute set, but it was a show that was to transform them from Aberdeen hicks to Olympia's most beloved band. Kurt's intensity—something that had been lacking in other performances—found a new depth, and not a person in the room could take their eyes off him. "As reserved as he was when he was offstage," remembered Slim Moon, "when he wanted to be *on*, he went all out. And on this one night, he played with an intensity that I had never seen." They were the same songs and riffs the band had been performing for some time, but with the added attraction of a possessed lead singer, they were mesmerizing. He had, surprisingly, a confidence now in front of the microphone that he had nowhere else in his life. Kurt's increased energy seemed to egg on Krist, who bounced around so much he smacked several members of the crowd with his bass.

But the coup de grâce was to come. At the end of their short set, right after they played "Love Buzz," Kurt lifted his relatively new Fender Mustang guitar and brought it down to the ground with such violence that pieces shot through the room like projectiles from a cannon. He paused for five seconds, hoisted the remnants in the air, and held it there while eyeing the crowd. Kurt's face appeared serene and spooky, as if you'd taken a Casper the Friendly Ghost Halloween mask and plastered it onto the body of a 21-year-old man. The guitar went up into the air, and, *smash*, it hit the floor once more. Kurt dropped it and walked out of the room.

He had never smashed a guitar before, probably never even thought about such an act, since guitars were expensive. "He never explained why he freaked out," recalled John Purkey, "but he was smiling. There was a finality to it—it was like his own little private celebration. No one got hurt, but when he smashed the guitar, it was as if he didn't really care if he hurt anyone. It was completely out of the blue. I was talking to him after the show and the guitar was laying there on the floor, and people kept grabbing pieces of it." The Greeners now couldn't get enough of Nirvana.

Three weeks later Kurt got a call from Sub Pop telling him the "Love Buzz" single was finally ready. He and Krist drove to Seattle to pick it up, and Sub Pop's Daniel House recalled he insisted on hearing it on the office stereo: "We played it for them and I don't think I ever saw Kurt happier." Both Kurt and Krist were particularly happy about the inside jokes on the release: Kurt's name was spelled "Kurdt," forever confusing reviewers and fans, and there was a tiny message scratched into the run-on groove of the vinyl that read, "Why don't you trade those guitars for shovels?" This was a line Krist's father would frequently yell at them, in his broken Croat-inflected English, during their Aberdeen practices.

Guitars for shovels, guns for guitars, from Aberdeen to Sub Pop. It seemed like a blur, now that Kurt was holding his very own record in his hand. Here was the final tangible proof he was a real musician. Like his guitar that he used to take to school in Montesano even when it was broken, the outcome or success of the single mattered little: Its very physical existence was what he had strived for over many years.

The band kept almost 100 of the edition of 1,000 "Love Buzz" singles, and while still in Seattle, Kurt dropped a copy off at the college radio station KCMU. He had high hopes for the single, describing it to the station as "a beautifully soft and mellow, crooning, sleep jingle. Incredibly commercial." He expected KCMU to immediately add the track to rotation, so he kept listening all day. Tracy had come up to Seattle to drive Kurt back to Olympia, and as they prepared to go home, the song still had not come on. As they drove south and reached the outer range of KCMU's signal, Kurt simply couldn't wait any longer: He ordered Tracy to pull over at a gas station. There he used a pay phone to call in and request his own single. As to whether the station's DJ thought this odd—getting a single from a band and then having an apparently random listener request it two hours later—isn't known. Kurt waited more than a half hour in the car, and then finally the station played "Love Buzz." "He sat there hearing himself coming out of the radio," Tracy remembered, "with a big smile on his face."

Kurt began December 1988 in some of the best spirits of his life. The single had buoyed his mood and people were still talking about the K-Dorm show. When he'd go to the Smithfield Café or the Spar coffee shop, college kids would whisper to themselves when he walked in. People started to ask him to play their parties; they still weren't offering to pay him, but they were asking. And *The Rocket* had given the band their first review, calling the single "one hell of a first effort." *The Rocket* piece was laudatory but warned that with all the attention other Sub Pop bands were getting, Nirvana could be overshadowed, both in the scene and within their label. "Serious traces of musicianship leak through," Grant Alden wrote. "Nirvana sit sort of at the edge of the current Northwest sound—too clean for thrash, too pure for metal, too good to ignore." It was the first evidence of something Kurt suspected but couldn't confirm without outside validation: The band was getting better.

Inside Sub Pop, where label-mates Soundgarden and Mudhoney were clearly the favorites, Nirvana's stock went up. The "Singles Club" had turned out to be a smart marketing move after all—the first pressing of "Love Buzz" sold out, and though the band didn't make a dime off it, it sounded impressive. There was other good news: Poneman and Pavitt had slated a remixed version of "Spank Thru" for the three-EP collection *Sub Pop 200*, the label's highest-profile release so far. And Sub Pop now were interested in talking to Kurt about a full-length album. There was one big caveat: Since the label was broke, Nirvana would have to pay the upfront costs for the recording. This was contrary to the way most record labels worked, and contrary to the way Sub Pop operated with their other bands. Though Kurt never sent one of his "we're willing to pay you to put out our record" letters to Sub Pop, his combination of hunger and ignorance was apparent to the more savvy Poneman. Checkbook in hand, the band excitedly made plans to go back into the studio with Jack Endino again at the end of December.

Once Kurt had an album to focus on, he immediately began to distance himself from the "Love Buzz" single, which only two weeks before had been his most precious possession in the world. He talked about it with Slim Moon, who said he was left with the impression that "Kurt didn't like anything about it, except the fact that they now had something that was out." Kurt sent a copy of the single to John Purkey and included the following note: "Here's our very commercialized rock star/stupid, fuzzy, Sub Pop picture sleeve, limited edition single, featuring Kurdt Kobain on front and back. I'm glad only 1000 were printed. The LP will be different. Very different. A rawer production and raunchier songs." Even writing to a friend, he spoke of himself in the third person. His love/hate relationship with the single mirrored his approach to all his work. Nothing the band ever did, either in the studio or onstage, matched the way it sounded in his head. He loved the idea of a record until it came out, and then immediately he had to find something wrong with it. It was part of a larger dissatisfaction.

This was most evident in his relationship with Tracy. She loved him completely, yet he rejected her sentimentality and told her she shouldn't love him so much. Note exchanges continued as their main method of communicating, and her to-do lists for him grew longer, since he rarely did anything she asked, even though he was unemployed and living off her. In December 1988 she left him the following note: "Hi Kurt! I'll be home at 2:30 or 3. Before you turn on the TV, could you straighten up the bedroom? You could fold my clothes and put them in my drawer or just inside the closet on the left. 1) Put fresh newspapers down, 2) Shake rugs in bathroom and kitchen, 3) Clean tub, sink, and toilet. I'm sorry, sorry, sorry I'm a nag and a bitch lately. I love you, let's get drunk (semi) and fuck tonight. Love you."

Kurt and Tracy struggled with the messy breakup between Krist and Shelli. From Kurt's perspective, it gave Krist more time for the band, but for Tracy the split had removed their best couple buddies: It was as if Lucy and Ricky had to watch Ethel and Fred divorce. Tracy found herself frequently worrying whether she and Kurt were next, if only because she knew a breakup would allow him to devote every waking hour to the band. She decided to test his commitment by threatening to break up. She didn't really want to split; she just wanted him to tell her he was committed. But any test of wills with Kurt was a mistake. Obstinate, he responded practically when she told him he had to move out. "If you want me to move out, I'll go live in my car," he said. He'd lived in cars before, and he would again. She, of course, told him this was nonsense. But Tracy had mistakenly begun a game of "Who will blink first?" with the reigning Grays Harbor champion.

Even with the band finally happening, life for Kurt went on much as it had before: He rose late and spent all day writing songs or playing his guitar while watching television. One afternoon, Tracy complained that he'd written songs about almost everything in his world—from masturbation to characters on "Mayberry R.F.D." ("Floyd the Barber")—except her. He laughed at the suggestion, but pondered it in his journal: "I would love to write a pretty song for her, even though I have no right to speak for her." On the same page, he was less romantic when he portrayed himself as a character with no arms: "I gesture and grunt for your affection, wielding my flippers in a windmill circle; my bib is soiled with lost attempts to contact you through saliva communication, drivel drying to my chest." One of his many obsessions was "flipper babies," infants born without arms; he wrote about the topic regularly and drew freakish illustrations of what he imagined they looked like.

A week later, he wrote a song about his girlfriend. The chorus went, "I can't see you every night for free," a direct reference to their argument. Strangely, though he rehearsed and played the song in front of her, he never admitted it was about her. Instead he told her, "I just write what comes in my head, and I don't write anything about you or anyone else." He was lying, of course, but the fact that he would create this gift for her, but not be willing to risk the intimacy of presenting it, says much about their relationship and his commitment to it. It was like a junior-high-school boy who leaves a valentine for a girl but doesn't have the courage to sign his name. When he played the song for Chad and Krist, they liked it immediately and asked its name. "I have no idea," Kurt said. "What's it about?" Chad asked. "It's about a girl," Kurt said, and they decided that would do for a title. Most of Kurt's titles had only a minor relationship to the lyrics anyway.

"About a Girl" was an important song in Kurt's development as a writer—it was his first straight-ahead love song, and even if the lyrics were twisted, it was so unabashedly melodic that in Nirvana's early live performances, audiences mistook it as a Beatles' cover. Kurt told Steve Shillinger that on the day he wrote "About a Girl," he played *Meet the Beatles* for three hours straight to get in the mood. This was hardly necessary: Ever since he was a toddler he'd studied their work, even though they were considered passé in punk circles.

By the end of 1988 Kurt's musical influences were a strange potpourri of the punk he'd learned at Buzz Osborne's knee, the heavy metal he listened to as a teenager, and the pop he'd discovered in his early childhood, with little rhyme or reason to their grouping. There were huge hunks of music history he'd missed simply because he hadn't been exposed to them (he still hadn't heard Patti Smith or the New York Dolls), yet in other small pockets, like when it came to Scratch

Acid, he was the sort of expert who could tell you every track they released. He had a tendency to fall in love with a group and embrace their music above all others, proselytizing to his friends like a doorstep preacher. Krist had a better grasp of the larger rock oeuvre, one reason Krist remained essential to the band—Krist knew what was kitsch, while Kurt sometimes erred in this category. In late 1988 Kurt summoned his friend Damon Romero to his apartment by telling him, "There's this great record I've discovered that you *have* to hear." When Romero arrived, Kurt pulled out the Knack's album *Get the Knack*, and moved toward the turntable with it. Romero, who was well familiar with this 1979 release, which couldn't have been considered more mainstream, thought Kurt was being sarcastic, and inquired, "Are you serious?" "No, you've got to listen to this—it's an *awesome* pop album," was Kurt's deadpan reply. Kurt put the record on, and Romero uncomfortably sat through both sides of the disc, wondering the whole while if there was some sort of punch line yet to come. But Kurt closed his eyes and was silent as it spun, playing air drums with his hands in a quiet homage.

Shortly after "Love Buzz" was released, Kurt made a mixed tape for his friend Tam Orhmund that displayed his favorite current music. Side A included songs from Redd Kross, Ozzy Osbourne, Queen, the Bay City Rollers, Sweet, Saccharine Trust, the Velvet Underground, Venom, the Beatles, and the Knack; he retitled the Knack's "My Sharona," as "My Scrotum." Side B included tracks from such dissimilar bands as Soundgarden, Blondie, Psychedelic Furs, Metallica, Jefferson Airplane, the Melvins, and "AC-Fucking-DC," as he wrote the name. It took hours to make a tape like this, but Kurt had nothing but time.

With the gift he was hoping to interest Orhmund in managing Nirvana. Realizing that Sub Pop wasn't looking out for his interests, he thought Ohrmund, who had no prior experience but was outgoing, might better represent them. At one point he and Tracy considered moving to Tacoma with Tam. After looking at several houses, Kurt nixed the idea when he saw a bullet hole in a wall.

Orhmund had instead moved to Seattle, which to Kurt seemed to be the only qualification needed to be the band's manager. On the day they picked up the "Love Buzz" single, they stopped by her place and Kurt announced she was their new manager. He gave her a stack of records and asked her to send them to Touch and Go and anyone else she might think would be interested. She put together a crude press kit, which included pictures from the K-Dorm show and their paltry press clippings. Even on the day the single came out, Ohrmund remembered, "Kurt acted like he hated Sub Pop."

That fall Kurt had ordered Donald Passman's book "All You Need to Know About the Music Business" from the library. After reading it and sharing the information with Krist, he became more suspicious of his label and decided they needed a contract. The next week, Krist drove to Seattle and drunkenly pounded on Bruce Pavitt's door, yelling, "You fuckers, we want a contract!" Sub Pop drafted a short contract that went into effect on January 1, 1989. It called for three albums over three years—a schedule Kurt thought too slow—and the label was to pay the band $6,000 for the first year, $12,000 for the second, and $24,000 for the third.

The band spent most of December rehearsing for the upcoming session. Since their practice space was in Aberdeen, travel could take up most of the day. Chad only occasionally had a car, and Kurt's vehicle was hardly dependable. Most days, Krist would drive his van from Aberdeen to Olympia to pick up Kurt; head north to Seattle to pick up Chad, who would take the ferry in from Bainbridge; and then they'd all drive back to Aberdeen. At the end of the day, the route would be reversed. Some days they'd drive as many as 400 miles to accomplish a three-hour practice. Still, there were benefits to this commuting: It began to foster a sense of togetherness, and gave them uninterrupted time to listen to music. "We listened to Mudhoney, Tad, Coffin Break, the Pixies, and the Sugarcubes," remembered Chad. The list of bands they listened to is as good a description of Nirvana's sound in 1988 as any. They managed to sound both derivative and original, at times within the same song. But Kurt was learning, and learning quickly.

On December 21, 1988, the band returned for their first official home-town show in Grays Harbor as Nirvana. Though they were starting to draw crowds in Olympia and Seattle, for this appearance they played to an audience of twenty, mostly "Cling-Ons." The venue was the Hoquiam Eagles hall, just two blocks away from the Chevron station where Kurt's father had once worked. Krist stripped down to his underwear and again poured blood on himself. They played Led Zeppelin's "Immigrant Song" for the first and only time in concert, and the cover elicited a bigger response than any of Kurt's originals. The show marked the first time Kurt's sister, who was still in high school, had seen her brother in concert. "I sat on the edge of the stage, singing along," Kim recalled. "I lost my voice. I was supposed to get up the next day in class and give a book report, but I couldn't."

That week Kurt sent his grandparents Leland and Iris a Hallmark Christmas card. Inside the card, he included a note, updating them on his professional progress:

Dear long lost grandparents: I miss you very much. Which is no excuse for my not visiting. I'm very busy living in Olympia when I'm not on tour with my band. We put out a single just recently and it has sold-out already. We are recording for a debut LP this Monday, which will be released in March. In February we are going on tour again in California and then we will be back in April only to take a break. Then on the road again. I'm happier than I ever have been. It would be nice to hear from you as well. Merry Christmas, love Kurt.

Kurt exaggerated the band's touring schedule—their shows were still infrequent, but increasing in pace. But he wasn't exaggerating when he described himself as "happier than I ever have been." The anticipation of an upcoming career milestone was always more joyous to him than the actual event, and the idea of having his own full-length album— something far more significant than a single he presumed—filled him with enough levity that he uncharacteristically talked about his inner emotions. It was rare for him to acknowledge how he felt about himself—rarer still for him to describe himself as happy.

Two days after the Hoquiam gig the band drove to Seattle to record their album. It was Christmas Eve. "We had nothing else to do," explained Krist. They spent the night before at Jason Everman's house, a friend of Chad and Dylan's. As typical for Kurt, he'd written the melodies but few lyrics, so he stayed up most of the night finalizing his words. He told his bandmates he couldn't sleep anyway.

They arrived at the studio the next afternoon and worked deep into the night. During this session they laid down basic tracks for ten songs, but Kurt didn't like his vocal takes. The only track he fancied was "Blew," which had been the victim of a bit of serendipity: Krist had forgotten which key he was in, and had mistakenly tuned down one notch below the Drop-D tuning the song was written in. The result was a sound that was heavier and deeper than anything they'd done before, a perfect mistake. Like many of the early songs Kurt wrote, the lyrics to "Blew" didn't make sense—they were, as Kurt later explained, simply "cool things to sing"—but the melody and lyrics effectively communicated hopelessness and despair, themes that were prevalent through most of Kurt's songs.

About midnight the band called it quits and headed back to Aberdeen. On the long drive home they listened to the session six times in a row. Krist dropped Kurt back in Aberdeen at Wendy's house at 1:30 in the morning on Christmas Day, 1988. He had planned to spend the holiday there before heading back to see Tracy. On the surface, Kurt and Wendy's relationship seemed improved. That fall, he wrote in his journal: "We get along great now that I've moved out. I've done what my mother wants. She thinks I have a respectable job, a girlfriend, a car, a house. I need to retrieve some old stuff that I left at home, my old home, my *real* home, now simply my mother's home."

Kurt usually made Christmas presents for his family by hand, both out of artistic preference and economic necessity; in 1987 he'd crafted keychains. But gifts in 1988 were a no-brainer: he gave everyone, including his aunts and uncles, copies of the single. Having the record created a homecoming of sorts for him—he now had evidence to prove to the relatives he was making something of himself. Wendy played the single on the family stereo, but it was clear she wasn't impressed. She told him he needed "something else to fall back on." Kurt would hear none of it.

More exciting than Christmas was yet another high-profile show the band played on December 28 at the Underground in Seattle for the release of the Sub Pop 200 box set. Even while struggling to pay their bands, Sub Pop threw lavish parties, and this event was no exception: It was an eight-band, two-day affair at a U-District club. Nirvana were on the first night and were introduced by Steven Jesse Bernstein as "the band with the freeze-dried vocals." The show marked one of the first times Nirvana was on equal billing with the rest of Sub Pop's roster— previously they had been considered a baby band. They stayed in Seattle and, during the next three days, spent another fifteen hours in the studio with Endino. Working until the early evening on New Year's Eve, Kurt finally retreated to Olympia to start 1989 with Tracy.

The second week of January, the band was back at work for two more sessions of mixing, and with this they were close to done. After almost 30 hours in the studio, they had nine tracks. They chose to use three of the Crover demos on the album, and they remixed those. Kurt had decided the album would be called *Too Many Humans*, which wasn't the name of any individual song but summed up the dark thesis of his work. But in early February the band headed to California on tour, and while driving through San Francisco, Kurt saw an AIDS prevention poster that struck him as funny: It read "Bleach Your Works." "*Bleach*," he said to his two bandmates as the van drove down the street. "That's going to be the name of our new album."

10 | ILLEGAL TO ROCK 'N' ROLL

OLYMPIA, WASHINGTON
FEBRUARY 1989–SEPTEMBER 1989

If it's illegal to rock 'n' roll, throw my ass in jail.
—A line Kurt wrote on a guitar, July 15, 1989.

The day before his 22nd birthday, Kurt wrote a letter to his mother that read: "It's a rainy Sunday afternoon and, as usual, there's not much to do, so I thought I'd write a little letter. Actually, since every day is rainy and slow, I've been writing a lot lately. I guess it's better than nothing. I either write a song, or write a letter, and I'm sick of writing songs, for now. Well, tomorrow is the 22nd birthday (and I still can't spell)." He didn't finish the letter, and he didn't send the fragment.

Despite the boredom expressed in the letter, Kurt's inner artistic life was blossoming. His 22nd year would be one almost completely devoted to creating—in the form of music or art. He had long ago given up aspirations of being a commercial artist, but in a way this freedom allowed his art to develop unfettered. He didn't have a job for most of 1989, unless you consider running Nirvana a job. Tracy had become his benefactor, a role she would assume for most of their relationship.

Walking into his apartment any afternoon during 1989, you were as likely to find him with a paintbrush in his hand as a guitar. But he wasn't actually a painter as much as he was a creator. He used whatever implement was in front of him as his brush, and whatever flat object he found as canvas. He couldn't afford actual canvas or even quality paper, so many of his works were done on the back of old board games he

found in thrift stores. Instead of paint—which he could rarely manage—
he used pencil, pen, charcoal, magic marker, spray paint, and occasionally even blood. One day a neighbor, Amy Moon, came by only to be
greeted at the door by Kurt wearing the grin of a mad scientist who
recently had birthed his first creature. He had just finished a painting,
he told her, this time done with acrylic paint, but with one special
addition, "my secret ingredient." He told Amy he added this to every
one of his paintings as the final touch, the fait accompli, once the work
was to his liking. The secret sauce, he explained, was his semen. "My
seed is on this painting," he told her. "Look, you can see how it glis-
tens!" he motioned. Amy didn't dare ask what method Kurt used to
apply his "seed," but she noticed no brush or palate in the area.

This unusual ritual didn't stop Amy from employing Kurt to create
a painting for her; it was the only commission he ever took. She described a dream and asked him to depict it. He took the assignment,
and she paid $10 for materials. The resulting painting was crudely
painted but so evocative of her dream, Amy could barely imagine Kurt
had created it from her description. "It's the middle of the night," Amy
described, "and there is an eerie force at work. In the background are
not well-defined trees, just shadows. In the foreground are the headlights of a car, and a freshly hit deer. You can see the breath coming
out of the animal, and the heat coming off its body. There is a very thin
female figure in the front, eating the flesh of the animal that is probably
not dead yet. His painting is exactly as I saw the dream."

Most of Kurt's creations were unsettling, sometimes strikingly so.
Many were of the same themes he'd explored in high-school art class,
but there was a darker edge to them now. He still painted aliens and
exploding guitars, but his sketchbook also included Dalí-esque land-
scapes with melting clocks, pornographic body parts on creatures with
no heads, and illustrations of severed limbs. Increasingly during 1989,
his art began to take on three-dimensional qualities. He shopped Olympia's many thrift stores every week, and anything cheap and bizarre was
likely to make its way into one of his constructions. On the back of an
Iron Butterfly album, he painted an image of Batman, affixed a naked
Barbie doll to it with a noose around her neck, and presented this to
Tracy as a birthday gift. He began to collect dolls, car models, lunch-

boxes, old board games (some he kept intact, like his beloved Evel Knievel game), toy action-figures, and other assorted objects found on the cheap. These collectibles were not treasured or put away on a shelf; they could be melted in the backyard during a barbecue or glued to the back of a board game. Tracy complained she couldn't turn around without having a doll stare at her. The entire apartment began to take on the look of a roadside museum of kitsch, but one in a constant state of both construction and destruction. "He had this clutter thing," remembered Krist. "His whole house was cluttered, and there were things everywhere. Yet he was a serious artist, and that was one of the ways he expressed himself; how he filtered the world. It came out a lot of ways, and some of it was morbid and twisted. In fact, all the art is decadent and twisted. His theme was pretty consistent. Everything was just a little fucked up and dark."

One of Kurt's favorite twists was switching sexual organs on figures he'd drawn. Male bodies would have vaginas for heads, women might get penises as well as breasts. One work from this period shows four naked women sitting around an oversized Satan, who sports a mammoth erect penis. Though the image is drawn in pencil, the women's heads are pasted from ads in *Good Housekeeping* magazine. The figures touch each other in one massive human chain: one woman is defecating; another has her hand in her vagina; a third has a hand in the next woman's anus, and the final woman has a baby coming out of her womb. All have devil horns, and they are drawn so realistically as to look like the work of the nineties-era San Francisco artist Coop.

Most of Kurt's artwork was never titled, but one particular piece from this period did garner a carefully lettered title. Drawn in black crayon on white twenty-pound bond, it shows a stick figure with a huge smiley face for a head, chopping off his left leg with an axe. The title reads: "Mr. Sunshine Commits Suicide."

Though Kurt complained of boredom, 1989 was one of the busiest periods for the band. By the end of 1988, Nirvana had only done two dozen shows during their entire two-year history, under various names, and using four different drummers (Burckhard, Foster, Crover, and

Channing). But in 1989 alone, they would play 100 gigs. Kurt's life shifted into the routine of a working musician.

Their first tour in 1989 was a West Coast swing that brought them to San Francisco, where they saw the "Bleach Your Works" sign. They were touring at the time on the basis of a single, an unheard-of proposition considering the mathematics of their possible fan base; with fewer than a thousand singles sold in the entire world, the chance of a crowd in San Jose, for example, having heard of them and liking them enough to go see them was beyond absurd. Some of these first gigs attracted an audience of literally a half dozen people, usually musicians interested in Sub Pop, since the label was a bigger draw than the band. Dylan Carlson went along on the tour and remembered Kurt's frustration. "It was kind of a fiasco," he said. "There were lots of shows that got cancelled." The plug was always pulled by club owners, since the band was willing to play for the bartender and doorman. The biggest crowd was when Nirvana opened for Living Color, a more mainstream rock band with a Top 40 hit, before 400 people. The audience hated them.

If there was a low among lows on this first tour, it came in San Francisco. There the band opened for the Melvins at the Covered Wagon, a reunion that Kurt had long been looking forward to. But when he discovered that the Melvins weren't a bigger draw in California than they had been in Grays Harbor, his faith was dashed. As on every other tour date, they struggled to find gas money, a floor to crash on, and food to eat. Tracy had followed the band down to California in her car, taking friends Amy Moon and Joe Preston. There were seven people in the band's entourage, and among them they couldn't afford a burrito. Someone on the street told them about a free soup kitchen. "It may have been run by the Hare Krishnas; Kurt was really creeped out by it," Amy remembered. While everyone else ravenously scarfed down the free soup, Kurt just dejectedly stared at his bowl. "He wouldn't eat it," Amy said. "He finally just got up and left. It depressed him." Hare Krishna food, crowds of ten people, begging for gas money, the Melvins as commercial failures, calling up to request your own single—these represented a level of degradation Kurt had not imagined or prepared for. That night, all seven people slept on a friend's floor in a studio apartment.

They returned to Seattle to play a more successful show on February 25 at the University of Washington. Billed as "Four Bands for Four Bucks," it was Nirvana's biggest crowd to date, an audience of about 600. They were playing with the Fluid, Skin Yard, and Girl Trouble, all of whom were better known, but it was during Nirvana's set that the crowd went wild. Seattle audiences had begun to slam-dance in the late eighties: This entailed a kind of violent, mad twist, usually performed in front of the stage by a swirling mass of teenagers. When the crowd was large enough, waves of people would begin to slam off each other, as if a hurricane had developed inside the audience. Nirvana's frenzied sound made the perfect soundtrack for slam-dancing, since they never slowed down, and rarely even paused between numbers. When the occasional fan would climb onstage and then jump back into the audience—called stage diving—the ritualistic dance was complete. Kurt calmly sang and played while dozens of kids jumped onstage, only to jump right off. At times there were so many kids jumping off the stage, it appeared Kurt was standing in the middle of some kind of airborne training facility for aspiring paratroopers. It was organized confusion, but *this* was exactly what Kurt had dreamed of: using his music to create chaos. Many other bands attracted a similar slam-dancing audience but few musicians were able to lackadaisically stand in the midst of these stage invasions the way Kurt was. He gave off the impression he was used to playing while the audience took over the stage; and in Seattle it had become so commonplace that he was.

That day Kurt conducted a brief interview with the *Daily*, the University of Washington student newspaper, wherein he addressed the Northwest scene, calling it "the last wave of rock music," and "the ultimate rehash." Kurt told writer Phil West the band's music had a "gloomy, vengeful element based on hatred." This article was the first occasion of what would become one of Kurt's favorite sports: spewing mythology to gullible journalists. "In Aberdeen, I hated my best friends with a passion, because they were idiots," Kurt announced. "A lot of that hatred is still leaking through." Kurt did give credit to Tracy for supporting him, but swore one day he'd "live off the band." If not, he pledged, "I'll just retire to Mexico or Yugoslavia with a few hundred dollars, grow potatoes, and learn the history of rock through back issues of *Creem*."

That spring the band added Jason Everman as a second guitarist, making them a four-piece for the first time. Kurt wanted Jason to cover guitar parts he felt weren't getting justice as his songs became more complicated. Jason had been in earlier bands with Chad, and had a reputation as a hot guitar player. He also had ingratiated himself to the band by loaning Kurt $600, used to pay the recording bill for *Bleach*. It had no strings attached—Everman was, in fact, never repaid—but Kurt listed Jason on the *Bleach* album cover, even though he did not play at the sessions.

With Jason in the lineup, Nirvana played Sub Pop's "Lamefest" on June 9, at Seattle's Moore Theater. It found them opening for Mudhoney and Tad, the two biggest Sub Pop groups, and it marked the official release of *Bleach*. Nirvana played first—their set was uneventful except for Kurt getting his guitar strings caught in his hair. The highlight of the night came when Kurt witnessed kids lining up to buy *Bleach*.

By mid-1989 the Northwest music scene began to gain international attention, greased by some smart moves from Pavitt and Poneman, who were showing that their real brilliance wasn't in running a label as much as it was marketing one. Their very concept of calling their annual showcase "Lamefest" was a stroke of genius: It immediately disarmed any possible criticism, while appealing to disaffected music fans who wore T-shirts that read "Loser" (the label sold as many of these as they did records). Despite the poor state of Sub Pop's bank account, in early 1988 they'd sprung for plane tickets for a few British rock critics to take a holiday in Seattle. It was money well spent: Within weeks, Sub Pop bands were in the English music weeklies, and bands like Mudhoney were stars, at least in Britain, of the "grunge" movement. The term was meant to describe loud, distorted punk, but it was soon used to categorize virtually every band from the Northwest, even those like Nirvana, who were in truth more pop. Kurt hated the term, but the hype machine had begun in earnest, and the Northwest scene grew. Though there were few venues to play in Seattle, each show became an event, and the crowds became exponentially larger.

Reflecting years later on why the scene exploded when it did, Kurt speculated in his journal: "Lots of flattering hype from multiple occupational English journalists . . . catapulted the Sub Pop regime into instant fame (just add water, or hype.)" Nirvana was usually mentioned in the early wave of 1989 press, but in most articles—like one in *Melody Maker* in March 1989 titled "Seattle: Rock City"—they were relegated to a tiny sidebar as also-rans. When Kurt read his first little bit of English press, he was probably most shocked to see Everett True's speculation on what the band would be doing if they weren't musicians: "You're talking about four guys . . . who, if they weren't doing this, would be working in a supermarket, or lumber yard, or fixing cars." Two of the three professions listed were jobs Kurt's father had held; the third was Buzz's old job.

Bleach had much to do with Nirvana moving out from under the shadow of their contemporaries. It was an inconsistent album, putting songs Kurt had written four years previously right next to the recent "About a Girl," but it had flashes of inspiration. On sludgy numbers like "Sifting," the chord progression was crude while the actual lyrics—when they could be heard—were smart and clever. When *The Rocket* reviewed the album, Gillian Gaar pointed out the different directions the band was going in: "Nirvana careens from one end of the thrash spectrum to the other, giving a nod towards garage grunge, alternative noise, and hell-raising metal without swearing allegiance to any of them." In his journal around the time of the release, Kurt expressed similar sentiments: "My lyrics are a big pile of contradictions. They're split down the middle between very sincere opinions and feelings that I have, and sarcastic, hopeful, humorous rebuttals towards cliché, bohemian ideals that have been exhausted for years. I mean to be passionate and sincere, but I also like to have fun and act like a dork."

Kurt accurately described *Bleach* as a mixture of sincere and cliché sentiment, but there was enough of each to get it airplay on divergent college radio stations. The band had used one of Tracy's photos on the cover, printed as a reverse image in negative, and the look was appropriate for the extreme contrast between the dark songs and the pop tunes. Kurt's dualism was key to the band's success: There were enough different-sounding songs that stations could play several cuts without wearing the band out. The album built slowly, but eventually songs like "Blew," "School," "Floyd the Barber," and "Love Buzz" became staples on college radio stations around the nation.

The band still had a long way to go. The day after Lamefest, the group stepped in as a last-minute replacement for Cat Butt for a gig in Portland. Along for the ride was eighteen-year-old Rob Kader, a fan who was at every one of their shows, and Kader led the band in joyously singing the theme song from "The Brady Bunch" on the van ride down. But when they arrived at the gig, only twelve people had purchased tickets, all of them Cat Butt fans. Kurt made a last-minute decision to forgo a set list and announced to Kader: "We're just going to ask you at the end of each song what you want to hear, and then we'll play that." As each tune wound down, Kurt would walk to the edge of the stage and point at Kader, who would shout out the next number. Other than Kader—who was in his glory—the rest of the audience gave the band a cold response, except on one Kiss song, "Do You Love Me?," which Nirvana had recently recorded for a covers album, and which Kader wisely requested.

In late June 1989 the band packed up Krist's Dodge van for their first major tour, a scheduled two-month jaunt that would take them across the United States. Kader and a group of friends gave them a send-off. Kader brought a 24-pack of Mountain Dew as a going-away present, always a band favorite because of the caffeine kick. They had stuffed the van with their new band T-shirts, which read: "Nirvana: Fudge Packin', Crack Smokin', Satan Worshipin' Motherfuckers." Krist and Shelli had just recently gotten back together, and their parting was tearful. And even Kurt was a bit broken up about leaving Tracy—it would be the longest they had been apart since they started dating.

They had no manager, so Krist had begun to take on more of the booking work, and the van was solely his domain, governed by a hard set of rules. One instruction was tacked inside the van: "No use of any gas corporation services besides Exxon—no exceptions." To save money, the air-conditioning could never be turned on, and no one was allowed to drive over 70 miles per hour. On this first tour, they split the driving assignments, but Kurt rarely made it into the rotation: His bandmates thought he drove too slowly. "He drove like a little old lady," Tracy recalled. It was just one of the many contradictions in Kurt's character; he might be willing to huff the fumes from the bottom of an Edge Shaving Gel can, but he wasn't going to get in a car accident.

Their first show was in San Francisco, where they found themselves playing to a small audience but enough to avoid the soup kitchen. Though they were now touring behind an album, Sub Pop's distribution was so bad they rarely found their album for sale. When they played an in-store in Los Angeles at Rhino Records two days later, the store only had five copies of the album in stock. In L.A. they were interviewed by the fanzine *Flipside*, and even though Kurt's name was misspelled as "Kirk" in the printed piece, they felt the clip gave them punk credibility. In the article, the writer asked Kurt about drugs: "I kinda reached my end of things to do, as far as acid and pot and stuff," Kurt replied, sounding downright temperate. "I just reached a maximum on that stuff. Once you go past the learning experience, then you go into the downhill part. I never took drugs as an escape, I always took drugs for learning."

As they headed east toward the Midwest and Texas, they played to progressively smaller crowds—some as tiny as a dozen people—mostly musicians who would see any band. "We measured our shows, not so much by how many people were there," recalled Chad, "but more by what people said. And a lot of people would say they liked us." They were improving as a live act, winning over audiences that weren't familiar with them. Like the Velvet Underground before them, they would soon find that an audience of a thousand musicians is more powerful than 10,000 casual fans. When possible they would hook up with other punk bands they knew of, to sleep on their floors, and these personal connections were as important in boosting their spirits as the shows were. In Denver, they stayed with John Robinson of the Fluid, who already noticed a shyness about Kurt. "Everyone would be in the kitchen eating, happy to have a home-cooked meal," Robinson said.

"I'd ask Krist where Kurt was. He said, 'Oh, don't worry about him; he's always off somewhere.' My house wasn't that big, so I went looking for him and found him in my daughter's room with the lights off, staring into space."

While driving through Chicago, Kurt purchased a large crucifix at a garage sale—probably the first religious artifact he didn't steal. He'd stick the crucifix out the window of the van, shake it at pedestrians, then snap a picture of their expression as he drove away. Whenever Kurt was in the passenger seat of the van, he held the crucifix in his hand, as if it were some weapon he might need at a moment's notice.

Many nights the band slept in the van or camped by the side of the road, so solitude was rare. They struggled to find enough money for gas and food, so staying in a motel was out of the question. The only way they were able to buy gas was when they sold enough T-shirts— the "fudge-packin'" shirts saved the tour. One night in Washington, D.C., they arrived late and pulled the van behind a gas station, planning to spend the night. It was too hot to sleep in the van, so they all slept outside on what they thought was a strip of grass in a residential neighborhood. The next morning, they found they had camped on a traffic median.

"We usually had the choice of buying food or gas, and we had to choose gas," Jason recalled. "Most of us did pretty well with it, but Kurt hated it. He seemed to have a low constitution—he would get sick easily. And once he got sick, it would make everyone miserable." Kurt's stomach condition flared up on the road, perhaps from infrequently eating, plus he seemed to consistently catch colds, even in the summer. His health problems weren't from lack of care; during 1989, he was the most health-conscious band member, infrequently drinking and not even letting his bandmates smoke near him for fear of losing his vocal abilities.

When the band hit Jamaica Plain, Massachusetts, they stayed at the house of photographer J. J. Gonson and her boyfriend Sluggo, from the band Hullabaloo. The band's show that night at Green Street Station was one of the few times Kurt played without a guitar: He'd broken his instrument the night before. He was angry about the guitar, suffering from such stomach pain he drank Strawberry Quik to soothe the inflammation, and he was homesick. He called Tracy after the show and told her he wanted to come home. The next morning, Gonson shot a photo of the band asleep on her floor: They shared one mattress, and Kurt and Krist had cuddled up next to each other during the night like two puppies.

Sluggo had a broken guitar on his wall, and Kurt asked if he could have it. "The neck isn't even snapped off, so I can fix it," Kurt observed. He traded Sluggo an old Mustang guitar, first autographing the Mustang, "Yo, Sluggo, thanks for the trade. If it's illegal to rock 'n' roll, throw my ass in jail." He signed it "Nirvana," thinking his own autograph meant nothing.

Later that day Kurt created a new guitar. It was patched together like Frankenstein, just in time for their next gig, which itself was something out of a horror story. They had agreed to play a fraternity party at MIT because it paid better than their club shows. Before the show, Kurt lay down on a pool table and kicked his legs like a two-year-old throwing a fit, screaming "I'm not playing! This is stupid. We are better than this. We are wasting our time." His tantrum subsided only when Krist told him that without the gig, they wouldn't have enough gas money to get home. As if to spite the crowd, the band played an energetic show, though Krist dismantled a sign that spelled out the fraternity's name in bones, handing the bones to the audience. The brothers insisted Krist apologize and fix the sign. Novoselic was never one to back down from a fight, even if the odds were greatly against him, but he sheepishly grabbed the microphone, asked the crowd to return the bones, and said he was sorry. The fraternity audience ended up loving the show.

It was also in Massachusetts where the first outward conflict between Kurt and Jason sprang up. Jason had made the mistake of inviting a girl home after the gig, something considered in poor taste by the rest of the band. Both Kurt and Krist had surprisingly old-fashioned attitudes about fidelity and groupies. A musician who was in a band for the girls— a large category but one that did not include Jason—they considered compromised.

In truth, Kurt and Jason had never gotten along famously because, in many ways, they were too much alike. Both were prone to brooding and spending time alone, and each felt threatened by the other's solitude. Jason had long, curly hair, which he would thrash about as he played, and Kurt claimed he found this annoying, though he was guilty of the same head movements. Like Foster before him, Jason represented a part of Kurt that the singer didn't want reflected back. Though Kurt wrote all the songs, he complained over this pressure, yet never allowed the other members to have much input. "He didn't want to give up any control. Everyone knew it was 'the Kurt show,' " observed Chad. Kurt asked Jason to come up with some new guitar solos, but when Jason did as requested, Kurt acted as if he'd overstepped his role. Instead of talking about it, or even yelling at each other, both became sullen and unresponsive. As in many conflicts in his life, Kurt turned the professional into the personal, and a blood feud of sorts began.

In New York the band played a show at the Pyramid Club, as part of the New Music Seminar. It was their highest-profile gig to date, in front of an industry crowd including Kurt's idols Sonic Youth. Yet the performance was compromised when a drunk climbed onstage, yelling into the microphone and knocking over the band's equipment. Jason threw the guy offstage and jumped into the audience to chase him.

The next day Kurt decided to fire Jason. They were staying at Janet Billig's Alphabet City apartment, which was known as the punk rock Motel 6 in New York City. Jason and Chad had gone off to sightsee, but Kurt and Krist used their remaining money to buy cocaine, breaking Kurt's tour-long sobriety. Kurt decided Jason was out of the band, though as typical with his non-confrontational style, he failed to announce this to anyone other than Krist. He simply told the other members that the tour was over and they were going home, and, as was usual, no one challenged him. The band cancelled two weeks' worth of gigs—the first time they'd ever pulled out of a show. The van ride home was hell. "No one said a word for the entire drive," remembered Jason. "We drove nonstop, only stopping for gas." They made it home from New York to Seattle, a drive of almost 3,000 miles, in less than three days. Kurt never actually told Jason he was fired—he simply never called again.

. . .

Kurt had a warm reunion with Tracy. He told her he missed her more than he realized, and while he was never one to talk about his feelings, Tracy was one of the few people he revealed himself to. That August Kurt wrote a letter to Jesse Reed and bragged about what a great girl-friend she was: "My girlfriend now has a brand new '88 Toyota Tercel, a microwave, a food processor, a blender, and an espresso machine. I am a totally pampered, spoiled bum." To Kurt, the Tercel seemed like a luxury car.

With Kurt's return, a sense of romance came back into their rela-tionship, though after living alone for almost two months, Tracy wasn't as keen on Kurt's moodiness. She felt they had outgrown the tiny studio apartment, particularly with Kurt's collecting habit. Early in August she wrote him a note, which read: "I'm not staying here in MOLD HELL any longer than the fifteenth. It's fucking gross." Even though it was the middle of the summer in the Northwest, their apartment was suf-fering a mold infestation.

It was a wonder anyone noticed mold since, with all their animals, the apartment had taken on the smell, according to Damon Romero, of "a vivisection lab." There were, of course, turtles, rats, and cats, but the strongest odor came from the rabbit. Stew was a female bunny and she served as Kurt and Tracy's surrogate baby, spoiled like an only child. Stew managed frequently to escape her cage, which always led Kurt or Tracy to post a warning, advising visitors they might be stepping on rabbit feces. One day in early August Kurt was on the phone with Michelle Vlasimsky, a booker they had hired to help reschedule their cancelled dates, when the phone went dead. Kurt called her back a minute later and explained: "The rabbit unplugged the phone." He joked that his apartment was nicknamed "the Animal Farm." A few weeks later Slim Moon witnessed Kurt frantically rushing his pet cages outside. "I was defrosting the freezer with a knife when I poked a hole in it, and I didn't want the Freon to kill the animals," he explained.

When a one-bedroom apartment in the same house became avail-able, they moved the traveling Cobain museum. It was $50 more a month, but it was bigger and directly across from the house's garage, which Kurt took over. There was a workbench he utilized to fix the guitars he'd already broken, and to cut more wooden necks for guitars he had yet to break. Within the week, the garage was filled with broken amps, smashed speaker cabinets, and other remnants of Nirvana's road show.

In the middle of August Kurt made his first attempt to seek medical help for his stomach condition, and for advice on gaining weight. His gauntness had become an obsession for him, so much so that he'd bought many remedies from late-night television ads and tried them all without success. He saw a specialist at Tacoma's St. Joseph's Medical Center, in the facility's Eating Disorder Clinic, but despite extensive tests, no physical cause for his stomach pain could be determined. Kurt went to see another physician later that summer, but Tracy found him home ten minutes after his appointment. Kurt's explanation: "They wanted to take some blood and I hate needles, so I left." Tracy recalled he was "terribly afraid of needles." His stomach condition came and went, and there were many nights where he threw up all night. Tracy was convinced it was his diet, which, despite his doctor's advice, consisted of fatty and fried foods. Her thoughts were shared at the time by Krist and Chad, who were always urging Kurt to eat vegetables, a category he avoided completely. "I won't eat anything green," he announced.

The first week of August, the band went into the Music Source Studio with producer Steve Fisk to cut an EP to promote an upcoming tour of Europe. The sessions lasted two days and found the band recovered from losing Jason, even if their gear was a little worse for wear from touring. "They had those big North drums," recalled Fisk, "and the kick drum was held together with two rolls of duct tape because it had been cracked so often. They joked that it was the 'Liberty Bell drum.'"

They cut five new Cobain compositions: "Been a Son," "Stain," "Even in His Youth," "Polly," and "Token Eastern Song." The quality of these songs represented a huge leap forward in Kurt's development as a writer. Where many of his early tunes had been one-dimensional rants—usually discourses on the sorry state of society—a song like "Polly" found Kurt taking a newspaper clipping and crafting an emotional back story to go with the headline. The song, originally titled "Hitchhiker," had its roots in a real-life incident from 1987, when a young girl was kidnapped, brutally raped, and tortured with a blow torch. The song is written, surprisingly, from the perspective and in the voice of the perpetrator. Kurt managed to capture the horror of the rape ("let me clip your dirty wings"), yet at the same time subtly pointed out the humanness of the attacker ("she's just as bored as me"). Its literary strength was that it concerned itself with internal dialogue, much in the way Truman Capote found a measure of empathy for the murderers in his book *In Cold Blood*. The song's subject is in marked contrast to the melody, which, like "About a Girl," is sweet, slow, and melodic, almost as if it were designed to catch the audience off guard and result in the listener unknowingly singing a pleasant melody about a horrific crime. Kurt ends the song with a line that could stand as an epitaph for the rapist, for the victim, or for himself: "It amazes me, the will of instinct." Years later, upon first seeing Nirvana in concert, Bob Dylan picked "Polly" out of the entire Nirvana catalog as Kurt's most courageous song, and one that inspired him to remark of Kurt, "The kid has heart."

The other tunes cut in the session were equally impressive. "Been a Son" is a song about how Don Cobain would have preferred Kurt's sister to have been a boy. Both "Even in His Youth" and "Stain" are also autobiographical songs about Don, addressing Kurt's feelings of rejection. In "Even in His Youth," Kurt writes of how "Daddy was ashamed he was nothing," while in "Stain," Kurt has "bad blood" and is "a stain" on the family. "Token Eastern Song" was the only throwaway—it's about writer's block, essentially a song version of the unsent birthday letter he'd written to his mother.

These songs were also Kurt's most complex musical compositions to date with riffs that were fleshed out and varied. "We want a big rock sound," Kurt told Fisk, and they achieved this. When they played back the tape, Kurt excitedly announced, "We're in a big studio and we have a big Top 40 drum sound." To celebrate, the band asked if they could jump on the tables. "It felt like this high, significant in some way, and worthy of celebration," Fisk recalled. He joined Kurt, Krist, and Chad as they climbed up on the tables and bounced up and down for joy.

Later that August Kurt formed an offshoot band with Mark Lanegan, of the Screaming Trees, Krist on bass, and the Trees' drummer Mark Pickerel on drums. Kurt and Lanegan had been writing songs with each other for several months, though most of their time together was spent talking about their love of Leadbelly. The band rehearsed several times in a Seattle practice space Nirvana had rented above the Continental Trailways bus station. "Our first rehearsal must have been exclusively dedicated to Leadbelly," Pickerel recalled. "Both Mark and Kurt brought Leadbelly tapes, and we listened to them on this little boombox." Kurt and Krist wanted to call the new band "Lithium," while Pickerel suggested "The Jury," the name they ultimately chose. But when the group went into the studio on August 20, with Endino producing, the project misfired. "It was as if both Mark and Kurt had too much respect for each other to tell the other what to do, or even make suggestions for what they should be doing," Pickerel said. "Neither of them wanted to take on the position of being the decision maker." The two singers couldn't even decide on who should sing what song. They eventually cut "Ain't It a Shame," "Gray Goose," and "Where Did You Sleep Last Night?," all Leadbelly songs, but they never followed through to finish a record. Kurt became distracted with another non-Nirvana project: He briefly went to Portland to play with Dylan Carlson's band Earth for a studio session.

Nirvana then had to go back out on the road and complete two weeks of Midwest dates. On this jaunt, much to their amazement, the crowds were a little larger and more enthusiastic. *Bleach* had begun to get college radio airplay and at some shows they drew as many as 200 fans who seemed to know the songs. They sold many T-shirts and actually made money for the first time in their history. When they arrived back in Seattle, they tallied up their income versus their expenses, and went home with several hundred dollars. Kurt was amazed, showing off his earnings to Tracy as if making $300 made up for the years of financial support she'd given him.

Sub Pop planned Nirvana's first tour of Europe for that summer.

Bleach had been released in the United Kingdom to glowing reviews. Kurt had never been overseas and was convinced the band would be bigger in Europe. He promised Tracy he'd come home with thousands of dollars, and that he'd send her postcards from every country he visited.

11 CANDY, PUPPIES, LOVE

LONDON, ENGLAND
OCTOBER 1989–MAY 1990

At a store near you:
Nirvana. Flowers. Perfume. Candy. Puppies. Love.
—From an imaginary ad for Nirvana's second album.

On October 20, 1989, Kurt arrived in London. He had three days off before the first show and would have liked to visit the British Museum, yet he felt ill so he settled for getting his photograph taken at the entrance. His bandmates explored the British pubs, but Kurt—who didn't drink or smoke pot at the time because of his stomach problems—stayed in the hotel with bronchitis, a recurring condition. To try to cure himself, he would beat on his chest with his fist, thinking this violence would loosen his phlegm.

The band was touring Europe with Tad, another Sub Pop band, who were fronted by Tad Doyle, a 300-pound former butcher from Idaho. Since the two bands shared a deep and heavy sound, and because of Tad's almost freakish obesity, a clever U.K. promoter advertised one gig as "Heavier Than Heaven." The play on words became the official title of the tour, used on posters and in newspaper adverts. It was an apt summation of the sonic assault both bands created: If the sheer volume did not subdue you, the dark themes of songs like Nirvana's "Downer" and Tad's "Cyanide Bath" surely would. They had planned to co-headline, switching off as openers, in a show of brotherhood.

Kurt had expected fame and fortune in Europe: What he found instead was a low-budget tour that called for the band to play 37 shows in 42 days in nine different nations, a routing that was only possible if they drove all night. Their vehicle, rented by Sub Pop, was a shrunken ten-seat Fiat van, which had to carry their equipment, tour merchandise, three members of Nirvana, four members of Tad, and two crew members. Considering Tad's girth, Krist's height, and the fact that Tad's drummer insisted on standing up in the van, the daily loading could take an hour and resembled something out of a Marx Brothers' routine. And prior to departing, due to many gastrointestinal problems, Tad Doyle had to go through an almost ritualistic daily vomiting. This last malady was so regular it could have been written into the tour schedule: "10 a.m., load the van; 10:10, Tad vomits."

Kurt was bewitched by Tad's internal workings. He was suffering his own stomach pains, but he vomited only bile or blood. Tad's vomit, Kurt would declare, resembled a work of art. "Before Tad would get in the van, Kurt would hold this plastic basin," Kurt Danielson of Tad remembered. "He would stand there patiently, holding this plastic tub, with a delightful glitter in this eyes. He'd look up at Tad expectantly, and finally Tad would puke, and it would just come out in a glorious, colorful flow, and Kurt would catch it all. No one else got to hold the tub; it was Kurt's job and it was his delight." Tad also frequently had bathroom emergencies which meant trips to the side of the road, much to the amazement of the English drivers who passed a 300-pound man relieving himself in the median strip. In some ways, Tad's gastrointestinal system became Kurt's muse that fall: He wrote the song "Imodium" about Doyle's diarrhea medication.

Elimination continued as a theme when the band explored Hamburg's notorious red-light district and its porno supermarkets. Kurt was a bit of an amateur pornographer himself: Obsessed with the female derrière, he had photographed Tracy's rear on several occasions. He found common porn sexist, but was enraptured by deviant porn the way an anthropologist sought out undiscovered tribes. He was particularly enthralled by magazines depicting what he called "shit love," the sexual fetish more formally called scatophilia. "Kurt was fascinated by anything out of the ordinary: anything anomalous, psychologically strange or unusual, physically or socially strange," observed Danielson. "If it involved bodily functions, so much the better. Instead of drinking or smoking pot, he'd get high watching the peculiar idiosyncrasies of humanity unfolding around him." Kurt was too poor to purchase any porn, but Tad did buy one magazine featuring Ciccolina, a sex-industry star who gained international attention after being elected to the Italian Parliament. One pictorial showed Ciccolina getting out of a limousine while in the process of urinating in a man's mouth. Each morning in the Fiat van, Tad would pull the magazine out and announce, "the library is open," whereupon the coveted journal would be passed around.

These adolescent antics were the only diversions to a schedule that was numbing and demoralizing. "We went to Paris, but didn't have time to see the Eiffel Tower," recalled Chad. The schedule, Kurt asserted, seemed designed to physically and psychologically break them. The hectic pace began to affect their shows: Sometimes they played exceptionally well (as in Norwich, where a rabid crowd called them back for encores), and sometimes it all fell apart (as in Berlin, where Kurt smashed his guitar six songs into the set). "They were either phenomenal or kind of atrocious," recalled road manager Alex MacLeod. "But even when they were atrocious, there was an energy about them." Most of the crowds were enthusiastic and familiar with their songs, and many shows were sold out—a first for Nirvana. But since the venues were small, neither band made much money.

They did get a lot of press, and that, along with extensive airplay from influential DJ John Peel, propelled *Bleach* into the Top Ten of the U.K. independent label charts. While in Berlin, Nirvana got their first magazine cover, back in Seattle on *The Rocket*. Kurt told writer Nils Bernstein his current influences were "cutie bands" like Shonen Knife, the Pixies, and the Vaselines, his latest and greatest crush. He also addressed what he described as the prejudice he felt Seattle hipsters had against Nirvana: "I feel like we've been tagged as illiterate redneck cousin-fucking kids that have no idea what is going on at all. That's completely untrue."

Though he was finally playing to adoring audiences, a terrible melancholy overtook Kurt. On the occasions when they could afford a hotel, he would frequently room with Kurt Danielson, and the two would stay up all night in the darkness of their room, staring at the ceiling, and talking about what led them to the hell of a Fiat van. Kurt told fantastic stories of his early life, of the Fat Man, of the Aberdeen jail, and of a strange religion Dylan Carlson had created, mixing Scientology and Satanism. But the most outlandish stories he told were of his own family: tales of Don and Wendy, of guns in the river, of his high-school buddies hitting on his mother. During one restless night, Kurt confessed he wished he was home. "I've wanted to go home since the first week of this tour," he said, lying on his hotel bed. "I *could*, you know. I could go to my mom's right now, if I wanted to—she'd *let* me. She'd wire me the money." His voice cracked as if he were telling an elaborate lie. "*She'd* have me, you know."

A few days later in Rome, Kurt broke down onstage. Tad had played first and fired up the crowd with chants of "Fuck the Pope," always popular with punk rockers in Italy. By the time Nirvana came on, the sold-out audience was riled up. But problems with the sound system infuriated Kurt, and after playing 40 minutes, he climbed a 30-foot stack of speakers and screamed to the crowd, "I'm going to kill myself!" No one in the room, not even Krist, Chad, or Poneman and Pavitt (who had come over for the gig), knew what to make of this. Nor did Kurt, who suddenly found himself with an audience shouting "jump" in broken English. He was still strumming his guitar—the rest of the band having stopped to watch—and seemed unsure of what to do next. "He would have broken his neck if he would have jumped, and at some point he realized that," observed Danielson. Kurt eventually climbed down but his freak-out wasn't over. Backstage, the promoter complained that a microphone had been broken. Road manager MacLeod was disputing this and demonstrating the microphone worked fine— they could ill afford to replace it. Kurt grabbed the microphone, twirled it around like Roger Daltry, and smashed it to the floor. "There, *now* it's broken," he exclaimed as he walked away.

He recovered enough to play another five shows in Europe, and the tour ended in London for another Lamefest. Kurt pulled out all the stops for this last date, jumping up and down on the stage until his knees were bloodied. But psychologically, the tour was over for Kurt after Rome. He didn't have another guitar player to fire, so this time he essentially fired his label. Pavitt and Poneman had flown into Rome; Kurt couldn't stop contrasting the conditions in the van with the jet-setting style these two traveled in. Though Nirvana would stay on Sub Pop for another year, in a progressively worsening marriage, Kurt had already emotionally jettisoned his label.

By the time Nirvana returned to America in early December, Krist and Shelli had announced their engagement, with a wedding set for New Year's Eve at their house in Tacoma. Kurt and Tracy attended, though the drive from Olympia to Tacoma was one of the worst 30 minutes of their relationship. Tracy couldn't witness Shelli's marriage without broaching the subject of commitment with Kurt, even while she knew it was a topic destined to pain her. During the European tour, Krist had phoned Shelli frequently; all Tracy got from Kurt was an occasional postcard, though one of those said "I love you" twenty times. But on the drive to Tacoma the only way he'd address marriage was to joke about her marrying someone else. "I'd still like to have sex with you, because I really like it," he told her, thinking he was giving her a com-pliment. At the wedding, Kurt spent most of the evening on the roof by himself, uncharacteristically drunk, welcoming in the new year.

That Christmas, Kurt and Tracy had celebrated almost three years of togetherness. Though he was hard-pressed to afford it, he had given her *The Art of Rock*, a $100 coffee-table book, as a present. Outwardly they looked like a tight couple, but something had shifted within Kurt, and both he and Tracy knew it. When he'd return from tours, he took longer to warm up to her, and the contrast between their away-time and together-time was testing her patience. She felt she was losing him to the rest of the world.

And in a way, she was. As things continued to improve for Nirvana, the band increasingly provided him with the self-esteem and financial support that previously had come from her. By the beginning of 1990, Kurt had band-related business that needed to be done every day, and Tracy knew not to test where she ranked in comparison. But in truth, she also was moving away from him. She was a level-headed girl, and Kurt just kept getting weirder and weirder. She wondered where it might all end. That February he wrote an entry in his journal, half-fantasy and half-reality, that would have concerned any lover: "I am a male age 23 and I'm lactating. My breasts have never been so sore, not even after receiving titty twisters from bully schoolmates. I haven't masturbated in months because I've lost my imagination. I close my eyes and I see my father, little girls, German Shepherds, TV news commentators, but no voluptuous pouty-lipped naked female sex kittens wincing in ecstasy. I see lizards and flipper babies." This, and other entries like it, made her worry about his mental state.

Kurt had never slept well, grinding his teeth at night and complaining of recurrent nightmares. "Ever since he could remember, he had dreams about people trying to kill him," Tracy recalled. "In the dreams, he'd be trying to fight people off with a baseball bat, or people with knives coming after him, or vampires." When he awoke, sometimes with tears in his eyes, Tracy would comfort him the way a mother would soothe a small boy, holding him in her arms and stroking his hair. She would always be there for him, she told him; she was never going to leave. Yet he'd lie there looking at the ceiling, soaked with sweat. "He had those dreams all the time." She worried about how he calmed himself when he was on tour.

Outwardly, during the day, he looked fine, never talking about bad dreams, instead giving the appearance of someone who dreamt of only the band. Nirvana began the year with a brief studio session where they recorded the song "Sappy." As early as the European tour, they were already talking about a new album by summer. For the first time in Kurt's career, he wasn't the solitary force pushing for a new release—now Sub Pop, the press, college radio, and even a growing cadre of fans were asking him for new music. He was still writing at a prodigious rate, and the songs kept getting better. Nikki McClure had moved into the apartment next to his, and she used to hear him through the walls, constantly playing his guitar. One afternoon that winter, she overheard a beautiful melody coming through the heat vent; he kept starting and stopping the song, as if he were constructing it on the spot. That evening she tuned the radio to KAOS and heard Kurt playing the song he'd been rehearsing that day, live on the air.

On January 19, 1990, Nirvana played yet another Olympia show that would go down in the history books, though this one for different reasons from the others. The show, at a grange hall outside of town, would pair Nirvana with the Melvins and Beat Happening. As a costume, Kurt used stage blood to draw needle marks on his arms. He wasn't certain what a junkie looked like, so he overdrew the marks, which gave him a ghoulish appearance, more like a zombie from an Ed Wood film than a drug addict. "He was wearing short sleeves, and both arms from the wrists to the sleeves had these bruises," observed Garth Reeves. "It looked like he had a disease." Nonetheless, Kurt's attempt at a joke would have unintended consequences: His parody was lost on many in the crowd, and rumors began to circulate that he was *indeed* a junkie. Still, the show represented a watershed of sorts: Though the Melvins headlined, Nirvana were now more popular than their mentors. The Melvins ended their set with a dynamic cover of Neil Young's "Rockin' in the Free World." Kurt was in the front row, raising his fist with the rest of the audience, yet he couldn't help but notice that a third of the crowd had left after Nirvana's set.

Something even more shocking happened the next night when the Melvins and Nirvana played in Tacoma at a hall called Legends. The concert was completely sold out and earned Nirvana a payday of $500, one of their biggest checks to date. There were a hundred people stage diving, creating chaos. One of the most obnoxious was Matt Lukin of Mudhoney, who used his backstage pass to walk onstage, then dive headfirst into the audience. Nirvana's set had to be stopped three times to break up fights between Lukin and the bouncers. "He's our friend," Kurt kept telling the bouncers, sounding both concerned and embarrassed. By the end of Nirvana's performance, which included part of Lynyrd Skynyrd's "Sweet Home Alabama," there were five security guards standing in front of the band. That didn't seem odd to Kurt, but what positively amazed him was seeing Mark Arm of Mudhoney, standing stage right, bopping his head back and forth during all of Nirvana's set.

Mark Arm, whose real name was Mark McLaughlin, was certifiably *the* tastemaker for Seattle punk rock. While Pavitt and Poneman had craftily capitalized on grunge, Arm, with his band Mudhoney and his previous group Green River, had virtually invented the musical style, and had even come up with the term "grunge," writing in a Seattle fanzine in the early eighties. Arm was bright, sarcastic, talented, notorious for his partying, and exuded the kind of confidence that made people think he was destined for stardom. In short, he was everything an insecure kid from Aberdeen imagined he could never be. For Arm to appear at your concert, and to be seen enjoying himself, was to have Jacqueline Kennedy Onassis come to your wedding and dance all night. Kurt's adoration of Arm was obvious to everyone, but it had to be most obvious to Buzz Osborne, who was watching his former charge move on.

Kurt had attempted to foster a friendship with Arm, with limited success. When in Seattle, he'd frequently stop by Arm's apartment, where he was intimidated by Arm's collection of punk rock singles—the ultimate status symbol in their circle. "He obviously idolized Mark," remembered Carrie Montgomery, Arm's girlfriend. "Mark wasn't all that impressed by it, of course." At the time, Mudhoney remained Sub Pop's priority and the kings of the Northwest scene. A number of major record labels were interested in them, but they pledged to stick with Sub Pop, owing to Arm's friendship with Pavitt.

But even for Mudhoney, this friendship was tested during 1990, when Sub Pop's financial problems threatened to sink the label and every band on it. Though records by Tad, Nirvana, and Mudhoney had been consistent sellers, their sales were nowhere near the level required to fund the large operation Pavitt and Poneman had built. "Sub Pop actually asked to borrow half of our first European advance," Mudhoney's Steve Turner remembered. The label was so broke they offered bands stock in lieu of royalties owed. "We said, 'What's the point of that?'" recalled Matt Lukin. "You're going to be bankrupt in two weeks." It was particularly hard for Lukin to watch how poorly Sub Pop treated his friends in Nirvana. "I saw how long Bruce had been promising to put out another record from them, and he kept putting them off," Lukin recalled. "They got put on the back burner."

The money Kurt had made from touring was quickly spent. That spring he started applying for jobs again, circling ads in the *Daily Olympian* for such occupations as cleaning apartments and hosing down dog kennels at a vet's; he applied for this last position but was turned down.

He and Krist decided to start their own janitorial business they would call "Pine Tree Janitorial." It was one of Kurt's many get-rich-quick schemes, and he went so far as to draw up a flyer for their new business with illustrations of Kurt and Krist pushing brooms. The ad touted, "we purposely limit our number of commercial offices in order to personally clean while taking our time." Despite putting flyers up all over Olympia, no client ever employed them.

When he wasn't being the CEO of Pine Tree Janitorial, Kurt was writing songs and touring. They left the first week of February for a West Coast tour with Tad that was their most successful yet, drawing large, enthusiastic crowds in Portland and San Francisco (for a Valentine's Day gig that billed the bands as "hot hunks"). Even in cynical Hollywood, people clamored to get into their show at Raji's. "That was the night they won over L.A.," recalled Pleasant Gehman, who booked the room. "People were just in awe. The club only held 200 people, but I swear there were 400 there." In Los Angeles they stayed with Jennifer Finch of the band L7, who described their appearance at the time as "looking like the Great Dane and Poodle act at the circus: Chad was tiny, his hair was down to his ass, and his eyes were feral; Kurt was a bit taller than Chad, but with hair that was stringy and long; and then there's Krist, who is so tall it hurt your neck to look up at him."

The tour also saw Kurt reunite with his old buddy Jesse Reed, who was now living outside of San Diego. They met up at the San Ysidro McDonald's, infamous for being the sight of a bloody shooting, and a place Kurt insisted on making part of their travels. Jesse drove with the band to Tijuana for a show, and later that night, a couple of days before Kurt's 23rd birthday, the two old friends celebrated by drinking a half gallon of booze and snorting crystal meth. Despite continued stomach problems, by early 1990, Kurt had started to drink again, and though his use of alcohol was still infrequent, when he drank he did so to excess.

When Kurt returned to Olympia, he had only three weeks before heading out on yet another long tour, which was to include a stop in Wisconsin to record the follow-up to *Bleach*. Kurt and Tracy tried to rekindle their romance, but the strain was obvious to all around them. "They didn't interact much in public anymore," recalled Slim Moon. Kurt complained to Slim that Tracy wanted to have sex more often than he did. To her, it was part of the bonding of their relationship; to him, it meant an emotional commitment he could no longer give.

That March, Damon Romero stopped by one night, and they rented videos, a frequent activity for a homebody like Kurt. Kurt had picked the latest film by Alex Cox, titled *Straight to Hell*—it starred Joe Strummer and Elvis Costello. During the film, Romero gestured at an actress and said, "Hey, there's that girl from that band down in Portland." Romero was pointing at Courtney Love. Despite the savage reviews the movie had garnered from critics, Kurt enjoyed the film. "It had just enough kitsch for Kurt to like it," Romero remembered.

On March 20 the band snuck into an Evergreen classroom with a few friends to film what Kurt imagined would be an official video release of his own. Kurt's plan was that the band would perform while vignettes he had taped off of television would be projected in the background. "He had hours and hours of this wacky shit," director Jon Snyder recalled. "He had recorded 'Star Search' with an old Donny and Marie routine, bits of 'Fantasy Island,' and all these insane late-night 'Lee Press-On Nail' commercials." For the first song, "School," the band played while Donny and Marie tap-danced behind them. For "Big Cheese" the background images came from a silent film about witches Kurt had sent away for, along with some of Kurt's Super-8 films from his childhood. "He had broken dolls, dolls on fire, or stuff like in *Toy Story* where the dolls are all put together wrong," remembered Alex Kostelnik, who operated one of the cameras. Kurt discussed extending the taping and going to Aberdeen to add more footage from his childhood haunts. Like many of his ideas, it was never pursued.

A week later, they packed up the van again and headed back on tour. Tracy was sleeping when Kurt left, but she had written a note in his journal: "Goodbye, Kurdt. Have a good tour and a great recording. Hang in there. I'll see you in seven weeks. Miss you. Love, Tracy." It was endearing, but even in her affection one could sense a defeat. Even Tracy was now spelling his name as his alter-ego "Kurdt." She had lost her Kurt.

In Chicago, on April 2, the band premiered "In Bloom." After the show, they drove all night to arrive in Madison, Wisconsin, home of Smart Studios and producer Butch Vig. They had only a week to cut their album, but Kurt reminded everyone of how many tracks they had managed during five hours for their first demo. Most of their new songs were still embryonic, a fact Kurt tried to downplay. Yet they had every confidence that Vig—who had worked with hundreds of alternative rock bands—could transform their ideas. Vig did impress the band; as a drummer himself, he managed to capture the drum sound Kurt thought was missing from their other efforts.

Working at a frantic pace, they cut eight songs, including a cover of the Velvet Underground's "Here She Comes Now," recorded for a compilation album. They did five new songs, and re-recorded two old ones in just a handful of days. Kurt was, of course, disappointed they hadn't done more. Five of the songs they cut at Smart would eventually end up on the *Nevermind* album.

The new songs found Kurt plumbing the emotional depths of his own life for material, and writing about the characters around him. "In Bloom" was a thinly disguised portrait of Dylan Carlson, while "Pay to Play" mocked the practice of clubs charging bands to play. "Breed" was the most complex song of the session: It had begun under the title "Imodium" about Tad's diarrhea medicine, yet there is little in the version recorded at Smart to connect it with Tad; Kurt instead used the title to suggest a running on of the mouth. More elaborate than Kurt's early screeds, it ended with the line "she said," implying the song was captured dialogue, and adding another layer of narrative to decipher.

Kurt had come up with an album title: *Sheep*. The name was his inside joke on the masses he was convinced would be buying his next effort. "Because you want to not; because everyone else is," he wrote in a fake advertisement for *Sheep*. The ad read: "May women rule the world. Abort Christ. Assassinate the greater and lesser of two evils. Steal *Sheep*. At a store near you. Nirvana. Flowers. Perfume. Candy. Puppies. Love. Generational Solidarity. And Killing Your Parents. *Sheep*." Around the same time, he wrote out yet another fake biography of the band, one that would prove strangely prophetic, even as it was filled with adolescent jokes. It described the band as "three-time Granny

Award Winners, No. 1 on *Billbored* Top 100 for 36 consecutive weaks in a row. Two times on the cover of *Bowling Stoned*, hailed as the most original, thought-provoking and important band of our decade by *Thyme* and *Newsweak*."

A few hours after finishing their final mixing at Smart, they were back on tour, and Vig sent the masters to Sub Pop, even though the band had grave doubts as to whether they wanted the label to release the session. Two weeks later, in Massachusetts, Kurt called Tracy and a long phone conversation ensued—one they both knew was coming but one she had hoped to postpone or avoid: He told her things weren't working out between them, and that maybe they should no longer live together. It wasn't an out-and-out breakup; honesty wasn't Kurt's way of dealing with conflict. "He thought maybe we should live apart for a while because we needed a bigger place," recalled Tracy. Kurt's suggestion was peppered with "maybes" and tempered with the assurance that "even if we aren't living together, we'll still be going out." But they both knew it was over.

Within the next month Kurt slept with a young woman while on the road. It was the only instance of infidelity his bandmates ever witnessed. As it was, the sex was crummy and Kurt hated himself for having been so weak. He told Tracy about it when he returned; there had been plenty of opportunities for him to have been unfaithful over the years, and the timing of this one infraction suggests he was trying to emotionally distance himself, to give her a reason to hate him, which would make breaking up easier.

As with all Nirvana tours, after about a month on the road, the band—and Kurt—seemed to fall apart. At a show at the Pyramid Club near the end of April, they had another bout of sound problems. Kurt's spirits were lifted when he saw one person among the crowd of New York hipsters who was bouncing away, even during their long tunings; he couldn't believe his eyes when he realized it was Iggy Pop. But his elation lasted only a moment before turning into embarrassment: Kurt was wearing an Iggy Pop T-shirt. Other people might have been able to laugh this coincidence off, but to Kurt, it corroborated the rock idolatry he desperately wanted to hide. He ended the show by demolishing Chad's drum kit.

Chad had to pay close attention to Kurt's moods to discern when he might torpedo himself into the drums. It was both a self-flagellation and an aggressive act—Kurt had grown dissatisfied with Chad's drumming. In Boston, Kurt threw a full pitcher of water at Chad and missed the drummer's ear by inches.

By the time the band arrived back in the Northwest in late May, it almost didn't have to be said that Chad was out of the band. Nothing, of course, *had* been said. But about two weeks after the tour ended, Channing looked out the window of his Bainbridge Island home, saw the van edging its way up the long driveway, and, like a doomed character in an Ernest Hemingway short story, knew the end was near. He was actually surprised Kurt had even come along—it was a testament to how much Kurt liked Chad, despite how he soon would claim Chad "didn't fit in with the band." Many times they had all three slept in the same bed, with Kurt and Chad flanking Krist so they could share the one blanket. Krist did the talking; Kurt hardly said a word and spent most of the conversation staring at the ground. But even for Chad, it came as a bit of a relief. "I'd spent the last three years with these guys in really close quarters," Chad recalled. "We'd gone through hell together. We'd been in shit together, in little vans, playing for no money. There wasn't any big daddy with the big bucks bailing us out." Kurt hugged Chad good-bye. Chad knew there had been a friendship, but he also realized it was now gone. "I knew that when we said good-bye, I wouldn't see them for a long time."

12 | LOVE YOU SO MUCH

OLYMPIA, WASHINGTON
MAY 1990–DECEMBER 1990

Love you so much it makes me sick.
—From "Aneurysm," 1990.

The same week Kurt fired Chad, he also broke up with Tracy. It too was a firing of sorts, and he handled all such partings poorly. Kurt's edict to Tracy was that they shouldn't live together: In saying this, however, he had neither the money nor the ability in his lethargy to move out. And since she'd spent all her money paying their bills, she couldn't afford to move. They continued to share the apartment until July, when she found a new place in Tacoma. During those three months, they lived in alternate universes, in the same physical space, but miles apart emotionally.

His was also a world of betrayal, because while Kurt had informed Tracy about his infidelity in Texas, he had neglected to tell her the greater betrayal, that he was in love with another woman. The new object of his desire was twenty-year-old Tobi Vail, an Olympia musician. Kurt had known Tobi for two years, but it wasn't until early 1990 that he had the occasion to spend an entire evening with her. He told Dylan the next day that he'd met the first woman who made him so nervous he threw up. He put that experience into the song "Aneurysm," with the lyric, "Love you so much it makes me sick." Though she was three years younger, she was more educated than he was, and he'd listen for hours to Tobi and her friend Kathleen Hanna prattle on about sexism and their plans to start a band called Bikini Kill. Tobi had her own fanzine, and in its pages she had coined the phrase "riot grrrl" to describe the 1990 model of punk feminism. She was a drummer primarily, but could play guitar; she had an extensive punk rock record collection; and she was, Kurt imagined, his female counterpart. "You just never met a girl that knew so much about music," observed Slim Moon.

Yet despite their shared musical interests, Kurt had fallen for someone who could never love him the way Tracy had, and who, more important, would never need him. Tobi took a more casual view toward relationships than Kurt; she wasn't looking for a husband, nor was she about to mother him. "Boyfriends were more like fashion accessories for Tobi," observed Alice Wheeler. What Kurt was searching for in a relationship was the kind of family intimacy he had lacked since early childhood; but Tobi rejected the traditional relationship he sought as sexist.

Even the word "girlfriend" meant something different in the Olympia punk rock community, where few would admit to being in a couple. It was as if to act like you were going steady was to adopt the traditional patterns of a society that everyone had come to Olympia to get away from. "No one dated in Olympia," observed Dylan. By these standards, Kurt's relationship with Tracy was downright old-fashioned; his union with Tobi would not conform to such stereotypical roles.

Their relationship had begun in secrecy—he was still living with Tracy when he first slept with her. But even after Tracy moved out, their coupling didn't seem to progress beyond coffeehouse discussions and occasional late-night sex. He thought of her all the time, obsessively, and he infrequently left the apartment, afraid she might call. She rarely phoned. Their relationship mostly entailed going to concerts, working on the fanzine, or talking about politics. He began to interpret her views of punk rock through his own lens, which inspired him to write lists of things he believed in, of things he hated, and of records he should listen to. One slogan he repeated again and again was, "Punk rock is freedom." He began to emphatically state this in every interview, though never explaining what he was seeking freedom from: It became a mantra to resolve every contradiction in his life. Tobi thought it sounded great.

Yet despite their intellectual joining, many in Olympia never knew they were a couple. "The whole time they were dating," said Slim, "it was confusing to me whether they were officially dating. Maybe it was inconvenient to her when he broke up with Tracy, in a way, because it put her on the spot. I don't think she really intended to be with him for a long period of time." Tobi, Kurt found out, was allergic to cats, so his animal farm was usually off-limits. It was also filthy by now: Once Tracy left, the whole apartment took on the look of a garbage dump, with unwashed dishes piled up, dirty clothes littering the floor, and Kurt's mutilated dolls watching over the scene with their crazed, busted eyes.

A year earlier, Kurt had complained that feminists were threatening to him. But once Kurt began sleeping with Tobi, riot grrrl feminism was easier for him to swallow, and he soon embraced it as if it were a newly discovered religion. The same man who read Ciccolina pornography now used words like "misogyny" and talked about the politics of oppression. In his notebook, Kurt wrote out two rules of rock that were quotations from Tobi: "1: learn *not* to play your instrument; 2: don't hurt girls when you dance (or any other time)." The "learn not to play" was one of the many teachings of Calvin Johnson, who argued that musicianship was always second to emotion.

Kurt had originally met Tobi while playing with the Go Team, an Olympia band centered around Calvin, but then most of the Olympia music scene was centered around Calvin. With his boyish short hair and propensity for wearing white T-shirts, Johnson resembled a wayward Marine recruit. But when it came to punk rock, he had the manner, if not the look, of a dictator, creating policy the way a newly crowned despot crafted a constitution. He was leader of Beat Happening, co-owner of K Records, DJ on KAOS, and promoter of local rock shows. He preached a low-fi, indie rock ethic, and he ruled Olympia the way Buzz Osborne had commanded Grays Harbor. "Calvin was very non-rock," remembered John Goodmanson. "The joke was that if you had a bass player in your band, you couldn't be on K." Calvin's followers even had their own name: "Calvinists." Tobi was not only a Calvinist, she had once been Johnson's girlfriend.

Every step of Kurt's relationship with Tobi presented challenges to his self-esteem. It was hard enough for Kurt to fit into the cosmopolitan

Seattle scene, but even in tiny Olympia he felt as if he were a contestant on a punk rock version of "Jeopardy!" and that one wrong answer would send him packing back to Aberdeen. For a kid who grew up wearing Sammy Hagar T-shirts, he found he had to constantly use his "Kurdt" self as a disguise to protect his real past. He admitted as much in a rare moment of self-disclosure in his journal: "Everything I do is an overly conscious and neurotic attempt at trying to prove to others that I am at least more intelligent and cool than they think." When asked to name his influences during press interviews in 1990, he listed an entirely different roster of music than he had one year earlier: He'd grown to understand that in the world of punk rock elitism, the more obscure and unpopular a band was, the hipper it was to drop their name. Friends began to notice the divided self more: When Kurt was around Tobi, he might criticize a band that earlier the same day he'd advocated for.

That summer both Krist and Kurt were fastidiously dubbing cassettes of the Smart Studios demos, but they weren't wasting postage sending them to Touch and Go; they sent them to Columbia Records and Warner Brothers. After all the problems with Sub Pop, Kurt and Krist had committed to signing with a major label, if only to get decent distribution. To Tobi, this was anathema. She announced her band would never be on a major label. Influenced by her position, Kurt tempered his major label aspirations by telling interviewers Nirvana would sign with a major, cash the advance check, break up, and then put a record out on K. It was a magnificent fantasy, and like the many grand ideas that floated through his head, he had no intention of acting in so foolish a way as to jeopardize his chance at fame and fortune.

Since their brief employ of Tam Ohrmund, Nirvana had managed themselves, using Michele Vlasimsky as booker, with Krist handling most of the financial arrangements. "I was the only member of Nirvana who graduated from high school," Krist explained. In May 1990, Sub Pop sent the band a new proposed contract—it was 30 pages long and gave numerous unequivocal rights to the label. Kurt knew he didn't want to sign this document. He and Krist turned to Susan Silver, the respected manager of Soundgarden. She took one look at the contract and told them they needed a lawyer.

Silver was surprised at how adamant they were about not wanting to be on Sub Pop anymore. They complained *Bleach* had gotten no promotion, and that the label had never provided them with an accounting for how many copies had sold. Kurt declared he wanted a big-money deal on a major label with the muscle of a big corporation behind him, even though the band was still without a drummer. Such a statement was grounds for public hanging in the court of Calvin, but it was even in contrast to most Seattle bands. It also contradicted what Kurt had said in the press as recently as three weeks before. On April 27, when radio station WOZQ asked whether the band would consider signing with a major, he replied: "We don't have any interest in a major label. It would be nice to have better distribution, but anything else that goes on major labels is just a bunch of shit."

But in the time since that interview, his split with Tracy had deprived him of his benefactor. He now declared he wanted a "million-dollar deal," but perhaps in a nod to the influence of Tobi, he proclaimed that even when Nirvana got their huge deal, they would "still tour in a van." Kurt had heard of Peter Paterno, one of the industry's heaviest lawyers, and asked if Susan could put in a word for them. "I'm going to Los Angeles tomorrow," she said. "If you come sometime while I'm there, I'll take you to meet him." Krist replied, "We'll start driving tonight and see you in a couple of days."

Two days later, they met Silver in Los Angeles. Silver introduced them to Don Muller, a well-known agent, and when Paterno was unable to make time in his schedule, she connected them with attorney Alan Mintz. He found them "naïve but ambitious." Mintz's specialty was new bands, but he discovered that even as new artists, "they were definitely among the scruffiest that ever came through the door." Sub Pop was also talking to lawyers, attempting to use Nirvana's growing reputation to get a major label to invest in them. Mintz mentioned this to the band, suggesting they might get the distribution they wanted on Sub Pop. Kurt leaned forward and resolutely replied, "Get me off this label!" Kurt declared he wanted to sell lots of records. Impressed by their tape, Mintz began working to find them a deal that day.

It wasn't a difficult job. Even by mid-1990, Nirvana's standing as a dynamic live act, and the budding success of *Bleach* on college radio, had attracted the interest of "artist and repertoire" agents, employees hired by labels to sign bands. The first A&R man interested was Bret Hartman of MCA, who in early 1990 had been having discussions about their contract with Poneman and Pavitt. Hartman realized his interest wasn't being passed on to the band, so he acquired Kurt's home number and started leaving messages on Kurt's answering machine.

When they returned to Seattle from L.A., Krist and Kurt headed back into the studio, on July 11, to record the single "Sliver," to release in advance of another U.K. tour. They had hired Dan Peters, Mudhoney's drummer, for this gig, though they were still auditioning drummers. This would be their ultimate quick-and-dirty studio session, recorded in the middle of a Tad album while that band was on a dinner break. The title was yet another Cobain composition with no relation to the lyrics, but this time the name was the only thing obtuse about the song: It was straightforward and a creative breakthrough. For subject matter, Kurt had mined what he knew best—his family. Like Richard Pryor, who struggled in his comedy career until he started telling jokes about growing up in a whorehouse, Kurt had finally discovered his unique voice, which evolved when he wrote about his family. He had found his gift as a writer, almost by accident.

"Sliver" tells the story of a boy dropped off with his grandparents who doesn't want his parents to leave. He pleads for his grandmother to take him home, but to no avail. He eats mashed potatoes for dinner. He has problems digesting his meat. He rides his bike, only to stub his toe. He tries watching television, but falls asleep. "Grandma take me home / I wanna be alone," was the unadorned chorus. The song ends as the boy wakes up in his mother's arms. "It's probably the most straightforward song we've ever recorded," Kurt explained to *Melody Maker*. It also was one of the first Nirvana songs to use contrasting dynamics, which would become a signature for the band: The verses were quiet and slow, but the chorus came in as a thunderous wall of sound. After its release, Kurt was quizzed about its meaning, and he had the audacity to claim it wasn't autobiographical. But no one, certainly not anyone who knew him, believed this: "It was about being a little boy and wanting to be at home with Mom, not wanting to be baby-sat by his grandparents," explained his sister Kim.

In August Nirvana went on the road for a short West Coast tour, opening for Sonic Youth, with Dale Crover as their temporary drummer. The tour was a chance for Kurt to meet Thurston Moore and Kim Gordon of Sonic Youth, whom he considered just short of royalty. His self-esteem rose when he found they treated him as a peer. The two bands immediately struck up a friendship, and best of all, Moore and Gordon offered business advice, suggesting Nirvana consider their management company, Gold Mountain.

They certainly needed help. Despite the honor the tour afforded, they were paid poorly, following Sonic Youth's huge bus in their absurd little Dodge van, looking more like starstruck fans than stars themselves. At the Los Angeles show, MCA's Bret Hartman and his boss Paul Atkinson went backstage to visit the band after their set, and found Kurt and Krist packing up their gear; they were too poor to afford roadies. Atkinson invited the band to tour MCA, but Krist said they had to drive back for his job. The conversation came to a halt when Krist explained he had to go sell T-shirts—they needed gas money to get out of town.

When the tour arrived in the Northwest, interest in the hometown boys was greater than for Sonic Youth. In Portland and Seattle, they were burgeoning stars; after each show a growing number of fans were speaking their praises. Yet Kurt's personality didn't seem to change with the attention, observed Sally Barry, who was in an opening band on this tour. "He was the first person I ever saw fling himself into the crowd with his guitar and not give a rat's ass," she recalled. "With other people, you could see a conscious thought to it. But with Kurt, it was instant and honest." Almost every show ended with Kurt leaping into the audience, or the audience leaping into him. This tour, Kurt spared his drummer, since Crover had announced he would pound Kurt within an inch of his life if his kit was damaged.

Crover had to return to the Melvins, so Nirvana hired Dan Peters as their new drummer, and began planning a U.K. tour. But even as Peters pounded the drums for the band at a September 22 concert, in the audience was another candidate Kurt and Krist had flown in to audition. The gig, for which Peters had played well, was his one and only show with Nirvana.

The newly arrived drummer was 21-year-old Dave Grohl. Originally from Virginia, Grohl had played with the bands Scream and Dain Bramage. The transposed letters of the latter name was probably enough to endear him to Kurt, since it showed, if nothing else, that Grohl shared his sense of humor. It was Buzz who had hooked Grohl up with Nirvana, stepping back into his mentor role, and it may have been the greatest gift he ever bestowed. The instant Kurt and Krist practiced with Grohl, they knew they had their final drummer.

Just twenty days later, Dave Grohl was playing his first show with Nirvana, barely familiar with the names of the songs, much less the drum parts. But with Grohl it hardly mattered: As Krist and Kurt had discovered, he was an animal behind the kit. Kurt had struggled with drummers in the past, his perfectionism stemming from his own tenure playing drums. During most soundchecks, Kurt regularly moved to the drum kit and pounded out a few songs for kicks. But Grohl was the kind of drummer who made Kurt glad he'd picked up the guitar.

Grohl's first show was in Olympia's North Shore Surf Club. The night marked some of the worst technical snafus of Nirvana's entire history; an electrical malfunction caused the power to blow repeatedly, and the band had to turn off half their amps to avoid further blackouts. The only illumination available came from audience members holding flashlights, creating an eerie effect like something out of a cheap independent film. Playing with a tiny kit, Grohl proved too strong: He hit the drums so hard he destroyed the snare.

A week later, the band toured England to promote the "Sliver" single, which, in typical fashion, didn't come out until the tour was over. Still, they played to rabid audiences, their fame in England being far greater than in the U.S. at the time. While in London, Kurt went to see the Pixies, one of his favorite groups. The next day he called up Pixies manager Ken Goes and asked if he would manage Nirvana. Goes wasn't familiar with Kurt but agreed to meet.

When they met in a hotel lobby, Goes found Kurt was more interested in talking about the Pixies than in promoting his own group. "He wasn't your average fan, like the type we always see outside of stage doors," Goes recalled. "In fact, he wasn't so much a fan; he was a *student* of the band. He obviously had a massive amount of respect for what they were doing. He went on and on about it." During their conversation, a commotion ensued when Charles Thompson, the lead singer of the Pixies, walked into the hotel. Goes offered to introduce Kurt to his idol, but Kurt froze at the suggestion. "I don't think so," Kurt said, backing away slightly. "I, uh, I can't." And with that, Kurt beat a hasty retreat, acting as if he wasn't worthy to be even in the presence of such talent.

When Nirvana returned from England, Dave Grohl decided to move to the Pear Street apartment—he had been staying with Krist and Shelli. That same week, MCA sent tickets for Kurt and Krist to fly to Los Angeles to tour their offices. The label wasn't the band's first choice—it had been so long since MCA had a hit, people joked their name stood for Music Cemetery of America—but they couldn't turn down a free ticket. The label put them up at the Sheraton Universal Hotel, and after they arrived Bret Hartman went to inquire if the accommodations were satisfactory. He found the mini-fridge ajar, and Kurt and Krist sitting on the floor surrounded by tiny bottles of liquor. "Who put this stuff in our room?" Kurt asked. Despite the fact that the band had toured the U.S. five times and Europe twice, Kurt had never seen an honor bar. When Hartman explained he could have anything in the fridge and MCA would pay, Kurt looked at him incredulously. "I realized," Hartman recalled, "that perhaps these guys weren't as experienced as I thought they were."

They didn't know honor bars, but they knew they were being slighted the next day when they toured MCA. Hartman and Atkinson had circulated copies of *Bleach*, along with a memo urging the staff to be warm and gracious. Yet when they escorted the band through the building, it appeared every bigwig was at lunch. Angee Jenkins, who ran the publicity department, spoke with them briefly and encouraged them, as did the guys in the mailroom, who were among the handful of MCA employees who had listened to *Bleach*. The topper came when the group was wheeled into the office of Richard Palmese, who briefly shook hands with them before muttering, "It's really great to meet you guys. I really like your music but I've got a lunch appointment in five minutes. I'm going to have to excuse myself." Kurt wasn't even sure who he was meeting, so he turned to Atkinson and asked, "Who is that guy?" "That's the president of MCA," Atkinson replied with a grimace. And with that, MCA was out of the running. While in Los Angeles, Kurt and Krist hooked up with Sonic Youth, who again pushed Gold Mountain Management and told them they should sign with their label, DGC, part of Geffen Records, one of the few labels who so far hadn't expressed interest.

By the time Kurt returned to the Northwest, Grohl had moved in, and his presence temporarily lifted Kurt's spirits. Living alone was never good for Kurt's mental health, and his isolation reached a peak during the summer of 1990. He bore all the signs of a child who had gone through a severe trauma: He stopped talking except when spoken to, and he spent hours every day doing nothing but stroking his wisp of a beard, staring into space. He and Tobi weren't seeing each other as much, and when they did get together he seemed unable to move the relationship to the next level. He bitterly observed in his journal, "The only difference between 'friends who fuck every once in a while' and 'boyfriend/girlfriend' is the official titles given."

When Grohl moved in, things improved provisionally; he was as easygoing as Kurt was withdrawn. "The house," remembered Nikki McClure, "became boy-land. Now Kurt had someone to hang out with all the time. It kind of had this husband-and-wife feel to it." Since Kurt was virtually incapable of picking up anything, Grohl did things like wash Kurt's clothes for him. Few others could have handled the state of the apartment, but Grohl had spent the last several years on the road. "Dave was raised in a van by wolves," explained Jennifer Finch. He taught Kurt how to create homemade tattoos using a needle and some India ink. However, when Kurt decided to imprint his arm with the K Records logo—a "K" inside a shield—he went to an Olympia tattoo parlor one day with another friend.

The tattoo was yet another attempt to impress Tobi—and Calvin. To anyone who wasn't familiar with K Records, Kurt explained the tattoo by pronouncing his love of the Vaselines. Curiously, the Vaselines weren't on K, though they were distributed by the label. "Who knows what he was thinking with that tattoo," said Dylan Carlson. "I think he liked the records K distributed better than the records they put out. He should have had the tattoo read, 'K Distribution.' "

A better idea would have been to etch "the Vaselines" on his arm. Ever since Kurt added the band's "Molly's Lips" to Nirvana's repertoire, he'd been singing this group's praises. They were the perfect band for Kurt. They were childish, amateurish, and unknown outside of the U.K. and a small U.S. cult. Soon after hearing the Vaselines, Kurt began one of his many multi-draft letter-writing campaigns in his journal, attempting to befriend Eugene Kelly of the band. These letters were always chatty (in one Kurt mentioned his "ridiculous sleeping schedule where I retire in the wee hours of the morning and successfully avoid any hint of daylight") and inevitably ended with some laudatory comments about how brilliant the Vaselines were: "Without trying to be too embarrassingly sappy, I have to say the songs you and Frances have written are some of the most beautiful songs ever."

Grohl shared Kurt's musical taste, but not his obsession with courting favor with legends. He was far more interested in girls, and they were interested in him. He began dating Kathleen Hanna of Bikini Kill— Dave and Kurt would then do the Olympia version of double dating with Kathleen and Tobi; they'd drink beer and make up lists of the most important punk rock records. Most of Dave and Kurt's amusements were adolescent, but with Tobi and Kathleen around, everyone was more sociable. The situation made Kurt more attractive to Tobi, since the prospect of hanging out as a gang was less serious than individual dating. "Tobi and Kathleen would literally say, 'Let's go out with Nirvana,' " neighbor Ian Dickson recalled. During one rambunctious night of partying at Kurt's house, Hanna spray-painted "Kurt smells like teen spirit" on the bedroom wall. She was referring to a deodorant for teenage girls, so her graffiti was not without implication: Tobi used Teen Spirit, and by writing this on the wall, Kathleen was taunting Kurt about sleeping with her, implying that he was marked by her scent.

Yet despite an occasional night of revelry, Kurt was lonely and disenchanted—he spent a few nights secretly watching Tobi's window from the street like a shy Cyrano. For the first time in years, he was feeling less hopeful about his career, even though labels had continued calling. Strangely, after years of anticipation, as he approached actually signing a contract, he was filled with self-doubt. He missed the togetherness he'd had with Tracy, and their friendship. A few weeks after Tracy moved out, Kurt had finally confessed that he'd been sleeping with Tobi all along, and Tracy was furious. "If you'd lie about that, you'd lie about anything," she yelled, and a part of him believed her.

He did, very briefly, consider buying a house in Olympia. He couldn't actually complete any sort of purchase until he got an advance check, but he was confident enough he would elicit a large deal that he paid a fee to procure a list of available properties. He drove around with his friend Mikey Nelson of Fitz of Depression, looking at dilapidated commercial buildings, planning to build a recording studio in the front and live in the back. "He seemed only interested in the houses that looked like businesses," Nelson said. "He didn't want to live in a normal house."

But that idea, and all the other fantasies he had for the future, went out the window during the first week of November, when Tobi broke up with him. He was devastated; when she told him the news, he was barely able to stand up. He'd never been dumped, and he took it badly. He and Tobi had gone out for less than six months. It had been casual dating, casual sex, and a casual romance, but through it all he hoped deeper intimacy was just around the corner. He fell back on his old pattern of internalizing his abandonment, and back into self-hatred. She didn't leave him because she was young; she left him, he imagined, because he didn't deserve her. He was so nauseated that, helping Slim move a week later, he had to stop the car to throw up.

In the wake of the breakup, Kurt became more sullen than ever. He filled an entire notebook with stream-of-consciousness ranting, much of it violent and distressed. He used writing, music, and artwork to express his despair, and with his pain, he wrote songs. Some of them were crazy and angry songs, but they represented yet another level of his craft, since the anger was no longer clichéd and now had an authenticity his early work lacked. These new songs were filled with rage, remorse, pleading, and utter desperation. In the four months following their breakup, Kurt would write a half dozen of his most memorable songs, all of them about Tobi Vail.

The first was "Aneurysm," which he wrote hoping to win her back. But he soon gave up on that, and instead used his songs, as countless songwriters had before, to express his deep level of hurt. One song was called "Formula," but was eventually retitled "Drain You." "One baby to another said, 'I'm lucky to have met you,' " went the lyrics, quoting words Tobi had told him. "It is now my duty to completely drain you," was the chorus; it was both an acknowledgment of the power she had over him and an indictment.

There were other songs inspired by Tobi, sometimes not as clearly connected, but all haunted by her ghost. " 'Lounge Act' is about Tobi," Krist observed. One line in the song references Kurt's tattoo: "I'll arrest myself, I'll wear a shield." Another sums up how their relationship was more about learning than love: "We've made a pact to learn from who-ever we want without new rules." In an earlier, unrecorded lyric of "Lounge Act," Kurt more directly addressed his former paramour: "I hate you because you are so much like me." "Lithium" was written before Tobi, but the lyrics changed over time and eventually reflected her. Kurt later told Chris Morris of *Musician* that the song included "some of my personal experiences, like breaking up with girlfriends and having bad relationships, feeling that death void that the person in the song is feeling—very lonely, sick."

Though Kurt never specifically addressed it, his most famous song, "Smells Like Teen Spirit," could not have been about anyone else, with the lyrics "She's over-bored and self-assured." "Teen Spirit" was a song influenced by many things—his anger at his parents, his boredom, his eternal cynicism—yet several individual lines resonate with Tobi's pres-ence. He wrote the song soon after their split, and the first draft included a line edited from the final version: "Who will be the king and queen of the outcast teens?" The answer, at one point in his imagination, had been Kurt Cobain and Tobi Vail.

His songs were the most fruitful aspect of the breakup; his writings and artwork showed a more enraged and pathological outcome. One drawing shows an alien with his skin being slowly ripped off; in another a woman with a Ku Klux Klan hat lifts up her skirt and flashes her vagina; another depicts a man stabbing a woman with his penis; and yet one more shows a man and a woman having sex above the caption, "Rape, Rape." There were dozens of such depictions, and pages and pages of stories with tragic endings and disturbing imagery. Not atypical is the following screed:

> When I grow up I want to be a faggot, nigger, cunt, whore, jew, spic, kraut, wop, sissie, whitey hippie, greedy, money-making, healthy, sweaty, hairy, masculine, quirky new waver, right wing, left wing, chicken wing, chicken shit, ass kickin, dumb fuck, nuclear physicist, Alcoholics Anonymous Counselor, psychiatrist, journalist, stink fist, romance novelist, gay, black, cripple, junkie, HIV positive, hermaphrodite, flipper baby, overweight, anorexic, king, queen, pawnbroker, stock broker, pot smoker, (all is swell, less is more, God is gay, harpoon a catch) journalist, rock journalist, stuffy, cranky, middle-aged, bitter, little, scrawny, opinionated, old, booking agent and editor of a fanzine that segregates the small percent into even a smaller percent. Keep em divided, Ghettoize, united we stand, do not respect others sensitivities. Kill yourself kill yourself kill kill kill kill kill kill kill rape rape rape rape rape rape is good, rape is good, rape kill rape greed greed good greed good rape yes kill.

Most of the rage was turned inward, though. If there was one central theme to his writing that fall, it was self-hatred. He imagined himself as "bad," "faulty," "diseased." One page told a crazy tale—completely fantastical—of how he enjoyed kicking elderly women's legs because "these ankles have a plastic bottle full of urine strapped on them and a tube running up into the old worn-out muscled vagina; the yellow stain goes flying everywhere." Next, he sought out "50-year-old fags who have the same muscle malfunction but in a different cavity. . . . I kick their rubber underwear and the brown stuff soaks into their beige slacks." But this disturbing story eventually turned the violence toward the writer: "Then people with no particular fetishes kick me all over the body and head and watch the red shit splat and run and soak my blue jeans and white shirt." The story ended with him writing repeatedly, "I am bad," and then, twenty times in big characters, the size of the letters he used to spray-paint on the walls of Aberdeen, "ME, ME, ME," until he finally ran out of space, having filled every inch of the page. He wrote this with so much pressure the pen went through the paper. He made no effort to hide these stories, and instead, his journals would lie open around the apartment. Jennifer Finch began dating Grohl, and she read some of the writings left on the kitchen table and noticed his torment. "I was worried about Kurt," she remembered. "He was just out of control."

The hatred he had for others was mild compared to the violence he described against himself. Suicide came up as a topic repeatedly. One diatribe detailed how he might turn himself into "Helen Keller, by puncturing my ears with a knife, then cutting my voice box out." He repeatedly fantasized about heaven and hell, both embracing the idea of spirituality as an escape after death, but just as often wholeheartedly rejecting it. "If you want to know what the afterlife feels like," he speculated, "then put on a parachute, go up in a plane, shoot a good amount of heroine into your veins, and immediately follow that with a hit of nitrous oxide, then jump or set yourself on fire."

By the second week of November 1990, a new character had begun to spring forth in Kurt's journal writing, and this figure would soon make its way into almost every image, song, or story. He intentionally misspelled its name, and in doing so he was granting it a life of its own. Oddly, he gave it a female persona, but since it became his great love that fall—and even made him throw up, just like Tobi—there was a fairness in this gender choice. He called it "heroine."

13 THE RICHARD NIXON LIBRARY

OLYMPIA, WASHINGTON
NOVEMBER 1990–MAY 1991

It might be time for the Betty Ford Clinic or the Richard Nixon Library to save me from abusing my anemic rodent-like body any longer.
—From a letter to Tobi Vail, May 1991.

"Heroine," Kurt's own bastardization of the word heroin, had first appeared back in his rude cartoons in eighth grade. Having grown up fascinated by rock 'n' roll, he was well aware that many of the musicians he idolized had succumbed to drug abuse. And though he had addictively smoked pot, frequently drank too much, and was known to huff inhalant from the bottoms of shaving cream cans, he pledged that he would never suffer a similar fate. In 1987, during one of Kurt's sober purging periods, he chastised Jesse Reed when his friend suggested they try heroin. "Kurt wouldn't hang out with me after that," Jesse remembered. "I was trying to find heroin, a drug I'd never tried, and he'd never tried, and he would lecture me: 'Why do you want to kill yourself? Why do you want to die so badly?' " In a personal drug history constructed later in life, Kurt wrote that he first had used heroin in Aberdeen in the late eighties; his friends contest this, since he had a fear of needles at the time and there was no heroin to be found in his circle. He did occasionally take Percodan in Aberdeen, a prescription narcotic; he may have romanticized and exaggerated this opiate when recalling it later.

By the fall of 1990, brokenhearted over Tobi, the same questions Kurt asked of Jesse earlier could have been put to him. In early November he overcame his fear of needles and first injected heroin with a friend in Olympia. He found that the drug's euphoric effects helped him temporarily escape his heartache and his stomach pain.

The next day, Kurt phoned Krist. "Hey, Krist I did heroin," Kurt told his friend. "Wow! What was that like?" Krist asked. Kurt said, "Oh, it was all right." Krist then told him, "You shouldn't do it. Look at Andy Wood." Wood was the lead singer of Mother Love Bone, an up-and-coming Seattle band, who died of a heroin overdose in March 1990. Novoselic cited other Olympia friends who had died of heroin addiction. Kurt's reply: "Yeah, I know." Novoselic, playing the role of older brother, warned Kurt that heroin wasn't like the other drugs he'd done: "I remember literally telling him that he was playing with dynamite."

But the warning fell on deaf ears. Though Kurt promised Krist he wouldn't try the drug again, he broke this promise. To avoid Krist's or Grohl's finding out, Kurt used the drug at friends' houses. He found a dealer named José, who was selling to many of the Greeners in Olympia. Coincidentally, Dylan Carlson had experimented with heroin for the first time that fall, though not with Kurt. But soon their bonding also extended to heroin—usually done only once a week, owing to several factors including their poverty and their desire to not become addicts. But they would go on occasional binges, like the time they rented a cheap hotel room in Seattle to nod off in private without alarming their friends or roommates.

But Kurt's friends *were* alarmed by his drug use. Tracy had finally forgiven Kurt, and they were occasionally hanging out. When Shelli told her Kurt was doing heroin, she couldn't believe her ears. That week, Kurt phoned Tracy late at night, obviously high, and she challenged him directly: "He told me he'd done it a few times. He said he really liked it, and that it made him more sociable. But he said he wasn't going to do it all the time. I tried to walk the fine line by telling him he shouldn't do it, without making him feel bad for having done it." A week later, they spent an evening together attending several parties. In between events, Kurt insisted they stop by his place so he could use the toilet. When he didn't return, Tracy went looking and found him on the floor, with a bottle of bleach sitting next to him and a needle in his arm. She was furious: Kurt had turned into something Tracy couldn't have imagined in her worst nightmare. The joke of Nirvana's first album title no longer seemed funny to anyone. But heroin was only a small part of 1990 for Kurt, and for the most part, he kept his promise to use it only occasionally. He was distracted from all else by the fact that his career was taking off like never before. He signed a contract in the fall with Virgin Publishing, which brought him his first big check. Kaz Utsunomiya, president of Virgin, flew to the Northwest to ink the deal. Though Kaz was a longtime industry veteran and had worked with everyone from the Clash to Queen, he was shocked to see the squalor of Kurt's apartment. They talked about Kurt's influences, particularly the Clash; Kurt said *Sandinista!* was one of the first records he owned that was remotely punk.

Kurt's initial share of the publishing deal came in the form of a check for $3,000. He paid his rent, and then drove to South Sound Mall with Mikey Nelson and Joe Preston. Kurt spent almost $1,000 in Toys "R" Us on a Nintendo system, two Pixelvision video cameras, two automatic BB guns that looked like M16 rifles, and several Evel Knievel plastic models. He also bought fake dog feces, fake vomit, and rubber severed hands. "He threw it all into a basket," remembered Preston. "It was just a bunch of junk he could destroy." It was as if an eight-year-old boy had been set loose in the store and told he could have anything he wanted. Kurt used the BB gun to immediately shoot out the windows on the Washington State Lottery building across the street. He also bought, for $20, a used child's Swinger bicycle, a style that at the time was remarkably unhip: It was so tiny that pedaling it required him to scrunch over with his knees to his shoulders. Kurt gleefully rode the bike until it was dark.

He was still riding the bike a few days later in the midst of what at the time was the most important business meeting he'd ever had. On Thurston Moore's recommendation, the band had contacted Gold Mountain Management. The firm was run by Danny Goldberg and John Silva. Silva, as the younger manager, was assigned the job of negotiating with Nirvana. It was an easy task—because of his connection with Sonic Youth, he already had Kurt's stamp of approval. Silva and his girlfriend Lisa Fancher came to Seattle to meet the band face-to-face and take them to dinner. Kurt loved being taken to dinner by music industry honchos because it was the only way he could guarantee eating a decent meal. But this night, Silva and the rest of the band sat around for hours while Kurt rode his Swinger bike in a circle in the Lottery parking lot. "We all decided he was going to break a limb," recalled Fancher. Though the long delay seemed like just another childish pastime, a more cynical observer might have suggested it was Kurt's first move in what would become a battle of wills with his soon-to-be manager.

Kurt put his bicycle down to go to dinner, but afterwards announced Beat Happening was playing across town. It was a test of Silva's interest, and like any good businessman, Silva acted enthused and went to the show with Kurt. Silva protested to Fancher later that he detested Calvin's band (she also remembered he initially hated Sonic Youth, complaining about their "major egos"). Yet he'd passed Kurt's acid test, and within the week, Nirvana had signed with Gold Mountain.

On November 25, Nirvana played a show at Seattle's Off Ramp that attracted more A&R representatives than any concert in Northwest history. Representatives from Columbia, Capitol, Slash, RCA, and several other labels were bumping into each other. "The A&R guys were in full-court press," observed Sony's Damon Stewart. The sheer number of A&R reps altered the way the band was perceived in Seattle. "By that time," explained Susan Silver, "there was a competitive feeding frenzy going on around them."

The show itself was remarkable—Kurt later told a friend it was his favorite Nirvana performance. During an eighteen-song set, the band played twelve unreleased tunes. They opened with the powerful "Aneurysm," the first time it was played in public, and the crowd slam-danced and body-surfed until they broke the light bulbs on the ceiling. "I thought the show was amazing," recalled Kim Thayil of Soundgarden. "They did a cover of the Velvet Underground's 'Here She Comes Now' that I thought it was brilliant. And then, when I heard 'Lithium,' it stuck in my mind. Ben, our bass player, came up to me and said, 'That's the hit. That's a Top 40 hit right there.' "

The A&R men were just as impressed. As the set ended—after a break for a fire alarm—Jeff Fenster of Charisma Records managed to convince the band his label was the best choice. Two days later, Nirvana's lawyer, Alan Mintz, called and said the band was going to sign with Charisma. The deal was for $200,000, a healthy but not outrageous advance. But before Fenster could have a contract prepared, the band decided, at the last minute, to sign instead with DGC, an imprint of Geffen Records. Though DGC's A&R rep Gary Gersh had not been one of the early bidders, the endorsement of Sonic Youth ultimately proved to be the deciding factor. Geffen also had a strong promotion department, headed by Mark Kates, and Gold Mountain knew promotion was the key to breaking the band. The Geffen deal called for Nirvana to be paid $287,000, at the time one of the largest advances for a Northwest band. Mintz extricated the band from the vestiges of their Sub Pop contract: As part of the Geffen agreement, Sub Pop would be paid $75,000 and get 2 percent of sales from the next two albums.

Though Kurt had read music industry books, even he wasn't prepared for how long the deal took to be finalized—the contract wasn't signed until April—and how little money it initially meant for him. By the time fees for lawyers, managers, taxes, and debt were deducted, Gold Mountain put him on a retainer of $1,000 per month. He immediately got behind on his bills, and complained he could only afford corn dogs—the floor of the apartment was now littered with their sticks.

Grohl had gone back east for most of December, and minus his roommate, Kurt sought to relieve his boredom by any means necessary. He hung out a lot with Dylan, and soon broke another barrier he'd sworn never to cross. Dylan was a gun nut, and Kurt consistently preached that guns were barbaric. A few times Kurt agreed to go into the woods with Dylan, but he wouldn't touch the guns, and on one occasion even refused to leave the car. But eventually Kurt began to let Dylan show him how to aim and fire. It was harmless stuff: putting holes in cans with shotguns, or shooting up art projects Kurt had decided to sacrifice.

Kurt also began to hang out a lot with Mikey Nelson to shop at thrift stores. "There was always some record he was hoping to track down," said Nelson. "One of his favorites had a bunch of truckers talking over the CB radio. He had the Charles Manson record *Lie*. And he was a huge fan of 'H. R. Pufnstuf.' " Even in late 1990, Kurt was still pushing the merits of the Knack's *Get the Knack*. "He told me all the great songs on that record were the ones people hadn't heard of."

John Purkey stopped by the apartment that month and helped Kurt shop for Christmas presents. Kurt's biggest purchase that year was a large custom aquarium for his turtles. They smoked marijuana before shopping, but Purkey was surprised when Kurt asked, "Do you know where I can get some heroin?" Purkey replied, "You're not shooting up are you?" "Oh, no," Kurt lied. "I'll just smoke anything." In many ways, his meager budget helped curb his addictive desires: He simply couldn't afford to become a drug addict.

On December 11 Kurt again sought medical help for his stomach condition, seeing a doctor in Tacoma. This time the diagnosis was irritable bowel syndrome, and Kurt was prescribed Lidox, a form of clidinium. The drug didn't seem to help his pain, and he discontinued it two weeks later when he got bronchitis.

The year ended with a New Year's Eve show in Portland at the Satyricon. Slim traveled down with the band and saw what he remembered as a knockout show, despite the fact that Kurt was drunk on whiskey and Coke, against his doctor's orders. It was now noticeable that Kurt was attracting groupies. Slim watched one young woman locking eyes on him for the whole show: "Her demeanor said, 'I'm the girl in the audience who wants to fuck you tonight.' " Kurt however, didn't notice and, like most nights, went home alone.

They began 1991 with the three-hour late-night drive from Portland since they had a studio session scheduled the next day. They finished two songs, "Aneurysm" and a re-recording of "Even in His Youth." They also worked up several songs Kurt had just written, including an early "All Apologies." "They had a bunch of ideas they wanted to throw down," remembered Craig Montgomery, who produced the tracks. "But their gear was in horrible shape, and they were all pretty fried."

Kurt's friend Jesse Reed returned to the Northwest for the holiday, and the day after the recording session they went to Aberdeen to visit Jesse's parents. On the drive, Kurt found himself talking about his future with his old friend, and as the car entered Grays Harbor County, he admitted his love for this landscape and the people, contradicting all he

said in interviews. As they passed some of the farms outside of Satsop—
an idyllic valley, despite an abandoned nuclear plant—Kurt told Jesse
his dream was to use his label advance to buy a farm. He saw a large
ranch house and pointed to it: "What do you think of that house over
there? If I buy that, then we can play as loud as we want, have big
parties, have people over, and no one will care." The house wasn't for
sale, and Kurt had no money yet, but he swore to Jesse that if he ever
did hit the big time, he'd come back to the harbor and buy a ranch,
"just like Neil Young has in California."

Early in 1991 Kurt made a telephone call he'd been putting off for
years: He phoned his father. Since moving to Olympia, most of his
contact with Don had been through his grandparents.

The conversation—as was typical of communication between two
stoic Cobain men—was short. Kurt mostly talked about the band, telling Don he'd signed a major label deal; Don wasn't sure what that
meant, but when he asked Kurt if he had enough money, his son said
yes. Kurt inquired of Don's other children, and they briefly chatted
about Don's latest job, working as an investigator with the Washington
State Patrol. Kurt told his father he'd been performing a lot; Don said
he'd enjoy going to see him some time. The conversation lasted only a
few minutes and was remarkable more for what the two men didn't say
than what they did. Don wasn't able to talk about the hurt he felt that
his firstborn had drifted away, and Kurt wasn't able to talk about any
of the hurts he felt: not the divorce, the remarriage, or their many other
struggles.

Kurt had stayed in better touch with his mother; her interest in his
career, and her acceptance of him as a musician, seemed to increase as
his fame did. Kurt and Wendy were drawn closer yet that year when
another family tragedy struck on January 2, 1991—Wendy's brother
Patrick died of AIDS in California, at 46. Patrick's homosexuality had
always been a deep secret within the Fradenburg family; he was so good-
looking and popular with girls, his parents seemed unable to believe it
when he announced he was gay. Even prior to his diagnosis, he had
suffered from clinical depression, but when he developed full-blown
AIDS, it sent him into an emotional tailspin. His anger at his parents
was so great he planned to write a treatise on his lifelong sexual history—

which included that he'd been sexually abused by his Uncle Delbert—and send it to the *Aberdeen Daily World* to embarrass his family. As it was, the family decided to leave the cause of death out of his obituary and to list his domestic partner as "a special friend." Kurt was invited to the memorial ceremony, but he did not attend, citing his need to work on his upcoming album.

For once, Kurt wasn't lying to get out of a family commitment. He was indeed preparing for his album, and as 1991 began he was fastidiously working. Nirvana had rented a new practice space in Tacoma, and every day they rehearsed for hours. Some of their playing was to teach Grohl the songs in their catalog, but much of it was honing new material Kurt was writing. In January, Sub Pop released their last official Nirvana single, a live recording of the Vaselines' "Molly's Lips." In the run-on groove the label had etched a one-word farewell: "Later."

In February Kurt turned 24, and for the occasion he sat down and began to write the story of his life, one of dozens of short attempts he undertook over the years. This version ran three pages before petering out. "Hi, I'm 24 years old," he wrote. "I was born a white, lower-middle-class male off the coast of Washington State. My parents owned a compact stereo component system molded in simulated wood grain and a four-record box set featuring AM radio's contemporary hits of the early seventies called *Good Vibrations* by Ronco. It had such hits as Tony Orlando and Dawn's 'Tie a Yellow Ribbon' and Jim Croce's 'Time in a Bottle.' After years of my begging, they finally bought me a tin drum set with paper heads out of the back of a Sears catalog. Within the first week, my sister poked holes in the heads with a screwdriver."

Kurt's history went on to note that he remembered his mother playing Chicago songs on the piano and that he'd forever be grateful to his Aunt Mari for giving him three Beatles albums. He wrote that one of his first disappointments was when he found out, in 1976, that the Beatles had dissolved six years earlier. His parents' divorce seemed to have less of an effect: "My parents got a divorce so I moved in with my dad into a trailer park in an even smaller logging community. My dad's friends talked him into joining the Columbia Record Club and soon records showed up at my trailer once a week, accumulating quite a large collection." And with that, this attempt at telling his life story ended.

He went back to his favorite journal subject at the time: writing liner notes for the upcoming album. He wrote many different versions—the album ultimately didn't include any—but one draft of a dedication for the record said more about his childhood than his attempt at biography: "Thanks to unencouraging parents everywhere," he wrote, "for giving their children the will to show them up."

In March Nirvana played a four-date Canadian tour, and then immediately went back into rehearsals. After much debate with their managers and label bosses, they settled on Butch Vig again as producer, using Sound City, a studio outside of Los Angeles. The label would be picking up the expenses, though these would come out of Nirvana's advance.

Before they headed for California, the band had one more Seattle show, on April 17, at the O.K. Hotel. Kurt organized it after hearing his friend Mikey Nelson had so many unpaid traffic citations he was in danger of going to jail. The line-up included Bikini Kill and Fitz of Depression, and Kurt insisted all proceeds go to Nelson. The show did not completely sell out, owing to a party for the movie *Singles* the same night. Nirvana's set included covers of Devo's "Turnaround," the Troggs' "Wild Thing," and the Wipers' "D7," but the surprise came when the band played a new composition. Kurt slurred the vocals, perhaps not even knowing all the words, but the guitar part was already in place, as was the tremendous driving drum beat. "I didn't know what they were playing," recalled Susie Tennant, DGC promotion rep, "but I knew it was amazing. I remember jumping up and down and asking everyone next to me, 'What is this song?' "

Tennant's words mimicked what Novoselic and Grohl had said just three weeks earlier, when Kurt brought a new riff into rehearsal. "It's called 'Smells Like Teen Spirit,' " Kurt announced to his bandmates, stealing the Kathleen Hanna graffiti. At the time, no one in the band knew of the deodorant, and it wasn't until the song was recorded and mastered that anyone pointed out it had the name of a product in it. When Kurt first brought the song into the studio, it had a faster beat and less focus on the bridge. "Kurt was playing just the chorus," Krist remembered. It was Krist's idea to slow the tune down, and Grohl instinctively added a powerful beat.

At the O.K. Hotel, Kurt just hummed a couple of the verses. He was changing the lyrics to all his songs during this period, and "Teen Spirit" had about a dozen drafts. One of the first drafts featured the chorus: "A denial and from strangers / A revival and from favors / Here we are now, we're so famous / We're so stupid and from Vegas." Another began with: "Come out and play, make up the rules / Have lots of fun, we know we'll lose." Later in the same version was a line that had no rhyming couplet: "The finest day I ever had was when tomorrow never came."

A week later the band headed to Los Angeles. On the drive down, Kurt stopped by Universal Studios, and went on the same rides he'd taken with his grandparents fifteen years before. The group moved into the Oakwood Apartments for the next six weeks, not far from Sound City Studios. Vig visited them during pre-production and found chaos. "There was graffiti on the walls," he remembered, "and the couches were upside down. They would stay up every night and go down to Venice Beach until six in the morning." The nervousness the band felt about recording was alleviated by drinking, which all three members did to excess. One night, Krist was arrested for driving while intoxicated; John Silva had to scramble to bail him out and get him back in the studio.

Most of the sessions began at three in the afternoon and ran until midnight. During breaks, Kurt wandered the halls of the studio and stared at gold records for albums like Fleetwood Mac's *Rumours* and Tom Petty's *Damn the Torpedoes*, though he was most impressed by the Evel Knievel record cut there. The lite-metal band Warrant had rented the studio before Nirvana; when the group came back to pick up gear during Nirvana's session, Kurt grabbed the studio's paging system and started screaming "Bring me some 'Cherry Pie,' " the title of Warrant's hit. One night Kurt stole the original master tapes to the Evel Knievel album and took them home to Olympia.

They spent that first week trying to get basic tracks down, mostly concentrating on the drum sound, which was Vig's specialty. After two weeks, they'd laid down ten songs, though most had no more than three takes because Kurt's voice would wear out after so much screaming. Many of the songs were ones they cut previously during the Smart Studio sessions, and it was more technical work than creative.

Compared to the band's other sessions, there were few problems. During the recording of "Lithium" Kurt struggled to get his guitar parts right and became progressively more frustrated, eventually smashing his guitar on the studio floor. In the end, Vig decided to use the take recorded during Kurt's meltdown; it was titled "Endless, Nameless" and put on the compact disc as a hidden track.

The biggest problem of the session was Kurt's own procrastination: He still hadn't settled on lyrics for many of the songs, though a few tunes, like "Polly" and "Breed," the band had been playing for years. When he did finish a lyric, most were as paradoxical as they were revelatory. Many lines left the listener unclear as to whether he was singing about external or internal circumstances, defying explanation though communicating an emotional tone. In his journals, Kurt wrote a letter to the long-dead critic Lester Bangs, complaining about the state of rock journalism—a profession that both fascinated and repulsed him—by asking, "Why in the hell do journalists insist on coming up with a second-rate Freudian evaluation of my lyrics, when 90 percent of the time they've transcribed them incorrectly?" Despite the wisdom in Kurt's question, he spent hours trying to figure out the songs of his idols. He also labored over his own compositions, variably inserting messages or editing himself when he thought he had been too revealing.

Such was the case with "Something in the Way," the last song recorded during the sessions. The lyrics recounted Kurt's mythical period living under the bridge. He had written this song a year earlier, but he had kept it hidden from his bandmates. In his first imagining of the album, Kurt had wanted a "Girl"-side (composed of all the songs about Tobi) and a "Boy"-side (to include "Sliver," "Sappy," and "Polly" among others, all the songs about his family or his inner world). He had always planned to end the album with "Something in the Way," though he never mentioned this to his producer. Instead, he brought forth the song during the Sound City sessions as a last-minute surprise and wrote the lyrics out in the studio, making it appear to all as if he were crafting them on the spot, when he had worked on them for years. Despite his letter to Lester Bangs, no single individual analyzed the Freudian implications of his lyrics more than Kurt himself, and he knew very well that releasing a song implying he lived under a bridge would cause much pain for his family.

As they finished up the sessions, a friend of Grohl's visited and offered to bet Kurt he'd be on the cover of *Rolling Stone* within six months. Kurt replied, "Ah, forget it." Mikey Nelson and his bandmates from Fitz of Depression also showed up and stayed with Nirvana at the Oakwood, as did the Melvins—during one weekend there were 22 people sleeping in their two-bedroom apartment. The Fitz had run into more bad luck: A club had promised a much-needed show but cancelled at the last minute. "Call him back," Kurt insisted, "and tell him we'll play, too." Two days after finishing their record, Nirvana played a tiny Los Angeles club called Jabberjaw and debuted "On a Plain" and "Come As You Are" in front of an astonished audience. They insisted that all the door money go to Nelson. Kurt described the show in a letter to Tobi as "indescribably fucked-up on booze and drugs, out of tune, and rather, uh, sloppy. It took me over fifteen minutes to change my guitar string while people heckled me and called me drunk. After the show, I ran outside and vomited." At the club, Kurt noticed Iggy Pop in the audience, and this time Kurt wasn't wearing an embarrassing shirt. "It was probably the most flattering moment of my life," he observed.

Yet the most revealing part of Kurt's letter was his admission of increasing drug abuse, including Quaaludes, which he'd been ingesting like candy. "I've been taking a lot of drugs lately," he wrote Tobi. "It might be time for the Betty Ford Clinic or the Richard Nixon Library to save me from abusing my anemic rodent-like body any longer. I can't wait to be back home (wherever that is) in bed, neurotic and malnourished and complaining how the weather sucks and it's the whole reason for my misery. I miss you Bikini Kill. I totally love you." He signed it "Kurdt."

This letter—like so many others he wrote—went unsent, perhaps because of a woman he had run into two weeks before the Jabberjaw show. She would play a far larger role in his life than Betty Ford, Richard Nixon, or Tobi Vail. He remembered her from her small part in *Straight to Hell.*

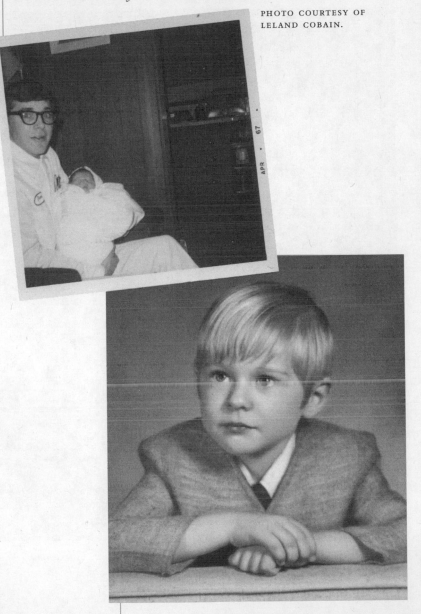

Kurt Cobain at two months old with his father, Don. Don is wearing his service station uniform with his name above the breast.

PHOTO COURTESY OF LELAND COBAIN.

Even as a child, Kurt had the most remarkable eyes.

PHOTO COURTESY OF LELAND COBAIN.

Wendy, Kim, Don and Kurt Cobain, Christmas 1974.
PHOTO COURTESY OF LELAND COBAIN.

Dave Foster, Kurt and Krist Novoselic outside the Vogue after their first Seattle show in 1988.

PHOTO © RICH HANSEN.

Tracy Marander and Kurt in a Woolworth's photo booth portrait, 1988. Kurt was going through a phase of wearing scarves on his head.

PHOTO © TRACY MARANDER.

Kurt in the kitchen of his Olympia apartment. He covered the cabinets with clippings from magazines.

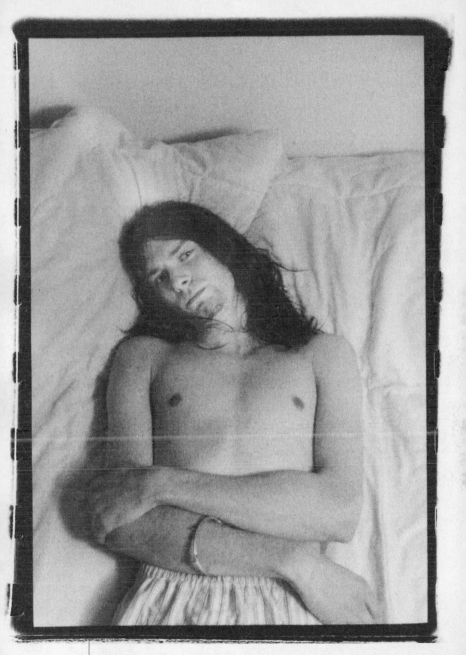

Kurt in pajamas, 1988.
PHOTO © TRACY MARANDER.

Kurt, Chad Channing, Jason Everman and Krist Novoselic in March of 1989 by the Seattle waterfront.

Chad Channing, Krist Novoselic, Kurt and his half-sister Brianne in the Nirvana van.

Kurt in the backyard of his house in Olympia, summer 1989.
PHOTO © TRACY MARANDER.

Kurt, his sister Kim and their Aunt Mari, Christmas 1989.

Kurt in front of a sign in Olympia.

Nirvana live at the Motorsports Speedway in Seattle, September 1990.

PHOTO © ALICE WHEELER.

Courtney Love, Dave Grohl and Kurt on the beach at Waikiki on February 24, 1992, moments after Kurt and Courtney were married.

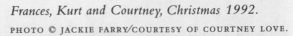

Frances, Kurt and Courtney, Christmas 1992.
PHOTO © JACKIE FARRY/COURTESY OF COURTNEY LOVE.

Kurt arriving back at Sea-Tac airport after his Rome suicide attempt—one of the last known photographs of him.

PHOTO © DUANE DEWITT.

Frances, Kurt and nanny Michael "Cali" Dewitt at Sea-Tac, March 1994.

PHOTO © DUANE DEWITT.

The greenhouse at the Lake Washington home, April 1994.
PHOTO © ALICE WHEELER.

Kurt and Frances, 1992.

PHOTO © LELAND COBAIN.

14 BURN AMERICAN FLAGS

Maybe we can tour together in the States and burn American flags on stage?
—From a letter to Eugene Kelly, September 1991.

Kurt Cobain and Courtney Love first locked eyes on each other at eleven in the evening on Friday, January 12, 1990, and within 30 seconds they were tussling on the floor. The setting was the Satyricon, a small, dimly lit nightclub in Portland, Oregon. Kurt was there for a Nirvana gig; Courtney had come with a friend who was dating a member of the opening band, the wonderfully named Oily Bloodmen. Already an infamous character in Portland, Love was holding court in a booth when she saw Kurt walk by a few minutes before his band was set to appear onstage. Courtney was wearing a red polka-dot dress. "You look like Dave Pirner," she said to him, meaning the remark to sound like a small insult, but also a flirt. Kurt did look a bit like Pirner, the lead singer of Soul Asylum, as his hair had grown long and tangled—he washed it just once a week, and then only with bar soap. Kurt responded with a flirt of his own: He grabbed Courtney and wrestled her to the ground. "It was in front of the jukebox," Courtney remembered, "which was playing my favorite song by Living Color. There was beer on the floor." She was glad her comment had gotten attention, but she hadn't expected to be pinned to the floor by this little waif of a boy. For his part, Kurt hadn't counted on his opponent being so tough: She was three inches taller than he was, and stronger. Without his high-school wrestling experience, she might have won the tussle.

But the roll on the floor was all in jest, and he pulled her up with his arms and gave her a peace offering—a sticker of Chim Chim, the "Speed Racer" monkey he had made his mascot.

As Kurt later told the story to Michael Azerrad, he had an immediate attraction to Courtney: "I thought she looked liked Nancy Spungen. She looked liked a classic punk rock chick. I did feel kind of attracted to her. Probably wanted to fuck her that night, but she left." Kurt's suggestions were no doubt apocryphal—Tracy was with him in Portland, and despite his enchantment, it would have been unlike him to cheat. But the connection between Kurt and Courtney was sexual: Wrestling was a fetish of Kurt's, and an opponent as worthy as Courtney was a major turn-on.

They parted that night but Courtney followed Nirvana's career the way a baseball pitcher in the American League might follow the exploits of a National League player. She read Nirvana's clips in the rock press, and she put Kurt's Chim Chim sticker on her guitar case, even though she remained unconvinced about the band—their early material was too metal for her. Like most rock critics at the time, she preferred Mudhoney, and after listening to "Love Buzz" in a record store, she passed on buying the single. Seeing the band in concert later, she was more struck by their strange physical appearance: "Krist was really, really big," she observed, "and he dwarfed Kurt to the point where you couldn't see how cute Kurt was because he looked like a tiny boy."

Her opinion of Nirvana, and the tiny boy, changed entirely when she bought the "Sliver" single in October 1990. "When I played it," she recalled, "I was like, 'Oh, my God—I *missed* this!' " On the B-side was "Dive," which became her favorite Nirvana song. "It is so sexy, and sexual, and strange, and haunting," she noted. "I thought it was genius."

When Courtney's friend Jennifer Finch became involved with Dave Grohl in late 1990, Nirvana and Kurt became a frequent topic of their girl talk. They nicknamed Kurt "Pixie Meat," because of both his diminutive size and Kurt's worship of the Pixies. Courtney confessed to Grohl that she had a crush on Kurt, and when Dave told her Kurt was suddenly single, Courtney sent Kurt a gift meant to move their wrestling match to a different arena. It was a heart-shaped box filled with a tiny porcelain doll, three dried roses, a miniature teacup, and shellac-covered seashells. She had purchased the silk-and-lace box at Gerald Katz Antiques in New Orleans, and before sending it she rubbed her perfume on it like a magical charm. When the fragrant box arrived in Olympia, it was the best-smelling thing in the Pear Street apartment, though this distinction wasn't difficult to achieve. Kurt was impressed with the doll; by 1990 dolls were one of the many mediums he used for his art projects. He would repaint their faces and glue human hair onto their heads. The resulting creatures were both beautiful and grotesque, looking as much like child corpses as dolls.

Kurt and Courtney met the second time in May 1991 during an L7 concert at the Palladium in Los Angeles. Kurt was backstage drinking cough syrup directly from the bottle. In a bit of fate that was reminiscent of his first meeting with Tracy and their shared rats, Courtney opened her purse and displayed her own vial of cough syrup, a more powerful brand. They wrestled to the ground again, but this time it was more of a grope than a physical challenge. The vibe, according to those who witnessed it, was very sexual. When Kurt let her up, the tension lessened and they talked shop. Courtney was quick to brag that her band, Hole, had finished recording *Pretty on the Inside*, with Kim Gordon of Sonic Youth producing; Kurt talked about his own album, which was still in production. Kurt was usually meek when meeting someone for the first time, but in his efforts to impress Courtney, he pulled out every name and credential he could—he clearly wanted to one-up her. As Kurt soon discovered, few could gain a verbal advantage over Love. She knew far more about the music business than he did, and Hole's career was accelerating as quickly as Nirvana's at the time. She was a peer, if not a mentor to Kurt, in ways that went far beyond Tobi.

In their conversation, Kurt disclosed he was staying at the Oakwood Apartments; Courtney told him she lived just a few blocks away. She wrote down her phone number on a bar napkin and told him to call her sometime. She was earnestly flirting, and he was flirting back.

Breaking every rule of dating, he called her later that night at three in the morning, sounding like the desperate brokenhearted loser in *Swingers*. "There was a lot of noise in the background," Courtney recalled. Kurt pretended as if he were phoning only because he wanted to discover where she got her cough syrup—he'd begun to prefer this to all other intoxicants that spring. But what he really wanted was to talk to her more. And as Kurt found out, Courtney could talk. This night, her normally booming voice was just a whisper—her ex-boyfriend and bandmate Eric Erlandson was sleeping in the next room. At the time, she was also in a long-distance relationship with Billy Corgan of the Smashing Pumpkins.

They talked for almost an hour, and it was a conversation Kurt would remember for weeks and weeks. Though he was typically direct and short-tempered on the phone, there were occasional individuals who could bring out the conversationalist in him, and Courtney was one of these. He was able to say things over the phone he'd been unable to speak in person just a few hours earlier. Kurt mentioned the heart-shaped box and thanked Courtney for it. It touched her that he'd noticed, but soon she went on to other topics, spewing forth a stream-of-consciousness rap that included producers, critics, Sonic Youth, guitar-playing, cough syrup brands, and songwriting, among other brief stops. She switched from subject to subject the way someone might flick the channels of a television remote control. When Kurt described the conversation to his friend Ian Dickson, he began by declaring, "I've met the coolest girl in the whole world." As Dickson, and his other friends, came to complain that May, "Kurt would not stop talking about her. It was 'Courtney says this,' and 'Courtney says that.'" It would be five months before they would see each other again, but during that time Kurt would recall their conversation frequently, wondering if it was real or just a drug-induced dream caused by too much cough syrup.

In early June Vig finished Nirvana's album, and the band began the laborious process of overseeing mixing, mastering, and creating the cover and video. The initial budget for recording had been $65,000, but by the time the record was completed two months later, expenses were over $120,000. Vig had done an admirable job capturing the power of Nirvana's live shows on a studio album, yet his mixes weren't to the liking of the label or Nirvana's managers.

Nirvana's career was now being directed by three men: co-managers John Silva and Danny Goldberg from Gold Mountain, and DGC's Gary Gersh. The trio took on the difficult task of convincing Kurt that the album needed remixing. Andy Wallace, who had worked with acts as diverse as Slayer and Madonna, was brought in. "Wallace's mix was a big factor in making that record what it was," Goldberg observed. Wallace mixed the basic tracks in a way that made them sound powerful on the radio: He created separation between the guitar and the drums, which created a sonic punch that had been missing from Nirvana's previous recordings. Kurt agreed with this direction at the time, though he would later claim it made the album sound "candy-ass." "Uniformly," Wallace recalled, "we all wanted the recording to sound as big and powerful as possible."

It wasn't until early June that Kurt settled on a definitive title for the record. He had abandoned *Sheep*, thinking it sophomoric. One day he suggested to Krist they call it *Nevermind*. For Kurt, the title worked on several levels: It was a metaphor for his attitude about life; it was grammatically incorrect, combining two words into one, always a plus for Kurt; and it came from "Smells Like Teen Spirit," which was becoming the most-talked-about song of the sessions. Though the band had gone into the studio convinced "Lithium" was the hit, by the time the album was finished, "Teen Spirit" was being touted as the first single.

Kurt had spent two years planning liner notes and various concepts for the album cover, but in early 1991 he threw out all his ideas and started from scratch. That spring he'd seen a television show about underwater childbirth and he had the label try to acquire footage from the program, without success. Finally, Kurt drew out a slightly different idea on a sheet of notebook paper: It was a baby boy swimming underwater, chasing a dollar bill. It was a striking image, and initially there was some controversy about how prominent the baby boy's penis was. For the back cover, Kurt insisted on a picture of Chim Chim resting on a vagina/meat collage.

For photos of the band, Kurt had hired New York–based photographer Michael Lavine, who flew to L.A. in early June. Kurt greeted him with a hug and then immediately showed off a huge sore inside his mouth. He also had badly infected gums, the result of infrequent tooth-brushing. Never a fan of having his photograph taken, Kurt buttressed himself for the shoot by drinking an entire bottle of Jim Beam bourbon. But despite the infection, Kurt was in a good mood and smiled a lot. "He was really funny and friendly," Lavine remembered. "We ate tacos and walked around and shot pictures." When it came time to select the final pictures for the inner sleeve, Kurt chose a photograph in which he displays his middle finger.

By the second week of June, Nirvana were back on tour, their only real source of income. They did a two-week West Coast swing with Dinosaur Jr. and the Jesus Lizard. They were now playing the *Nevermind* songs, even though the album was months away from release, and at every show "Teen Spirit" grew in crowd response. Kurt returned to Olympia with enough money to buy a car; his old Datsun had been hauled to the junkyard. On June 24, he purchased a beige 1963 Plymouth Valiant for $550 from a friend. Though it had 140,000 miles on it, the car was in good shape and Kurt's friends remarked that it looked like a car a grandmother would drive. He drove it very slowly as he tooled around Olympia—he thought driving ten miles under the speed limit would lessen the wear and tear on the engine.

Kurt and Tobi maintained a friendship, and both continued to talk about the record they wanted to make together. The only other woman in Kurt's life at the time was Carrie Montgomery, Mark Arm's old girlfriend, whom he had become close to. This relationship was platonic, though everyone in the scene, including Mark Arm, thought otherwise. Without a girlfriend, Kurt was more gloomy than usual, which was notable in itself. All his friends were excited for his success, but he didn't share in their enthusiasm. It was as if the world was holding a parade in his honor, and everyone in town came to celebrate except the man himself.

When a young girl from England showed up in Olympia that summer, having flown over specifically to track Kurt down and bed him, he uncharacteristically slept with her. After just a couple of days, he realized his mistake, though since he avoided conflict, it took him almost a week to kick her out. When he did, she stood outside the Pear Street apartment screaming and cursing. It was the kind of incident that immediately became the talk of Olympia. Combined with his decision to sign to a major label, this infraction damaged his relationship with the Calvinists; increasing rumors of his heroin use only added fuel to the fire.

In July Grohl moved to West Seattle; Kurt was alone again and retreating even more from the world, if that were possible. He no longer limited his drug binges to one night a week—if he could afford heroin and find it, he'd do the drug all weekend and nod out by himself in the apartment. He wrote in his journal less, he practiced guitar less, and he escaped from the world more.

Even when he was sober, Kurt was getting more eccentric, or so observed his friends. He had a little white kitten named Quisp, and he dyed the cat's fur (along with his own hair) red, white, and blue with Kool-Aid. He allowed Quisp, who was male, to have sex with the rabbit, Stew, who was female. Stew had an unusual vagina, which fascinated Kurt—her uterus was inverted, which meant it frequently stuck out. "He used to take a pencil and push it back in," observed Ian Dickson. Kurt's theory was that the cat having sex with the rabbit had messed up the rabbit's reproductive tract, though he had made no attempt to stop their antics, and watching their cross-species mating had become one of his favorite pastimes.

That month Kurt and Dickson went swimming at a quarry outside of Olympia, and Kurt came home with dozens of tadpoles he'd captured. He dropped them in the aquarium, watching with glee as his turtles ate the tadpoles. "Look," Kurt told Dickson, "you can see their little arms and pieces floating in the tank." A young man who used to save birds with broken wings was now delighting in watching tadpoles being devoured by turtles.

The second week of July Kurt did something so uncharacteristic that when Tracy initially heard the news, she had to be told twice, since she couldn't imagine she was hearing this about the man she once loved: Kurt sold his turtles. He claimed he sold them because he needed the money; it wasn't because of his schedule, since he always managed to find friends to care for his animals when he traveled. He told anyone who would listen that he was poorer than he had ever been, despite having signed a major-label deal. He had asked $100 for the turtles, but when the buyer only came up with $50, he accepted that. Tracy visited the Pear Street apartment and found the fancy aquarium on its side in the yard. Curiously, some of the tadpoles used for turtle food had survived, and the grass was covered with tiny frogs.

On July 15 Kurt flew to Los Angeles for more work on the album cover and promotional photos. When he returned to Olympia on July 29, he found his material possessions sitting in boxes beside the curb; he had been evicted. Despite recording his major label debut that spring and signing a record deal, he had gotten behind on the rent. His neighbors, thankfully, had contacted Tracy to come and rescue the animals, but Kurt's artwork, his journals, and much of his musical equipment were sitting in cardboard boxes beside the apartment. That night, and for several weeks afterward, he slept in his car.

While Kurt was sleeping in the backseat of his Valiant in Olympia, his managers and label bosses were in Los Angeles debating how many copies *Nevermind* was going to sell. Expectations within Geffen had begun very low, but inched up as an advance tape circulated. In truth, expectations were actually higher outside of Kurt's own label than within the company. During 1990 and early 1991, Nirvana had become the hip band, and the advance spread like a virus among music industry employees in the know. John Troutman was one such example: Even though he worked for RCA, he dubbed several dozen copies and gave them to radio programmers and friends simply because he was enthusiastic about the band. Nirvana had built an audience the old-fashioned way, through their unceasing touring. On the eve of the release of the new album, they had a loyal fan base waiting.

Nirvana was signed to DGC, a smaller imprint of the Geffen label having only a few employees and just a couple of hit acts. In contrast, Geffen had Guns N' Roses, the most successful rock group of the era. Geffen employees called DGC the "Dumping Ground Company," instead of what the initials really stood for, the David Geffen Company, jesting that lame bands were put on DGC so as to not smear the Geffen name. Few at the label expected Nirvana to score a hit the first time out. "In the marketing meetings at the time," observed John Rosenfelder, DGC radio promotion, "sales of 50,000 were what was planned, since Sonic Youth had sold 118,000 of *Goo*. We figured if it could sell half that, we were doing good." The enigmatic label head, David Geffen, let his A&R staff run the label, but Rosenfelder slid a cassette of *Nevermind* to Geffen's chauffeur, hoping to get the label's boss behind the band.

Kurt and the rest of the band flew back to Los Angeles in mid-August to begin promotional efforts for the record and prepare for a tour of Europe. DGC was footing the bill for their hotel, a single room at the Holiday Inn. It only had two beds, so Kurt and Dave flipped a coin each night to see who would share with Krist. But to Kurt, any bed, even one shared with a gigantic bass player, was better than the backseat of his car.

On August 15 they played an industry showcase at the Roxy. Though the gig was organized primarily to allow Geffen executives to see their new property, it drew a crowd of movers and shakers from all walks of the industry. "It was strange," remembered Mark Kates, DGC promotions director, "because *everybody* had to see them, *everybody* had to get in." Their performance impressed even the normally staid Geffen executives. After the show, a Geffen vice president announced, "We'll sell 100,000," which was twice what he had been predicting two weeks before.

On the day of the Roxy show, the band had done their first radio interview for *Nevermind* at college station KXLU. John Rosenfelder drove them while they pelted Reese's Peanut Butter Cups at passing cars. When Rosenfelder told Kurt *Nevermind* "was good music to get stoned to," Kurt responded, "I want a tie-dyed shirt made with the blood of Jerry Garcia." Like his "Punk rock is freedom" line, this comment, about the lead singer of the Grateful Dead, was repeated so often Kurt might as well have put it on bumper stickers. At the station, Rosenfelder produced a vinyl test-pressing of what they had now decided was the first single—it represented the very first public airing of "Smells Like Teen Spirit." On the way back to the hotel, Kurt raved about how great it sounded.

The band began the music video for "Smells Like Teen Spirit" two days after the Roxy show. The concept for the video—a pep rally gone wrong—was Kurt's. He wrote a basic treatment, detailing it down to the idea of using prostitutes as cheerleaders, with anarchy symbols on their sweaters. He told John Gannon, a cameraman he knew, that he wanted a "mosh-cam" to film him, "something I can smash my head against." But Kurt struggled from the start with director Sam Bayer, whom he called "a little Napoleon." Truth was, Kurt wanted to be directing the video himself. Bayer and Cobain got into a yelling match, but the director was able to use this to his benefit: Kurt was clearly angry, which helped sell the song. He was also drunk, having downed half a bottle of Jim Beam between takes. Kurt helped edit the final version and added the shot that showed his face almost pressing into the camera—it was the only time in the video his good looks were apparent. When the crowd careened out of control and into the band, it accurately recreated some of the band's early shows played without a stage.

There was even a hidden joke in the clip, one that was lost on most who saw it other than Kurt, Krist, and a few of the Aberdeen "Cling-Ons." A school custodian appeared in the video, pushing a mop and bucket. This was Kurt's depiction of his former job at Aberdeen's high school. Weatherwax High's worst janitor was now America's newest rock star.

Two days after the video shoot, the band left for a ten-date tour of Europe with Sonic Youth. Kurt had convinced Ian Dickson to accompany the band on the road. Since money was tight, Kurt promised his managers Dickson would share his room. "I know John Silva thought we were lovers," Dickson recalled. At the time Silva wasn't the only one who suspected Kurt was a homosexual: Many at Geffen and Gold Mountain wrongly assumed he was gay.

The European tour, much of which was captured in Dave Markey's film *1991: The Year Punk Broke*, was a watershed of sorts—Nirvana played to rabid crowds, and Kurt was uncharacteristically joyful. Advances of *Nevermind* had circulated, and the future success of the record hung in the air as if it had been preordained. This brief two-week tour was Kurt's happiest time as a musician. "Even on the plane ride over there," Markey remembered, "Kurt was bouncing up and down with happiness." When Nirvana played the Reading Festival—England's most influential rock event—Eugene Kelly of the Vaselines agreed to come onstage and do a duet on "Molly's Lips." As Kurt would later say, it was the greatest moment of his life.

Hole also played Reading; they were touring England, too. Kurt had run into Courtney the night before, when Hole opened up for Mudhoney. To spite Courtney, Kurt left the club with two groupies, though he later claimed he didn't have sex with either of them. At Reading, Courtney was more generous. When Markey put his camera on her and asked if she had anything to say, she replied, "Kurt Cobain makes my heart stop. But he's a shit."

Reading was the first show where Kurt found Nirvana getting comparable attention to Mudhoney. Only four years earlier, Kurt had played his first public concert at a kegger and struggled to play loud enough to drown out the noise from the crowd—now he was playing to festival audiences of 70,000, and the instant he went to the microphone the entire massive crowd fell silent, as if a prince were about to speak. "There was this kind of cockiness about Nirvana that day," remembered road manager Alex MacLeod. "They had a confidence."

And for once, that confidence extended to Kurt's feelings about himself. He had a glorious time on the tour, taking full advantage of his ascendant popularity. Most dates were festivals featuring five or six bands, and the atmosphere was one of an all-day party. "They joined what seemed like a traveling circus," Markey observed, "and it didn't feel like a burden to them—it seemed more like a vacation." But it was a vacation out of a Chevy Chase movie: Every tour stop included a food fight or some form of drunken debauchery. Nirvana's set was usually early in the day, and after playing they spent the afternoon drinking liquor provided by the promoters. By the time Nirvana made it to the Pukkelpop Festival in Belgium on August 25, they were acting like fraternity brothers on spring break, trashing their dressing rooms and knocking over food trays. During a set by Charles Thompson of the Pixies, Kurt grabbed a fire extinguisher backstage and shot it. A year earlier he had been too shy to even meet Thompson; now he was trying to hose his former idol off the stage.

On the tour, Kurt rarely walked by a fire extinguisher he didn't fire off. On earlier tours, his destructive tendencies had been fueled by frustration with his playing, problems with sound, or fights with his bandmates. But destruction during this brief flash in his life was driven by joyous exuberance. "The most exciting time for a band is right before they become really popular," Kurt would later tell Michael Azerrad. In Nirvana's case, this was undoubtedly August 1991.

When the tour hit Rotterdam on the first of September, it was almost with a nostalgic wistfulness that Kurt approached the last show. He was wearing the same T-shirt he'd had on two weeks earlier—it was a bootlegged Sonic Youth shirt—which had gone unwashed, as had his jeans, the only pair of pants he owned. His luggage consisted of a tiny bag containing only a copy of William S. Burroughs's "Naked Lunch," which he had found in a London bookstall. Perhaps inspired by his bedtime reading, the Rotterdam show turned into something out of a Burroughs novel after Kurt discovered some costumes backstage. "Kurt and Ian Dickson were drinking vodka in copious amounts," recalled MacLeod. "They stole these doctor's jackets and face masks, and they were storming around the place, bothering people. People would walk into the dressing room and get doused with orange juice and wine. At one point, Ian was wheeling Kurt around in a hospital bed. They'd be two floors up in this atrium pouring orange juice on these security guards and then running." It was MacLeod's job to control these antics, but he just threw up his hands: "We were 22 or 23 years old and in a situation that none of us ever imagined being in."

In Rotterdam Kurt again encountered Courtney at a club. She was quick to ask for a ride back to England in the Nirvana van. Her coy dance with Kurt continued, and on the ferry over, as the band watched *Terminator*, Courtney flirted with Dave in an effort to get a rise from Kurt. When that failed, she left her purse with her passport in Nirvana's van, and had to call the next day to retrieve it. Courtney found herself disappointed when Dickson and MacLeod returned the bag, rather than Kurt. He was playing coy too.

On September 3 Nirvana recorded another radio show for John Peel and then went out to celebrate their final night in England. Kurt insisted they find the drug Ecstasy, which he took for the first time. The next day he flew back to Olympia, ending one of the most joyous tours he would ever undertake. Still without a place to live, he fell asleep that night curled up in the backseat of his Valiant.

He returned to an Olympia that was much changed in the three weeks that he'd been gone, at least for him. While Nirvana was playing huge festivals in Europe, Olympia was staging its own festival, the 50-act International Pop Underground. Nirvana had originally been scheduled to play the IPU, but after their major label deal they were no longer an indie act, and Kurt's absence at the biggest ball Olympia ever staged was notable. It marked the end of his relationship with the Calvinists, and the end of his time living in a city he loved more than any other, yet one he never felt welcome in.

But in a way, he was ready to leave. Just as Kurt had needed to break free of the orbit of Buzz, he had hit a developmental stage where he had to leave Olympia, Calvin, and Tobi. It wasn't an easy transition, because he had believed in the Calvinist indie ideals and they had served him when he needed an ideology to break out of Aberdeen. "Punk rock is freedom," he had learned, a line he would continue to repeat to any journalist who would listen. But he always knew that punk rock was a different freedom for kids who had grown up privileged. To him, punk rock was a class struggle, but that was always secondary to the struggle to pay the rent, or find a place to sleep other than in the backseat of a car. Music was more than just a fad for Kurt—it had become his only career option.

Before he left Olympia, Kurt sat down and wrote a final letter to Eugene Kelly of the Vaselines, thanking him for playing with Nirvana at Reading. In the letter, he demonstrated he had already begun emotionally departing Olympia. Surprisingly, he criticized KAOS, the much-loved radio station that had been one of his first public forums: "I've realized that . . . DJs have bloody awful taste in music. Oh, yes, and to prove my point, right now they're playing a Nirvana song from an old demo."

He wrote of the recent conflict with Iraq: "We won the war. Patriotic hypocrisy is in full effect. We have the privilege of purchasing Desert Storm trading cards, flags, bumper stickers, and many video versions of our triumphant victory. When I walk down the street I feel like I'm at a Nuremberg rally. Hey, maybe [we] can tour together in the States and burn American flags on stage?"

He ended the letter with yet another description of his circumstances, which, if Kurt had mailed the letter—as usual, he never put it in the post—probably would have shocked Kelly and anyone else who saw Kurt onstage in Reading, playing to 70,000 adoring fans. "I got evicted from my apartment. I'm living in my car so I have no address, but here's Krist's phone number for messages. Your pal, Kurdt." That same week, the "Smells Like Teen Spirit" single went on sale in record shops.

15 EVERY TIME I SWALLOWED

*Every time I swallowed a piece of food, I would experience an
excruciating, burning, nauseous pain in the upper part of my
stomach lining.*
—An inventory of Kurt's drug and stomach problems from his
journal.

The second Friday of September—a Friday the thir-
teenth—was one of the most extraordinary days of Kurt's life. It was a
day that would encompass two food fights, a fire extinguisher duel, and
the destruction of gold record awards in a microwave oven. All of this
divine chaos was in celebration of the release of *Nevermind* in Seattle.

The day began with a series of radio interviews on Seattle's biggest
rock stations. Kurt sat still for the first one on KXRX, but barely said
a word and started throwing pizza around the control room. Earlier in
the week he had been willing to talk with any interested journalist.
"Even if it was a writer they didn't like," recounted publicist Lisa
Glatfelter-Bell, "Kurt would say, 'That guy's a prick, but he loves the
record, so we'll give him ten minutes.' " His attitude changed after just
a few phone interviews. He tired of trying to explain himself, and each
progressive interview turned into a game to see what new fiction he
could fabricate. When he talked with Patrick MacDonald of the *Seattle
Times*, he claimed to have purchased an inflatable love-doll, cut off the
hands and feet, and intended to wear it onstage. Yet, by the end of the
week, even deceiving journalists bored him. Where he had been joyous
in Europe two weeks previously, being back in America—and promoting the album—seemed to tire him. The exuberance of Rotterdam
had quickly given way to reticence and resignation. Kurt stayed in the

car during the next two interviews, leaving Krist and Dave to chat up the DJs.

At six o'clock, the band had their much anticipated invitation-only record release at the Re-bar, an event Kurt had been waiting his whole life for (*Bleach* had no such celebration). The invitations read, "Nevermind Triskaidekaphobia, here's Nirvana." The phobia referred to a fear of Friday the thirteenth, but what was truly scary was how packed the club was with musicians, music journalists, and the power brokers of the scene.

It was Kurt's chance to bask in glory, having finally conquered Seattle, yet he seemed uncomfortable with the attention. On this day, and during many to follow, he gave the impression that he'd rather be anywhere than promoting his record. As a boy who had grown up the center of attention in his family, only to lose that distinction in adolescence, he responded with suspicion to his change of fortune. He sat in a photo booth at the party, physically present, but hidden from view by a cloth curtain.

The band had smuggled in a half gallon of Jim Beam, a violation of Washington liquor law. But before any liquor inspector could bust them, mayhem erupted, when Kurt started throwing ranch dressing at Krist, and a food fight ensued. A bouncer grabbed the offenders and threw them out, unaware he'd ejected the very three men the party was being held for. Before DGC's Susie Tennant was able to straighten matters out, Krist had to be dragged away from a confrontation with the bouncer. "We were laughing," Krist recalled, "saying, 'Oh my God, we just got kicked out of our own record release party!' " For a time, the band stood in the alley behind the club and talked to their friends through a window. The party was still raging inside, and most of the attendees never noticed the guests of honor had been banished.

The celebration resumed at the loft of a friend, until Kurt shot off a fire extinguisher and the place had to be evacuated. They then moved to Susie Tennant's house, where the destruction continued until dawn. Susie had a gold record by the band Nelson on her wall; Kurt took the plaque down, calling it "an affront to humankind," rubbed lipstick on it, and stuck it in a microwave on defrost. The night ended with Kurt trying on one of Susie's dresses, applying makeup, and walking around in drag. "Kurt made a great-looking woman," Susie recalled. "I had this one dress, my Holly Hobby dress, and Kurt looked better in it than I did, better than anyone I'd ever seen."

Kurt spent that night at Susie's, as did many of the revelers. He fell asleep under a Patti Smith poster wearing the dress. When he arose the next morning, he announced that he and Dylan planned to spend the day shooting holes in a rump roast. "After we shoot it all to hell, we're going to eat it," he said. He departed, asking for directions to a supermarket.

Two days later, Nirvana held an "in-store" at Beehive Records. DGC expected about 50 patrons, but when over 200 kids were lined up by two in the afternoon—for an event scheduled to start at seven—it began to dawn on them that perhaps the band's popularity was greater than first thought. Kurt had decided that rather than simply sign albums and shake people's hands—the usual business of an in-store—Nirvana would play. When he saw the line at the store that afternoon, it marked the first time he was heard to utter the words "holy shit" in response to his popularity. The band retreated to the Blue Moon Tavern and began drinking, but when they looked out the window and saw dozens of fans looking in, they felt like they were in the movie *A Hard Day's Night*. When the show began, Beehive was so crowded that kids were standing on racks of albums and sawhorses had to be lined up in front of the store's glass windows to protect them. Nirvana played a 45-minute set—performing on the store floor—until the crowd began smashing into the band like the pep rally in the "Smells Like Teen Spirit" video.

Kurt was bewildered by just how big a deal it had all become. Looking into the crowd, he saw half of the Seattle music scene and dozens of his friends. It was particularly unnerving for him to see two of his ex-girlfriends—Tobi and Tracy—there, bopping away to the songs. Even these intimates were now part of an audience he felt pressure to serve. The store was selling the first copies of *Nevermind* the public had a chance at, and they quickly sold out. "People were ripping posters off the wall," remembered store manager Jamie Brown, "just so they'd have a piece of paper for Kurt to autograph." Kurt kept shaking his head in amazement.

Kurt retreated to the parking lot for a smoke and some downtime. But there, the day became even more freakish when he saw two of his old Montesano schoolmates, Scott Cokely and Rick Miller, holding copies of "Sliver." Though Kurt signed hundreds of autographs that day, none made him feel more surreal than putting his signature on a single about his grandparents for two guys from the town his grandparents lived in. They talked about their mutual friends from the harbor, but the conversation made Kurt wistful—Cokely and Miller were a reminder of a past Kurt thought he had left behind. "Do you get back to the harbor much?" Cokely asked. "Not very often," Kurt replied. Both Cokely and Miller were confused when they looked at their singles and noticed Kurt had signed them "Kurdt."

Kurt later cited this exchange as one of the first moments he realized he was famous. Yet rather than comfort him, this realization set off something just short of a panic. Though he had always wanted to be famous—and back when he was in school in Monte, he had promised his classmates one day he would be—the actual culmination of his dreams deeply unnerved him. Krist would recall this particular show—a free show in a record store a week before the album's official release date—as a turning point in Kurt. "Things started to happen after that," Krist said. "We weren't the same old band. Kurt, he just kind of withdrew. There was a lot of personal stuff that was going on. It got complicated. It was more than we bargained for."

It wasn't that the Beehive audience was more intrusive than most; in fact, as the band discovered when their tour began, the Seattle crowd was subdued, compared to what they encountered elsewhere. The tour had been booked before the success of the record, so most of the venues were tiny, leading to hundreds, if not thousands, of fans coveting tickets they couldn't get. Each show was a circus. When they rolled into Boston on September 22, Kurt was looking forward to seeing the Melvins on this rare night off. Yet when he tried to talk his way into the club, the doorman hadn't heard of Nirvana. Mary Lou Lord, a Boston singer-songwriter who was standing by the door, chirped in to say she'd heard of Nirvana and they were playing the next night. This failed to sway the doorman, and Kurt finally paid the cover.

Once inside, Kurt turned his attention to Lord, rather than his old friends. When Lord said she was a musician who played the subway platform, he asked her favorite bands, and she listed the Pastels, the Vaselines, Daniel Johnston, and Teenage Fanclub. "Bullshit," replied Kurt. "Those are *my* favorite bands, in order!" He forced her to name songs by each artist to prove she wasn't jesting. They talked for hours, and Lord gave him a ride on her bicycle's handlebars. They ended up talking all night, and the next day Kurt went to her apartment, where he saw a picture of Lester Bangs hanging on the wall. He asked Lord to do a song, and when she performed two tunes from the yet-to-be-released *Nevermind*, he felt like he'd been bewitched by this rosy-cheeked girl from Salem, Mass.

As they walked around Boston, the stories of his life sprang forth from him in a torrent. He told Lord about his father kicking a dog once, about how miserable he was growing up in his family, and about Tobi. If one of the cardinal rules of flirting was never to talk about your last girlfriend with your potential next, Kurt broke this rule. He told Lord that Tobi was "awesome," but that she was "a real heartbreaker." He admitted he wasn't over her.

Kurt also told Lord how enraptured he had become with an Eastern religion called Jainism. He had seen a documentary on late-night television that enchanted him because the official Jain flag featured an ancient version of the swastika on it. He had since read everything he could find on the Jains, who worshipped animals as holy. "He told me," Lord recalled, "that they had hospitals for pigeons. He said he wanted to join them. He planned to have this big career, and that when everything was all done, he was going to go off and join the Jains." One of the concepts of Jainism Kurt was most taken with was their vision of the afterlife. Jainism preached of a universe that was a series of heavens and hells layered together. "Every day," Kurt told Lord, "we all pass through heaven, and we all pass through hell."

As they walked through Boston's Back Bay, Kurt couldn't keep up with Lord. "He was like an old man," she observed. "He was only 24, but there was a weariness about him far beyond his years." He told Lord that certain drugs helped temper his stomach pain. She didn't do drugs, and didn't inquire further, but a half hour later he revisited the topic and asked her if she'd ever tried heroin. "I don't even want to hear you talking about that kind of shit," she said, cutting off the conversation.

That night they went to the Axis, where Nirvana shared a bill with the Smashing Pumpkins. As Kurt and Lord approached the club, he grabbed her guitar and held her hand. "I'm sure people in line were thinking, 'That's Kurt with the dorky subway girl,' " Lord said. "I'd been there for years and everybody knew me, and they all probably thought I was awful. But then here I was, walking down this street, holding hands with him."

The next day, September 24, *Nevermind* officially went on sale. An MTV crew filmed a brief news segment of Krist playing Twister in his underwear covered with Crisco shortening. Kurt blew off most of the interviews and promotions DGC had set up and instead spent the day with Lord. When DGC's Mark Kates took Novoselic and Grohl to Newbury Comics, Boston's hippest record store, they found a long line. "It was amazing," Kates recalled. "There were like a thousand kids trying to buy this record."

It took two weeks for *Nevermind* to register in the *Billboard* Top 200, but when it did chart, the album entered at No. 144. By the second week it rose to No. 109; by the third week it was at No. 65; and after four weeks, on the second of November, it was at No. 35, with a bullet. Few bands have had such a quick ascendancy to the Top 40 with their debuts. *Nevermind* would have registered even higher if DGC had been more prepared—due to their modest expectations, the label had initially pressed only 46,251 copies. For several weeks, the record was sold out.

Usually a quick rise on the charts is attributable to a well-orchestrated promotional effort, backed by marketing muscle, yet *Nevermind* achieved its early success without such grease. During its first few weeks, the record had little help from radio except in a few selected cities. When DGC's promotion staff tried to convince programmers to play "Teen Spirit," they initially met with resistance. "People at rock radio, even in Seattle, told me, 'We can't play this. I can't understand what the guy is saying,' " recalled DGC's Susie Tennant. Most stations that added the single slated it late at night, thinking it "too aggressive" to put on during the day.

But radio programmers took notice of the number of listeners who phoned in requests. When Seattle's KNDD did research on "Smells Like Teen Spirit," the song received the highest positive response the polling company had ever registered. "When a song like that is being re-searched," observed KNDD's Marco Collins, "we're talking about play-ing this track through a phone line, and people only hearing a fifteen-second clip. Try to imagine what it would be like to hear 'Teen Spirit' for the first time through the phone."

Within MTV, the video caused a stir when it was considered in early September. Amy Finnerty, a 22-year-old programmer, felt so strongly about the video, she announced that if the channel wouldn't play the clip, then MTV wasn't the kind of place she wanted to work. After some heated debate, the video was added to the specialty show "120 Minutes." It went into regular rotation in November as one of the channel's first "Buzz Bin" videos.

The first time Kurt saw himself on television was in New York City a few days after the Boston shows. He was staying in the Roger Smith Hotel, and Mary Lou Lord was in his room. When the video came on "120 Minutes," Kurt phoned his mother. "There's me," he gleefully said. "There's me again," he repeated when ten seconds later he reap-peared. "And there's me again." He kept playfully announcing this every time he saw himself on the television, as if his presence were a surprise.

That afternoon Nirvana played a rare acoustic in-store at Tower Records. During the short set, Kurt pulled Oreos from a bag of groceries one fan was carrying, and washed those down with milk he also pilfered from the sack. That same night, they played a sold-out show at the Marquee Club, which was followed by a party at the home of MTV's Amy Finnerty. Word of the celebration leaked out to the club audience, many of whom showed up uninvited. Kurt snuck out of the party and went with Finnerty and Lord to a bar across the street. "This place has the best jukebox I've ever seen," Kurt declared, though the machine had only disco tunes. For one of the few times in his entire life, perhaps in honor of the official release of *Nevermind*, Kurt stood up and danced.

After New York the tour accelerated, and so did Nirvana's fame. As both the single and video of "Teen Spirit" vaulted up the charts, every show was sold out and signs of a greater mania appeared. Kurt stayed in touch with Lord by phone and described her to soundman Craig Montgomery as his "girlfriend." Two weeks after New York she came to Ohio, only to discover Kurt in a meltdown. He was sitting on a pool table, kicking his legs and cursing. "What's wrong?" she asked. "Everything," he replied. "Nobody can get the fucking sound right. This fucking sucks. I've been doing this for so fucking long. And the show fucking sucked. I couldn't hear myself at all." Used to busking on the subway for quarters, she told him to enjoy his success, but she was unable to cheer him. "I'm tired of this fucking shit, these fucking ratholes," he announced. What she didn't know was that Kurt was suffering from drug withdrawal. It was a dirty secret he hadn't told Lord or his bandmates. She followed the tour for two more dates, but in Detroit, on the morning of October 12, she left to return to her job at a record store in Boston. Kurt and the band headed for Chicago and a show at the Metro.

On that same morning of October 12 Courtney Love boarded a plane in Los Angeles and flew to Chicago to visit Billy Corgan. Love and Corgan had a tempestuous relationship—she was more enthralled by the love letters he wrote than his actual presence. When she arrived at his apartment, she found him unexpectedly back with another girlfriend. A ruckus ensued and Courtney fled amidst a hail of shoes.

She spent her last $10 on a cab to the Metro, where she was surprised to find Nirvana on the bill. After talking her way past the doorman, she called Corgan from a pay phone: In later tellings, she'd claim the call was to make sure she was completely broken off with Billy before becoming romantically involved with Kurt. Corgan told her he couldn't see her, and she slammed down the phone.

All the signs of Courtney and Kurt's sexual attraction had been present in earlier meetings, just not the opportunity. She watched the final fifteen minutes of Nirvana's set, which basically involved Kurt smashing the drum kit, all the time wondering what made this boy so angry. He was a mystery to her, and Courtney was attracted by the unexplained. She was not the only woman to fall under this spell. As Carrie Montgomery observed: "Kurt made women want to nurture and protect him. He was a paradox in that way, because he also could be brutally and intensely strong; yet at the same time he could appear fragile and delicate."

After the show she made her way to a backstage party, where she beelined for Kurt: "I watched her walk across the room and sit on his lap," recalled manager Danny Goldberg. Kurt was happy to see her, and particularly happy when she asked to stay at his hotel. If Kurt was bad about confessing past romantic entanglements, Courtney was his equal in this department, and she told him the whole sorry tale of the fight with Corgan. As they conversed, Kurt was reminded of the "coolest girl in the world" description he had bestowed on her after that long talk in Los Angeles five months before. They left the club together and walked along Lake Michigan, eventually ending up at the Days Inn.

The sex, as Kurt later described it to his friends, was amazing. He told Courtney he could count his previous lovers on one hand. She was as shocked by this fact as anything else he said; she came from a Sunset Strip world where sex was as casually offered as a ride home from a gig. Courtney was also surprised to see that Kurt wore zebra-striped briefs for underwear. "You have got to get boxers," she told him.

But their bond, even in that post-intercourse languor, was considerably more than sexual—it was an emotional connection, one that none of their friends or bandmates understood. Ironically, Kurt's confidantes thought he was slumming to become involved with her; Courtney's friends felt the same about her dating him. Their individual stories had a familiar feel, and when Courtney described a childhood that included neglect, being shuttled between divorced parents, and struggles in school, it was a terrain Kurt knew. She was the first woman he'd ever met that when he told her the stories of his youth—mythologized at this point beyond simple exaggeration—she responded by saying, "I can top that." It became almost a game of "Who had the worst childhood?" but in their union Kurt felt a normalcy about his life.

Like anyone, what Kurt wanted most in a partner was unconditional love; but that night in the Days Inn he discovered something else in Courtney that had eluded him in other relationships—understanding. He felt Courtney intrinsically knew the smell of the shit he'd crawled through. Mary Lou Lord had liked the Vaselines, but she had never lived in a cardboard box. Tracy, for all her unwavering love of Kurt, had always been accepted by her family, even when she did something as crazy as date a punk rocker from Aberdeen. Kurt had tried everything to make Tobi love him, but their paths had been so different he couldn't even make her understand his nightmares, much less the reason he did drugs. But Courtney knew the gelatinous flavor of surplus government cheese given out with food stamps; she knew what it was like to tour in a van and struggle for gas money; and during her time working as a stripper, at "Jumbo's Clown Room," she had come to understand degradation of a sort not many people taste. Both of them later joked that their bonding was over narcotics—and it would certainly include drugs—but the initial attraction was something far deeper than a shared desire to escape: It was, instead, the very fact that Courtney Love, like Kurt Cobain, had something to escape from.

They parted that next morning, Kurt continuing on the tour, and Courtney heading back to Los Angeles. But over the next week, they exchanged faxes and phone calls, and were soon chatting every day. Despite Nirvana's success, Kurt was not happy on the road, and bitched constantly about the state of their van, the "rat-hole" clubs, and a new complaint—the frat boys who were now coming to their shows after seeing the band's video on MTV. Some in the Nirvana camp initially greeted Courtney's involvement with Kurt enthusiastically—at least he had someone to talk to (he was communicating with Novoselic and Grohl less and less).

In Dallas, on October 19, Kurt went into meltdown mode again, this time onstage. The show was doomed from the start because it was oversold and the audience spilled onto the stage. Frustrated, Kurt destroyed a monitor console by whacking his guitar against it. When a few minutes later he dived into the crowd, a bouncer named Turner Van Blarcum attempted to help him back onstage, which Kurt mistakenly read as an aggressive act. He responded by smashing the butt end of his guitar on Van Blarcum's head, drawing blood. It was a blow that might have killed a smaller man, but it only stunned Van Blarcum, who punched Kurt in the head, and kicked him as the singer fled. The audience began to riot. Kurt hid upstairs in a closet until promoter Jeff Liles finally convinced him Van Blarcum had gone to the hospital and could do him no harm. "I know he had drunk a ton of cough syrup that night," Liles explained. Kurt finally reappeared and finished the set.

But the action was far from over. After the show, Liles managed to get the band into a waiting cab, which sped off only to come right back: No one in the band knew what hotel they were in. Just as the cab returned, so did Van Blarcum—complete with a bloody bandage on his head. He shattered the taxi windows with his fist as the driver frantically tried to pull away. The cab escaped, but as they drove off—with no destination still—the members of Nirvana sat in the backseat covered with broken glass. This was not an isolated event—the band's road manager soon found himself paying out thousands of dollars every week to cover damages caused by the band.

A week later Kurt was reunited with Courtney at a pro-choice benefit in Los Angeles. Backstage they seemed very much together, and many remarked how they made the perfect rock 'n' roll couple. Yet later in the evening, behind closed doors, their relationship took a more destructive bent. For the first time, Kurt brought up the idea of doing heroin. Courtney paused for a moment, but then agreed. They scored dope, went to his hotel, the Beverly Garland, prepared the drugs, and he injected her—Courtney couldn't stand to handle a needle herself, so Kurt, the former needle-phobe, handled things for himself and her. After getting high they went out walking and came upon a dead bird. Kurt pulled three feathers off the animal and passed one to Courtney, holding the two others in his hand. "This is for you, this is for me," he said. And then holding the third feather in his hand he added, "and this is for our baby we're gonna have." She laughed and later remembered this as the point when she first fell in love with him.

But Kurt already had another mistress. By the fall of 1991 heroin was no longer a recreational weekend escape for him and was instead part of an ongoing daily addiction. He had "decided" several months before he met Courtney to become a "junkie," as he wrote in his journal. Later, Kurt sat down and, for the sake of a treatment program he was enrolled in, detailed his entire drug history. It begins:

> When I got back from our second European tour with Sonic Youth, I decided to use heroine on a daily basis because of an ongoing stomach ailment that I had been suffering from for the past five years, [and that] had literally taken me to the point of wanting to kill myself. For five years, every single day of my life, every time I swallowed a piece of food, I would experience an excruciating, burning, nauseous pain in the upper part of my stomach lining. The pain became even more severe on tour, due to lack of a proper and regimented eating schedule and diet. Since the beginning of this disorder, I've had ten upper and lower gastrointestinal procedures, which found an enflamed irritation in the same place. I consulted 15 different doctors, and tried about 50 different types of ulcer medication. The only thing I found that worked were heavy opiates. There were many times that I found myself literally incapacitated, in bed for weeks, vomiting and starving. So I decided, if I feel like a junkie as it is, I may as well be one.

What was extraordinary about Kurt's recounting of his journey into addiction was his consciousness regarding the choices involved. He wrote of his addiction as a "decision," one undertaken because of the suicidal thoughts he had after chronic stomach pain. His timing put the start of his full-fledged addiction at the beginning of September 1991, the month of the release of *Nevermind*.

Courtney had struggled with drug addiction herself during the summer of 1989, when heroin had been the rage in the Los Angeles rock scene: She had used 12-Step groups and Buddhist chanting to help her break her habit. But her sobriety was tenuous by October 1991, the main reason friends like Jennifer Finch warned her to stay away from Kurt. Love's drug issues were different from Kurt's—to her, heroin was a social drug, and the very fact that she couldn't stand to inject herself was a barrier to daily abuse. But because Courtney had previously struggled with the drug, many in the rock community gossiped that she had gotten him hooked on drugs, when in many ways the opposite was true. "People blame Courtney, that Courtney turned him on to heroin, but that's not true," asserted Krist. "He did it before he even met Courtney. Courtney did not get Kurt on drugs."

After their first night doing heroin together, he came by the next evening and wanted to get high again. "I had a rule about not doing drugs two nights in a row," Courtney recalled, "that that was bad. And I said, 'No, that's not going to happen.' So he left."

The third night, Kurt phoned her, sobbing, and asked if she could come over. When Courtney arrived at the hotel, she found him shaking uncontrollably, having a breakdown. "I had to put him in the bath," she remembered. "He was about to get famous, and it freaked him out. And he was really thin and skinny. And I had to sort of pick him up with my arms because he collapsed. He wasn't on drugs. But he went back and pouted because I wouldn't do heroin with him." Courtney did heroin with him again that night. "I'm not saying it was his fault, but I am saying that there was a choice I made. I thought, 'I'll go back to this, I guess.' "

As Nirvana continued with the *Nevermind* tour, record sales increased exponentially. Each morning, as their tour progressed up the West Coast, they would hear a new report of the latest figures. The album had sold 100,000 copies by San Diego, 200,000 by L.A., and by the morning they hit Seattle, for a Halloween show, it had gone gold, selling half a million. Just over a month before, Kurt had been destroying Nelson gold records in a microwave—soon he would have one of his own.

But despite the attention and his mushrooming fame, that afternoon Kurt had other pressing concerns—he was out of socks. He and Carrie Montgomery walked from the theater to Bon Marché. In the department store, Kurt selected several pair of underwear (he was now buying boxers) and socks (white). When he brought his purchases to the counter, a scene worthy of a Samuel Beckett play unfolded: "He starts taking off his shoes and socks to get the rest of his money out," recalled

Carrie. "He's got these crumpled bills in his shoe. He is literally dump-ing his shoe out on the counter in the Bon, and the salesperson is looking at him like he's insane. In this crotchety, old, crusty way, he starts unfolding these bills, and it took him forever to count them out. He had to reach into another pocket to find more. There's this big pile of lint on the counter next to his money. The salesman, in a suit, is looking at Kurt as if he were a homeless person." Despite his gold record, Kurt *was* still homeless—staying in hotels or with friends like Carrie when the band wasn't touring.

That evening's show was a blur for Kurt: With a documentary crew filming, media attention, radio promo people, and his family and friends backstage, it seemed like everywhere he turned, someone was asking him for something. He had complicated matters by two of his own decisions: He invited Bikini Kill to open the show, so Tobi was around, plus he had convinced Ian Dickson and Nikki McClure to act as go-go dancers in full body suits—his said "girl," and hers said "boy." When the camera operators kept pushing Kurt's dancers out of the way, he became frustrated and it showed in his performance. *The Rocket* review noted: "These guys are already rich and famous, but they still represent a pure distillation of what it's like to be unsatisfied in life."

After the show, Kurt looked shell-shocked. "He reminded me of a cat in a cage," observed photographer Darrell Westmoreland. When Westmoreland posed Kurt with his sister Kim, Kurt yanked her hair at the moment the shutter snapped. "He was all pissed off and being a dick," Kim recalled.

But the strangest moments of the day were reserved—as at the Bee-hive in-store—for a couple of ghosts Kurt couldn't escape. Later in the evening, he hung out with Tobi, and she ended up sleeping on the floor of his hotel room. She wasn't the only one in his room—like always, there were a half dozen friends who needed a place to crash—but it was no small irony that Tobi was sleeping on his floor the day he'd sold half a million copies of an album that was ostensibly about how she didn't love him.

And after the show, Kurt ran into another familiar face from the harbor. There, standing by the stage door smoking pot with Matt Lukin, was Steve Shillinger, once one of Kurt's closest friends and a member of the family that had given him shelter when he was sleeping in a cardboard box. Shillinger spoke the words that were now painfully obvious to Kurt no matter how much he wanted to deny them: "You're really famous now, Cobain. You are on television, like, every three hours."

"I didn't really notice," Kurt said, pausing for a moment to search for the classic "Cling-On" comeback that would disarm this condition of fame, as if words alone could halt something that was now unstoppable. "I don't know about that," Kurt replied, sounding very young. "I don't have a TV in the car I live in."

16 BRUSH YOUR TEETH

SEATTLE, WASHINGTON
OCTOBER 1991–JANUARY 1992

Please don't forget to eat your vegetables or brush your teeth.
—From a letter Kurt's mom wrote the *Aberdeen Daily World*.

The real substance of the courtship of Kurt and
Courtney commenced during November 1991, when Nirvana began
another tour of Europe, and Hole followed two weeks later, playing
many of the same venues. The two lovers would talk on the phone
every night, send faxes, or leave cryptic messages written on the dressing
room walls. Their inside joke was that when he called her, he pretended
to be funk-rocker Lenny Kravitz. When Courtney called, she claimed
to be Kravitz's once-wife, "Cosby Show" actress Lisa Bonet. This
led to much confusion for hotel night managers, who might be instructed to immediately stick a certain fax under the door of a room
that they knew very well did not contain Lenny Kravitz. "That's when
we started really falling in love—on the phone," Kurt told Michael
Azerrad. "We called each other almost every night and faxed each other
every other day. I had, like, a $3,000 phone bill."

Yet while this love affair by fax was evolving, Kurt had unfinished
business to attend to, something he was always wretched at. After Nirvana finished their first U.K. show, in Bristol, he was astounded to find
Mary Lou Lord backstage. She had flown over to surprise him, something she did with aplomb. She knew from that instant something was
wrong: He was different, and it wasn't just his level of fame, though
this too was in marked contrast to even a month before. A month prior,

in Boston, Kurt could walk around without being bothered; now he had someone tugging at his sleeve every minute. At one point, a record company rep grabbed Kurt to announce: "We've just sold 50,000 units this week." For the United Kingdom, it was a remarkable statistic, but Kurt responded by looking perplexed: Was there something he was supposed to *do* about this?

The next day Lord inquired: "Have you met someone else?" "I'm just tired," he lied. She chalked it up to his stomach, which he was complaining about famously, asserting it hurt worse than ever. That night, the phone in his room rang at three in the morning: It was Courtney, but Kurt never announced this. A DJ had told Courtney that Kurt's "girlfriend" was Mary Lou Lord. "Kurt's girlfriend?" Courtney had yelled back, close to tears. "*I'm* Kurt's girlfriend." The first words out of Courtney's mouth on the phone were, "Who the *fuck* is Mary Lou Lord, and why are people saying she's your girlfriend?" Courtney's voice swirled around Lord's name as if it were a particularly bad case of parasites. Kurt managed to deny having a relationship with Mary Lou without mentioning her name directly, since she was four feet away as he spoke. Love told Kurt, in no uncertain terms, that if she ever heard about a Mary Lou Lord again, they were history. The next morning, Kurt coldly asked Lord how she was getting to London—she discerned that in asking, he was as good as announcing they were kaput.

A day later Lord was watching a television program called "The Word," where Nirvana were making a much-touted appearance. Prior to playing an abbreviated 90-second version of "Teen Spirit," Kurt grabbed the microphone and, in a dry monotone that sounded like he was ordering lunch, uttered: "I just want everyone in this room to know that Courtney Love, of the pop group Hole, is the best fuck in the world." His words, as he well knew, went out far beyond the room. A British television audience of millions gasped, though the loudest sounds had to come from Mary Lou Lord, who was beside herself.

Kurt was already the subject of considerable media coverage in the U.K., but this one declarative statement got him more attention than anything he uttered in his career—not since John Lennon had asserted the Beatles were bigger than Jesus Christ had a rock star so outraged the British public. Kurt's intention wasn't to increase his infamy—instead, he had simply chosen this television show to tell Lord it was over, and to pledge his love to Courtney. His review of Love's sexual abilities accomplished something he most certainly didn't intend—it moved him from the front page of the music weeklies to the front page of the daily tabloids. Combined with the phenomenal sales of *Nevermind*, what he *said* now became news. He both embraced this turn of events and cursed it, depending on whether it was working to his advantage.

Three weeks later, on November 28, the day *Nevermind* hit sales of one million in the U.S., the band appeared on another highly rated British television show, "Top of the Pops." The producers had insisted Nirvana play "Teen Spirit," and the program required performers to sing live vocals over a backing track—just a step up from lip-syncing. Kurt hatched a plan with Novoselic and Grohl to make a mockery of their performance. As the backing track played, Kurt sang the vocals in a slowed-down, almost Vegas-like lounge version; he was attempting, he later claimed, to sound like Morrissey.

The producers were furious, but Nirvana escaped their wrath by quickly departing for a gig in Sheffield. As they drove away, Kurt smiled for the first time that day. "He was highly amused," observed Alex MacLeod. "There was no question that they were the biggest thing happening in music. And he took advantage of that. He knew he had the power."

If audacity was Kurt's occasional vice, it was in daily orbit around Courtney. In this came a small part of his adoration for her. She walked into most social settings with all the grace of a wolverine thrown into a henhouse, yet simultaneously she could be witty and funny. Even those in the Nirvana crew and organization who disliked her—and there were many in this category—found her entertaining.

Kurt was by nature a voyeur and loved nothing better than to create a ruckus, sit back, and watch it unfold. But when Courtney was in a room—particularly a room backstage at a venue—people simply could not take their eyes off her, least of all Kurt. Few were foolish enough to take Courtney on in a game of verbal one-upmanship, and those who did found she could sarcastically skewer even the quickest-witted opponent. Kurt had a major attachment to being a bad boy, and thus required a bad girl. Even though he knew at best Courtney would be but a dark hero, he loved her all the more for it. "He worked out some of his aggression through her," explained Carolyn Rue, Hole's drummer. "He got off on it, vicariously, because he didn't have the courage to do it himself. He needed her to be his mouthpiece. He was passive-aggressive." Love, for her part, was simply aggressive, a characteristic that earned her many cruel reviews in a punk rock world that, despite declarations of equality, was still male-dominated and had defined roles for how even liberated females were to act. When Courtney coupled with Kurt, the press accused her of hooking up to a rising star. And while that charge was essentially true, the gossip failed to note that Hole's early reviews were as glowing as Nirvana's. Kurt was more famous than she was in November 1991, and Courtney's friends had warned her not to get involved with him because of the likelihood his career would overshadow hers. But being self-possessed, she didn't consider that possible, and was offended when such suggestions were offered. Truth was, they were *both* ambitious, which was part of their attraction toward each other.

Though theirs was an unusual love story, at points it touched on traditional sentiment. Some of the faxes they sent were X-rated, but others were straight out of a dime-store romance. As writers, they were attempting to win the other's heart. One fax of Courtney's from early November read: "I want to be somewhere above you with all the candy in my hands. You smell like waffles and milk. . . . I love and miss your body, and your twenty-minute kisses."

Both parties in this union were also self-effacing to a degree that approximated stand-up comedy. Close intimates told tales of their debauched senses of humor, something the public rarely saw. That fall Courtney wrote a list of Kurt's "most annoying traits," and her insights were both wicked and flirty: "1. Plays cutesy with journalists and they all fall for it all the time. 2. Plays helpless cutesy punk hero for teenage fans who already think he is a God anyway, and don't need anymore convincing. 3. Has the entire world convinced that he is humble and shy and modest when, in fact, he is a secret big-mouthed narcissist which is why I love him anyway but no one knows but me. 4. Is a Pisces, and the object of my intense desires and repulsions at once." She ended another fax by promising to buy him flowers every day when she hit it rich. Many of her faxes contained lines that years later ended up in her best-known songs. "I am doll parts, bad skin, doll hearts, it stands for knife, for the rest of my life, peel my little heart off and soak it in your left hand and call me tonight," she faxed on November 8. Other messages were simple and sweet: "Please comb your hair tonight, and remember I love you," she wrote one night.

He sent her copies of Oscar Wilde's *The Picture of Dorian Gray* and Emily Brontë's *Wuthering Heights,* and faxes that were equally romantic, though owing to his essential strangeness, much of what he wrote was also just plain weird. He frequently obsessed on his favorite off-color topics: human waste, "butt-fucking," birth, babies, and drugs. He reveled in the possibility that their indiscretions might make the tabloids. One fax he sent in mid-November spoke to a greater truth. It began with Courtney's name inside a heart and read:

> Oh, stinking, bloody cum. I'm hallucinating way too often. I need oxygen. Thank Satan, we've found a script-happy doctor who's willing to call-in prescriptions whenever the handler can't score on the street. I think I'm getting some kind of clammy mold, skin disease because I keep passing out in the wee hours of morning covered in little boy blood and wearing the same sweaty clothes that I had worn from the show the night before. Little Oliver, the Indian boy I bought last week, is becoming quite the professional nurse except the needles he uses are so big that it makes my arms swell up like golf balls. I mean, snooker balls. He's also a lot better at sucking my cable now that I've bashed his teeth out. Guido is sending that receptionist at the hotel a fish tomorrow. I hope she's a good swimmer. I love you. I miss you. P.S.: I've convinced Lenny Kravitz that the baby is his and he's willing to pay for the abortion. Love me.

He signed the letter with a fish. Of course, he didn't have an Indian boy love-slave, and there was no November pregnancy. The addiction he spoke of, though, was real and he had found a British physician to prescribe pharmaceutical morphine.

Courtney was infatuated enough that by the end of November, after not seeing Kurt for two weeks, she uncharacteristically cancelled a Hole gig and flew to Amsterdam. There, they bought heroin and spent the day nodding out and having lazy sex. Courtney didn't do drugs just because she loved Kurt—she had her own demons worthy of running from—but she rarely did drugs when he wasn't around. Around Kurt she dropped all boundaries as she was well aware that to be in an intimate relationship with him meant living in an opiate-soaked world of escapism. She chose Kurt and, in doing so, chose drugs.

After Amsterdam and a brief stop in London she rejoined the Hole tour, and Nirvana continued their U.K. dates. Not since the Sex Pistols had a band on the road gotten so much attention. Every show contained something newsworthy, or at least something that got them in the papers. In Edinburgh, they played an acoustic show to benefit a children's hospital. In Newcastle, Kurt announced from the stage, "I am a homosexual, I am a drug user, and I fuck pot-bellied pigs," another classic Cobainism, though only one of his three claims was true. By the time the tour hit London again, Kurt was incapacitated by stomach pain and decided to cancel six dates in Scandinavia. Considering the state of his health and the increasing state of his addiction, it was a wise call.

While Kurt was in Europe, his mother had written a letter to the *Aberdeen Daily World*. It represented the first mention of Kurt in his hometown paper since his Little League team won the Timber League championship the year his parents divorced. The letter ran under the headline LOCAL "TWANGER" MAKES GOOD, MOM REPORTS:

> This letter is directed more or less to all of you parents out there who have kids bangin' or twangin' away on drums or guitars out in your garage or up in their rooms. Watch what you say, for you may have to eat every one of those concerned parental lecturing words. Like, "Get a life." "Your music is good but chances of mak-

ing it are slim to none." "Further your education, then if you still want to play in a band you can, but if it doesn't work out you'll have something to fall back on." Do those words sound familiar?

Well, I just received a phone call from my son, Kurt Cobain, who sings and plays guitar with the band "Nirvana." They are presently touring Europe. Their first album with Geffen Record Co., just went "Platinum" (over one million sales). They are No. 4 on the Top 200 albums in *Billboard*. Well, I know the chances of making it are still slim-to-none for many, but two boys who never lost sight of their goals, Kurt and [Krist] Novoselic, have something to really smile about these days. The hours and hours and hours of practice have paid off.

Kurt, if you happen to read this, we are so proud of you and you are truly one of the nicest sons a mother could have. Please don't forget to eat your vegetables or brush your teeth and now [that] you have your maid make your bed.

—Wendy O'Connor, Aberdeen

Kurt didn't read the *Aberdeen Daily World*, rarely in his entire life did he eat vegetables, and his drug addiction was so bad by December 1991 that he usually taped a note to his hotel room door warning the maids not to enter—if they did, they frequently found him passed out. He also, strangely, did not brush his teeth, one of the reasons he had a gum infection during the *Nevermind* album cover sessions. "Kurt hated to brush his teeth," said Carrie Montgomery. "Still, his teeth never looked gnarly and he never had bad breath." Carrie recalled Kurt telling her eating apples worked as well as brushing.

On December 21, Kurt, Carrie, and a group of friends planned a trip to Portland to see the Pixies. Kurt had rented a Pontiac Grand Am for the long drive, worrying his Valiant wouldn't handle the distance. He rarely drove the Valiant, putting only 3,000 miles on it the first year he owned it. Instead, he used it as a mobile hotel room, occasionally sleeping in the backseat and storing all his possessions in the trunk. His friends met up with him in Aberdeen, where Kurt had gone to get a meal of his mother's pot roast.

The dynamic within the house on First Street had undergone a continental shift since Kurt's last visit to Aberdeen: He was being treated, for the first time since early childhood, like the most important person in Wendy's life. Even Kurt was struck by the hypocrisy of the situation, especially when he saw his stepfather, Pat O'Connor, kiss up to him: It was like a bad episode of "All in the Family," where Meathead is given Archie's beloved La-Z-Boy. When his friends arrived, they stayed long enough for Kurt to give his six-year-old half-sister Brianne some art supplies—he adored her—before they quickly departed.

The next day Courtney arrived in Seattle, and Carrie was recruited to act as a buffer when Courtney went to visit Kurt's family. They first met at Maximilien's, a fine French restaurant, in the Pike Place Market to strategize how to handle this important introduction. When Courtney got up to go to the bathroom, Kurt asked Carrie what she thought of his new love. "You guys are like a natural disaster," she replied. Carrie was one of Kurt's only female friends, so she had a rare perspective on their union. "I enjoyed being around them in the way it was interesting to watch a car crash," she observed.

When Courtney returned, another diner inquired, "Are you guys Sid and Nancy?" Kurt and Carrie looked at each other, both knowing that Courtney was about to erupt. Love stood up and yelled: "My husband has the number-one record in the entire country, and he has more money than any of you people ever will have!" He was, of course, not her husband, and he also didn't have a number-one record—it was at No. 6 that week—but her point was clear. The waiter came running, and the sarcastic patron ran for cover. Despite this outburst, and in part because of it, Carrie found Courtney bright and funny, and thought they made a sweet couple. The trip to Aberdeen went well, and Wendy liked Courtney and told Kurt she was good for him. "They were like clones, glued to each other," Wendy later told writer Tim Appelo. "He was probably the only person who loved her totally and completely unconditionally."

One week later, Kurt and the other members of Nirvana headed back out on the road, with Courtney in tow, for another tour. They were playing their biggest arenas to date—20,000-seat halls—but since the tour was booked before the album exploded, they had the middle slot on a three-band bill. Pearl Jam was opening—they were just beginning to become stars themselves—while the Red Hot Chili Peppers headlined.

Before the December 27 date at the Los Angeles Sports Arena, Kurt conducted an interview with *BAM* magazine's Jerry McCully. McCully's piece caused a sensation, if only because his description of Kurt was consistent with the rumors that had begun to circulate about drugs. McCully wrote that Kurt kept "nodding off occasionally in midsentence." The article never mentioned heroin, but the writer's description of Kurt's "pinned pupils; sunken cheeks; and scabbed, sallow skin" was concerning. He described Kurt as looking "more like 40 than 24."

When he wasn't nodding off, Kurt was surprisingly lucid about his career. "I wanted to at least sell enough records to be able to eat macaroni and cheese, so I didn't have to have a job," he declared. He mentioned Aberdeen—he rarely did an interview without discussing the city, as if it were a lover he'd left behind—and pronounced, "ninety-nine percent of the people [there] had no idea what music was, or art." He claimed the reason he didn't become a logger was because "I was really a small kid." While he didn't manage to get his "punk rock is freedom" line in print, he did assert, "To mature, to me . . . is to wimp out. . . . [I] hope I die before I turn into Pete Townshend." He was making a play on Townshend's "I hope I die before I get old" from "My Generation," and perhaps in a nod to this, he opened the show with the Who's "Baba O'Riley."

As shocking as Kurt's appearance was, his announcement of future plans was the real surprise: "I'm getting married, and that's a total revelation—emotionally, that is. I've never felt so secure in my life, and so happy. It's like I have no inhibitions anymore. It's like I'm drained of feeling really insecure. I guess getting married has a lot to do with security and keeping your mind straight. My future wife's and my personalities are so volatile that I think if we were to get into a fight, we'd split just like that. Getting married is an extra bit of security." He ended the interview with another forecast: "There are plenty of things I would like to do when I'm older. At least, just have a family, that would satisfy me."

Kurt and Courtney had become engaged in December while lying in bed in a London hotel. Before speaking with McCully, Kurt hadn't made a formal announcement, but everyone else in the band already knew. No date had been set, since betrothal or not, the business of Nirvana couldn't be put on hold for anything.

Nirvana ended 1991 with a New Year's Eve show at San Francisco's Cow Palace. Pearl Jam opened the night with a bit of "Smells Like Teen Spirit," and Eddie Vedder joked, "Remember we played it first." This crack was an acknowledgment of something everyone in the building knew: As 1992 began, Nirvana was the biggest band in the world, and "Teen Spirit" was the biggest song. Keanu Reeves was at the concert and attempted to befriend Kurt, who rebuffed the efforts. Later that night at their hotel, Kurt and Courtney were so harassed by other guests they put a sign on their door: "No Famous People Please. We're Fucking."

By the time the group made it to Salem, Oregon, for the last date of the tour, *Nevermind* had been certified for sales of two million copies and was selling at an ever-accelerating pace. Every direction Kurt turned, someone was asking him for something—an endorsement deal, an interview, an autograph. Backstage, Kurt briefly caught the eye of Jeremy Wilson, the lead singer of the Dharma Bums, a Portland band Kurt admired. Wilson waved to Kurt, not wanting to interrupt him from a woman trying to convince him to appear in an ad for guitar strings. As Wilson walked away, Kurt screamed "Jeremy!" and fell into Wilson's arms. Kurt didn't say a word, he just rested in Wilson's bear hug as Jeremy repeated, "It's going to be okay." Kurt wasn't sobbing, but he didn't seem far from it. "It wasn't just a short hug," recalled Wilson. "He was there for a full 30 seconds." Finally a handler grabbed Kurt and dragged him to another meeting.

After a couple of days off in Seattle, Kurt's spirits seemed to improve. On Monday, January 6, 1992, super-fan Rob Kader was riding his bike down Pine Street when he suddenly heard someone shout his name. It was Kurt, walking with Courtney. Kader congratulated Kurt on the success of the album and the news Nirvana was to be on "Saturday

Night Live." But as soon as Kader said the words, he knew he'd made a mistake—Kurt's warm mood turned sour. Two years earlier, when Kader had congratulated Kurt on the fact that twenty people had come to a Community World Theater show—two more than their previous gig—Kurt greeted the news with a beaming smile. By the beginning of 1992, the last thing he wanted to hear was how popular he was.

That next week, Kurt's fame was amped up considerably as the band flew to New York City to be the musical guests on "Saturday Night Live." Kurt's mood seemed upbeat in their Thursday rehearsal as they ran through some of their early songs. Still, everyone knew that on the show, they had to play "Teen Spirit," no matter how much Kurt had grown tired of the hit.

He had paid for his mother and Carrie Montgomery to fly to New York with him. When the rest of the Nirvana crew met Wendy for the first time, he was again razzed. "Everybody was always saying, 'Wow, Kurt, your mom is hot,'" recalled Carrie. It was the last thing Kurt wanted to hear; it was even more grating than being told how famous he was.

While Kurt rehearsed, Courtney, Carrie, and Wendy went clothes shopping. Later, Kurt went shopping for drugs, which were as easy to find in New York as a sale on dresses. In Alphabet City, Kurt was shocked to find lines of customers waiting for the man, just like in the Velvet Underground song. He was in love with the ritual of using now, and seductively drawn to the seamy netherworld it brought him into. The China white heroin in New York City (West Coast heroin was always black tar) made him feel sophisticated, and it was cheaper and more powerful. Kurt became gluttonous.

That Friday, when Wendy knocked on the door of her son's room at noon, he answered in his underwear, looking like hell. Courtney was still under the covers. There were deli trays everywhere, and after just two days in the suite, the floor was covered with refuse. "Kurt, why don't you get a maid in here?" Wendy asked. "He can't," Courtney replied. "They steal his underwear."

The week marked a turning point in Kurt's relationship with the band and crew. Up until then, everyone was aware that Kurt was messed up—and Courtney had usually been the scapegoat for Kurt's increasingly sour attitude. But by New York, it was clear it was Kurt who was on a self-destructive course, and that he had all the hallmarks of an active addict. Though everyone knew Kurt was abusing drugs—they assumed heroin—no one knew what to do about it. It was hard enough to convince Kurt to do a soundcheck or comb his hair, much less get him to listen to advice regarding his private affairs. Kurt and Courtney moved to a different hotel from the rest of the entourage; they were only a few blocks away, but the action would serve as a metaphor for a growing divisiveness inside the band. "By that time," Carrie recalled, "there had already been a separation within the Nirvana camp between the 'good' people, and the 'bad' people. Kurt, Courtney, and myself were the bad people. We had this feeling of not being welcomed, and it got more negative."

Nirvana's managers were also at a loss for what to do. "It was a very dark time," said Danny Goldberg. "It was the first time I was aware of him having a drug problem." At the same time Gold Mountain was working to get attention for the band's appearance on "Saturday Night Live," his managers were privately praying Kurt's drug problem wouldn't embarrass them or derail their growing financial success. "I was just hoping that things wouldn't spin out of control publicly," recalled Goldberg.

And then, as if things weren't turbulent enough, the news came that in the next issue of *Billboard* magazine, *Nevermind* would hit the No. 1 spot, pushing out Michael Jackson's *Dangerous*. Though *Nevermind* had been hovering near No. 6 all December, it had bounced to the top based on sales of 373,520 the week after Christmas. Many of those purchases came in an unusual manner, according to Tower Records' Bob Zimmerman: "We saw an incredible number of kids returning the CDs their parents had given them for Christmas, and buying *Nevermind* in exchange, or using money they'd gotten as a present to buy the CD." *Nevermind* may be the first record to ever hit No. 1 buoyed by exchanges.

That Friday Kurt and Courtney did an interview for the cover story of *Sassy*, a teen magazine. Kurt had turned down requests from the *New York Times* and *Rolling Stone*, yet he'd agreed to this piece because he felt the magazine was so silly. After the interview, they rushed off for a filming at MTV. But Kurt didn't feel well and what was scheduled to be an hour show ended after 35 minutes. Kurt asked Amy Finnerty, "Can you get me out of here?" He wanted to visit the Museum of Modern Art.

His mood picked up considerably once he was inside the MOMA— it was the first time he'd ever visited a major museum. Finnerty had a hard time keeping up as Kurt dashed from wing to wing. He stopped when an African-American fan approached and asked for an autograph. "Hey man, I love your record," the guy said. Kurt had been asked for his autograph a hundred times that day, but this was the only time he responded with a smile. Kurt told Finnerty, "No one black has ever said they liked my record before."

After the museum, Kurt returned to NBC for yet another "Saturday Night Live" rehearsal. This time the show's producers wanted the band to perform only the songs they were going to do on the broadcast, so Nirvana played "Teen Spirit" and "Territorial Pissings." This second choice was not to the network's liking and a debate ensued. Kurt had enough of working for the day and departed.

On Saturday afternoon, the day of the television show, the band had a photo session scheduled at Michael Lavine's studio. Kurt arrived but was so high he kept falling asleep while standing up. He complained that he felt ill. "He was so messed up at that one," Lavine recalled, "he couldn't keep his eyes open."

By early January Kurt was so seriously addicted to heroin that a normal dose no longer made him feel euphoric: Like all addicts, he needed an increasing daily supply simply to stop withdrawal symptoms. But New York heroin was powerful, and Kurt was using more than was prudent in an attempt to reach euphoria. He had decided to shoot up early that Saturday so he'd be functional by the time "Saturday Night Live" began. In his attempt to properly regulate his dose—an impossible task from one bag of heroin to the next—he had taken too much and was in a stupor by the afternoon. By the time the band drove to NBC, Kurt was outside the studio throwing up. He spent the hours before the show lying on a sofa, ignoring host Rob Morrow, and refusing to sign an autograph for the daughter of NBC's president. His only joy came when he talked on the phone to "Weird Al" Yankovic and agreed to a parody of "Teen Spirit." By showtime, he was sober again, and miserable.

Before their first number, there was a noticeable hush in the studio as Morrow introduced the band. Kurt looked awful—his complexion was pasty, a bad dye-job left his hair the color of raspberry jam, and he appeared moments away from barfing, which he was. But as happened many times during his life, with his back against the wall, he responded with an admirable performance. As Kurt launched into the first "Teen Spirit" guitar solo, "Saturday Night Live" bandleader G. E. Smith turned to Nirvana's soundman Craig Montgomery and said, "Jesus, that guy can sure play."

While it was not the best version of "Teen Spirit" Nirvana ever played, there was enough raw energy in the song to survive even a lackluster performance and still sound revolutionary. It worked on live television because the appearance of the band told half the story of the song: Krist bopped around with his beard and long hair, resembling a mad, elongated Jim Morrison; Grohl, shirtless, pounded the drums with the spirit of John Bonham; and Kurt looked possessed. Kurt may not have been at 100 percent, but anyone watching the broadcast knew he was pissed off about something. The kid who spent his youth playing with Super-8 movies knew how to sell himself to the camera, and in both his aloofness and intensity he was mesmerizing to watch.

When the band came back for the next number, it was all about catharsis. They played "Territorial Pissings," against the producer's wishes, and ended with the destruction of their instruments. Kurt began the assault by puncturing a speaker with his guitar; Grohl knocked his drum set off the riser; and Krist threw the drums in the air. It was certainly calculated, but the anger and frustration weren't faked. In one final "fuck you" to America, as the program's credits rolled, Kurt and Krist French-kissed (NBC would edit this ending out in all repeat broadcasts, fearing it was offensive). Kurt later claimed the kiss was his idea, done to piss off "the rednecks and homophobes" back in Aberdeen, but in truth he had refused to come out for the final good-bye until Krist pulled him onstage. "I walked right up to him," Krist remembered, "and grabbed him and stuck my tongue in his mouth, kissing him. I just wanted to make him feel better. At the end of it all, I told him, 'It's going to be okay. It's not so bad. Okay?' " Though Kurt Cobain had just won over the few youths in America who weren't already in love with him, he didn't feel like a conqueror. He felt, as he did most days, like crap.

Kurt skipped the SNL cast party and quickly left the studio. He was scheduled to do an interview, but as usual he was hours late. Amy Finnerty was sitting in Janet Billig's apartment in the early hours of the morning when Kurt called, asking if he could borrow money. He had a No. 1 record, had just played "Saturday Night Live," but said he had no money. They went to the cash machine, and Billig gave Kurt $40.

An hour later, when Kurt showed up at DJ Kurt St. Thomas's room, he was in the mood to talk, and gave one of the longest interviews of his life. The purpose of the conversation was to create a promotional CD for radio stations. Kurt told the "guns in the river" story, tales of eating corn dogs while living with Dave, and accounts of Aberdeen as a city of hicks and rednecks. When Kurt left two hours later, DGC's Mark Kates turned to St. Thomas and said, "Wow, I can't believe how much you got from him. He never talks like that. But I don't know if everything is true."

Several hours later, as the sun was rising on Sunday morning, Courtney discovered Kurt had overdosed on heroin he'd done after the interview. Whether it was intentional can't be known, but Kurt was an addict with a reputation for recklessness. She saved his life by reviving him, after which he seemed as good as ever. That afternoon, the couple did another photo shoot with Lavine for the cover of *Sassy*—one shot captured Kurt kissing Courtney on the cheek and the magazine used it for the cover. Less than eight hours earlier Kurt had been comatose.

In the interview with *Sassy*'s Christina Kelly, Kurt discussed their engagement: "My attitude has changed drastically, and I can't believe how much happier I am and how even less career-oriented I am. At times, I even forget I'm in a band, I'm so blinded by love. I know that sounds embarrassing, but it's true. I could give the band up right now.

It doesn't matter. But I'm under contract." When Kelly asked if his relationship had changed his writing style, Kurt gushed even more: "I'm just so overwhelmed by the fact that I'm in love on this scale, I don't know how my music's going to change."

But the most ironic comment came when Kelly asked if the couple would consider having a baby. Kurt answered: "I just want to be situated and secure. I want to make sure we have a house, and make sure we have money saved up in the bank." He didn't know Courtney was already carrying their child.

LITTLE MONSTER INSIDE

*There is a little monster inside your head that says, "you know
you'll feel better."*
—Kurt describing addiction to his sister, April 1992.

It was all those drawings of "flipper babies" he'd done
over the years that made Kurt panic upon hearing the news of the
pregnancy; that and knowing that they'd been using heroin during the
period the child was conceived in early December. Kurt's harshest critic
was always his own inner voice, and this tainted pregnancy, his friends
observed, caused him some of the most potent shame of his life.
Through all the rottenness in his life—both internal and external—he'd
held two things sacred: a pledge he would never turn into his parents
and a vow that if he ever had children he'd offer them a better world
than the one he grew up in. Yet, in early January 1992, Kurt couldn't
stop thinking of all the "flipper baby" drawings he'd done and wondering if he was being given one of his own as divine retribution.

Concurrently, even within Kurt's despair, there was a hopefulness
around the pregnancy. Kurt truly loved Courtney and thought they
would have a child with many gifts, including above-average intelli-
gence. He believed the affection he had for her was deeper than the
love he witnessed between his own parents. And despite Kurt's freak-
out, Courtney seemed surprisingly calm, at least calm by Courtney standards. She told Kurt the baby was a God-given sign, and she was
convinced it would not be born with flippers, no matter how many
drawings of deformed fetuses Kurt had sketched in his youth. She said

his nightmares were just fears, and that her dreams showed them having a healthy, beautiful child. She held these beliefs even as those around her suggested otherwise. One drug treatment doctor she consulted offered to "give her morphine" if she'd agree to an abortion. Courtney would have none of it, and sought another opinion.

She visited a Beverly Hills specialist in birth defects who said that heroin, when used in the first trimester of pregnancy, posed few risks for birth defects. "He told her if she followed a course of treatment and tapered off, there was no reason in the world she couldn't have a healthy baby," recalled her lawyer, Rosemary Carroll. With the "flipper baby" images fading from his head, Kurt joined Courtney in the conviction that the pregnancy was a blessing. If anything, the disapproving attitudes of others only strengthened Kurt's resolve, just as it had done in his coupling with Courtney. "We knew it really wasn't the best of times to have a child," Kurt told Michael Azerrad, "but we were just determined to have one."

They had rented a two-bedroom apartment in Los Angeles for $1,100 a month at 448 North Spaulding, between Melrose and Fairfax. It was a quiet neighborhood, and they were relatively isolated because neither could drive: Kurt had failed to pay some traffic tickets and had temporarily lost his license; Courtney had never learned to operate a car. It was the first time Kurt had lived outside of Washington state, and he found himself missing the rain.

But soon after moving in, they departed for the confines of a Holiday Inn. They had hired a drug doctor who specialized in quick detox therapy and he recommended they check into a motel—it would be messy, he had told them. And it was. Though later Kurt tried to downplay this withdrawal, claiming he "slept for three days," others painted a far darker picture of the detox, which entailed hours of vomiting, fever, diarrhea, chills, and all the symptoms that one would associate with the worst influenza. They survived by copiously using sleeping pills and methadone.

Though both were detoxing for the sake of the baby, Kurt had to leave in two weeks for a tour of the Far East. "[I] found myself realizing that I wouldn't be able to get drugs when we got to Japan and Australia," he wrote in his journal. In the middle of his detox, Kurt had to film a video for "Come As You Are." He insisted all shots of his face appear obscured or distorted.

Before leaving for the tour, Kurt called his mother to tell her the news of the pregnancy. His sister Kim answered the phone. "We're having a baby," he declared. "I better give you to Mom," Kim replied. When Wendy heard the news, she announced: "Kurt, you can't shock me anymore."

The first few concerts in Australia went smoothly, but within a week Kurt was suffering from stomach pain, forcing the cancellation of dates. He went to the emergency room one night, but walked out after overhearing a nurse say, "He's just a junkie." As he wrote in his journal, "the pain left me immobile, doubled-up on the bathroom floor, vomiting water and blood. I was literally starving to death. My weight was down to about 100 pounds." Desperate for a solution, he went to an Australian doctor who specialized in rock bands. On the office wall, proudly displayed, was a photograph of the physician with Keith Richards. "I was taken to a doctor at the advice of my management, who gave me Physeptone," Kurt wrote in his journal. "The pills seemed to work better than anything else I've tried." But a few weeks later, after the tour hit Japan, Kurt noticed the label on the bottle: "It read: 'Physeptone—contains methadone.' Hooked again. We survived Japan, but by that time opiates and touring had started to take their toll on my body and I wasn't in much better health than I was off of drugs."

Despite his physical and emotional struggles, Kurt adored Japan, sharing the nation's obsession with kitsch. "He was in a completely foreign country, and he was fascinated with the culture," recalled Virgin Publishing's Kaz Utsunomiya, who was on the tour. "He loved cartoons and 'Hello Kitty.' " Kurt didn't understand why Japanese fans gave him presents, but announced he would accept only "Hello Kitty" gifts. The next day, he was deluged with trinkets. Before a gig outside Tokyo, Utsunomiya had to help Kurt buy new pajamas. When Kurt told the salesman he wanted the pajamas to wear onstage, the staid clerk looked at the singer like he was truly insane.

In Osaka, on a rare night off, Nirvana reunited with one of their favorite touring partners, Shonen Knife, a pop group made up of three Japanese women. They gave Kurt gifts of toy swords, a new motorized

Chim-Chim monkey, and took him to dinner at a bratwurst restaurant he had selected. He was disappointed to learn Shonen Knife had a gig the next night, as did Nirvana. Uncharacteristically, Kurt ended the Nirvana set early and announced from the stage he was planning to go see Shonen Knife. Leaving the venue, his cab was mobbed by Japanese girls grasping at the car, just wanting to touch it. At the Shonen Knife show, things were just as surreal, because as the only blond, blue-eyed boy there, he was easy to spot. "He was still wearing his pajamas," remembered Shonen Knife's Naoko Yamano.

Courtney had rejoined the tour in Japan, and they spent Kurt's 25th birthday flying to Honolulu for two scheduled shows. On the plane they decided to get married in Hawaii. They had fantasized about a Valentine's Day wedding, but didn't finish their prenuptial agreement in time. Kurt had suggested a pre-nup after strong lobbying from manager John Silva, who never liked Courtney. The pre-nup was mostly to cover future earnings, because at the time of their marriage they were still "fuck poor," as Courtney described it. When Kurt filed his 1991 taxes, owing to the arcane way the music industry pays royalties so late and the huge percentage taken by managers and lawyers, his gross income was just $29,541. He had deductions of $2,541, giving him a taxable income of $27,000 during a year he played before hundreds of thousands of fans and sold almost two million records.

Courtney was negotiating her own record deal with DGC, which gave Hole an advance of a million dollars and a royalty rate considerably higher than Nirvana's, a matter of great pride to her. She still had reservations about how she might not be perceived as an artist in her own right married to someone as famous as Kurt. In Japan, she had jotted her melancholia in her journal: "My fame. Ha ha. It's a weapon, kiss my ass, just like morning sickness. . . . Could it just be the commercial effect of too many sales and a semi-freak accident, semi-meant to be, but I'm starting to think I can't sing, can't write, that esteem is at an all-time low, and it isn't his fault. God, how could it be. . . . Don't you dare dismiss me just because I married a ROCKSTAR."

They were married on Waikiki Beach at sunset on Monday, February 24, 1992. The ceremony was conducted by a non-denominational minister found through the wedding bureau. Kurt had done heroin before the wedding, though he told Azerrad he "wasn't very high. I just did a little teeny bit so I didn't get sick." Courtney wore an antique silk dress that had once belonged to actress Frances Farmer. Kurt wore blue-plaid pajamas and a woven Guatemalan purse. With his gauntness and bizarre clothing, he looked more like a chemotherapy patient than a traditional groom. Yet the wedding was not without meaning to him, and he cried during the short ceremony.

Since the wedding was hastily arranged, most of the eight guests were from the band's crew. Kurt had Dylan Carlson fly in to serve as best man, though this was partially precipitated by Kurt wanting Dylan to bring heroin. Dylan had not yet met Courtney, and his first encounter with her was the day before the wedding. He liked Courtney and she liked him, though neither would be able to get over a belief that the other party was a negative influence on Kurt. "In some ways, she was very good for him," Dylan recalled, "and in other ways, she was terrible." Dylan brought his girlfriend, and the two were the only attendees not on the Nirvana payroll.

But of more significance were those missing: Kurt hadn't invited his family (nor had Courtney), and Krist and Shelli were noticeably absent. The morning of the wedding, Kurt had banned Shelli and a few crew members because he felt they were gossiping about Courtney—the effect of this edict was to also uninvite Krist. "Kurt was changing," recalled Shelli. That month, Kurt had told Krist, "I don't want to even *see* Shelli, because when I look at her, I feel bad about what I'm doing." Shelli's analysis of this: "I think looking at me was like looking at his conscience."

Shelli and Krist left Hawaii the next day, assuming the band was broken up. "We thought it was over," recalled Shelli. Krist was just saddened and felt shunned by his old friend: "Kurt was in his own world at that point. After that, I was pretty estranged with him. It was never the same. We talked about the direction of the band somewhat, but there really was *no* direction of the band after that." It would be four months before Nirvana would perform again in public, and almost two months before Krist and Kurt would see each other.

· · ·

Kurt and Courtney honeymooned in Hawaii, but the sunny island was not Kurt's idea of paradise. They returned to Los Angeles, where his drug habit was easier fed. Kurt later downplayed his increasing abuse as "a lot less turbulent than everyone thinks." He told Azerrad he decided to continue being an addict because he felt "if I quit then, I'd end up doing it again for at least the next couple of years all the time. I figured I'd just burn myself out of it because I hadn't experienced the full junkie feeling yet. I was still healthy." His chemical and psychological dependency were so great at this stage, his comments were an attempt to minimize what had become a debilitating addiction. His own description of himself in his journal was anything but healthy, at least as he imagined others saw him: "I'm thought of as an emaciated, yellow-skinned, zombie-like, evil, drug-fiend, junky, lost cause, on the brink of death, self-destructive, selfish pig, a loser who shoots up in the backstage area just seconds before a performance." This was what he imagined people thought of him; his own self-talk was even darker, summed up by a line that would repeatedly show up in his writings: "I hate myself and I want to die." By early 1992, he had already decided this would be the title of his next album.

Heroin became, in many ways, the hobby he'd never had as a child: He methodically organized his "works" box the way a small boy might shuffle his baseball card collection. In this sacred box he stored his syringe, a cooker to melt the drugs (West Coast heroin had the consistency of roofing tar and needed to be cooked), and spoons and cotton balls used in preparing the heroin for injecting. A seamy underworld of dealers and daily deliveries became commonplace.

In the spring of 1992 he did virtually nothing involving the band, and refused to schedule future shows. The band was offered outrageous sums to do a headlining arena tour—*Nevermind* was still near the top of the charts—but Kurt turned down all overtures. Though Courtney had kicked drugs during their January detox, with Kurt buying heroin daily and filling their apartment with the smell of it cooking, she found herself falling down a slippery slope again. The combination of their weaknesses helped pull each into a spiral of abuse, and their mutual emotional dependence made breaking that cycle nearly impossible. "With Kurt and Courtney, it was like they were two characters in a play, and they'd simply switch parts," observed Jennifer Finch. "When one would get sober and better, the other would slip. But Courtney could control herself more than Kurt. With him, it was this train wreck that was going down and everyone knew it, and everyone just wanted to get out of the way."

In early March, Hole's Carolyn Rue visited their apartment to get high. When Rue asked for an extra syringe, Kurt replied, "We broke them all." In an effort to control their addictions, Courtney would frequently destroy every syringe in the apartment, which only had the effect of forcing Kurt to buy new ones when he bought his daily heroin. Even to Rue, who had her own struggles, Kurt's addiction seemed full-throttle. "Kurt talked about taking drugs like it was so fucking natural," she recalled. "But it wasn't." Even within the confines of drug culture, Kurt's level of use seemed abhorrent.

The prospect of the baby gave Kurt a small beacon of hope in what had become an increasingly bleak existence. To ensure the fetus was properly developing, they'd gotten several sonograms, pictures of the baby in the womb. When Kurt saw them he was visibly shaken, and wept with relief that the child was developing normally. Kurt took one of the sonograms and used it as the centerpiece of a painting he began working on. When a second test produced an ultrasound video of the fetus, he asked for a copy and watched it obsessively on his VCR. "Kurt kept saying, 'look at that little bean,'" recalled Jennifer Finch. "That's what they were calling her, 'the bean.' He would point out her hand. He knew every single feature of that graphic image." Early in the pregnancy, after determining the child's gender, they had selected a name: Frances Bean Cobain. Her middle name was their nickname, while her first name came from Frances McKee of the Vaselines, or so Kurt would later tell reporters. Her sonogram photo later was reproduced on the sleeve of the "Lithium" single.

By March concern over Kurt's increasing dependence on drugs and its effect on Courtney pushed his managers to attempt their first formal intervention. They brought in Bob Timmins, an addiction specialist whose reputation was built on working with rock stars. Courtney recalled Timmins being so starstruck by Kurt he paid little attention to her. "He literally ignored me, and was drooling over Kurt," she said. Timmins suggested Kurt consider an inpatient chemical dependency program. "My advice was taken," Timmins said. "Why I recommended that particular one was because it happened to be Cedars-Sinai Hospital, and I felt that some medical issues presented themselves in my evaluation. It wasn't just a simple 'go to treatment, get clean and go to meetings.' There were a lot of medical issues going on."

Initially, Kurt's stay at Cedars-Sinai helped considerably, and soon he appeared sober and healthy. But though he agreed to continue on methadone—a drug that stops withdrawal without producing a high— he ended treatment early and balked at 12-Step meetings. "He definitely wasn't a joiner," observed Timmins. "That part of his personality probably got in the way of the recovery process."

In April Kurt and Courtney traveled to Seattle, where they shopped for a house. They appeared one evening in Orpheum Records and caused a scene when they seized all the Nirvana bootlegs in the store. Courtney rightly claimed that the CDs were illegal, but the clerk protested that he'd be fired if the owner found the CDs were missing. Ironically, Kurt had come in the store searching for a CD by the band Negativland that itself had been ruled a bootleg after a lawsuit. The clerk asked if they could write a note to his boss, so Courtney wrote: "I need for you not to make money off my husband so I can feed my children. Love, Mrs. Cobain." Kurt added: "Macaroni and cheese for all." The note was so odd, the worried clerk asked Kurt, "If I lose my job can I work for you?" The next day the store received a phone call from a man who asked, "Is that guy with the long hair who was working there last night still employed?"

While the couple were in Seattle, the Fradenburgs threw a combo wedding reception/baby shower for them. It would be the first time many of Kurt's uncles and aunts would get a chance to meet Courtney, but several left before she arrived: The party had been scheduled for 2 p.m., but the guests of honor didn't show until seven. Courtney told Kurt's relatives they might purchase a Victorian mansion in Grays Harbor. "Then we can be the king and queen of Aberdeen," she joked.

Marriage seemed initially to mellow both Kurt and Courtney. When they were away from the spotlight, and away from drugs, their relationship had many moments of tenderness. Stripped of their fame, they both turned back into the scared lost children they'd been prior to being discovered. Each night before bed they would pray together. Once in bed, they would read each other books. Kurt said he loved to go to sleep listening to the sound of Courtney's voice—it was a comfort he had missed for much of his life.

That month, Courtney returned to Los Angeles for Hole business; Kurt stayed in Seattle and even did a short one-day recording session with Nirvana, at Barrett Jones's home studio. They cut "Oh, the Guilt," "Curmudgeon," and "Return of the Rat," the final song slated for a tribute album for the Portland band the Wipers. The day after the session, Kurt drove his Valiant to Aberdeen for his first visit to Grays Harbor in months.

Two days later Kurt drove back to Seattle to retrieve his sister and bring her to Aberdeen. He had a subtext to this long day of travel, a six-hour round trip, which he did not announce to Kim until the car drove past "Think of Me Hill" just minutes from Wendy's home. "You know your best friend Cindy?" he asked. "She told Mom you and Jennifer were having an affair."

"It's not an affair," Kim answered. "We're girlfriends. I'm *gay*." Kurt knew this, or at least suspected it, but his mother had not. "Mom's kind of flipped out right now," he told his sister. Kurt told Kim to pretend as if their mother didn't know. Kurt, like Wendy, preferred a nonconfrontational style—Kim, however, told her brother she would do no such thing.

As they drove into Aberdeen, Kurt decided they needed to confer before walking into the house. He drove to Sam Benn Park, where they sat on a swing, and he decided to use this moment to drop his own bombshell. "I know you've tried pot, and you've probably done acid and cocaine," he told her. "I've never touched cocaine," Kim argued. "Well, you will," her brother replied. Their conversation devolved into a debate about whether Kim, just two weeks away from turning 22, would end up using cocaine. "Well, you *will* use cocaine," Kurt insisted.

"But if you ever touch heroin, I'll go get a gun, and I'll come find you, and I'll kill you." It did not sound like he was joking. "You don't have to worry about that," Kim told him. "I'd never stick a needle in my arm. I'd never do that." Kim realized that in the way Kurt had constructed the warning, he'd been broadcasting a message about himself.

After the kind of long silence only natural among siblings, Kurt finally announced, "I've been clean about eight months." He didn't specify what he'd been clean from, but Kim had heard the rumors just like everyone else. She also suspected he was lying about having eight months clean-time—it was actually less than a month, and he was still on a daily dose of methadone.

"I don't know much about heroin," she told her brother. Kurt sighed and it was as if a door had opened, and the brother Kim had always loved came through and revealed himself to her once more. He didn't hide behind his constructed self or lies or fame as he told her about the pain he felt trying to kick heroin. He described it as similar to cigarette smoking, where each progressive attempt at quitting becomes harder and harder. "The more you do it," he explained, "and the more you quit, the harder it gets to quit on the third, and the fourth time, and the fifth, and the sixth time. There is a little monster inside your head that says, 'You know you'll feel better, and you know I'll feel better.' It's like I have another person in my head who is telling me that everything will be okay if I just go and do a little."

Kim was speechless. She knew from his mentioning how hard it was to quit the "fifth" or "sixth" time that he was far more gone than she had supposed. "Don't ever worry about me, Kurt, because I'm *never* touching that shit," she said. "I'll never get near it. You've been clean for eight months—that's *great*. Please continue." She was running out of words, and reeling from the shock of "finding out your brother is a junkie," as she remembered it. Despite the rumors, Kim had a difficult time accepting that her brother, who had grown up with her and suffered many of the same indignities, was an addict.

Kurt moved the topic back to Kim's sexuality and the prejudice he knew she would encounter on the harbor. He tried to talk her out of being a lesbian. "Don't totally give up on men," he urged. "I know they're assholes. I would never date a guy. They're dicks." Kim found this hilarious, since despite keeping her secret from her family, she had always known she was gay, and felt little shame. Even with all the "Homo sex rules" graffiti Kurt had spray-painted around Aberdeen, he struggled to accept that his sister was gay. As the conversation wound down and they headed toward home, he gave her a long brotherly embrace and pledged he'd love her forever.

On April 16, 1992, Nirvana made their first appearance on the cover of *Rolling Stone*. Though the piece was ostensibly about the band, even the headline—"Inside the Heart and Mind of Kurt Cobain"—was evidence everything Nirvana did was focused on Kurt. For the cover photo he wore a T-shirt reading "Corporate Magazines Still Suck." The fact that the story came together at all was a testament to how hard Kurt's managers had worked to convince him that corporate magazines didn't suck. He had rejected *Rolling Stone*'s interview requests in 1991, and in early 1992 he wrote the magazine a letter: "At this point in our, uh, career, before hair loss treatment and bad credit, I've decided I have no desire to do an interview. . . . We wouldn't benefit from an interview because the average *Rolling Stone* reader is a middle-aged ex-hippie turned hippiecrite, who embraces the past as 'the glory days' and has a kinder, gentler, more adult approach towards the new liberal conservatism. The average *Rolling Stone* reader has always gathered moss." He didn't mail the letter, and a couple of weeks after writing it, he was sitting down with the magazine's Michael Azerrad, talking once again about how he wanted a tie-dyed T-shirt made from the blood of Jerry Garcia.

He initially had given Azerrad an icy reception, but when Kurt started reciting tales of getting beaten up in high school, Azerrad stood and displayed his five-foot six frame and joked, "I don't know what you're talking about." They bonded after that, and Kurt answered Azerrad's questions, managing to get in print many of his major life revisions, including that "Something in the Way" was about the time he lived under a bridge. When asked about heroin, Kurt replied: "I don't even drink anymore because it destroys my stomach. My body wouldn't allow me to take drugs if I wanted to, because I'm so weak all the time. Drugs are a waste of time. They destroy your memory and your self-respect and everything that goes along with your self-esteem. They're no good at all." As he spoke, sitting in the living room of the Spaulding apartment, his beloved "works box" sat like a bejeweled family heirloom in the closet.

Though the *Rolling Stone* article downplayed tensions within the band, between the time of the interview and its publication, Nirvana had temporarily ceased to exist. When the band signed their original publishing deal, Kurt had agreed to evenly split songwriting royalties with Novoselic and Grohl. This was generous, but at the time no one imagined the record would sell millions. With the phenomenal success of *Nevermind*, Kurt insisted these percentages be shifted to give him the bulk of the revenue—he proposed a 75/25 split on the music, with him getting 100 percent of the lyrics—and he wanted the agreement to be retroactive. "I think once *Nevermind* was playing itself out, Kurt began to realize that [publishing contracts] weren't just theoretical documents; that this was real money," observed attorney Alan Mintz. "The publishing splits meant lifestyle issues."

Krist and Dave felt betrayed that Kurt wanted the new deal to be retroactive, but they eventually agreed, thinking the other option was dissolving the band. Kurt had resolutely told Rosemary Carroll—now simultaneously serving as lawyer for Kurt, Courtney, and Nirvana—he would break up the band if he didn't get his way. Though Grohl and Novoselic blamed Courtney, Carroll remembered Kurt being unmovable on the issue. "His focus was laser-like," she observed. "He was very clear and very persistent, and knew to the penny what he was talking about. He knew what he was worth, and he knew he deserved all the money, [since] he wrote all the lyrics and the music." Ultimately, the percentages didn't leave as deep a hurt as the manner in which Kurt chose to handle it: As with most conflicts, he avoided the issue until he was in a rage. Several of the band's crew members were shocked to hear Kurt talking badly about Krist, who had been one of the greatest anchors in his life.

By May Kurt was back on heroin again, having managed to stay sober for less than six weeks. His addiction was common knowledge in rock circles, and eventually rumors made their way to the *Los Angeles Times*. On May 17, in an article headlined "Why is Nirvana missing from a heavenly tour season?" Steve Hochman wrote "[Nirvana's] low profile has renewed public speculation that singer/guitarist Kurt Cobain has a heroin problem." Gold Mountain dismissed the rumors, issuing what would become the standard denial, blaming the band's absence on Kurt's "stomach problems."

Kurt's old friend Jesse Reed visited that month, and on the day Jesse was there, Kurt had to shoot up twice. Both times he went into the bathroom so as not to use in front of his oldest friend or Courtney, who was suffering from morning sickness and didn't want to witness Kurt getting high. But Kurt wasn't shy about discussing his habit with Jesse, and they spent most of the day waiting around for a new supply of heroin to be delivered. Kurt was clearly over the fear of needles Jesse remembered from their youth—Kurt even begged his old friend to find him some illegal injectable steroids.

Jesse found the apartment not that differently furnished from the pink apartment back in Aberdeen—there was graffiti on the walls, the furniture was cheap, and, in general, "it was a shit-hole." But one aspect of the domicile did impress Jesse: Kurt had begun to paint again, and the living room was filled with his work. "He had 100 square feet of canvas," Jesse recalled. "He was talking of quitting music and opening his own gallery." The art Kurt painted in 1992 showed dramatic growth. One painting was a 24-by-36-inch canvas of bright orange with a brown dog tooth hanging from a string in the middle. Another featured crimson blotches with pressed flowers in the center of the paint smears. Yet another showed blood-red crosses with ghostly white alien images behind them. One giant canvas featured an alien hanging like a marionette with a tiny nub of an exposed penis; a small cat was in a corner looking at the viewer, and in another corner Kurt had lettered: "rectal abscesses, conjunctivitis, spinabifida."

Kurt's royalty checks had finally started to come in, and money for canvas and paint was no longer a problem. He told Jesse he was doing $400 worth of heroin a day, an extravagant amount that would have killed most users; part of the reason for that figure was that most dealers overcharged Kurt, knowing he could pay. Jesse detected that when Kurt fixed, there was little impairment to his motor functions: "He didn't nod off. There was no change."

Jesse and Kurt spent most of the afternoon watching a videotape of a man shooting himself in the head. "He had this video of a senator," Jesse recalled, "blowing his brains out on TV. This guy takes a .357 magnum from a manila envelope, and blows his brains out. It was pretty graphic. Kurt got it at some snuff shop." The video was actually the suicide of R. Budd Dwyer, a Pennsylvania state official who, upon being convicted of bribery in January 1987, called a press conference, thanked his wife and children, handed an envelope to his staff containing his suicide note, and told the reporters, "Some who have called have said that I am a modern-day Job." With the cameras filming, Dwyer inserted a gun into his mouth and pulled the trigger—it took off the back of his head and instantly killed him. Bootlegged copies of the live television coverage had circulated after Dwyer's death, and Kurt had purchased one. He watched the suicide obsessively during 1992 and 1993—almost as often as he watched the ultrasound of his daughter in the womb.

After Kurt's heroin delivery arrived, Jesse accompanied Kurt on some errands. One stop was Circuit City, where Kurt dropped almost $10,000 buying the latest video equipment. Jesse left that night to return to San Diego, and gave the frail Kurt a hug as he parted. They continued to stay in touch over the phone, but though neither knew it at the time, it would be the last time the two old friends would see each other.

In June, Nirvana began a ten-date European tour to make up for cancelled 1991 shows. By the first date in Dublin, Kurt was already complaining of stomach pain and was rushed to the hospital. There he claimed the pain was caused by failing to take his methadone pills; during other incidents he would claim methadone caused some of his stomach pain. This being the first concert on the tour, it was well attended by journalists who had interviews scheduled with Kurt: When they were told he was "unavailable," they smelled a story. The band's U.K. publicist, Anton Brookes, found himself almost comically trying to shuffle reporters out of the lobby without anyone seeing Kurt leaving the hotel on a stretcher. When one reporter declared, "I just saw Kurt in an ambulance," Cobain's health problems were suddenly hard to deny. "I remember getting back to the office, and CNN had been on the phone," Brookes recalled. "I'd say, 'He had stomach problems. If it was heroin, I'd tell you. He's on medication.' " To outwit persistent reporters Brookes would display Kurt's prescription bottles. After an hour in the hospital, Kurt improved and went on to play the next day's show without incident. But management had hired two guards to follow Kurt—and he immediately gave them the slip.

Before a show in Spain, the band did an interview with Keith Cameron for the *NME*. Cameron's article mentioned the drug rumors and questioned whether it was possible for Nirvana to go "from nobodies to superstars to fuck-ups in the space of six months." It was their most damning press yet, and seemed to encourage other U.K. writers to include allegations of heroin abuse in their pieces, a topic previously considered taboo. But despite Cameron's description of Kurt as "ghoulish," the photos accompanying the article found him looking boyish, with bleached short hair, and sporting thick Buddy Holly–style glasses. He didn't need the glasses but thought they made him look intelligent; he also wore a similar pair in the "In Bloom" video. When his aunt told him the spectacles made him look like his father, Kurt never wore them again.

On July 3, still in Spain, Courtney began to have contractions though her due date wasn't until the first week of September. They rushed her to a Spanish hospital, where Kurt was unable to find a doctor who could speak English well enough to comprehend him. Finally, by phone they reached Courtney's physician, who recommended they take the next plane home. They did, and Nirvana cancelled two dates in Spain for the second time.

When they arrived in California, doctors assured them everything was fine with the pregnancy, but nonetheless they returned to catastrophe: Their bathroom had flooded. Kurt had stored guitars and journals in the bathtub, and they were ruined. Disheartened, he and Courtney decided to move immediately, even though she was eight months pregnant; there were also heroin dealers knocking on their door at all hours, a temptation Kurt found hard to resist. Kurt marched down to Gold Mountain's office to insist Silva find them a new place to live. Despite his increasing wealth, Kurt hadn't yet been able to establish credit, and he left all his financial matters to his managers.

Silva helped them locate a house, and they moved in late July, leaving all their trash in the Spaulding apartment and the word "patricide" written on the wall above the fireplace. Their new home, at 6881 Alta Loma Terrace, was something straight out of a movie; it had been used as a location for several films including *Dead Again*, and Robert Altman's version of *The Long Goodbye*. It sat on a small bluff in the hills of North Hollywood, overlooking the Hollywood Bowl. The only way to reach the bluff, which had ten apartments and four houses, was by a shared Gothic-looking elevator. The Cobains rented their house for $1,500 a month. "It was yucky in a lot of ways," remembered Courtney, "but it was okay. It wasn't an apartment, anyway."

Distraught over his increasing stomach pain, Kurt contemplated suicide. "I instantly regained that familiar burning nausea and decided to kill myself or stop the pain," he wrote in his journal. "I bought a gun, but chose drugs instead." He abandoned methadone and went right back to heroin. When even drugs didn't seem to relieve him of the pain, he eventually decided to try treatment again, after lobbying by Courtney and his managers. On August 4 he checked into the drug rehabilitation unit of Cedars-Sinai hospital for his third rehab. He had begun using a new physician—he saw a dozen different chemical dependency specialists during 1992—and had agreed to a 60-day intensive detox program. It was two months of "starvation and vomiting, I looked to an IV and moaning out loud with the worst stomach pain I have ever experienced." Three days after Kurt's admission, Courtney checked into a different wing of the same hospital under an assumed name. According to her medical records, which were leaked to the *Los Angeles Times*, she was being given prenatal vitamins and methadone. Courtney was suffering from both a complicated pregnancy and emotional exhaustion: Earlier that week she had received a fax of a profile of her, set to appear in the next month's issue of *Vanity Fair*.

Rosewater, diaper smell. . . . Hey, girlfriend, detox. I'm in my
Kraut box, held up here in my ink penitentiary.
—From a 1992 letter to Courtney.

Frances Bean Cobain was born at 7:48 a.m. on August 18, 1992, at Cedars-Sinai Medical Center in Los Angeles. When the doctor announced she appeared to be in excellent health at seven pounds and one ounce, an audible sigh of relief could be heard from both mother and father. Not only was Frances healthy, she was also cute, being born with her father's blue eyes. She cried upon birth and responded like a normal baby.

But Frances's birth story and the events that unfolded that week were anything but normal. Courtney had been in the hospital for ten days of bedrest, but her fame had drawn tabloid reporters who had to be shooed off. Even though she'd been ordered to stay in bed, once her contractions began, at four in the morning, she managed to pull herself up, grab the IV-stand she was connected to, and walk through the halls of the huge medical facility until she found Kurt in the chemical dependency wing. His rehab had not been going well; he found himself unable to keep food down and spent most of his time sleeping or vomiting. When Courtney arrived at his room, she pulled the covers off his face and yelled, "You get out of this bed and you come down now! You are not leaving me to do this by myself. Fuck you!"

Kurt sheepishly followed her to the labor and delivery wing, but he wasn't much assistance. He was in such fragile health—at 105 pounds and still hooked up to an IV—he was unable to inhale deeply enough to serve as a breathing coach. Courtney found herself turning her focus away from her contractions and caring for her ailing husband: "I'm having the baby, it's coming out, he's puking, he's passing out, and I'm holding *his* hand and rubbing *his* stomach while the baby's coming out of me," she told Azerrad. Kurt fainted moments before Frances's head crowned, and he missed her passing through the birth canal. But once the baby was out, suctioned off, and cleaned up, he held her. It was a moment he described as both one of the happiest of his life and the most fearful. "I was so fucking scared," he told Azerrad. As Kurt inspected her more thoroughly and saw that she had all her fingers and was not a "flipper baby," some of that fear subsided.

Yet even the sweeping joy of holding his newborn couldn't pull Kurt out of the increasing hysteria set off by the *Vanity Fair* article. The next day, in a scene that could have been written for a Sam Shepard play, Kurt escaped the hospital's detox unit, bought heroin, got high, and then returned with a loaded .38 pistol. He went to Courtney's room, where he reminded her of a vow the two had made—if it appeared they would lose their baby for any reason, they would kill themselves in a double suicide. Both feared Frances would be taken from them, and Kurt feared he'd be unable to kick heroin. He had pledged not to live with such a fate. Courtney was distraught over the magazine article, but not suicidal. She tried reasoning with Kurt, but he was mad with fear. "I'll go first," she finally told him as a ploy and he handed her the pistol. "I held this thing in my hand," she recalled in a 1994 interview with David Fricke, "and I felt that thing that they said in *Schindler's List*: I'm never going to know what happens to me. And what about Frances? Sort of rude. 'Oh, your parents died the day after you were born.' " Courtney gave the gun to Hole's Eric Erlandson, who was the one friend they could count on no matter how sordid things became, and he disposed of it.

But Kurt's feelings of despair didn't go away; they only increased. The next day he snuck a drug dealer into Cedars-Sinai, and in a room off the labor and delivery wing, he overdosed. "He almost died," Love told Fricke. "The dealer said she'd never seen someone so dead. I said, 'Why don't you go get a nurse? There's nurses all over the place.'" A nurse was found and Kurt was revived, beating death yet another time.

But he couldn't escape the September issue of *Vanity Fair*, which hit the streets that week. Written by Lynn Hirschberg, the article was head-lined "Strange Love: Are Courtney Love, lead diva of the postpunk band Hole, and her husband, Nirvana heartthrob Kurt Cobain, the grunge John and Yoko? Or the next Sid and Nancy?" It was a damning portrait, calling Love a "train-wreck personality," and painting her mar-riage to Kurt as nothing more than a career move. But the deepest wounds came from several anonymous quotes, obviously from a person close to the couple, which raised concerns about the health of Frances and their drug problems during the pregnancy. The allegations were bad enough; Kurt and Courtney felt doubly betrayed that someone in their organization would slander them in a public forum.

Worse yet, the article was treated as news by other media outlets, including MTV. Kurt told Courtney he felt deceived that the network would make him famous, only to destroy him. That week he sat down and wrote a letter to MTV attacking Hirschberg and the network:

Dear Empty TV, the entity of all corporate Gods: How fucking dare you embrace such trash journalism from an overweight, unpopular-in-high-school cow who severely needs her karma bro-ken. My life's dedication is now to do nothing but slag MTV and Lynn Hirschberg, who by the way is in cahoots with her lover Kurt Loder (Gin Blossom–drunk). We will survive without you. Easily. The old school is going down fast.

—Kurdt Kobain, professional rock musician. Fuck face.

For her part, Courtney was still reeling from the fact that she had so wrongly read Hirschberg. Most of the issues the article raised had already been brought up in other stories, but it was the tone of the piece that felt like class warfare. In 1998, Courtney posted the following reflection on America Online:

I had NO fucking clue how a "boomer mentality" like *Vanity Fair/Hirschberg* would receive me and my family. I was sheltered from the mainstream in every possible way my entire life: Feminism, punk rock, and subcultural living did not enable me to have a value system that understood mainstream thought or that understood how us "dirty punks" had no rights to the American dream; that, plus I thought it would be neat to get famous; I had NO IDEA about the archetype I would get slammed into. . . . But the fact remains that most of that article was unsaid and untrue.

The attention moved Kurt and Courtney out of the rock magazines and into the newspapers in the U.S., where the court of public opinion was quick to damn any parent considered unfit. *The Globe* tabloid ran a story headlined "Rock Star's Baby is Born a Junkie," complete with a picture of a deformed newborn they deceptively implied was Frances. Though Courtney wasn't the first mother with drug problems to have a child, she was soon the most public, and "the Cobain baby" was as talked about across lunch counters and supermarket checkout lines as the Lindbergh baby had been decades before. Axl Rose, of Guns N' Roses, even weighed in from the stage: "Kurt Cobain is a fucking junkie with a junkie wife. And if the baby's born deformed, I think they both ought to go to prison."

Two days after Frances's birth, the couple's worst fears were realized, when a social worker from the Los Angeles County Department of Children's Services appeared in the hospital, holding a copy of *Vanity Fair*. Courtney was crestfallen, and felt—more than at any other moment in her life—she was being judged, which she was. Kurt had spent most of his life feeling judged, but this time it was his skills as a parent being evaluated and his drug addiction. The conversation between the social worker and Love immediately became testy. "Within five minutes of meeting this woman," Rosemary Carroll remembered, "Courtney created an atmosphere wherein the woman wanted to bring her down and hurt her. And unfortunately the ammunition was there." The county petitioned to take Frances away and to have Kurt and Courtney declared unfit parents, based almost entirely on the *Vanity Fair* article. As a result of the county's actions, Courtney wasn't even allowed to take Frances home when she left the hospital three days after the birth. Instead, Frances had to stay for observation—despite the fact that she was healthy—and only left a few days later in the care of a nanny, as the court would not release her to Kurt and Courtney.

On August 24, 1992, six days after Frances's birth, the first court hearing was held. Though they hoped to retain custody of Frances as a couple, Kurt and Courtney were prepared for the possibility the court might put restrictions on one parent, and therefore had separate lawyers. "This is done strategically," recalled Neal Hersh, Kurt's attorney, "so if there is a divergence of interests or issues, you can separate the parents and make sure the child stays with family." As it was, the judge ruled Kurt and Courtney would not be allowed to see their own child without the supervision of the court-appointed guardian. Kurt was ordered to undergo 30 days of drug treatment, and both parents were required to give random urine tests. Kurt had been clean for several days, yet he told Courtney he felt the ruling had broken his heart in two. "It was horrible," recalled Carroll. "That child was very wanted. Courtney had gone through a whole lot to have that child. Almost everyone she knew and trusted had told her *not* to have that child with varying degrees of intensity, obviously excluding Kurt. She'd gone through physical pain, much more than a regular pregnancy, because of the struggles to withdraw and stay healthy, at a time when nothing around her was healthy. To go through that and have the baby, and then have the baby taken away from you. . . ." Hersh recalled, observing Kurt with Frances, "You should have seen him with that kid. He just could sit and stare at her for hours. He was as adoring as any father would be."

They had already planned on having a nanny; soon they developed a complex plan to put Frances into the temporary care of nannies and relatives, as required by the judge. This presented another problem: What relative? Both Kurt and Courtney had so many issues with their own families, they weren't willing to trust Frances to their respective parents. Eventually the idea of Courtney's half-sister Jamie Rodriguez came up. "There was no issue that they were not going to take good care of this child," observed Carroll. "That was not an issue. The only issue was drugs. It was this insane American puritanical 'war-on-drugs' mentality. The assumption is that you can't be an addict and be a good parent."

After considerable finagling, Jamie was flown in to satisfy the letter of the court decree. "She barely knew Courtney," recalled Danny Goldberg, "and she couldn't stand her. So we had to kind of bribe her to pretend she gave a shit. We rented her a place right next to Kurt and Courtney, so officially she had custody for a few months, while the legal system decided it was okay for them to raise their own kid. I was frequently the one who Jamie would come to, to write another check."

Jackie Farry, a friend of Gold Mountain's Janet Billig, was hired as nanny and for the next eight months she would have the primary responsibility of parenting Frances. Though Farry had no previous nanny experience—and had never even held a baby before—she took the job seriously and attempted to give Frances consistent care in a situation of high drama. "It was crucial, because of what [Kurt and Courtney] were going through in their lives, that somebody always be there to take care of Frances," Farry recalled. Jackie, Jamie, and Frances all moved to the Oakwood—the same apartment complex where Kurt stayed during the making of *Nevermind*—while Kurt continued in rehab, and Courtney returned to the Alta Loma house without her child.

Two days after the court hearing, Kurt flew to England. New baby, drug rehab, *Vanity Fair* article, and court hearings aside, he was needed onstage.

Not only did Nirvana headline the 1992 Reading Festival, Kurt essentially programmed the line-up, which included the Melvins, Screaming Trees, L7, Mudhoney, Eugenius, and Bjorn Again, an Abba-cover band Kurt adored. But most of the 60,000 fans had come for Nirvana, and Kurt was the king of this punk-rock prom.

There was more frenzy around this show than any concert Nirvana ever played. Much of it was generated by the English press, which had been reporting stories about Kurt's personal life as if they were breaking international news flashes. Several newspapers claimed Nirvana was broken up, and Kurt was described as in ill health. "Every day there were new rumors going around that Nirvana weren't going to play," Anton Brookes remembered. "People would come up and ask me, every five minutes, 'Are they playing?' And I'd say, 'Yes.' And then someone else would come up and say that they'd heard Kurt was dead."

Kurt was very much alive, having arrived in London that week. J. J. Gonson was walking through Piccadilly Circus two days before the festival when she ran into him. They chatted for a while, Kurt showed off baby pictures, then said he had to go the bathroom. They were directly in front of the Rock 'N' Roll Wax Museum, so Kurt walked up the stairs to the entrance, and very politely asked if he could use the bathroom. "No," the guard told him, "our restroom is for patrons only." Kurt stormed away. In the window of the museum sat a wax replica of Kurt holding a guitar.

At the concert, anticipation built during the opening acts and rumors continued to circulate that Nirvana was going to be a no-show. It rained, and the crowd greeted Mudhoney by pelting them with mud. "The body heat was so intense," recalled Gonson, "clouds of steam rose off the crowd as the rain continued to fall in the night." People waited to see whether Nirvana would actually appear and if Kurt was still breathing. "The energy level was so incredibly high," Gonson remembered. "When any figure came onstage, there was a ripple of shock through the audience."

Kurt had decided to play to the rumors, and arranged to appear onstage in a wheelchair and a disguise of a medical smock and a white wig. As he rolled onto the stage, he fell out of the chair and collapsed. Krist, always the perfect straight man, said into the microphone, "You're gonna make it, man. With the support of his friends and family . . . you, guy, are going to make it." Kurt tore off the disguise, jumped into the air, and ripped into "Breed." "It was such an electric moment," recalled Brookes, "it made you want to cry."

The show itself was revelatory. The band had not played together, or even rehearsed, for two months, yet they performed a 25-song set that spanned their entire catalog. It even included a snippet of Boston's 1976 hit "More Than a Feeling" to introduce "Teen Spirit," appropriate since Kurt claimed in interviews he'd stolen his riff from Boston.

Several times they appeared on the brink of breakdown, but always edged away from the precipice. Kurt dedicated "All Apologies" to Frances, and asked the crowd to chant "Courtney, we love you." During a song break, the band joked about their own demise in a way that didn't seem funny. "I don't know what you guys have heard, but this isn't our last show or anything," Krist told the audience.

"Yes, it is," asserted Kurt. "I would like to officially and publicly announce that this is our last show . . ."

". . . until we play . . . ," chimed in Krist.

". . . again . . . ," added Grohl.

". . . on our November tour," finished Kurt. "Are we going to tour in November? Or are we going to record a record?"

"Let's do a record," responded Krist.

It was no surprise when they ended the night with "Territorial Pissings" and demolished their instruments. They walked offstage as conquering invaders, while road manager Alex MacLeod pushed the abandoned wheelchair. "They had something to prove and they wanted to prove it," observed MacLeod. "They wanted to stand up, in front of all these people who were saying, 'It's over, he's a fuck-up, he's useless,' and say to them, 'Fuck you. It's not over.' "

Kurt returned to Los Angeles on September 2, but despite having wooed the United Kingdom for the third time, he was feeling less than victorious. He was still on methadone and in rehab, though he had switched treatment centers and was now a patient at Exodus in Marina Del Rey. Krist visited him at the center and found his friend looking ill: "He just laid there on the bed. He was just worn-out. He got better after that, because he'd gotten really strung-out. Everything was so heavy; he was a father; he was married; he was a rock star; and it all happened at one time. For anybody to go through all that stuff, it was a lot of pressure, but to be addicted to heroin while you were going through it is another matter."

Kurt spent his time in Exodus attending individual therapy, group therapy, and even 12-Step meetings. Most nights he wrote in his journal, producing long treatises on everything from the ethics of punk rock to the personal price of heroin addiction. "I wish there was someone I could ask for advice," he wrote one night. "Someone who wouldn't make me feel like a creep for spilling my guts and trying to explain all the insecurities that have plagued me for, oh, about 25 years now. I wish someone could explain to me why, exactly, I have no more desire to learn anymore."

Though Kurt was allowed to check out for brief day visits with Frances and Courtney, his nights seemed endless. Their marriage had the not-uncommon dynamic that when Kurt was weak and needy, he romanced Courtney more. The letters he wrote her from rehab were a combination of poetry and stream-of-consciousness ranting. He covered them with candle wax, blood, and, occasionally, his semen. One he penned during this period read:

> Rosewater, diaper smell. Use your illusion. Speak in tongue and cheek. Hey, girlfriend, detox. I'm in my Kraut box, held up here in my ink penitentiary. Kinda starving and kinda bloated. My water broke. Selling my body of water every night in a full house. Sell out in dark in bed, missing you more than an Air Supply song. Doll steak. Well done. . . . Your milk is so warm. Your milk is my shit. My shit is your milk. I have a small man's complexion. I'm speechless. I'm toothless. You pull wisdom from my teeth. My mom is the tooth fairy. You give me birth and dentures and fangs. I love you more than the tooth fairy.

But most of what Kurt wrote was about his struggle to free himself from heroin. Immediately prior to entering rehab, his journal entries reflected a growing state of denial, particularly in response to the media coverage of his drug problem. "I am not a heroine addict!" he penned one day, as if he were trying to convince himself. Another such entry read: "I am not gay, although I wish I were just to piss off homophobes. For those of you who are concerned with my present physical and mental state, I am not a junkie. I've had a rather inconclusive and uncomfortable stomach condition for the past three years, which, by the way, is not related. No stress, no fuss, and then, wham! Like a shotgun: stomach time."

Yet as soon as Kurt kicked heroin long enough to break the physical addiction, he took on the opposite slant, displaying a hatred and disgust at himself for getting hooked in the first place. "Almost everyone who tries hard drugs, i.e. heroine and cocaine, will eventually become literally a slave to these substances," he declared in one such self-examination. "I remember someone saying, 'if you try heroine once, you'll become hooked.' Of course, I laughed and scoffed at the idea, but now I believe this to be very true." And though when high, Kurt used his stomach as an excuse for drugs, when sober, he challenged this: "I feel real sorry for anyone who thinks they can use heroine as a medicine because, uh, duh, it don't work. Drug withdrawal is everything you've ever heard. You puke, you flail around, you sweat, you shit your bed just like that movie *Christiane F.*" Kurt was referencing a 1981 German film about drugs.

He found more success in his own treatment when he began seeing Dr. Robert Fremont, a Los Angeles chemical dependency counselor, who was also caring for Courtney. Fremont couldn't have been more controversial: He had once lost his medical license after prescribing himself narcotics. He eventually regained his license and started a practice treating some of Hollywood's biggest stars for their drug problems. He was successful in a profession where rates of relapse are extraordinarily high, perhaps because he understood addiction firsthand. He believed in generously prescribing legal drugs to clients detoxing from heroin, which was the methodology he used with Kurt.

In September 1992 Fremont began to use an experimental—and at the time illegal—treatment plan on Kurt that involved giving him daily doses of buprenorphine. This relatively benign narcotic stimulates the brain's opiate receptors, and thus can cut the craving for heroin, or so Fremont supposed. It worked in Kurt, at least temporarily. As Kurt described in his journal: "I was introduced to buprenorphine, which I found alleviates the [stomach] pain within minutes. It has been used experimentally in a few detox centers for opiate and cocaine withdrawal. The best thing about it is that there are no known side effects. It acts as an opiate, but it doesn't get you high. The potency range of buprenorphine is that of a mild barbiturate, and on a scale of one to ten, it's a one, and heroine is a ten."

. . .

On September 8 Kurt received a day-pass from Exodus to rehearse with Nirvana—despite his ongoing rehab, the business of the band didn't stop, and they were scheduled to play MTV's Video Music Awards the next day. The VMAs were the equivalent of the grunge Academy Awards—they were the highest-profile music awards, more respected at the time than the Grammy Awards, and came complete with a ceremony that attracted the power brokers of the industry. Nirvana had been nominated for three awards, and in July it had been announced they would play the show.

Still there were doubts whether Kurt could, or should, play an awards show in his state. Kurt chose, with pressure from management, to play. "He hated going to awards shows," explained manager Danny Goldberg, "and he didn't always like being recognized, but he worked very hard to get nominated for those awards shows, and he worked very hard to be recognized." Kurt whined in interviews that MTV played his videos too much; privately he called his managers and complained when he thought they didn't play them enough.

The huge television audience was guaranteed to sell more albums, but perhaps more important to Kurt, the awards were his first chance to stand on a podium and be recognized as the biggest rock star in the world. Though Kurt always downplayed his success and made out in interviews that he was trapped by his popularity, at every turn of his career he made critical choices that furthered fame and success; it was one of the greatest contradictions in his character. The absurdity of a man appearing on MTV and talking about how he hated publicity was lost on many of Nirvana's fans, who preferred to see Kurt as he successfully presented himself—as an unwilling victim of fame rather than someone who had skillfully sought it. Yet even in that desire for recognition, Kurt wanted things on his own terms, as events this week would prove.

Controversy erupted from the first rehearsal. As Kurt walked into UCLA's Pauley Pavilion, he went up to MTV's Amy Finnerty and told her, "I'm going to play a new song." "He was all excited about it, and acted like it was a gift," remembered Finnerty. Much to the surprise of

MTV's executives, who had expected to hear "Teen Spirit," they cranked out "Rape Me." It wasn't in fact a new song—Nirvana had been playing it in concert for two years—but it was new to MTV's brass. It had only eleven lines of lyrics, with a chorus of, "Rape me, my friend, rape me again." It had the same catchy soft/loud dynamic as "Teen Spirit," and with the odd chorus, it created a perfect Cobain aesthetic—beautiful, haunting, and disturbing.

Finnerty was immediately pulled into a production trailer where she was lectured by her bosses about the band's song choice: They thought "Rape Me" was about MTV. "Oh, *come on*," she protested. "I can assure you that he didn't write the song for or about *us*." Kurt had written it back in late 1990, but by 1992 he had altered the lyrics to include a slam at "our favorite inside source," a reference to the *Vanity Fair* article. Though he would defend the song in interviews as being an allegory of society's abuses, by September 1992 it had also come to represent a more personal metaphor for how he felt treated by the media, his managers, his bandmates, his addiction, and MTV (as the MTV executives had astutely realized).

A battle of wills began between MTV brass and the still-in-rehab Kurt, with Finnerty and Gold Mountain acting as go-betweens. MTV threatened to yank Nirvana from the show; Kurt said that was fine. MTV threatened to stop playing Nirvana videos; Kurt said that was fine, though he probably secretly feared it. And then the network upped the ante and threatened to stop playing videos by other artists managed by Gold Mountain. Finnerty was recruited to run between the two camps, and she drove out to Exodus with Courtney, Frances, and nanny Jackie to talk to Kurt, who had been whisked back to the facility immediately after the rehearsal. They sat on the lawn and discussed the options, but no resolution was found, and Kurt had to rush off to therapy. During each progressive rehab effort, therapy had become a larger part of his drug treatment, though he still refused to attend counseling when not in rehab.

Kurt reconsidered his song choice, but only after being told that Finnerty would be fired if Nirvana played "Rape Me." MTV's executives were visibly surprised when Nirvana showed up for the final rehearsal on the day of the show. All eyes in the hall turned to Kurt as he entered, and in that moment he reached down, grabbed Finnerty's hand, and defiantly walked down the center aisle, exaggeratedly swinging his arms with Amy's, like two toddlers on a day-care excursion. It was done entirely for the MTV honchos: Kurt was letting it be known that if they fired her, he wasn't playing their party.

This particular rehearsal was uneventful. The band played "Lithium," it sounded great, and the MTV staff clapped, perhaps a bit too enthusiastically. Yet as everyone waited for the show to start, a rumor circulated that once the show was live, Kurt planned to play "Rape Me." It was the kind of tension that enveloped most significant Nirvana performances, and Kurt thrived on it.

Meanwhile, a drama was unfolding backstage. Kurt, Courtney, nanny Jackie, and Finnerty were sitting with Frances when Axl Rose walked by, holding hands with his model-girlfriend Stephanie Seymour. "Hey Axl," Courtney beckoned, sounding a bit like Blanche Dubois, "will you be the godfather of our child?" Rose ignored her but turned to Kurt, who was bouncing Frances on his knee, and leaned down near his face. As the veins in Axl's neck thickened to the size of a garden hose, he barked: "You shut your bitch up, or I'm taking you down to the pavement!"

The idea that anyone could control Courtney was so laughable that a giant smile came to Kurt's face. He would have started chortling uncontrollably if it weren't for his own strong sense of self-preservation. He turned to Courtney and ordered, in a robot-like voice: "Okay, bitch. Shut up!" This brought a snicker to everyone within earshot, other than Rose and Seymour. Perhaps seeking to save face, Seymour created her own confrontation, asking Courtney, with as much sarcasm as she could muster, "Are you a model?" Love, who had just delivered her child three weeks before, was too quick for anyone to best her in this type of repartee—particularly Stephanie Seymour—and she fired back, "No. Are you a brain surgeon?" With that, Rose and Seymour stormed off.

Then it came time for Nirvana to take the stage. MTV's chiefs had already come up with a contingency plan to make sure they weren't duped by Kurt. The engineers had been instructed that if the band played "Rape Me," they should immediately go to a commercial. The only problem was, no one in the booth knew what the unreleased "Rape Me" sounded like. The show began, and Nirvana appeared on-stage. Suddenly, there was an awkward pause and in that moment one could see Kurt, Krist, and Dave locking eyes. Kurt lived for moments like this—all those hours during his youth doodling band logos in note-books and countless hours watching MTV had trained him well. He knew to never disappoint an audience, whether it be eighteen kids at the Community World Theater or a bunch of MTV suits sitting in a VIP section. He began slowly, strumming his guitar. At first it wasn't clear what song he was playing, but as Krist came in with the bass part, everyone in the hall, and over the airwaves, heard the opening chords to "Rape Me." What television viewers couldn't hear or see was an MTV executive running toward the control truck. But before they could be cut off, Nirvana shifted into the first chords of "Lithium." "We did that to fuck with them," Krist recalled. It had been less than twenty seconds—and MTV would edit it out when they replayed the show—but it was one of Nirvana's finest moments. As the song ended, Krist threw his bass in the air and it landed directly on his forehead. He staggered from the stage and collapsed, and many thought he was dead. When Finnerty found him backstage, he was shaking it off and laughing.

When Nirvana won the award for Best Alternative Music Video, they sent a Michael Jackson impersonator to accept. But all three band members did appear when they won Best New Artist, and Kurt said, "You know, it's really hard to believe everything you read." Rebutting the *Vanity Fair* piece had become an obsession for him. Sober for two weeks, he had a clear complexion and a preacher's clarity in his eyes. Later, while Eric Clapton played "Tears in Heaven," Finnerty and Courtney conspired to make Kurt and Eddie Vedder slow dance to-gether. When they were pushed together by the women, Kurt grabbed his rival and danced with him like an awkward teenager at the prom.

Novoselic, meanwhile, found himself confronted by Duff McKagan, of Guns N' Roses, and two bodyguards, looking for a brawl. Krist, Courtney, and baby Frances were inside the band's trailer when the entourage unsuccessfully attempted to topple it. Kurt missed this be-cause he'd left to make the Exodus curfew. "That was pretty funny, what you did," Finnerty said as he climbed into the van to leave.

"Yeah," Kurt said. He was smiling like a little boy who had embarrassed his teachers but escaped to annoy them again another day.

A week after the MTV Awards, Kurt sat down in his Alta Loma home with Robert Hilburn of the *Los Angeles Times* for his first major interview in six months. It was the first time he had been remotely honest with anyone in the press about his heroin addiction—over half the printed interview was concerned with his drug and health struggles. Kurt admitted to a heroin problem, but downplayed its extent. He said, correctly, that his experience with narcotics before he recorded *Nevermind* only amounted to "dabbling," but when he talked about his use since then, he minimized it, calling it "a little habit," and describing his addicted phase as "three weeks." He said he "chose to use drugs," mirroring the language from his own journals.

Many of his comments, on his health and his life, were shaded by the presence of Frances, who he held in his arms during the interview. "I don't want my daughter to grow up and someday be hassled by kids at school. . . . I don't want people telling her that her parents were junkies," he said. "I knew that when I had a child, I'd be overwhelmed, and it's true. . . . I can't tell you how much my attitude has changed since we've got Frances. Holding my baby is the best drug in the world."

He talked about how he'd come close to quitting Nirvana, but said the band was now on solid ground. They planned to record "a really raw album," and might tour again, he suggested. But he discounted the idea of a long tour, warning that his fragile health prevented him from it. "We might not go on any more long tours," he told Hilburn. "I would rather be healthy and alive. I don't want to sacrifice myself or my family."

The interview represented an emotional breakthrough for Kurt; by being truthful about his addiction, he had taken away some of the shame associated with it. Once Kurt found he was applauded for his honesty, rather than shunned, he felt like a man who had been condemned to a public execution only to be pardoned at the last moment. Shortly after the Hilburn article ran, he reflected in his journal on the current state of his life:

Sometimes I wonder if I could very well be the luckiest boy in the world. For some reason I've been blessed with loads of neat stuff within the past year, and I don't really think these baubles and gifts have been acquired by the fact that I'm a critically-acclaimed internationally-beloved teen idol demi-God-like blonde front man, cryptically honest. Stuttering outspoken speech impediment articulately award acceptance speech, Golden boy, rock star who has finally, and *finally* come out of the closet in regards to his viscous two month drug habit, showering the world with the classic, "I can no longer keep this a secret because it pains me to hide any part of my private life from my adoring, concerned, we-think-of-you-as-our-public-domain-cartoon-character-but-we-still-love-you-fans." Yes, my children, in the words of a total fucking geek, speaking on behalf of the world, "we really appreciate you finally admitting what we have been accusing you of, we needed to hear it because we were concerned because the catty gossip and jokes and speculation at our jobs, schools, and parties had become well, uh, exhausted."

19 THAT LEGENDARY DIVORCE

SEATTLE, WASHINGTON
SEPTEMBER 1992–JANUARY 1993

That legendary divorce is such a bore.
—From "Serve the Servants."

Two days after the MTV awards, Kurt, Courtney, and Frances—along with Jamie and Jackie—arrived in Seattle, where Nirvana was headlining a benefit to fight a music-censorship bill introduced into the Washington state legislature. The night before, they'd played a show in Portland to aid homosexual rights. The band's choice in benefits—mostly pro-gay and pro-choice organizations—had gained them a piece of baggage Kurt hadn't counted on: He was now receiving death threats. "It was mostly right-to-lifers," recalled Alex MacLeod. "We brought in metal detectors." One of the callers had warned that Kurt would be shot the moment he stepped onstage. This prospect was scary enough, but equally terrifying was being back in Seattle, where he would see his relatives for the first time since having the baby.

Kurt arrived at the sold-out, 16,000-seat Seattle Center Coliseum to find Wendy, Kim, and half-sister Brianne already in his dressing room. It was the first time they saw Kurt with Frances. "He was so excited, and he was such a good daddy," remembered Kim. "He just adored Frances and loved her so much. He would do anything to make her smile or laugh."

As his family doted on Frances, Kurt heard updates from his road manager. There had been more death threats; Fitz of Depression had problems in soundcheck (Kurt had of course insisted they open); and there were dozens of journalists hoping to interview him. Kurt eventually threw up his hands. Yet just when he thought he'd dispensed with all problems, Kim came running to him in a panic with one crisis Kurt didn't anticipate. "Dad's here!" she exclaimed. "What the *fuck* is he doing here?" Kurt cursed. Don had talked his way backstage by showing his driver's license and State Patrol I.D. to a security guard. "It's okay though," Kim assured Kurt. "I told him they weren't letting anyone in the dressing rooms." This was of course a lie, since even minor Sub Pop bands were walking around drinking free beer. Kim warned the head of security to not let Don anywhere near his son. Kurt hadn't seen his father for eight years, and hadn't spoken to him since February 1991. Don had tried contacting Kurt but their relationship was so estranged, he didn't even have his son's phone number but had left messages with neighbors and record company receptionists.

Don walked into the dressing room with Kurt's half-brother Chad. "Oh, hi, Dad," Kurt said, changing the tone of his voice to hide the anger he had been demonstrating moments before. For the first time in a decade, the four original Cobains—Don, Wendy, Kurt, and Kim—were in a room together. Their clan now included two other half-siblings, Courtney, and a couple of Kurt's employees. Three-week-old Frances Bean Cobain—cooing and grunting as she was passed around her relations—was the only one oblivious to all the tension; to everyone else, it seemed like the weigh-in at a particularly contentious boxing match.

The Cobain family soap opera did not disappoint the onlookers. When Don saw Wendy holding Frances, he said, "Well hello, *Grandma*," putting an emphasis on the "Grandma" as if it were a slur. "How's it feel to be a *Grandma*?" "Great, *Grandpa*," Wendy replied in the same sarcastic tone. "I love it, *Grandpa*." What in many families might have been a humorous or sentimental exchange turned into an uncomfortable confrontation. More than eighteen years had passed since Don and Wendy had divorced, but suddenly the original family was emotionally back in 1210 East First Street in Aberdeen, and the relationship between Mom and Dad was unchanged. For Kurt, it was a joining of his new family with the wounds of the original. "I was like, 'Oh, my God, not again,' " remembered Kim. The only different dynamic was Kurt's role; he was no longer the little, helpless boy. He had become—with 16,000 adoring fans waiting on the other side of the wall—the patriarch.

Courtney had never seen Don before, and found herself speechless observing how much he looked like his son—Don had the rough handsomeness of a middle-aged Steve McQueen. But Kurt was not without words, particularly for his elder lookalike: "You shut the fuck up," he yelled at his father, as forcefully as he had ever spoken in his life, using a curse word that in his childhood would have gotten him "thumped" on the temple. "Don't talk to her like that. Don't you put her down."

Quickly, Wendy, Kim, Courtney, and Brianne left the room. "Jeez, you look old," Kurt told his father when he calmed down. He immediately assumed Don was there to ask for money. "I didn't want anything," Don recalled. "I just wanted to make contact with him. I said, 'If you're happy, having fun, that's great. Just try to keep in touch.' "

Kurt signed a poster for his half-brother Chad—who, Kurt introduced to everyone as "his stepbrother," much to Don's consternation— and told his father he had to go: He was late for Nirvana's set. As production manager Jeff Mason walked Kurt toward the stage, Kurt had only a few seconds to leave behind his family, and to become "Kurdt Kobain," the rock star, his other self. He was about to walk out onstage in the very hall where he'd seen his first rock concert, Sammy Hagar with Quarterflash, only ten years before though it seemed like an eternity ago. Mason and Kurt always used these brief walks to discuss details of the show, or check in emotionally—this was one of the few times Kurt ever took that long walk toward the spotlight in complete silence.

The show itself was phenomenal, the best Nirvana had ever done in Seattle. The rustiness of Reading was gone, and Kurt seemed like a man with a burning desire to convert any non-believers. Hundreds of kids crowd-surfed, cascading over the barricades like lemmings over a cliff. During a song break, Krist told the story of how he'd been "banned for life" from the Coliseum for getting drunk at a Neil Young concert: Backstage he'd found a picture of himself on a bulletin board of individuals who should never be allowed inside.

After the show, Kurt blew off all interview requests except one: *Monk,* an irregularly published travel magazine. When *Monk*'s Jim

Crotty and Michael Lane made their way to his dressing room, they found it deserted except for Kurt and Frances. "There was this feeling," Crotty remembered, "akin to when I met the Dalai Lama: When you have somebody whose every move is dissected to such a degree, in your own mind they take on this incredible importance. There was all this activity outside, and then you open the door, and there's Kurt Cobain holding a child in an empty room. He seemed so sensitive, exposed, vulnerable, and tender, with him holding the child."

Where the Hilburn interview had found him in a serious mood, this conversation was the greatest myth-making session of Kurt's life. When asked about Aberdeen, he told a story of being run out of town: "They chased me up to the Castle of Aberdeen with torches, just like the Frankenstein monster. And I got away in a hot-air balloon." When Crotty asked if there was "a quintessential Aberdeen" place in his memory, he said "under the bridge." He described his favorite food as "water and rice." When asked if he believed in reincarnation, he replied: "If you're really a mean person you're going to come back as a fly and eat poop." And when Crotty asked Kurt what he might title his autobiography, his response was, " 'I Was Not Thinking,' by Kurt Cobain."

That fall Kurt and Courtney—with Frances, Jamie, and Jackie in tow—spent most of their time in Seattle, living in the Sorrento, the Inn at the Market, and a couple of other four-star hotels. They would register as "Simon Ritchie," Sid Vicious's real name. They had just purchased a $300,000 house on eleven acres near Carnation, 30 miles outside of Seattle. The house—which had a tree growing through it—was so run-down they began construction of a new home on the property.

It was while in Seattle Kurt learned two women from England were writing an unauthorized biography. Following on the heels of the *Vanity Fair* profile, this sent him into a furor, as his Aunt Judy had already been interviewed for the book. On October 22, Kurt, Courtney, Aunt Judy, and Dave Grohl phoned co-author Victoria Clarke and left a series of increasingly threatening messages. "If anything comes out in this book which hurts my wife, I'll fucking hurt you," Kurt warned. In another he raged, "I don't give a flying fuck if I have this recorded that I'm threatening you. I suppose I could throw out a few hundred thousand dollars to have you snuffed out, but maybe I'll try the legal way first." The messages filled the tape on Clarke's answering machine, which she turned over to the police. Asked about the threats by the *New York Times*, Danny Goldberg said, "Kurt absolutely denies the notion that he or any member of the band made such phone calls." But Kurt later admitted he made them. He also wrote Clarke a letter (never sent) that included such venom as, "You are both hideously jealous and hideously ugly. You are not writing a book about my band, you are writing a book about how jealous you are of my smart, beautiful, sexy, and talented wife, none of which either of you are. If one single solitary, tabloidesque or negative comment or statement in regards to my wife shows up in your book, I will (with more enthusiasm than I've ever had in my life) gladly devote every fucking waking hour of my life to make yours unlivable. If that doesn't work, well, let's not forget that I work for the Mafia."

In discussing the matter a few months later, Kurt was still unrepentant: "If I ever find myself destitute and I've lost my family, I won't hesitate to get revenge on people who have fucked with me," he told Michael Azerrad. "I've always been capable of that. I've tried killing people before in a fit of rage when I've gotten in fights with people. . . . When people unnecessarily fuck with me, I just can't help but want to beat them to death." A month prior he had received death threats; now he was making them.

Kurt's late-night phone calls became commonplace, though most were thinly veiled cries for help. Everyone from his lawyer to members of the crew would receive calls at four in the morning. He once called his Aunt Mari at 2:30 in the morning with a business proposition: He wanted to put out an album for her. "I figure I might as well throw my weight around while I have it," he explained.

Kurt phoned Jesse Reed frequently in the middle of the night—he knew Jesse would always be a sympathetic ear. There had been a gradual shift in Kurt's friendships as both his fame and drug usage grew. Kurt and Dylan were closer than ever, but many of his old friends had fallen by the wayside—most were now unable to contact him due to the walls of his fame and his travel schedule. Kurt's old friends complained that

Courtney had become a wedge: Sometimes when they called she hung up on them, thinking they were drug buddies and wanting to protect Kurt from his vices.

Kurt increasingly depended on those he employed for advice and friendship. Co-manager Danny Goldberg took on a more important role, as did crew members Alex MacLeod and Jeff Mason. But his confidences rarely extended to the other members of Nirvana now. Krist and Kurt's relationship had changed after the wedding: Though they would talk about band business, the days of social interactions were over. "I remember getting in big fights with Kurt over the phone," Krist recalled, "and at the end of the phone call he'd say, 'Well things are going to get better.' And I'd say, 'Yeah, things are going to get better.' That's what we'd agree upon, just to feel better about things." And while Dave and Kurt had been like brothers when they lived together, by the end of 1992, Kurt openly talked about firing Dave whenever he was unhappy with something the drummer had done, either off or on the stage.

One of the more unusual friendships Kurt forged during 1992 was with Buddy Arnold, a self-described "geezer-Jewish-jazz drummer-former junkie." Arnold ran the Musicians Assistance Program, which offered treatment referrals for musicians. Upon their first interaction in 1992, Kurt suspiciously looked at the bald, thin senior citizen and asked, "Did you ever use drugs?" "Only heroin," Arnold replied, "and only for 31 years." That was enough to cement Kurt's trust. When in Los Angeles, Kurt would stop by Arnold's condo, but rarely did he want to talk about treatment: Mostly he wanted to hear about Charlie Parker, Billie Holiday, and other legends Arnold had known. Arnold tried to insert cautionary tales of how drugs had destroyed them. Kurt listened politely, but always moved the conversation back to the greats.

On October 24 Kurt reunited with Krist and Dave to begin work on their next album. They had decided to return to do demos with Jack Endino on the same mixing board employed on *Bleach*. Though they worked on six songs, only "Rape Me" progressed very far. Courtney and Frances came by for the second night's session; Kurt did the final vocal take for "Rape Me" with Frances sitting on his lap. The session ended when a terminally ill seventeen-year-old from the Make-A-Wish Foundation came by and the band bought him pizza.

They ended October with a show in Buenos Aires, Argentina, for 50,000 fans. They were being offered huge paychecks to perform at such mega-concerts, and Kurt was now occasionally accepting them. But the show was painful for both band and audience: Nirvana hit the opening chords of "Teen Spirit" but did not play the song, and the crowd nearly rioted in their disappointment. Kurt also missed Frances— it was one of his first tour dates without her.

Early in November, Kurt and Courtney moved to the Four Seasons Olympic Hotel in Seattle, registering under the name "Bill Bailey," Axl Rose's real name. They would stay for almost two months and ring up a bill of $36,000 before the ritzy hotel kicked them out. Eventually they would be kicked out of every luxury hotel in Seattle and forced to move to more modest accommodations. It wasn't their drug use that typically got them in trouble, but instead their habit of leaving cigarette burns on the carpets and wrecking their rooms beyond repair. "I always would tip the maids," recalled nanny Jackie Farry, "but it would get to a point where the hotel would say, 'We don't want your business.' "

In the Four Seasons' Garden Court restaurant, Courtney sat for an interview with *The Rocket*'s Gillian Gaar a week before Thanksgiving. Mostly Courtney talked about the upcoming Hole album—but she had one comment on her husband: "This whole concept of the man being so weak, and not making any choices—has anybody ever put on his record? Has anybody ever put on my record? You're talking about two people who are absolutely not stupid!" She attacked the sexism of rock, where "a woman, of course, can only use her pussy to get anywhere. Men can get by just playing good songs."

The Rocket interview was the first in what would be a larger campaign of damage control—the couple felt so burned by the *Vanity Fair* piece that they began encouraging interview requests from sympathetic writers. Sub Pop's Jonathan Poneman was solicited by *Spin* to profile them, and his piece, titled "Family Values," painted a portrait of loving and overprotective parents. "We knew we could give [Frances] what we didn't get," Courtney told Poneman, "loyalty and compassion, encouragement. We knew we could give her a real home and spoil her rotten." But more effective than the article were the accompanying photographs of Kurt and Courtney playing with their child. The pictures showed they were a remarkably good-looking family, and Frances was a beautiful baby who looked both healthy and well cared for.

During October, Kurt spent many hours obsessively composing liner notes for *Incesticide*, an album of B-sides slated for release before Christmas; he also painted the album's cover of a baby clinging to an alien parent staring at poppy flowers. He wrote at least twenty different drafts of the liner notes, and used this forum to slam what he perceived as his growing list of enemies. In one draft, Kurt challenged the image of him as controlled by others: "A big 'fuck you' to those of you who have the audacity to claim that I'm so naive and stupid that I would allow myself to be taken advantage of and manipulated."

That October, Kurt's managers suggested he consider putting out an authorized biography, which might deter more damning press. He agreed, deciding that if he told the story of his life—even if it was controversial—it would give him spin control. Gold Mountain approached Michael Azerrad, who in October began work on a book done with Kurt's cooperation. For its cover, Kurt even created an oil painting, which wasn't used. He did a series of interviews with Azerrad that fall, and though he mostly told the truth, as in his interview with Hilburn, he many times directed the writer to a smaller light scene so as to ignore the larger dark landscape. As it was, Azerrad's book included Kurt's frank admissions of drug problems, though the extent of his addiction was downplayed. When Kurt read the final manuscript, he made only two factual changes, but let many of his own mythical stories, from guns in the river to living under a bridge, stand.

The second week of November Kurt did a photo session for *Monk*—he was to be on the cover of their Seattle issue. He arrived alone at Charlie Hoselton's studio and, unlike most photo sessions, cooperated fully. "Here's the deal," Kurt told Hoselton. "I'll stay as long as you want, I'll do whatever you want, you just have to do two things for me: Turn off your phone, and don't answer the door if anyone knocks." Courtney had already called the studio five times looking for him. The *Monk* editors convinced Kurt to dress like a logger and pose with a chainsaw. At one point during the shoot, Kurt dared to venture outside, and when Hoselton asked him to pose in front of the espresso machine, Kurt did one better—he pushed the barista aside and made a coffee.

A month later, when Kurt sat down for an interview with *The Advocate*, a weekly gay magazine, writer Kevin Allman found the couple looking surprisingly domestic—Courtney was getting ready to take Frances for a walk in a stroller. When Allman commented they looked nothing like Sid and Nancy, Kurt replied: "It's just amazing that at this point in rock-and-roll history, people are still expecting their rock icons to live out these classic rock archetypes, like Sid and Nancy. To assume that we're just the same because we did heroin for a while—it's pretty offensive to be expected to be like that." The interview was far-reaching and saw Kurt play to the magazine's gay readership. He falsely claimed he'd been arrested for spray-painting "Homo Sex Rules" in Aberdeen, and talked about his support of homosexual rights. He retold the Axl Rose/MTV Awards story, but exaggerated to claim that Rose had an entourage of "50 bodyguards: huge, gigantic, brain-dead oafs, ready to kill." When asked about heroin, Kurt admitted to once having struggled with the drug, but explained that the rumors about him continued because, "I am a skinny person. Everyone thinks we're on drugs again, even people we work with. I guess I'll have to get used to that for the rest of my life."

Kurt admitted the past year had been his least prolific period. At least he was reading books, he argued, including *Perfume*, by Patrick Suskind, for a second time; he also professed to being a fan of Camille Paglia's work—this was one of the many influences Courtney affected. He talked about painting, and said that making dolls had been his primary artistic expression of late. "I copy them from doll-collector magazines," he explained. "They're clay. I bake them, and then I make them look really old, and put old clothes on them." When asked for any final words, he responded with an answer that didn't sound like it came from a 25-year-old: "I don't have the right to judge anything."

By mid-November, the Los Angeles court relaxed their restrictions on the Cobains and Courtney's sister Jamie departed. During her three-month period of guardianship of Frances, Jamie had proven a strict master, rarely allowing Kurt and Courtney time with their daughter without supervision. With Jamie gone, Jackie continued to impose rules, shielding the baby from her parents when they were high. Jackie took care of the bulk of the diapering and feeding, though she would frequently deposit Frances, with a full bottle, with her parents at bedtime. "Sometimes, Kurt would say, 'I really want to see her,' " Farry recalled. "And I'd bring her in, but he'd not really be capable so I'd take her back because he was nodding off." Yet when Kurt and Courtney were sober, they were affectionate and doting parents.

During the final months of 1992, Kurt finalized many of the songs for his next record—which he was still calling *I Hate Myself and I Want to Die*—and most were about his family, old and new. Seeing his father haunted Kurt, and Don became a central character in this latest song cycle. In "Serve the Servants" Kurt crafted his most autobiographical lyrics, starting with a direct reference to the mania around *Nevermind*: "Teenage angst has paid off well / Now I'm bored and old." There were pokes at his critics ("self-appointed judges judge") and the way Courtney had been treated by the press ("if she floats, then she is not a witch"). But most of the song was about Don, with the infamous line: "I tried hard to have a father / But instead I had a dad." In the chorus, Kurt downplayed the most significant single event in his life: "That legendary divorce is such a bore." When he performed the song, he sang this phrase as if it were a cast-off, but in his very first draft of the lyrics, he wrote this line twice as big and underlined it three times.

Though no explanation was needed, Kurt penned extensive liner notes for the song. "I guess this song is for my father," he wrote, "who is incapable of communicating at the level of affection in which I have always expected. In my own way, I decided to let my father know that I don't hate him. I simply don't have anything to say to him, and I don't need a father/son relationship with a person whom I don't want to spend a boring Christmas with. In other words: I love you; I don't hate you; I don't want to talk to you." After writing this, Kurt had second thoughts—he crossed most of it out.

Kurt also wrote Don an unsent letter that next spring, reflecting on how Frances had changed him:

Seven months ago I chose to put myself in a position which requires the highest form of responsibility a person can have. A responsibility that should not be dictated. Everytime I see a television show that has dying children, or see a testimonial by a parent who recently lost their child, I can't help but cry. The thought of losing my baby haunts me every day. I'm even a bit unnerved to take her in the car in fear of getting into an accident. I swear that if I ever find myself in a similar situation [to what] you've been in (i.e. the divorce), I will fight to my death to keep the right to provide for my child. I'll go out of my way to remind her that I love her more than I love myself. Not because it's a father's duty, but because I want to, out of love. And if Courtney and I end up hating each other's guts, we both will be adult and responsible enough to be pleasant to one another when our child is around us. I know that you've felt for years that my mother has somehow brainwashed Kim and I into hating you. I can't stress enough how totally untrue this is, and I think it's a very lazy and lame excuse to use for not trying harder to provide your fatherly duties. I can't recall my mother ever talking shit about you until much later in the game, right around the last two years of high school. That was a time when I came to my own realizations without the need of my mother's input. Yet she noticed my contempt for you, and your family, and acted upon my feelings in accordance, by taking the opportunity to vent her frustrations out on you. Every time she talked shit about you, I've let her know that I don't appreciate it, and how unnecessary I think it is. I've never taken sides with you or my mother because while I was growing up, I had equal contempt for you both.

Even more telling was a collage Kurt created in his journal where he took Don's yearbook photo and pasted it next to a picture of his A&R man, Gary Gersh. Above Don, he wrote "Old Dad," with the caption, "Made me pawn my first guitar. Insisted I participate in sports." Above Gersh, he wrote "New Dad," without a description. Underneath this collage, Kurt pasted several pictures from old medical textbooks of deformed bodies, and headlined this, "The many moods of Kurdt Kobain." Under the mood "baby," he used an image of a retarded man;

for "pissy" he showed a man wetting himself; for a skinny man, he wrote "bully," to describe his mood; and for the only normal man, he doctored the man's shirt so it read "Bratmobile" and drew a syringe on it, for the mood "sassy."

Kurt and Courtney ended 1992 in Seattle seeing the Supersuckers at the RKCNDY club on New Year's Eve. Later, at a party, Kurt ran into Jeff Holmes, a local booking agent. They chatted about music, and when the subject of the Meat Puppets came up, Holmes told Kurt he knew the band. Holmes phoned Curt Kirkwood and handed the receiver to Kurt. It was the start of a friendship between the Meat Puppets and Nirvana that would eventually lead to collaboration.

With the year ending, Kurt and Courtney compiled a list of those they intended to send Christmas cards to. Included were all the usual suspects and a few unlikely recipients: Eddie Vedder, Axl Rose, and Joe Strummer. Near Strummer's name, Courtney suggested they write, "Thanks for siccing your friend Lynn Hirschberg on us, she's really fucking sweet and honest. Give her our best regards, won't you?" The card they sent to Susan Silver, Soundgarden's manager, was addressed to "our favorite inside source," since they believed—incorrectly—that Silver was the originator of the *Vanity Fair* quotes.

Also on their Christmas card list were two people the couple were truly close to—Dr. Paul Crane, who had delivered Frances, and Dr. Robert Fremont. In fact, by an accounting done for Kurt by Gold Mountain, the Cobains had spent $75,932.08 on medical bills between January 1 and August 31, 1992. Almost half went to doctors involved in their drug treatment, including $24,000 alone to Dr. Michael Horowitz, whom Courtney later sued, claiming he released her medical records to the press. Dr. Fremont collected $8,500 for his treatments and the buprenorphine he gave them. A few of the bills were pre-rehab and represented the fees charged by "Dr. Feelgood" physicians who had prescribed narcotics. Though Kurt finally was making big bucks from *Nevermind* (total sales had reached eight million copies), these medical bills demonstrated how much of 1992 had been absorbed with their health struggles.

Kurt revealed more financial details in the *Advocate* interview: He earned over a million dollars in 1992, "of which $380,000 went to taxes, $300,000 went to [buying the Carnation] house, the rest went to doctors and lawyers, and our personal expenses were $80,000. That's including car rentals, food, everything. That's not very much; that's definitely not what Axl spends a year." Their legal bills ran $200,000. Though Kurt's income had risen incredibly from the previous year, he was spending money as fast as he could make it.

Two weeks before Christmas, *Incesticide*, Nirvana's collection of outtakes and B-sides, was released. It entered the *Billboard* charts at No. 51, a remarkable feat considering it wasn't new material. Within two months it would sell half a million copies without major promotional effort or touring.

The only dates Nirvana played that January were two mega-stadium shows in Brazil undertaken for huge paydays. The January 16 show in São Paolo drew the largest crowd Nirvana ever played to—110,000—and both the crew and band recalled it as their single worst performance. It had been a while since the group had rehearsed, and Kurt was nervous; to make matters worse he had mixed pills with liquor, which left him struggling to play a chord.

Their set featured more covers than Nirvana songs. They played Terry Jacks's "Seasons in the Sun," Kim Wilde's "Kids in America," the Clash's "Should I Stay or Should I Go," plus Duran Duran's "Rio." For a cover of Queen's "We Will Rock You," Kurt changed the lyrics to "We will fuck you." Thirty minutes into the set, Krist threw his bass at Kurt and stormed off. "It was this comedy of errors," remembered guitar tech Earnie Bailey. "Everyone started throwing fruit at them, in this classic vaudeville gesture. We were wondering if we were going to get out of there without getting the van overturned." Eventually, Krist was located and shoved back onstage by the crew—if the band didn't play 45 minutes, they would not fulfill their contract, which would mean no paycheck. As it was, even the huge check didn't cover the costs of the equipment the band destroyed. Krist later described the show as a "mental breakdown," while a Brazilian magazine was less kind: "They were not the *real* Nirvana at all; instead it was only a depressing Cobain making noise with his guitar."

Kurt *was* depressed and had become suicidal that week. The band had a week before their next show in Rio, and the original plan was to work on the upcoming album. But when they checked into their high-rise hotel in Rio, Kurt, after an argument with Courtney, threatened to leap to his death. "I thought he was going to jump out a window," remembered Jeff Mason. Finally Mason and Alex MacLeod took him to find another hotel. "We checked into hotel after hotel, but couldn't stay because we'd walk into a room and there would be a balcony, and he would be ready to jump," Mason explained. Finally MacLeod found a first-floor room, not an easy task in Rio. While the rest of the band slept in a luxury high-rise, Kurt stayed in a single-story fleabag.

Much of Kurt's despondency came from drug withdrawal. On tour, with the watchful eyes of the band and crew upon him, he was unable to escape and score, at least without feeling shame. Even when he could slip away from the heightened surveillance, one of his greatest fears in life was that he'd be arrested buying drugs, and it would end up in the papers. It was one thing for rock critics to speculate that he was messed up—he could always deny that or do what he usually did, which was admit in interviews he'd used drugs in the past. But if he were busted, no denial he could fabricate would diminish an arrest. To lessen his heroin craving, he would use whatever intoxicants he could find—pills or booze—but this was a far less reliable formula.

A night in a ground-floor hotel seemed to help, and Kurt showed up at the studio the next day refreshed, wanting to work. Kurt played the first-ever version of "Heart-Shaped Box," a song that was the result of a collaboration with Courtney. Despite Kurt's mood earlier in the trip, once he began recording he came out of his melancholia. "There were some moments that were positive musically," Mason observed. During breaks between Nirvana songs, Courtney and Hole's new drummer, Patti Schemel, worked on some of Love's songs.

Their Brazil trip ended with another huge concert, on January 23, in Rio's Apoetose Stadium. This show was more professional than

São Paolo, and they debuted "Heart-Shaped Box" and "Scentless. Apprentice," which in this form stretched on for seventeen minutes. When they flew home the next day, Kurt and the other band members were once again upbeat about the upcoming sessions for their new album.

20 | HEART-SHAPED COFFIN

SEATTLE, WASHINGTON
JANUARY 1993–AUGUST 1993

I am buried in a heart-shaped coffin for weeks.
—An early version of "Heart-Shaped Box."

The line "I hate myself and I want to die" had been kicking around Kurt Cobain's verbal and written repertoire for some time. Like many of his lyrics, or the quips he threw off in interviews, before it appeared publicly it had been auditioned dozens of times in his journal. The line first appeared in his writing around the middle of 1992 in a list of rhyming couplets, and though he didn't come up with a rhyme to pair it with, like a scientist who had stumbled onto a breakthrough formula, he circled it. By mid-1992, he was fixated on the phrase, telling interviewers and friends it was to be the title of his next record. At best it was gallows humor.

What wasn't a joke were the expressions of self-hate that continually cropped up in Kurt's journals, including a poem that sounded similar to his childhood graffiti: "I hate you. I hate them. But I hate myself most of all." In another Jack Kerouac–styled sentence from this period, he wrote of his stomach pain as if it were a curse: "I've violently vomited to the point of my stomach literally turning itself inside out to show you the fine hair-like nerves I've kept and raised as my children, garnishing and marinating each one, as if God had fucked me and planted these precious little eggs, and I parade around them in a peacock victory and maternal pride like a whore relieved from the duties of repeated rape and torture, promoted to a more dignified job of just plain old every day, good old, wholesome prostitution." The remark "As if God had fucked me" came up often, and it was conjured without humor—it was Kurt's own explanation for his physical and emotional struggles.

It was only after Krist convinced Kurt that Nirvana might be opening themselves up to lawsuits with the title "I Hate Myself and Want to Die" that Kurt considered anything else. He switched titles, first to "Verse, Chorus, Verse," and then finally to "In Utero," which was from a poem of Courtney's.

Many of the songs Kurt had written in 1992 were affected by his marriage. "We feed off each other," he wrote in "Milk It," a line that summed up their creative and emotional union. As is common in the marriage of two artists, they began to think alike, share ideas, and use each other as editor. They also shared a journal: Kurt would write a single line, to which Courtney would add a couplet. He read her writings, and she read his, and each was influenced by the other's musings. Courtney was a more traditional lyricist, crafting tighter and less murky lines, and her sensibility greatly shaped "Heart-Shaped Box" and "Pennyroyal Tea," among others. She made Kurt a more careful writer, and it is not by accident that these stand as two of Nirvana's most accomplished works: They were crafted with more intent than Kurt had spent on the entire *Nevermind* album.

But Courtney's biggest role in Kurt's new songs was as a character— just as *Nevermind* was mostly about Tobi, so *In Utero* would be shaped by Don, Courtney, and Frances. "Heart-Shaped Box," of course, referenced Courtney's initial gift of the silk-and-lace box, but the song's line "forever in debt to your priceless advice" came from a note he sent her. "I am eternally grateful for your priceless opinions and advice," he wrote, sounding more sincere in the writing than he did singing the line. The album was his gift to her—he was returning her a "Heart-Shaped Box," though doing it in a musical form. It was not a Hallmark valentine though: "Heart-Shaped Box" evolved through several drafts, and Kurt had originally titled it "Heart-Shaped Coffin," including the line "I am buried in a heart-shaped coffin for weeks." Courtney advised him that was a bit dark. Yet theirs was a relationship where each urged the other to push boundaries, and the artistic risk of these new songs was a matter of pride to her as well as to him.

Prior to entering the studio, Kurt had a list of eighteen songs he was considering; twelve from the list would ultimately end up on the finished album, but with their titles shifted considerably. The song that eventually was called "Radio Friendly Unit Shifter" started life as "Nine Month Media Blackout," Kurt's not-so-veiled response to the *Vanity Fair* piece. "All Apologies" was originally titled "La, La, La . . . La" while "Moist Vagina," a B-side, began with a far longer and more descriptive name: "Moist vagina, and then she blew him like he's never been blown, brains stuck all over the wall."

The band flew to Minnesota on Valentine's Day to begin the album. Seeking a sparse and raw sound, they had hired Steve Albini to produce—Kurt intended to move as far away as he could from *Nevermind*. Albini had been in the influential punk band Big Black, and back in 1987 Kurt had traveled to a Seattle steam plant to witness Big Black's last performance. As a teenager, Kurt had idolized Albini, though as an adult it was at best a working relationship. Albini got along well with the rest of the band, but later described Courtney as a "psycho hose-beast." She countered that the only way he would think her attractive would be "if I was from the East Coast, played the cello, had big tits and small hoop earrings, wore black turtlenecks, had all matching luggage, and never said a word."

Gold Mountain had picked Pachyderm Studios in Cannon Falls, Minnesota, thinking the rural climes would minimize distractions. They did: By the sixth day of the session—February 20, Kurt's 26th birthday—the band had finished all basic tracks. When they weren't working, they made crank phone calls to Eddie Vedder and traveled to Minneapolis, an hour away. There Kurt searched the Mall of America for plastic anatomical models of The Visible Man, his latest collecting obsession. When the record was finished, only twelve days after they began, the band celebrated by setting their pants on fire. "We were listening to the final mixes," explained Pat Whalen, a friend who stopped by. "Everyone poured solvent on their pants, lit them, and then passed the flame from one pant leg to another, and from one person to the next." They were wearing their pants when they did this; to avoid burns they had to douse each other with beer the instant the flames shot up their legs.

The finished album had been recorded in half the time of *Nevermind.* "Things were on the upswing," Krist recalled. "We left all the personal stuff outside the door. And it was a triumph—it's my favorite Nirvana record." Novoselic's viewpoint was shared by many critics, and by Kurt, who thought it his strongest effort. At first, Kurt saw "Pennyroyal Tea" as the first single: It combined a Beatles-like riff with the slow/fast pacing Nirvana perfected. The title referred to an herbal abortion remedy. Though Courtney's lyrics had shaped the tune, it ended with a nonfictional description of Kurt's stomach: "I'm on warm milk and laxatives, cherry-flavored antacids."

In Utero also had a number of up-tempo rockers, but even these had lyrical depth. "Very Ape" and "Radio Friendly Unit Shifter" had the kind of crunchy riffs played during a three-second break in a basketball game, yet featured lyrics convoluted enough to inspire term papers and Internet debates. "Milk It" was a punk rock burner the band had pulled off in one take, yet Kurt spent days fine-tuning the lyrics. "Her milk is my shit / My shit is her milk," was his twisted way of connecting himself to his wife. The song also hinted at his rehab ("your scent is still here in my place of recovery"), plus he reprised a line that he'd been kicking around in various songs since high school: "Look, on the bright side is suicide." In his unused liner notes for "Dumb" he described his descent to drug addiction: "All that pot. All that supposedly, unaddictive, harmless, safe reefer that damaged my nerves, and ruined my memory, and made me feel like wanting to blow up the prom. It just wasn't ever strong enough, so I climbed the ladder to the poppy."

But no song on the album ranked with "Heart-Shaped Box." "I wish I could eat your cancer when you turn black," Kurt sang in what has to be the most convoluted route any songwriter undertook in pop history to say "I love you." With the line, "Throw down your umbilical noose, so I can climb right back," Kurt ended his most transcendent song with a plea that could be to Courtney, to his mother, from his daughter, from himself, or perhaps most likely, to his God. His own explanation in his unpublished liner notes fell completely apart (he crossed most of it out) but touched on *The Wizard of Oz,* "I Claudius,"

Leonardo da Vinci, male seahorses (who carry their young), racism in the Old West, and Camille Paglia. Like all great art, "Heart-Shaped Box" escaped any easy categorization and offered many interpretations to the listener, as apparently it did to its author.

What "Heart-Shaped Box" meant to Kurt is best surmised by the treatment he wrote for the song's video. Kurt envisioned it starring William S. Burroughs, and he wrote Burroughs begging him to appear in the video. "I realize that stories in the press regarding my drug use may make you think that this request comes from a desire to parallel our lives," he wrote. "Let me assure you, this is not the case." But exactly what Kurt hoped to achieve by casting the writer was never clear: In his attempt to convince Burroughs to participate, he had offered to obscure the writer's face, so that no one other than Kurt would know of his cameo. Burroughs declined the invitation.

Both the *In Utero* album and "Heart-Shaped Box" video were obsessed with images of birth, death, sexuality, disease, and addiction. There were several versions of the video made, and a battle over who originated the ideas eventually caused Kurt to split with video director Kevin Kerslake, who promptly sued Kurt and Nirvana; Anton Corbijn completed the final cut, which included shots of Kurt's growing collection of dolls. The released video centered around a junkie-looking elderly Jesus dressed as the Pope, wearing a Santa hat while being crucified in a field of poppies. A fetus hangs from a tree, and reappears crammed inside an IV bottle being fed into Jesus, who has moved to a hospital room. Krist, Dave, and Kurt are shown in a hospital room waiting for Jesus to recover. A giant heart with a crossword puzzle inside it appears, as does the Aryan girl, whose white KKK hat turns to black. And throughout these images, Kurt's face continues to charge the camera. It is an absolutely striking video, and all the more remarkable because Kurt privately told his friends that many of these images were from his dreams.

The first week of March, Kurt and Courtney moved into a $2,000-a-month house at 11301 Lakeside Avenue NE in Seattle. It was a modern three-story home, just up from Lake Washington, with views of Mount

Rainier and the Cascade Mountains. It was also gigantic, and at over 6,000 square feet of living space, it was bigger than all of Kurt's previous homes combined. Yet the Cobains quickly filled the house—an entire room became Kurt's painting space, there were quarters for guests and nannies, and Kurt's MTV awards decorated the second-floor bathroom. In the two-car garage, next to Kurt's Valiant, they now had a gray 1986 Volvo 240DL, which Kurt proudly told his friends was the safest family car ever made.

Soon after the move, Kurt and Courtney's ongoing case with the Department of Children's Services finally came to an end. Though the Cobains had initially followed the court's decrees, they still feared Frances would be taken from them. Moving to Seattle was a strategic chess-move in the battle—Courtney knew Interstate Compact law would prevent the Los Angeles judge from having control over them in Seattle. An L.A. social worker named Mary Brown flew to Seattle in early March to observe Frances in her new home. When she recommended the county drop the case, her decision was eventually accepted. "Kurt was ecstatic," lawyer Neal Hersh recalled. On March 25, just a week after Frances's seven-month birthday, Frances was legally returned to her parents' unsupervised care. Their daughter's return came with a price: They had spent over $240,000 on legal fees.

Frances had remained with her parents throughout the entire investigation, though Jamie or Jackie had been on-site to satisfy the court. Jackie had been a life-saver as a nanny, but by early 1993 she was exhausted. She had only been given a handful of days off during her tenure, though in the new home she had managed to institute stricter parameters on her duty: She insisted that when Frances woke during the night her parents care for her until 7 a.m. But Farry now had to handle many record company calls that Kurt wanted to avoid: "People would call and say, 'Can you have Kurt call me back?' And I'd say, 'I'll tell him,' but I knew he wasn't going to call them back. He just didn't want to deal with what was being forced upon him in his life. He just wanted to hang out with Courtney and not deal with the world." Farry announced she was leaving in April.

Jackie interviewed numerous professional nannies as potential replacements, but it was clear that most couldn't fit with the drama of the

Cobain home. "They'd ask, 'When is feeding time?' " Farry said. "I'd have to tell them that things didn't work exactly like that around their house." Eventually Courtney decided to hire Michael "Cali" DeWitt, a twenty-year-old former Hole roadie, as the new nanny. Despite his youth, Cali was an excellent caretaker for Frances, who bonded with him immediately. The Cobains additionally employed Ingrid Bernstein, the mother of their friend Nils Bernstein, on a part-time basis.

April 1993 was a busy month for both Hole and Nirvana. Hole released "Beautiful Son," a song Courtney wrote about Kurt, and used a childhood picture on the sleeve. Nirvana, meanwhile, traveled to San Francisco's Cow Palace to play a benefit for Bosnian rape victims, an issue of concern to Novoselic, due to his ethnic heritage. It was Nirvana's first show in the U.S. in six months, and they used it to showcase their upcoming album, playing eight of the twelve songs on *In Utero*, many for the first time in concert. Kurt decided to switch from his usual position, stage left, to stage right—it was as if he was attempting to re-craft the band's show. It worked, and hardcore fans cited this as one of the band's best live performances.

Though *In Utero* had been recorded, it was still waiting for release, and a dispute in April over its production overshadowed everything else the band did that spring. The band had solicited Albini because they wanted a rawer sound, but they found his final mixes too stark. News of this got back to the producer, who in April told the *Chicago Tribune*'s Greg Kot, "Geffen and Nirvana's management *hate* the record. . . . I have no faith it will be released." Kurt responded with his own press release: "There has been no pressure from our record label to change the tracks." But the controversy continued, and Kurt had DGC take out a full-page ad in *Billboard* denying allegations the label had rejected the album. Despite the denials, most at the label did think the production too raw, and in May, Scott Litt was hired to make "Heart-Shaped Box" and "All Apologies" more radio friendly. Once again, when challenged by a problem that might affect the success of his record, Kurt acquiesced to the path of least resistance and greatest sales.

That didn't stop him from quietly steaming. Though he continued to tell reporters he was in support of the Litt remixes and thought Albini did a great job—two contradictory statements—in his journal he outlined plans to release the album exactly as he wanted. He would first release the Albini version as *I Hate Myself and Want to Die*, but only on vinyl, cassette, and eight-track tape. His next phase of operations would come one month later. "After many lame reviews and reports on curmudgeonly, uncompromising vinyl, cassette, eight-track-only release, we release the remixed version under the title *Verse, Chorus, Verse*." For this, Kurt wanted a sticker reading, "Radio-Friendly, Unit-Shifting, Compromise Version." DGC, not surprisingly, declined to follow Kurt's plans. The remixed version of *In Utero* was slated for release in September.

On the first Sunday of May, at 9 p.m., King County's 911 emergency services center received a report from the Cobain house of a drug overdose. When police and an aid car arrived, they discovered Kurt on the living-room sofa babbling about "Hamlet." He was suffering, the officers observed, from "symptoms associated with an overdose of a narcotic. . . . Victim Cobain was conscious and able to answer questions, but was obviously impaired."

Just a few minutes prior to the arrival of police, Kurt had been blue and appeared, once again, to be dead. Courtney told officers Kurt had been at a friend's house where he had "injected himself with $30 to $40 worth of heroin." Kurt had driven home, and when Courtney confronted him about being loaded, he locked himself in an upstairs bedroom. Courtney had threatened to call the police or his family, and when he didn't respond, she followed through on the second threat. She reached Wendy on the first ring, and Kurt's mother and sister immediately got in their car and "bombed our asses up there," as Kim remembered.

In the two and a half hours it took Kim and Wendy to speed from Aberdeen to Seattle, Kurt's condition deteriorated. By the time Wendy and Kim arrived, Kurt was vomiting and in shock. He did not want 911 called, he told them in his slurred voice, because he would "rather die" than see it in the paper that he overdosed or got arrested. Courtney threw cold water on Kurt, walked him around the house, gave him Valium, and finally injected him with Narcan, a drug used to counteract heroin, but none of these efforts fully revived him (a supply of Narcan, itself illegally obtained, was always kept in the home for this purpose). Wendy tried to rub Kurt's back—her way of comforting her son—but the heroin made his muscles tighter than a plaster mannequin. "It was horrid," remembered Kim. "We finally had to call paramedics because he was starting to turn blue." When police arrived, they found, "his condition gradually deteriorated to the point that he was shaking, became flushed, delirious, and talked incoherently."

Once Kurt was in the aid car, the crisis seemed averted. Kim followed the ambulance to Harborview Hospital, where events took a farcical turn. "There he was hilarious," she recalled. "He was laying out in the hallway of this packed hospital, getting IV fluids, and the stuff to reverse the drugs. He's laying there, and he starts talking about Shakespeare. Then he'd nod out and wake up five minutes later, and continue his conversation with me."

Part of the reason Kim had been sent to chase the ambulance was because Courtney wanted to throw away the rest of Kurt's heroin but couldn't locate it. When Kurt came back to consciousness, Kim asked him where he put it. "It's in the pocket of the bathrobe hanging on the stairway," Kurt admitted, right before he passed out again. Kim ran to the phone and called the house, though by then Courtney had already discovered it. When Kim returned to Kurt's side, he had woken again and insisted she not divulge the location of the drugs.

After about three hours of Narcan, Kurt was ready to go home. "When he was able to leave the hospital, I couldn't light his cigarette fast enough," Kim said. There was a huge sadness for her in witnessing what at times had seemed like an almost comic brush with death: Overdosing had become ordinary to Kurt, part of the game, and there was a normalcy to this madness. Indeed, as the police report noted, Courtney told the officers the larger, sadder truth about this one episode: "This type of incident had happened before to Victim Cobain."

"Heroine" was now part of Kurt's daily existence, and sometimes, particularly when he had no band business and Courtney and Frances were gone, the central part. By the summer of 1993, he was using almost every day, and when not using he was in withdrawal and complaining vociferously. It was a period of more functional dependency than in the past, but his usage still surpassed most addicts'. Even Dylan, an addict himself, found Kurt's dosage level dangerous. "He definitely used a lot of dope," Dylan recalled. "I wanted to get high and still be able to do something, but he always wanted to do so much he couldn't do anything. He always wanted to do more than he needed to do." Kurt's interest was in escape, and the quicker and the more incapacitating, the better. As a result, there were many overdoses and near-death situations, as many as a dozen during 1993 alone.

The increase in Kurt's habit ran counter to an effort Courtney was making to sober up. In late spring, she hired a psychic to help her kick drugs. Kurt balked at paying the bills from the psychic and laughed at her advice that the couple both needed to rid themselves of "all toxins." Courtney took it seriously, however; she attempted to stop smoking, began drinking fresh-squeezed juice every day, and attended Narcotics Anonymous. Kurt taunted his wife at first, but then encouraged her to attend N.A. meetings, if only so he had more free time to get loaded.

The first of June, Courtney staged an intervention in the Lakeside house. In attendance were Krist, friend Nils Bernstein, Gold Mountain's Janet Billig, Wendy, and Kurt's stepfather, Pat O'Connor. At first, Kurt refused to leave his room and even look at the group. When he finally left his room, he and Courtney began screaming at each other. In a fit of rage, Kurt grabbed a red Sanford Magic Marker and scrawled "None of you will ever know my true intent" on the hallway wall. "It was obvious there was no getting through to him," Bernstein remembered. The assembled group went through a litany of reasons Kurt should stop doing drugs, one of the most repeated being the needs of his daughter. His mother told him his health was at risk. Krist pleaded with Kurt, talking of how he had limited his own drinking. When Pat O'Connor shared stories of his struggles with alcohol, Kurt was silent and stared at his sneakers. "You could see in Kurt's face that he was thinking, 'Nothing in your life relates to anything in my life,' " Bernstein recalled. "I thought to myself, 'this is *so* not working.' " When Kurt returned to his bedroom in a huff, those assembled began to argue among themselves about who was to blame for Kurt's addiction. For those closest to him, it was easier to blame each other than to put responsibility at his feet.

Kurt began to increasingly isolate himself that summer; friends jok-ingly called him Rapunzel because he so rarely came down from his room. His mother was one of the few people he'd listen to, and Court-ney increasingly made use of Wendy as mediator. Kurt still desperately needed mothering, and he regressed to an almost fetal state as he re-treated from the world. Wendy could soothe him by stroking his hair and telling him everything was going to be fine. "There were times when he would be nodded out upstairs, and nobody, neither Courtney or anyone else, could go near him," observed Bernstein. "But his mom would wander in, and he didn't shut her out. I think it was chemical depression." Depression ran in Wendy's family, and though several of Kurt's friends suggested he be treated, he chose to ignore their pleas and to self-medicate with drugs. Truth be told, it was hard for anyone to get him to do anything: If the world of Nirvana could be considered a small nation unto itself, Kurt was king. Few dared challenge the king's mental health for fear of being banished from the kingdom.

On June 4, after another horrible day of drama, Courtney called the police on Kurt. When officers arrived, she told them they had "an argument over guns in the household," she had thrown a glass of juice in his face, and he had shoved her. "At which time," the police report states, "Cobain pushed Love to the floor and began choking her, leaving a scratch." Seattle law required police to arrest at least one party in any domestic dispute—Kurt and Courtney began to argue over who would be the one arrested, since both wanted this distinction. Kurt insisted he go to jail—for someone passive-aggressive, this was a mother lode of an opportunity to both emotionally retreat and play the martyr. He won. He was transported to the North Precinct and booked into the King County Jail. Police also seized a large collection of ammunition and guns from the home, including two .38 pistols and a Colt AR-15 semi-automatic assault rifle.

But the real story of what happened that day illustrated the increasing strain within their marriage. Like two characters in a Raymond Carver short story, their fights increasingly included digs at each other's weak points, and on this day Kurt was flaunting his drug use in front of Courtney and her psychic. "He had to find, of course, the *one* drug that would drive me insane," Love recalled. "He decided he was going to try crack. He made this big insane production out of how he was going to acquire and try *ten dollars' worth* of 'rock.' "

To bait his wife, Kurt acted like "he was pulling down the drug deal of the century" with repeated phone calls to a dealer. Visions of him free-basing crack cocaine in their house enraged Courtney, and instead of throwing a glass at him, as the police report states, she actually threw a juicer. It wasn't much of a fight—physical battles between the two ended in draws, just like their first wrestling match on the floor of the Portland club. But Courtney called the police anyway, figuring that having him go to jail was better than having him burn down their house free-basing. "I'm sure Kurt got his crack eventually, somehow, somewhere, but I never did find out about it," she said. He spent only three hours in jail, and was released that night on $950 bail. Charges were later dropped.

They patched things up after the arrest, and as happened repeatedly in their relationship, the trauma brought them closer. On their bedroom wall she wrote the graffiti, "You better love me, you fucker," inside a heart. A month after the fight, Kurt described their relationship to Gavin Edwards of *Details* as "a whirling dervish of emotion, all these extremes of fighting and loving each other at once. If I'm mad at her, I'll yell at her, and that's healthy." Both were masters at pushing and testing limits—it was all Kurt did in childhood—and whenever he made Courtney angry, he knew he had to woo her back, usually with love letters. One such note began: "Courtney, when I say, 'I love you,' I am not ashamed, nor will anyone ever, ever come close to intimidating, persuading, etc., me into thinking otherwise. I wear you on my sleeve. I spread you out wide open with the wing span of a peacock, yet all too often with the attention span of a bullet to the head." The prose was self-deprecating, describing himself "as dense as cement," but also reminding her of his marriage commitment: "I parade around you proudly like the ring on my finger which also holds no mineral."

Two weeks after the domestic violence arrest, Neal Karlen arrived at the Cobain house to interview Courtney for the *New York Times*. When he knocked, Kurt answered, holding Frances, and announced his wife was "at her N.A. meeting." He invited Karlen in, and they sat and watched television. "It was this huge house," recalled Karlen, "but there were cigarette butts put out on plates, and this ugly, shitty furniture. In the living room was this huge, eighteen-foot television. It was as if someone had gone to the store and said, 'I want the biggest television in the catalog.' "

On TV was the latest episode of "Beavis and Butt-Head," MTV's popular show. "I *know* Beavis and Butt-Head," Kurt told Karlen. "I grew up with people like that; I recognize them." In a grand bit of serendipity, the video for "Smells Like Teen Spirit" came on the program. "All right!" Kurt exclaimed. "Let's see what they think about us." When the two cartoon characters gave Nirvana the thumbs up, Kurt seemed genuinely flattered. "They *like* us!"

As if on cue, Courtney arrived home. She kissed Kurt, bounced Frances on her knee, and with only a mild hint of sarcasm announced, "Ah, the perfect family—just like a Norman Rockwell picture." Even Karlen was struck with a domestic image. "I kept thinking of them as Fred and Ethel Mertz," he recalled. "He was more like Fred, with his hands in his pockets, while Ethel was running the household." Karlen also had caught Kurt on a day his eyes were clear. "I'd seen enough junkies to know he was straight."

As it was, Love didn't want to talk to the *New York Times*, but she did wish to voice her opinions for a book Karlen was writing on the band Babes in Toyland. Their interview went on for hours, and Kurt frequently chimed in when Courtney would prod him. "He was not as passive as people said," Karlen observed. Courtney used Kurt as she would a resident punk historian—when she made a point, and needed a date or a name, she would query Kurt, and he would inevitably know the answer. "It was like watching a quiz show where they would go to the professor to verify facts," Karlen noted.

Kurt had one quandary of his own: He was pondering whether to buy a guitar that once belonged to Leadbelly. It was for sale for $55,000, but he couldn't decide whether buying it was a "punk move" or an "anti-punk move." The only tension Karlen noticed between the couple was when Courtney stumbled upon a Mary Lou Lord album in Kurt's record collection. This set Love off telling a story of how she'd chased Lord down the street in Los Angeles, threatening to beat her up. Kurt was silent, and it was the only time Karlen thought Kurt acted like "the long-suffering husband."

Courtney's discourse on the history of punk rock went on for hours after Kurt went to bed. Karlen eventually spent the night in a spare bedroom. The morning brought the only evidence this wasn't the typical household: When Kurt went to prepare the morning meal, there was no food. After looking for several minutes, Kurt put some sugar cookies on a plate and announced it was breakfast.

On July 1 Hole played their first show in several months, at the Off-Ramp in Seattle. Courtney had retooled her band, and they were preparing to tour England and make a record. Kurt came to the show, but he was a mess. "He was so wasted he could barely stand up," recalled the club's Michelle Underwood. "We had to help him move around. It seemed like he was very nervous for her." His nerves were exacerbated by the fact that the day of the show, the *Seattle Times* published a story on his arrest the previous month in the domestic violence incident. Courtney joked onstage: "We're donating all the money you paid to get in tonight to Domestic Violence Wife Beaters Fund. *Not!*" Later she came back to the topic: "Domestic violence is not something that's ever happened to me. I just like to stick up for my husband. It's not a true story. They never fucking are. Why is it that every time we have a fucking beer, it's on the fucking news?" Despite the drama, her performance was riveting, and it was the first time she'd won over a Seattle audience.

Hole's set ended at fifteen minutes past one, but that wasn't the end of the evening for the Cobains. Brian Willis of *NME* came backstage and asked if Courtney might want to be interviewed. She invited him to their house but she spent most of the interview promoting Kurt's record. Love even played *In Utero* for Willis, the first time a journalist had heard the album. He was overwhelmed, writing, "If Freud could hear it, he'd wet his pants in anticipation." He called it "an album pregnant with irony and insight. *In Utero* is Kurt's revenge."

Willis's listening experience was interrupted when Kurt came into the room to report: "We were just on the news, on MTV. They were talking about the story in the *Seattle Times* and how Hole have just started their world tour in Seattle at the Off-Ramp." With that, Kurt made a snack of English muffins and hot chocolate, and sat at the counter watching the sun rise. When Willis wrote the late-night events up for the *NME*, he ended his piece with a bit of analysis: "For someone who's been through so much shit in the past two years, whose name's being dragged through acrimony once again, who's about to release a record the whole rock world's desperate to hear and be faced with astonishing attention and pressure, Kurt Cobain's a remarkably contented man."

21 A REASON TO SMILE

> *God damn, Jesus fucking Christ Almighty, love me, me, me, we*
> *could go on a trial basis, please I don't care if it's the out-of-the-in-*
> *crowd, I just need a crowd, a gang, a reason to smile.*
> —From a journal entry.

Like every other American family with a young child,
Kurt and Courtney purchased a video camera. While Kurt could construct a guitar out of a block of wood and spare wires, he never figured
out how to install the battery, so the camera was used only when they
were near an outlet. A single videotape charted the period from their
first Christmas together in December 1992, through to images of
Frances as a toddler in March 1994.

A few of the scenes on the tape were of Nirvana shows, or were
footage of the band offstage, hanging out. One short fragment captured
Kurt, Courtney, Dave, Krist, and Frances sitting in Pachyderm Studios
listening to the first play-back of "All Apologies," collectively appearing
battle-weary after a week in the studio. But most of the tape documented the development of Frances Bean and her interaction with their
friends: It showed her crawling around Mark Lanegan and talking while
Mark Arm sang her a lullaby. Some of the tape was humorous, as when
Kurt lifted up the baby's butt and made fart noises, or the footage of
him serenading her with an a cappella version of "Seasons in the Sun."
Frances was a beatific child, as photogenic as her parents, with her
father's mesmerizing eyes and her mother's high cheekbones. Kurt
adored her, and the video documents a sentimental side of him the
public rarely saw—the look he gave both Frances and Courtney during

these tender moments was one of unadulterated love. Though this was the most famous family in rock 'n' roll, much of the footage could have been from any household with a Toys "R" Us charge account.

But one segment on the tape stands out above all others and shows how extraordinarily different this family was. Shot by Courtney in the bathroom of their house in Carnation, the scene begins with Kurt giving Frances a bath; he's wearing a burgundy smoking jacket and looking like a handsome country squire. As he lifts Frances like a plane over the tub, she involuntarily snorts because she's having so much fun. Kurt wears the kind of ear-to-ear smile that was never captured by a still picture—the closest any photographer came was the photo of Kurt, Wendy, Don, and Kim from the Aberdeen days. In the video, Kurt looks to be exactly what he is: a caring, doting father, enthralled by his beautiful daughter, and wanting nothing more in life than to pretend she is an airplane, soaring over the bath and dive-bombing the yellow rubber ducks. He talks to her in a voice like Donald Duck—just like his sister Kim did when he was growing up—and she giggles and cackles, full of the kind of glee that only an eight-month-old can exude.

Then the camera turns toward the sink, and in the blink of an eye, the scene changes. To the right of the basin, mounted eight inches up the wall, rests a toothbrush holder—the same kind of white, porcelain toothbrush holder in 90 percent of all homes in America. Yet what makes this particular fixture so remarkable is that it isn't storing toothbrushes: It's holding a syringe. It is such an astonishing and unexpected object to see in a bathroom, most viewers wouldn't notice it. But it's there, hanging solemnly, needle-tip pointed down, a sad and tragic reminder that no matter how ordinary this family looks on the outside, there are ghosts that follow even the tender moments.

By July 1993 Kurt's addiction had become so routine, it was a part of life in the Cobain house, and things worked around it. The metaphor frequently used to describe the role of alcoholism within a family—that of a 10,000-pound elephant in the middle of the living room—seemed so obvious that few bothered to utter it. That Kurt was going to be messed up for at least part of the day had become the status quo; as accepted as the rain in Seattle. Even the birth of his child and court-ordered treatment had only served to temporarily distract him. Though he'd been on methadone and buprenorphine for weeks at a time, he hadn't been free of opiates long enough to completely detox for almost a year.

In the crazed logic that overtakes families caught up in addiction, it almost seemed better when Kurt was on drugs: In contrast, he was impossible when he was suffering the physical pain of withdrawal. Only a few actually voiced this theory—that the system orbiting around Kurt was more stable when he was using drugs rather than abstaining—but Kurt professed it himself. In his journal he argued that if he was going to feel like a junkie in withdrawal, he might as well be one in practice. And he had friends that agreed with him: "The whole 'getting him to stop using drugs' [theory] was absurd and ultimately damaging to Kurt," argued Dylan Carlson. "Drugs are a problem when they are impacting your ability to, say, have a house or maintain a job. Until they become a problem of that nature, you just leave the person alone and then they'll hit the emotional bottom on their own—you can't drive them to that bottom. . . . He didn't have any reason to *not* do drugs."

By the summer of 1993, addiction was a lens through which everything in Kurt's life was distorted. Yet though he was outwardly happier on drugs, in the crazy contradiction that is addiction, he was inwardly filled with remorse. His journals were marked by laments on his inability to stay sober. He felt judged by everyone around him, and he was correct in this perception: Every time his bandmates, family, managers, or crew encountered him, they did a quick survey to determine whether he was high or not. He experienced this ten-second once-over dozens of times during each day, and was furious when it was assumed he was stoned when he was not. He felt he was a functional addict—he could use drugs and play—so he hated the constant scrutiny and found himself spending more and more time with his junkie friends, where he felt less inspected.

Yet by 1993 even the drugs weren't working as well as they once had. Kurt found the reality of drug addiction a far cry from the glamour he had once imagined reading the works of William S. Burroughs, and even within the insular subculture of addicts, he felt he was an outsider. One journal entry from this period found him desperately pleading for friendship, and ultimately for salvation:

Friends who I can talk to and hang out and have fun with, just like I've always dreamed, we could talk about books and politics and vandalize at night, want to? Huh? Hey, I can't stop pulling my hair out! Please! God damn, Jesus fucking Christ Almighty, love me, me, me, we could go on a trial basis, please I don't care if it's the out-of-the-in-crowd, I just need a crowd, a gang, a reason to smile. I won't smother you, ah shit, shit, please, isn't there somebody out there? Somebody, anybody, God help, help me please. I want to be accepted. I have to be accepted. I'll wear any kind of clothes you want! I'm so tired of crying and dreaming, I'm soo soo alone. Isn't there anyone out there? Please help me. HELP ME!

That summer Kurt's drug rehabilitation physician, 60-year-old Robert Fremont, was found dead in his Beverly Hills office, slumped over his desk. His cause of death was ruled a heart attack, though Fremont's son Marc asserted it was suicide by overdose, and that his father had been again addicted to drugs. At the time of his death, Fremont was being investigated by the Medical Board of California, charged with gross negligence and unprofessional conduct for overprescribing buprenorphine to his patients. Fremont certainly made plenty of buprenorphine available to his most famous client—he would dispense it to Kurt by the carton.

On July 17, 1993, *Nevermind* finally fell off the *Billboard* charts after being on for just under two years. That week the band traveled to New York to do press and play a surprise appearance as part of the New Music Seminar. The night before the show, Kurt sat down and conducted an interview with Jon Savage, author of "England's Dreaming." Perhaps because Kurt admired Savage's book, he was particularly forthcoming about his family, describing his parents' divorce as something that made him feel "ashamed" and yearning for what he had lost: "I desperately wanted to have the classic, you know, typical family. Mother, father. I wanted that security." And when Savage asked if Kurt could understand how great alienation might lead to violence, he replied in the affirmative: "Yeah, I can definitely see how a person's mental state could deteriorate to the point where they would do that. I've gotten to the point where I've fantasized about it, but I'm sure I would opt to kill myself first." Virtually every interview Kurt did in 1993 had some reference to suicide.

When Kurt was asked the inevitable question about heroin, he told the inevitable lie: He talked in the past tense, said he did heroin "for about a year, off and on," and claimed he only did it because of his stomach problems. When Savage followed up on the stomach pains, Kurt declared they were gone: "I think it's a psychosomatic thing." Savage found Kurt particularly jovial this night. "I haven't felt this optimistic since right before my parents' divorce," he explained.

Twelve hours later, Kurt was lying on the floor of his hotel bathroom, having overdosed again. "His lips were blue and his eyes were completely rolled back in his head," recalled publicist Anton Brookes, one of the people who rushed to Kurt. "He was lifeless. There was a syringe still stuck in his arm." Brookes was shocked when he saw Courtney and the nanny Cali spring into action like experienced medical aides—they were so methodical he was left with the impression they did this regularly. While Courtney checked Kurt's vital signs, Cali held Kurt up and punched him violently in the solar plexus. "He hit him once, and he didn't get much reaction, so he hit him again. Then, Kurt started to come around." This, plus cold water to the face, got Kurt breathing. When hotel security arrived, drawn by the noise, Brookes had to bribe them to not call the police. Brookes, Courtney, and Cali dragged the still-groggy Kurt outside. "We started walking him," Brookes remembered, "but at first his legs weren't moving." When Kurt finally could speak, he insisted he did not want to go to the hospital.

After food and coffee, Kurt seemed fully revived, though still very high. He returned to the hotel, where he was scheduled to get a massage in his room. As Kurt was getting his rubdown, Brookes grabbed packets of heroin off the floor and flushed them down the toilet. Ironically, less than three hours after he was comatose in the bathroom, Kurt was back doing interviews, denying he used drugs. At soundcheck that evening, he was still way too high—perhaps due to a bag not found by his handlers. "He pretty much died right before that show," recalled soundman Craig Montgomery. When David Yow, of the opening band the Jesus Lizard, went to chat with Kurt before showtime, "Kurt couldn't talk. He could just mumble. I said, 'How are you?' and he said, 'buzz-colloddbed.' " In a pattern that was becoming all too familiar, despite Kurt's earlier impairment, he seemed fine onstage, and the show itself was a marvel. The band had added Lori Goldston on cello, and it was the first time they featured an acoustic interlude in their set.

Nirvana returned to Seattle the next week and played a benefit on August 6 to raise funds to investigate the murder of local singer Mia Zapata. That week, Kurt, Courtney, Krist, and Dave spent a rare night out together taking in Aerosmith at the Coliseum. Backstage, Aerosmith's Steven Tyler took Kurt aside and told him about his experience with 12-Step recovery groups. "He wasn't preaching," Krist remembered, "just talking about similar experiences he'd been through. He tried to give him encouragement." For once, Kurt appeared to listen, though he said little in response.

That same week, also at the Seattle Center, Kurt did an interview with the *New York Times*, conducted at the top of the Space Needle. Kurt picked this location because he'd never been to Seattle's most famous landmark. He was now insisting a representative from DGC's publicity department tape every interview—he thought this would cut down on misquotes. The talk with Jon Pareles, as with all of Kurt's 1993 interviews, sounded like a therapy session, as Kurt discussed his parents, wife, and the significance of his lyrics. He exposed enough of himself that Pareles wisely noted the contradictions: "Cobain ricochets between opposites. He is wary and unguarded, sincere and sarcastic, thin-skinned and insensitive, aware of his popularity and trying to ignore it."

The first week of September Kurt and Courtney returned to Los Angeles for a two-week stay, their first extended visit since moving. They attended the 1993 MTV Video Music Awards, and Nirvana won Best Alternative Video for "In Bloom." The band wasn't playing this night, and there were few of the histrionics of the previous year's awards. Much had changed in the music business during the last year, and Nirvana had been missing in action for most of it. Though *In Utero* was highly anticipated, they were no longer the biggest rock band in the world, at least commercially: Pearl Jam now held that honor.

That week, Kurt and Courtney appeared at a benefit for "Rock Against Rape" at Hollywood's Club Lingerie. Courtney was on the bill as a solo act, but after performing "Doll Parts" and "Miss World," she called out for "her husband Yoko" and Kurt came onstage. Together they did duets of "Pennyroyal Tea" and the Leadbelly tune "Where Did You Sleep Last Night?" It was the only occasion they would ever play together in public.

In Utero was finally released on September 14 in the U.K. and September 21 in the U.S., where it entered the charts at No. 1, selling 180,000 copies in the first week alone. It reached those sales figures without being carried by Wal-Mart or Kmart: Both chains had objected to the song title "Rape Me" and the back-cover collage of Kurt's fetus dolls. When his manager phoned with this news, Kurt agreed to revisions that would get the album into the stores. "When I was a kid, I could only go to Wal-Mart," Kurt explained to Danny Goldberg. "I want the kids to be able to get this record. I'll do what they want." Goldberg was surprised, but he knew to accept Kurt's word: "No one would dream of saying no to him at that point. No one made him do anything."

Yet Kurt did clash with his managers over concert dates. He began 1993 asserting he wasn't planning on touring. While not unheard of, this decision certainly would have diminished the new record's chances of hitting the top of the charts. On this issue, Kurt faced a juggernaut of opposition: Everyone who worked with him—from his managers to his crew to his bandmates—made most of their money from touring, and they urged him to reconsider. But when he discussed the matter with his lawyer, Rosemary Carroll, he seemed adamant. "He said he didn't want to go," she remembered. "And frankly, he was pressured to go."

Most of the pressure was from management, but some came from his own fear of scarcity. Though he was wealthier than he had ever imagined possible, a tour would make him richer still. A memo Danny Goldberg sent Kurt in February 1993 outlined details of his projected income for the next eighteen months. "Thus far, Nirvana has been paid a little over $1.5 million," the memo states on the subject of songwriting income. "I believe there is another $3 million in the pipeline to be paid out over the next couple of years." Goldberg estimated that Kurt's income after taxes in 1993 would include $1,400,000 from songwriting royalties, $200,000 for expected sales of two million of the new record, and if Nirvana toured, an additional $600,000 from merchandising and concert revenue. Even these figures, Goldberg wrote, were conservative: "I personally believe that [your] income for the next eighteen months will be double this amount or more, but for rational family planning I think it's safe to assume $2 million, which presumably gives you the breathing room to furnish your house very nicely and know that you will have a substantial nest egg." Despite his earlier protests, Kurt agreed to tour.

On September 25 Nirvana was back in New York to appear again on "Saturday Night Live." They played "Heart-Shaped Box" and "Rape Me," and though the performance was rocky, it was free of the tension of their first visit. In addition to cello player Goldston, they had added former Germs guitarist Georg Ruthenberg, known by his stage name of Pat Smear. Smear was eight years older than Kurt, and he'd already been through a long junkie drama with Darby Crash, his band-mate in the Germs. He gave the impression there was little that could unnerve him; his wry sense of humor lightened the band, and his solid playing helped Kurt fret less onstage.

The week before the *In Utero* tour began, Kurt flew to Atlanta for a visit with Courtney, who was recording Hole's album. When he came by the studio, producers Sean Slade and Paul Kolderie played him the songs from her record that were done. Kurt seemed proud of Courtney's effort and praised her lyrical skills.

Later that day, Courtney asked Kurt to sing background vocals on a few unfinished numbers. He protested at first, but relented. It was apparent to Slade and Kolderie that Kurt was not familiar with much of the material. "She said things like, 'Come on, sing on this one,'" recalled Kolderie. "He kept saying, 'Well let me hear it. How can I sing on it if I haven't heard it?' She'd say, 'Just sing off the top of your head.' " The results were less than impressive, and Kurt's vocals were used on only one song in the final mix. But Kurt warmed up considerably when the official session ended and a jam ensued. He sat down at the drums, Eric Erlandson and Courtney picked up guitars, and Slade grabbed a bass. "It was a blast," recalled Slade.

Kurt returned to Seattle, only to leave a week later for Phoenix to rehearse for Nirvana's upcoming tour. On a connecting flight to L.A., the band Truly were on the same plane, and Kurt had a warm reunion with his old friends Robert Roth and Mark Pickerel. Pickerel ended up in the seat next to Kurt and Krist—Grohl was in the front of the cabin—and Pickerel felt embarrassed for carrying a copy of *Details* with Nirvana on the cover. Kurt grabbed it and devoured the article. "He became agitated as he read," Pickerel recalled. Kurt was unhappy with Grohl's quotes. "He went on and on about it," Pickerel said. A few minutes into his rant, Kurt announced that for his next album, "I want to bring in other people just to create a different kind of record." He would revisit this subject repeatedly that fall, threatening to fire his bandmates.

The *In Utero* tour began in Phoenix at a 15,000-seat venue where Billy Ray Cyrus had performed the night before. It was the largest-scale tour Nirvana undertook, and included an elaborate set. When MTV asked Kurt why the band was now playing big arenas, Kurt was pragmatic, citing the increased production costs of the show: "If we were to just play clubs, we'd be totally in the hole. We're not nearly as rich as everyone thinks we are." When *USA Today* ran a negative review of the debut ("Creative anarchy deteriorated into bad performance art," wrote Edna Gunderson), Smear defused a Kurt fit by remarking, "That's fucked—they totally got us. That's the funniest thing I've read in my life." Even Kurt had to laugh.

Courtney begged Kurt not to read his reviews, yet he obsessively sought them out, even searching for out-of-town newspapers. He had become increasingly paranoid about the media and now demanded to inspect a writer's previous clippings before agreeing to an interview. Yet in Davenport, Iowa, Kurt ended up in a car coming home from a gig with publicist Jim Merlis and a *Rolling Stone* writer. Kurt was unaware a journalist was in his midst as he directed Merlis to a Taco Bell–like joint. The fast food restaurant was swarming with kids from the concert, all wide-eyed when they saw Kurt Cobain standing in line to order a burrito. "Taco day was my favorite day at school," he told everyone within earshot. The story, of course, ended up in the press.

During this first week of the tour, Alex MacLeod drove Kurt to Lawrence, Kansas, to meet William S. Burroughs. The previous year Kurt had produced a single with Burroughs titled "The Priest They Called Him," on T/K Records, but they'd accomplished the recording by sending tapes back and forth. "Meeting William was a real big deal for him," MacLeod remembered. "It was something that he never thought would happen." They chatted for several hours, but Burroughs later claimed the subject of drugs didn't come up. As Kurt drove away, Burroughs remarked to his assistant, "There's something wrong with that boy; he frowns for no good reason."

In Chicago, three days later, the band ended a show without playing "Smells Like Teen Spirit" and there were boos. Kurt sat down that night with *Rolling Stone*'s David Fricke and began, "I'm glad you could make it for the shittiest show on the tour." Kurt's interview with Fricke was so full of references to his emotional turmoil, it could have just as easily appeared in *Psychology Today*. He talked about his depression, his family, his fame, and his stomach problems. "After a person experiences chronic pain for five years," he told Fricke, "by the time that fifth year ends, you're literally insane. . . . I was as schizophrenic as a wet cat that's been beaten." He reported his stomach much healed now, and admitted to having eaten an entire Chicago pizza the night before. Kurt announced that during the worst of his stomach problems, "I wanted to kill myself every day. I came very close many times." When he discussed his hopes for his daughter, Kurt argued: "I don't think Courtney and I are that fucked up. We have lacked love all our lives, and we need it so much that if there's any goal that we have, it's to give Frances as much love as we can, as much support as we can."

After Chicago the shows improved, and so did Kurt's spirits. "We were on the upswing," recalled Novoselic. Everyone enjoyed playing the *In Utero* material, and they'd added "Where Did You Sleep Last Night?" and a gospel number called "Jesus Wants Me for a Sunbeam."

During parts of the tour fourteen-month-old Frances traveled with her father, and Kurt appeared happier when she was around. At the end of October the Meat Puppets opened seven shows, uniting Kurt with his idols Curt and Cris Kirkwood.

For some time Nirvana had been in negotiations with MTV about playing the network's "Unplugged" program. It was while touring with the Meat Puppets that Kurt finally acceded to the idea, inviting the Kirkwoods to join the show, thinking their supplementary presence in the band would help. The idea of playing a stripped-down show made Kurt nervous, and he worried more in advance about this particular performance than any since the band's debut at the Raymond kegger. "Kurt was really, really nervous," remembered Novoselic. Others were more direct: "He was terrified," observed production manager Jeff Mason.

They arrived in New York the second week of November and began rehearsals at a New Jersey soundstage. But as with every inter-action the band ever had with MTV, more time went to negotiations than rehearsal. The Kirkwoods found they spent most days sitting around waiting; additionally, they were warned by Nirvana's management to refrain from marijuana around Kurt. They found this particularly grating, since Kurt was consistently late for rehearsal and obviously was high. "He would show up looking like the apparition of Jacob Marley," Curt Kirkwood observed, "all bound up in flannel, in a cutting-up-a-deer hat. He looked like a little, old farmer. He thought *this* disguise would make him fit in with the locals in New York."

Though Kurt had agreed to do the show, he didn't want his "Unplugged" to look like the others in the series; MTV had the opposite agenda, and the debates became contentious. The day before the taping Kurt announced he wasn't playing. But MTV was used to this ploy. "He did it just to get us worked up," said Amy Finnerty. "He enjoyed that power."

On the afternoon of the show, Kurt arrived, despite threats otherwise, but he was nervous and in withdrawal. "There was no joking, no smiles, no fun coming from him," allowed Jeff Mason. "Therefore, everyone was more than a little concerned about the performance." Curt Kirkwood was worried because they hadn't rehearsed an entire set: "We played the songs through a few times, but never a rehearsal set. There was never any concerted practice." Finnerty was troubled because Kurt was lying on a sofa complaining about how poorly he felt. When he said he wanted Kentucky Fried Chicken, she immediately sent someone to locate some.

But he really desired more than just KFC. A member of Nirvana's crew told Finnerty Kurt was throwing up, and asked if she could "get something" to help him out. "They told me," Finnerty recalled, "that 'he's not going to make it on the show if we don't *help him* out.' And I was like, 'I've never done heroin, and I don't know where to find it.' " It was suggested that Valium would help Kurt through his withdrawal, and Finnerty asked another MTV employee to purchase a supply from a corrupt pharmacist. When Finnerty handed them to Alex MacLeod, he reported back, "These are too strong—he needs a Valium 5 milligram." Eventually a separate messenger showed up with a delivery Kurt himself had arranged.

Kurt finally sat down and did a brief soundcheck and blocking rehearsal. He was tentative about the acoustic format and filled with dread. His greatest fear was that he'd panic during the show and ruin the taping. "Can you make sure," he asked Finnerty, "that all the people who love me are sitting in the front?" Finnerty shuffled the audience so that Janet Billig and some of Kurt's other associates were in the front row. But even that wasn't enough to calm him; he stopped the soundcheck once again and told Finnerty, "I'm scared." He asked if the crowd was going to clap even if he didn't play well. "Of course, we're going to clap for you," Finnerty said. He insisted she sit so he could see her. He also asked a production person to locate some fretboard lubricant; he'd never used it previously, but said he'd watched his Aunt Mari apply it on her acoustic when he was kid.

Backstage, waiting for the show to begin, Kurt still seemed disturbed. To lighten his mood, Curt Kirkwood brought up what had been a running joke between them: Kirkwood would scrape gum off the bottoms of tables in restaurants and re-chew it. "Man, you are fucking weird," Kurt declared. As they prepared to walk toward the stage, Kirkwood pulled a wad of gum out of his mouth and offered Kurt half— this gag drew Kurt's first smile of the day.

As the cameras started rolling, that smile was long gone. Kurt had the expression of an undertaker, an appropriate look as the stage was set for a macabre black mass. Kurt had suggested Stargazer lilies, black candles, and a crystal chandelier. When "Unplugged" producer Alex Coletti asked, "You mean like a funeral?" Kurt said that was exactly what he meant. He had selected a set of fourteen songs that included six covers; five of the six cover songs mentioned death.

Though dour in expression, and with eyes that were slightly red, Kurt looked handsome nonetheless. He wore his Mister Rogers sweater, and though his hair hadn't been washed for a week, he appeared boyish. He began with "About a Girl," which was performed in a markedly different arrangement, stripping its volume to emphasize the basic melody and lyrics. It wasn't exactly "Unplugged," since Nirvana used amps and drums, albeit with pads and brushes. A more accurate title was suggested by Jeff Mason: "They should have called it 'Nirvana toned-down.' "

But Kurt's emotional performance was toned-up. Next was "Come as You Are" and then a haunting rendition of "Jesus Wants Me for a Sunbeam," with Novoselic on accordion. Only after this third song did Kurt speak to the audience. "I guarantee I will screw this song up," he announced before a cover of David Bowie's "The Man Who Sold the World." He did not screw up, and he felt relieved enough during the next break that he joked that if he messed up, "Well, these people are going to have to wait." You could almost hear the collective sigh of relief from the crowd. For the first time in the night he seemed present, though still addressing the audience in the third person.

Kurt's tension had manifested itself in the crowd: They were reserved, unnatural, and waiting for a cue from him to fully relax. It never came, but the tautness in the room—like that found during a championship game—served to make the show more memorable. When it came time to do "Pennyroyal Tea," Kurt asked the rest of the band, "Am I doing this by myself or what?" The band had never managed to finish a rehearsal of this song. "Do it yourself," Grohl suggested. And Kurt did, though halfway into the song he seemed to stall. He breathed a very short breath, and as he exhaled, he let his voice crack on the line "warm milk and laxatives," and it was in that decision—to let his voice break—where he found the strength to forge ahead. The effect was remarkable: It was like watching a great opera singer battling illness complete an aria by letting emotion sell a song, rather than the accuracy of the notes. At several turns it seemed as if the weight of an angel's wing could cause him to fold, yet the songs aided him: These words and riffs were so much a part of him he could sing them half dead and they'd still be potent. It was Kurt's single greatest moment onstage, and like all the high-water marks of his career, it came at a time when he seemed destined to fail.

After "Pennyroyal Tea" the rest of the songs hardly mattered, but he grew more confident after each one. He even smiled at one point, after a request from the audience for "Rape Me," joking, "Ah, I don't think MTV would let us play that." After ten songs, he brought the Kirkwoods on, introduced them as "the Brothers Meat," and performed three of their numbers with their backing. The Kirkwoods were venerable misfits, but their strangeness fit perfectly into the Cobain aesthetic.

For the final encore, Kurt chose Leadbelly's "Where Did You Sleep Last Night?" Before playing the song, he told the story of how he'd considered buying Leadbelly's guitar, though in this rendition the price was inflated to $500,000, ten times what he'd said three months before. Though Kurt was prone to exaggeration in telling any story, his offering of the song was understated, subdued, ethereal. He sang the tune with his eyes shut, and when his voice cracked, he turned the wail into a primal scream this time that seemed to go on for days. It was riveting.

As he left the stage, there was yet another argument with MTV's producers—they wanted an encore. Kurt knew he couldn't top what he'd already done. "When you saw the sigh on his face before the last note," Finnerty observed, "it was almost as if it was the last breath of life in him." Backstage, the rest of the band was exhilarated by the performance, though Kurt still seemed unsure. Krist told him, "You did a great job up there man," and Janet Billig was so moved she wept. "I told him it was his bar mitzvah, a career-defining moment, becoming the man of his career," Billig recalled. Kurt liked this metaphor, yet when she complimented his guitar playing, this seemed a step too far: He lambasted her, announcing that he was "a shitty guitar player" and that she was never to commend him again.

Kurt left with Finnerty, avoiding an after-show party. Yet even after a transcendent performance, his confidence seemed no higher. He complained, "No one liked it." When Finnerty told him it had been incredible and that everyone loved it, Kurt protested that the audience usually jumped up and down at his shows. "They just sat there silently," he grumbled. Finnerty had heard just about enough: "Kurt, they think you are Jesus Christ," she announced. "Most of these people have never had the opportunity to see you that close. They were totally taken with you." At this he softened, and said he wanted to phone Courtney. As they entered an elevator in his hotel, he nudged Finnerty and bragged, "I was really fucking good tonight, wasn't I?" It was the only time she ever heard him admit to his own skill.

Yet an event that occurred two days before the "Unplugged" taping was more indicative of the internal Kurt than anything on MTV. On the afternoon of November 17, the band prepared to leave their New York hotel to head to an "Unplugged" rehearsal. As Kurt walked through the lobby, he was approached by three male fans holding CDs, asking for autographs. He ignored their pleas, walking to a waiting van with his hands over his face in the manner used by countless felons to avoid being photographed leaving a courthouse. The trio seemed surprised he was so ungracious, though as cellist Lori Goldston recalled, "There was something about them that didn't seem completely displeased. Even though they hadn't gotten an autograph, they'd had a connection with Kurt, which was what they really wanted." Even a "fuck you" from their enigmatic hero was reason for celebration.

As the van filled with the rest of the group, a crew member was slightly delayed, so they waited. It was apparent that if the van were to idle there for days, these fans would remain for the duration, simply to stare at Kurt, who would not return their gaze. While they were waiting, Krist remarked to Kurt, "Hey, that guy called you an asshole." Novoselic most likely said this in jest—no one present remembers hearing anything disparaging. The missing crew member finally jumped into the van, and the driver began to pull away.

But at the moment the vehicle lurched into drive, Kurt yelled, "Stop!" with the same forcefulness a man might yell "Fire!" at the first sight of flames. The driver hit the brakes, and Kurt rolled down the passenger-side window. The fans on the sidewalk were stunned he was acknowledging their presence, and thinking, perhaps, that he was finally going to offer them a precious autograph. But rather than reach out the window, Kurt stretched his long, thin body out of it, not unlike Leonardo DiCaprio on the *Titanic*. Once fully extended, he arched his back and launched a huge wad of phlegm from the deep recesses of his lungs. It languished in the air, in what seemed like slow motion, before landing squarely on the forehead of a man who was holding in his hand a copy of the eight million–selling *Nevermind*.

22 | COBAIN'S DISEASE

*And the title of our double album is "Cobain's Disease." A rock
opera about vomiting gastric juice.*
—From a journal entry.

The day of "Unplugged," Kurt had a secret that col-
ored his mood: His stomach problems were back, and he was vomiting
bile and blood. He had returned to doctor-roulette, seeing multiple
specialists on both coasts, or wherever the tour stopped. While he received many different opinions on his ailments—a few thought it irritable bowel syndrome but the diagnosis was uncertain, and he had tested
negatively for Crohn's disease—none of the treatments gave him relief.
He still swore heroin helped, but whether he was off heroin long
enough to know if it was the problem or the cure was debatable.

The morning of "Unplugged" Kurt spent an hour filling out a physician's questionnaire on his eating habits. In it he told the story of a
lifetime of near starvation, both spiritual and physical. He wrote his
favorite flavor was "raspberry-chocolate," and his least favorite was
"broccoli/spinach/mushroom." When asked what dish his mother
made he liked the best, he replied "roast, potatoes, carrots, pizza." To
the question, "What did you feed the family dog under the table?" he
answered, "Stepmother food." He described his top take-out choices
as Taco Bell and thin-crust pepperoni pizza. The only cuisine he professed to hating was Indian food. When the questionnaire inquired
about his general health, he failed to mention his drug addiction and
simply wrote "stomachaches." As for exercise, the single physical activ-

ity he reported was "performance." And to, "Do you enjoy the great outdoors?" he wrote a two-word answer: "Oh, please!"

He recorded the progression of his gastrointestinal problems in his journal, spending pages on minute details like describing an endoscopy (a procedure whereby a tiny video camera is inserted through the throat into the intestines, something he'd had done three times). He was both tormented by his stomach and, in some small way, entertained by it. "Please Lord," he pleaded in one entry, "fuck hit records, just let me have my very own unexplainable rare stomach disease named after me. And the title of our double album is 'Cobain's Disease.' A rock opera about vomiting gastric juices, being a borderline anorexic, Auschwitz-grunge boy, with an accompanying Endoscope home video!"

Though "Unplugged" had been an emotional high, ten days later in Atlanta, he hit a physical low, lying on the dressing-room floor clutching his belly. The tour caterers had disregarded his request for Kraft Macaroni and Cheese—instead, they concocted a dish of pasta shells, cheese, and jalapeño peppers. Courtney carried the plate of pasta in to manager John Silva and demanded, "What the fuck are jalapeños and jack cheese doing in this macaroni?" As she held the plate aloft like a waitress, she displayed Kurt's rider where in bold type it stated "*only* Kraft Macaroni and Cheese." To emphasize her point, she tossed the food in the trash. "She didn't care what Silva thought of her, she just wanted to make sure Kurt got food he could eat," Jim Barber, who was in the room, recalled. "She said to John, 'Why don't you just let Kurt be who he is?' " To further illustrate her point, Courtney forced Silva to examine Kurt's vomit, which contained blood. After Love left the room, Silva turned to Barber, and said, "*See* what I have to deal with?"

The relationship between Kurt and his managers had deteriorated to the point where the Nirvana organization resembled a dysfunctional family—in truth, it bore a similarity to Kurt's own family, with his bandmates playing the role of step-siblings, while his managers were parents. "Kurt hated John," recalled one former Gold Mountain employee, perhaps because Silva reminded Kurt a bit of his father. By late 1993 Kurt's distrust of Gold Mountain was so strong, he routinely employed Dylan Carlson to look over his financial statements because he felt he was being cheated, and Kurt had most of his interactions with

Michael Meisel, Silva's assistant. For his part, Silva openly described his most famous client as "a junkie," which was accurate, yet, to those who overheard it, it seemed disloyal. It was also true that Silva—like everyone in Kurt's life, Courtney included—simply didn't know what to do about Kurt's addiction. Was tough love better than acceptance? Was it better to shame him or enable him?

Kurt's other manager, Danny Goldberg, had worked as the press agent for Led Zeppelin during the height of that band's debauchery; consequently, tasks like locating drug rehab doctors usually fell to him. Kurt grew to treat Danny as a father figure, even while he thought Danny's company—Gold Mountain—was screwing him. Their personal relationship was complicated by their professional one: Goldberg's wife, Rosemary Carroll, was attorney for both Kurt and Courtney. It was an incestuous situation that raised eyebrows. "I don't think it was in his overall best interest, and I say that without comment to [Carroll's] abilities as an attorney," observed Alan Mintz, Cobain's prior lawyer.

Yet there was no denying Kurt trusted both Rosemary and Danny. Not long after Frances was born, he wrote a draft "last will and testimony" (it was never signed), stating that if Courtney were to perish, he wished for Danny and Rosemary to be his daughter's guardians. After them, he gave the duty to his sister Kim, and following her, he designated a list of subsequent guardians: Janet Billig; Eric Erlandson of Hole; Jackie Farry, their previous nanny; and Nikki McClure, Kurt's old neighbor, whom he hadn't talked to in more than a year. Ninth in succession—only to be given responsibility for Frances if Courtney, Rosemary, Danny, Kim, Janet, Eric, Jackie, and Nikki were deceased themselves—was Wendy O'Connor, Kurt's mother. Kurt wrote that under absolutely no circumstances—even if every single other relative in his family was dead—was Frances to be turned over to his father or anyone in Courtney's family.

The U.S. leg of the *In Utero* tour lumbered on for another month after "Unplugged," hitting St. Paul, Minnesota, on December 10. Nirvana had another MTV filming at the end of the week, and Kurt decided to make peace with the network: He invited Finnerty and Kurt Loder to interview him. At the taping, the band got drunk and dog-piled each other until they knocked over the camera. "It never aired," Finnerty recalled, "because everyone, including Kurt Loder, was so fucked up on red wine it was unusable." Loder and Novoselic then destroyed a hotel room by smashing the television and dragging pieces of the furniture out into the lobby. The hotel later unsuccessfully sued to collect what they alleged was $11,799 in damages.

Three days later the band taped MTV's "Live and Loud" in Seattle. The network filmed Nirvana's set before a small crowd, using props to make it appear it was New Year's Eve, when the program would air. After the performance Kurt invited photographer Alice Wheeler back to the Four Seasons Hotel to chat. He ordered steak from room service, explaining "MTV's paying." He urged Wheeler to come visit him at a new home he and Courtney were purchasing, but he couldn't recall the address. He told her, like he now told most friends, to contact him through Gold Mountain. Giving out the number of his management had the inadvertent result of further isolating Kurt: Many old friends told of calling Gold Mountain but never hearing back, and eventually losing touch.

A week later, when the tour came to Denver, Kurt reunited with John Robinson from the Fluid. When Robinson revealed the Fluid had broken up, Kurt wanted to know every detail; he left the impression he was looking for tips. Robinson mentioned he had begun writing songs on piano and wanted to make a lush album using strings and horns. "Wow!" Kurt replied. "That's exactly what I want to do!" He declared he'd been discussing a similar idea with Mark Lanegan, and invited Robinson to collaborate with the two of them after the lengthy tour was over. He'd also been talking about working with R.E.M.'s Michael Stipe.

The tour finally took a break at Christmas, and Kurt and Courtney flew to Arizona to spend four days at the exclusive Canyon Ranch Spa, outside of Tucson. For a Christmas present, she gave him a video copy of Ken Burns's series "The Civil War," which fascinated Kurt. While at the spa, Kurt attempted his own self-policed detox and each day visited Dr. Daniel Baker, the facility's resident counselor. The therapist offered one insight that stayed with Kurt well after the long weekend:

He warned Kurt his addiction had progressed to the point where he had to get sober, or it would mean his death. Many others had given the same advice, but on this particular day Kurt appeared to listen.

The difference between sobriety and intoxication was never more clearly illustrated than on December 30, when Nirvana played a show at the Great Western Forum near Los Angeles. Filmmaker Dave Markey was videotaping that night and observed a display of inebriation so extreme, he turned his camera off in pity. And it wasn't Kurt who was a mess—it was Eddie Van Halen. The famed guitar player was backstage on his knees drunk, begging Krist to let him jam. Kurt arrived only to see his one-time hero collapsing toward him with his lips puckered, like a toasted Dean Martin in a bad Rat-Pack skit. "No, you can't play with us," Kurt flatly announced. "We don't have any extra guitars."

Van Halen didn't grasp this obvious lie and pointed to Pat Smear, shouting, "Well, then let me play the Mexican's guitar. What is he, is he Mexican? Is he black?" Kurt couldn't believe his ears. "Eddie went into this racist, homophobic banter, typical redneck," observed Dave Markey. "It was surreal." Kurt was furious, but finally came up with a worthy verbal response: "Actually, you *can* jam," he promised. "You can go onstage *after* our encore. Just go up there and solo by yourself!" Kurt stormed off.

As 1993 ended Kurt wrote several reflections on the significance of the passing year. He composed a letter to the *Advocate* thanking them for running his interview and listing his accomplishments: "It was a fruitful year. Nirvana finished another album (of which we are quite proud, although we took shit from people who claimed—before its release—that we were gonna commit 'commercial suicide'). My daughter, Frances, a cherubic joy, taught me to be more tolerant of all humanity."

He also composed an unsent letter to Tobi Vail. Tobi was still hoping to complete their oft-talked-about recording project, and this convinced Kurt—still hurting from her original snub—that she was only interested in him to further her career. He wrote her a bitter letter: "Make them pay while you're still beautiful, while they watch you break, and they make you burn." Referring to *In Utero*, he declared: "Every song on this record is not about you. No, I am not your boyfriend. No, I don't write songs about you, except for 'Lounge Act,' which I do not play, except when my wife is not around." Behind Kurt's wrath was the terrible wound he still felt from her rejection. These weren't his only stinging words for Tobi: In another unsent screed he blasted her, Calvin, and Olympia:

I made about five million dollars last year and I'm not giving a red cent to that elitist, little fuck Calvin Johnson. No way! I've collaborated with one of my idols, William Burroughs and I couldn't feel cooler. I moved away to L.A. for a year and came back to find that three of my best friends have become full blown heroine addicts. I've learned to hate riot grrrl, a movement in which I was a witness to its very initial inception because I fucked the girl who put out the first grrrl-style fanzine and now she is exploiting the fact that she fucked me. Not in a huge way, but enough to feel exploited. But that's okay because I chose to let corporate white men exploit me a few years ago and I love it. It feels good. And I'm not gonna donate a single fucking dollar to the fucking needy indie fascist regime. They can starve. Let them eat vinyl. Every crumb for himself. I'll be able to sell my untalented, very ungenius ass for years based on my cult status.

In early January, Kurt and Courtney moved to their new house at 171 Lake Washington Boulevard East in ritzy Denny-Blaine, one of Seattle's oldest and most exclusive neighborhoods. Their home was just up the hill from the lake in an area of luxurious waterfront estates and stately turn-of-the-century mansions. The house across the street had a "no parking" sign in French, while their next-door neighbor was Howard Schultz, CEO of Starbucks. Though Peter Buck of R.E.M. owned a house a block away, he and the Cobains were the exceptions in the neighborhood, which was occupied by old money scions, society matrons, and the sorts of people who have public buildings named after them.

Their home had been built in 1902 by Elbert Blaine—who the neighborhood was named for—and he saved the finest and largest piece of land for himself: It was nearly three quarters of an acre and lushly landscaped with rhododendrons, Japanese maples, dogwoods, hemlock, and magnolia trees. It was a stunning property, though it had the odd feature of being directly next to a small city park, which made it less private than many of the district's homes.

The house itself was a 7,800-square-foot, three-story, five-fireplace, five-bedroom monolith. With gables and gray shake shingles, it looked better suited to the coast of Maine, where it might have served as a vacation compound for a former president. As with most large, old houses, it was drafty, though the kitchen was certainly cozy—it had been extensively remodeled and featured a Traulson stainless-steel refrigerator, a Thermador oven, and oak flooring. The main floor contained a living room, dining room, kitchen, and a library that became a bedroom for the nanny Cali. The second floor had a bedroom for Frances, two guest bedrooms, and a master suite, with its own private bathroom, that accorded views of the lake. The top floor consisted of a large, unheated attic, while the basement had another bedroom and several cavernous, dimly lit storage rooms. The Cobains paid $1,130,000 for the home; their mortgage with Chase Manhattan was $1,000,000, with monthly payments of $7,000 and taxes of $10,000 a year. To the rear of the house was a separate structure, which held a greenhouse and garage. Kurt's Valiant—which once had served as his only home—soon found a place in the garage.

Each family member found a small corner of the house to call their own: The north yard became Frances's playground, complete with a jungle-gym; Courtney's collection of teacups went on display in the kitchen, while her assortment of lingerie filled an entire closet in the bedroom; and the basement became the depository for all of Kurt's gold record awards—they weren't exhibited, just stacked. In an alcove on the main floor, a fully dressed mannequin stood, like some strange corpse-like sentinel. Kurt didn't like large spaces, and his favorite part of the house was the closet off the master bedroom, where he would play guitar.

Soon Kurt found other places to hide away. He had a month break before the *In Utero* tour was to head to Europe, and he appeared to make a conscious decision to spend as much of that respite as possible taking drugs with Dylan. Their relationship went deeper than their mutual addictions: Kurt truly loved Dylan, and was closer to him than any friend in his life other than Jesse Reed. Dylan was also one of the few of Kurt's friends who was welcome in the Lake Washington house—Courtney couldn't very well ban him, since when she occasionally fell off the wagon, Dylan was her main drug connection. There were almost-comic scenes when Dylan served as a runner for both husband and wife: Kurt would call looking for drugs, while on call-waiting Courtney would be seeking intoxicants of her own, and each requested he not tell the other spouse.

By 1994 their nanny Cali was also heavily into cocaine. They kept him on the payroll since he was essentially family at this point, but turned most supervision of Frances over to other caregivers and talked to Jackie Farry about her coming back. Cali still did most of the shopping—buying Totino's mini frozen pizzas for Kurt and Marie Callender pies for Courtney—since on the rare occasions the Cobains went to the store by themselves, they struggled with this task. Larry Reid had the occasion to be behind Kurt and Courtney in Rogers Thriftway Grocery that January: "They were throwing this stuff in their basket, but there was no rhyme or reason to what they were buying. It was weird shit, like relish, ketchup, and stuff like that. It was as if you went blind and went to the store and just threw stuff in your basket."

When Courtney attempted to stop drug dealers from coming over, Kurt employed friends to stash deliveries in the bushes. Kurt's use of drugs had expanded over the course of his addiction: If he couldn't find heroin, he'd inject cocaine or methamphetamine, or use prescription narcotics, like Percodan, bought on the street. If all other sources were dry, he'd take massive amounts of benzodiazepines, in the form of Valium or other tranquilizers; these cut down on his heroin withdrawal symptoms. Any attempt to stop drugs from coming into 171 Lake Washington Boulevard had as much success as a plumber trying to shore up a pipe that was being riddled with bullet holes: As soon as one leak was fixed, another sprang forth.

And in the midst of these daily traumas, Nirvana continued on, planning the next tour and scheduling rehearsals, though Kurt infrequently showed. The band had been offered the headlining slot on the 1994 Lollapalooza Festival. Everyone in Kurt's life, from his managers to the rest of the band, thought Nirvana should embrace the opportunity, but Kurt balked at more touring. His reticence infuriated Courtney, who felt he should do the tour to shore up their financial future. Most discussions over this or other opportunities led to screaming and shouting matches between them.

Wendy called Kurt during the last week in January to announce her own ten-year shouting match with Pat O'Connor was finally over—they had divorced. Kurt, while sorry to hear of her grief, felt glee hearing his one-time challenger for his mother's attention had finally been ousted. But he also heard news that saddened him: His beloved grandmother Iris had been suffering heart problems, and was going into the hospital in Seattle for tests and treatment.

Leland called Kurt once Iris was in the hospital in Seattle. Kurt bought $100 worth of orchids and apprehensively ventured into Swedish Hospital. It was hard for him to see Iris so frail; she had been one of the only stable forces throughout his childhood, and the idea of her death scared him worse than his own. He sat with her for hours. While he was there the bedside phone rang; it was his father. Hearing Don's voice, Kurt motioned he was going outside. But Iris, even in her frail state, grabbed his arm and handed him the phone. No matter how much he wanted to avoid his father, he couldn't turn down the request of a dying woman.

Kurt and Don chatted for the first time since their dreadful encounter at the Seattle concert. Most of the conversation was about Iris—the doctors predicted she would pull through her current illness but she had irreversible heart disease. Yet something in their short exchange seemed to break down a barrier—perhaps it was that Kurt heard some of the same fear in Don's voice that he felt. Before Kurt hung up, he gave his father his home phone number and asked his dad to call. "We'll have to get together soon," Kurt said as he put the phone down, and looked at his grandmother, who was smiling. "I know a lot of that stuff is from my mother," Kurt told Iris and Leland. "I now know a lot of it was bullshit."

By January 1994 Leland's personality had dramatically changed—it pained Kurt to see Leland so humbled and scared. Though Leland had suffered many losses—stretching back to the early death of his father and the suicides of his brothers—the illness of his wife of 49 years seemed to be the hardest to bear. Kurt invited his grandfather to spend the night at his house, and when the two Cobain men arrived, Courtney was walking around in a slip. This was usual attire for a performer who made undergarments a fashion statement, but the old-fashioned Leland found it disturbing: "She had no pants on; it sure as hell wasn't ladylike." Leland ran into Cali in the living room, and was shocked when Kurt informed him this long-haired, stoned-looking young man was one of Frances's nannies.

Courtney left for a meeting, so Kurt treated his grandfather to his favorite restaurant: the International House of Pancakes. Kurt recommended I-Hop's roast beef, which they both ordered. As they ate, Kurt examined the itinerary for his upcoming European tour. The band was scheduled to play 38 shows in sixteen nations over a period of less than two months. While it wasn't as grueling as the "Heavier Than Heaven" tour with Tad, it felt more fatiguing to Kurt. He had intentionally asked for a halfway break, during which he hoped to see Europe as a tourist with Courtney and Frances. Kurt told Leland that when he returned, he wanted to plan a fishing trip. During their dinner, Kurt was interrupted on three occasions by other patrons asking for autographs. "He signed them and asked what they wanted him to say," observed Leland. "But he told me he didn't like doing it."

On the way back to the house, Kurt asked to drive Leland's Ford truck, and he told his grandfather he wanted to buy a similar model. That month he'd already been out looking at cars, and had purchased a black Lexus. Jennifer Adamson, one of Cali's girlfriends, remembered Kurt stopping by her apartment to show it off: "Courtney wanted to buy it but Kurt thought it was too fancy, and he didn't like the color. They ended up taking it back." Courtney later explained in an Internet posting: "We went out one day and bought a really spendy black car, drove it around, got totally stared at, and felt mortified like we were sellouts—so we returned it within eighteen hours of buying it."

The last week of January Nirvana had a recording session at Robert Lang Studios in northern Seattle. The first day, despite repeated phone calls, Kurt failed to show. Courtney had already gone overseas with Hole, and no one answered the phone in the Cobain house. Novoselic and Grohl used the time to work on songs Dave had written. Kurt also failed to appear the second day, but on the third, a Sunday, he arrived, making no mention of why he'd missed the previous sessions. No one questioned him: The group had long ago lost its democracy, and Krist and Dave had resigned themselves to waiting, thinking it a miracle to have any participation from Kurt.

On that third day they worked for a full ten hours, and despite low expectations, laid down tracks for eleven songs. During the morning, a black kitten walked into the studio. This arrival, who looked a bit like Kurt's old childhood pet Puff, lightened Kurt considerably. The band cut several songs written by Grohl (which later would end up re-recorded by the Foo Fighters), and on these, Kurt played drums. One song of Kurt's they recorded was titled "Skid-marks," referring to underwear stains; Kurt had never escaped his obsession with fecal matter. Another was called "Butterfly," but this, like most of the new songs, was without lyrics and not completely formed.

One singular Kurt composition was completed with vocals, and it stands as one of the high-water marks in his entire canon. He later titled it "You Know You're Right," but the only time it was played live—Chicago on October 23, 1993—he had called it "On the Mountain." Musically, it featured the same soft/hard dynamics of "Heart-Shaped Box," with quiet verses followed by a loud chorus of Kurt's screams. "We bombed it together fast," recalled Novoselic. "Kurt had the riff, and brought it in, and we put it down. We Nirvana-ized it."

Lyrically, the verses were tightly crafted, with a haunting, tormented chorus of "You know you're right." The first verse was a list of declarations beginning with, "I would never bother you / I would never promise to / If I say that word again / I would move away from here." One couplet—that could only come from Kurt Cobain—went: "I am walking in the piss / Always knew it would come to this." The second verse shifts to statements about a woman—"She just wants to love herself"—and closes with two lines that have to be sarcastic: "Things have never been so swell / And I have never been so well." The plaintive wail in the chorus couldn't be clearer: "Pain," he cried, stretching the word out for almost ten seconds, giving it four syllables, and leaving an impression of inescapable torment.

Near the end of the session, Kurt looked for the black cat, but it had vanished. It was early evening when they finished, and the band celebrated by going out to dinner. Kurt seemed elated and told Robert Lang he wanted to book more time when they returned from Europe.

The next day Kurt phoned his father. They talked for over an hour, the longest conversation between the two Cobain men in over a decade. They discussed Iris and her prognosis—the doctors had sent her back to Montesano—and their respective families. Don said he wanted to see Frances, and Kurt proudly recited all the latest things she could say and do. As for their own strained relationship, they avoided reviewing their disappointments in each other, but Don was able to utter the words that many times earlier had eluded him. "I love you Kurt," he told his son. "I love you too, Dad," Kurt replied. At the end of the conversation, Kurt invited his father to come see his new house when he returned from tour. When Don hung up, it was one of the few times Jenny Cobain had ever seen her usually stoic husband weeping.

Two days later Kurt flew to France. The first show had Nirvana scheduled to play a variety show. Kurt came up with a solution that allowed him to save face: They purchased black pinstripe suits—he called them their "Knack outfits." When the show began, they performed straight ahead versions of three songs, but dressed in their attire it had the same effect as a comedy skit. In Paris, the band did a photo session with photographer Youri Lenquette; one of the pictures showed Kurt jokingly putting a gun to his head. Even this early in the tour, those close to him noticed a change in Kurt. "He was a mess at that point," Shelli Novoselic recalled. "It was sad. He was just so worn out." Kurt traveled in a separate tour bus from Novoselic and Grohl, but Shelli thought their relationship seemed better: "It wasn't as tense as the previous tour, but maybe it all had just become normal."

The next shows were in Portugal and Madrid. By Spain—only three dates into a 38-date tour—Kurt was already talking about cancelling. He phoned Courtney in a rage. "He hated everything, everybody," Love told David Fricke. "Hated, hated, hated. . . . He was in Madrid, and he'd walked through the audience. The kids were smoking heroin off tinfoil, and going, 'Kurt! Smack!' and giving him the thumbs up. He called me crying. . . . He did not want to be a junkie icon."

He also did not want to split with Courtney, but their increasing fights over the phone—mostly about his drug use—plus the separation caused by the tour, made him fearful of this outcome. He had wanted her on the road with him, but she was finishing post-production on her album. Kurt went to Jeff Mason and asked what would happen if he cancelled the tour: Mason informed him that because of past cancellations, they would be liable for damages from any missed shows, unless there was illness. Kurt fixated on this point, and in the tour bus the next day, kept joking that since the insurance only covered illness, if he was dead, they'd still have to play.

Though Kurt was heartbroken at seeing European teenagers equate him with drug abuse, the anxiety that overcame him did in fact spring from his addiction. In Seattle he knew where to find heroin, and it knew how to find him. In Europe, even if he found a drug connection, he was terrified of being arrested at a border crossing. Instead Kurt employed the services of a London physician who was well known for his liberal prescribing of legal but powerful narcotics. Kurt had prescriptions for tranquilizers and morphine, and he used both to cut the pains of his withdrawal. When he ran into trouble on tour, all it took was one phone call to this physician, who immediately wrote out prescriptions without question, and international couriers were used to ferry these to Kurt.

On February 20, a travel day, Kurt turned 27. John Silva jokingly gave him a carton of cigarettes as a present. Four days later, while in Milan, Kurt and Courtney celebrated their second anniversary, but they did so apart: She was still in London doing press for her album. They did talk on the phone and planned to celebrate when they reunited a week later.

By February 25, their second of two nights in Milan, something had shifted in Kurt. He no longer just seemed depressed—there was a defeatism about him. He came to Krist that day and said he wanted to cancel the tour. "He gave me some bullshit, absurd reason for why he wanted to blow it off," Novoselic recalled. Kurt complained about his stomach, though Krist had heard this protest hundreds of times by now.

Krist asked why he'd agreed to the tour in the first place, and reminded Kurt a cancellation would cost hundreds of thousands of dollars. "There was something going on with him in his personal life that was really troubling him," Krist observed. "There was some kind of situation." But Kurt didn't share any specifics with Krist—he had long ago stopped being intimate with his old friend.

Kurt didn't cancel the tour that night, but the only reason he didn't, Novoselic theorized, was because the next date was in Slovenia, where many of Krist's relatives would attend. "He hung on there for me," Krist recalled. "But I think his mind was made up." During their three days in Slovenia the rest of the band toured the countryside, but Kurt stayed in his room. Novoselic was reading *One Day in the Life of Ivan Denisovich*, by Aleksandr Solzhenitsyn, and he explained the plot to Kurt, thinking it would distract him: "It's about this guy in a Gulag, who still makes the most of his day." Kurt's only response was, "God, and he wants to live! Why would you try to live?"

When the band arrived in Munich for two scheduled shows at Terminal Eins, starting March 1, Kurt complained he felt ill. He uncharacteristically phoned his 52-year-old cousin Art Cobain back in Aberdeen, waking him up in the middle of the night. Art hadn't seen Kurt in almost two decades, and they weren't close, but he was glad to listen. "He was getting really fed up with his way of life," Art told *People*. Art invited Kurt to the upcoming Cobain family reunion when he returned from Europe.

Everyone who saw Kurt that day reported a sense of desperation and panic to his every action. Adding to his woes was the venue they were playing: It was an abandoned airport terminal turned into a club, and had horrid acoustics. At soundcheck, Kurt asked Jeff Mason for an advance on his per diem, and announced, "I'll be back for the show." Mason was surprised Kurt was leaving, considering how loudly he'd complained about feeling ill, and he inquired where he was bound. "I'm going to the train station," Kurt answered. Everyone on the tour knew what this meant; Kurt might as well have announced, "I'm going to buy drugs."

When he returned several hours later, Kurt's mood was no better. Backstage he phoned Courtney and their conversation ended in a fight, as had all their talks over the past week. Kurt then called Rosemary Carroll and told her he wanted a divorce. When he put down the phone, he stood on the side of the stage and watched the opening act. Kurt picked all Nirvana's opening bands, and for this leg of the tour he had selected the Melvins. "This was what I was looking for," he'd written in his journal back in 1983, when he'd first seen this band and they had transformed his life. In many ways, he loved the Melvins more than he loved Nirvana—they had meant salvation at a time when he needed to be saved. It had been only eleven years since that fateful day in the parking lot of the Montesano Thriftway, but so much had changed in his life. Yet in Munich, their show only made him feel nostalgic.

When the Melvins finished, Kurt marched into their dressing room and unleashed a long list of problems to Buzz Osborne. Buzz had never seen Kurt so distraught, not even when Kurt had been kicked out of Wendy's house back in high school. Kurt announced he was going to break up the band, fire his management, and divorce Courtney. Before he walked onstage, Kurt announced to Buzz, "I should just be doing this solo." "In retrospect," Buzz observed, "he was talking about his entire life."

Seventy minutes later, Nirvana's show was over, prematurely ended by Kurt. It had been a standard set, but, strangely, had included two covers by the Cars—"My Best Friend's Girl," and "Moving in Stereo"—and after this latter tune, Kurt walked offstage. Backstage, Kurt grabbed his agent, Don Muller, who happened to be at the show, and announced, "That's it. Cancel the next gig." There were only two shows before their scheduled break, which Muller arranged to postpone.

Kurt saw a doctor the next morning who signed a slip—required for their insurance—stating that he was too ill to perform. The physician recommended he take two months off. Despite the diagnosis, Novoselic thought it all an act: "He was just too burned out." Krist, and several members of the crew, flew back to Seattle, planning on returning for the next leg of the tour on March 11. Kurt headed to Rome, where he was to meet up with Courtney and Frances.

· · ·

On March 3 Kurt checked into room 541 in Rome's five-star Hotel Excelsior. Courtney and Frances were slated to arrive later that night. During the day, Kurt explored the city with Pat Smear, visiting tourist attractions, but mostly gathering props for what he imagined would be a romantic reunion—he and Courtney had been apart for 26 days, the longest span of their relationship. "He'd gone to the Vatican and stolen some candlesticks, big ones," Courtney recalled. "He also kicked off a piece of the Colosseum for me." Additionally, he'd purchased a dozen red roses, some lingerie, rosary beads from the Vatican, and a pair of three-carat diamond earrings. He also sent a bellboy out to fill a prescription for Rohypnol, a tranquilizer that can aid heroin withdrawal.

Love did not arrive until much later than expected—she had been in London during the day doing press for her upcoming album. At one of those interviews, Courtney had taken a Rohypnol in front of the writer. "I know this is a controlled substance," she told *Select*. "I got it from my doctor; it's like Valium." Courtney was seeing the same London doctor as Kurt. When Courtney and Frances finally arrived in Rome, the family, their nannies, and Smear had a warm reunion, and ordered champagne to celebrate—Kurt didn't drink any. After a while, Cali and a second nanny took Frances to her room, and Smear left. Finally alone, Courtney and Kurt made out, but she was exhausted from traveling, and the Rohypnol put her to sleep. Kurt had wanted to make love, she later reported, but she was too exhausted. "Even if I wasn't in the mood," she told David Fricke, "I should have just laid there for him. All he needed was to get laid."

At six in the morning, she awoke and found him on the floor, pale as a ghost, with blood coming out of one nostril. He was fully dressed, wearing his brown corduroy coat, and there was a wad of $1,000 in cash in his right hand. Courtney had seen Kurt close to death from heroin overdoses on more than a dozen occasions, but this wasn't a heroin overdose. Instead she found a three-page note clutched in the tight, cold ball of his left hand.

23 | LIKE HAMLET

SEATTLE, WASHINGTON
MARCH 1994

Like Hamlet, I have to choose between life and death.
—From the Rome suicide note.

When Kurt sat down to compose his suicide note in the Excelsior Hotel, he thought of Shakespeare and the Prince of Denmark. Two months earlier, during his attempt to dry out at the Canyon Ranch, his doctor warned he had to choose whether to continue with his addiction—which would ultimately mean death—or get sober, and that his answer would determine his very existence. Kurt replied, "You mean, like Hamlet?"

In his Rome note, Kurt cited Shakespeare's most famous character: "Dr. Baker says that, like Hamlet, I have to choose between life and death. I'm choosing death." The rest of the note touched on how sick he was of touring, and how Courtney "didn't love him anymore." This final point he reinforced by accusing his wife of sleeping with Billy Corgan, who he had always been jealous of. In one of their conversations that week, she'd mentioned Corgan had invited her to go on vacation. She declined, but Kurt heard it as a threat, and his vivid imagination went wild with it. "I'd rather die than go through another divorce," he wrote, referencing his parents' split.

Upon discovering Kurt's lifeless body, Courtney called the front desk, and Kurt was rushed to Umberto I Polyclinic Hospital. Love had retrieved two empty blister packs of Rohypnol next to Kurt—he had taken 60 of the aspirin-size pills, individually removing each from a plastic-and-foil container. Rohypnol has ten times the potency of Valium, and the combined effect was enough to put him very close to death. "He *was* dead, legally dead," Love reported later. Yet after his stomach was pumped, Kurt had a slight pulse, though he was in a coma. Doctors told Courtney it was a matter of chance: He might recover uninjured; he might have brain damage; or he might die. During a break in her vigil, she took a cab to the Vatican, purchased more rosary beads, and got down on her knees and prayed. She called his family in Grays Harbor, and they too prayed for him, though his half-sister, eight-year-old Brianne, couldn't figure out why Kurt was "in Tacoma."

Later that day, Cable News Network interrupted a broadcast to report Kurt had died of an overdose. Krist and Shelli picked up their phone to hear a Gold Mountain representative with the same sad news. Most of the initial reports of Kurt's death had originated from David Geffen's office—a female identifying herself as Courtney had left a message with the label head saying Kurt was dead. After an hour of panic and grief, it was discovered the caller was an impersonator.

As friends in America were being told he was dead, Kurt showed his first signs of life in twenty hours. There were tubes in his mouth, so Courtney handed him a pencil and a notepad, and he jotted, "Fuck you," followed by, "Get these fucking tubes out of my nose." When he finally spoke, he asked for a strawberry milkshake. As he stabilized, Courtney had him moved to the American Hospital, where she thought he'd get better care.

The next day, Dr. Osvaldo Galletta held a press conference and announced: "Kurt Cobain is clearly and dramatically improving. Yesterday, he was hospitalized at the Rome American Hospital in a state of coma and respiratory failure. Today, he is recovering from a pharmacological coma, due not to narcotics, but the combined effect of alcohol and tranquilizers that had been medically prescribed by a doctor." Courtney told reporters that Kurt wasn't going to "get away" from her that easily. "I'll follow him through hell," she said.

When Kurt awoke, he was back in his own small piece of hell. In his mind, nothing had changed: All his problems were still with him, but now were accentuated by the embarrassment of a highly publicized fall from grace. He had always feared arrest; this overdose, and having been declared dead by CNN, was about the only thing that could have been worse.

And despite a near death experience and twenty hours in a coma, he still craved opiates. Later, he would brag that a dealer visited his hospital room and pumped heroin through the IV; he also phoned Seattle and arranged for a gram of heroin to be left in the bushes outside his home.

Back in Aberdeen, Wendy was much relieved to hear Kurt was better. Wendy told the *Aberdeen Daily World* her son was "in a profession he doesn't have the stamina to be in." She told reporter Claude Iosso that she had handled the news well until she looked at the wall: "I took one look at my son's picture and saw his eyes and I lost it. I didn't want my son gone." Wendy had health struggles of her own that year: She had been fighting breast cancer.

Kurt left the hospital on March 8 and four days later flew back to Seattle. On the plane, he asked Courtney for Rohypnol so loudly other passengers overheard him; she told him they were all gone. When they arrived at Sea-Tac airport, he was taken off the plane in a wheelchair, "looking horrible," according to Travis Myers, a customs agent. Yet when Myers asked for an autograph, Kurt consented, writing, "Hey, Travis, no cannabis." In America, the scrutiny he dreaded was mostly absent because the official Gold Mountain statement had declared Rome an accidental overdose—few knew he'd taken 60 pills or left a note. Kurt didn't even tell his best friend, Dylan. "I thought it was an accidental OD, which was the party line, and was believable," Dylan recalled. Even Novoselic and Grohl were told it was an accidental overdose. Everyone in the organization had witnessed Kurt's overdoses before; many were resigned his drug use would one day claim his life.

The European tour had been postponed, but the band and crew were told to prepare for Lollapalooza. Kurt had never wanted to play the festival, and he had yet to sign the contract, but management assumed he'd yield. "Nirvana had confirmed they were going to appear on the 1994 Lollapalooza," said promoter Marc Geiger. "Nothing was in writing at that point, but they were totally confirmed, and we were working on finishing up the contracts." Nirvana's take of box office revenues would have been around $8 million.

Kurt felt the offer wasn't fair; he didn't want to perform in a festival environment, and he simply didn't want to tour. Courtney felt he should take the money, arguing that Nirvana needed the career boost. "He was being threatened with being sued for the shows he didn't do in Europe," Dylan recalled. "And I think he felt like he was going to be financially ruined." Rosemary Carroll remembered Kurt emphatically announcing he didn't want to play the festival. "Everyone around him basically told him that he had to, in his personal life and his professional life," she said. Kurt handled this situation as he dealt with most conflict: He avoided it, and by stalling, he killed the deal. "He was withdrawing, not from drugs, but from dealing with people," Carroll recalled. "It was such a difficult time that I think people exaggerated and blamed his drug use when they weren't getting what they wanted out of him."

Yet the drugs were present, in quantities greater than ever before. Courtney had hoped Rome would scare Kurt—it had terrified her—so his heedless overuse alarmed her. "I flipped out," she told David Fricke. She decided to establish an iron-clad rule she hoped would keep Kurt, Cali, and herself clean: She insisted no drugs were to be done inside the house. Kurt's response was simple and typical: He left his $1.13 million-dollar mansion and checked into $18-a-night motels on seedy Aurora Avenue. Throughout the worst spans of his addiction, he had frequently retreated to these dark places, not even bothering in most instances to check in under an assumed name. He frequented the Seattle Inn, the Crest, the Close-In, the A-1, and the Marco Polo, always paying cash, and in the privacy of his room he would nod off for hours. He favored establishments in northern Seattle: Though they were less convenient to his home, they were close to a favorite dealer. On nights he wouldn't return home, Courtney became panicked, worried that he'd overdosed. She quickly rescinded her policy. "I wish I'd just been the way I always was, just tolerant of it," she later told Fricke.

But it wasn't just Courtney's disappointment driving Kurt; something was different about him after Rome. Novoselic wondered whether the coma had indeed left him with brain damage. "He

wouldn't listen to *anybody*," Krist recalled. "He was *so* fucked up."
Dylan noticed a shift as well: "He didn't seem as alive. Before, he had
more to him; after, he seemed monochromatic."

A week after Rome, Kurt's father phoned, and they had a pleasant
but short conversation. He invited his dad to visit, but no one was home
when Don arrived. Kurt apologized the next day by phone, claiming
he'd been busy. Yet when his father returned two days later, Cali reported Kurt again gone. Truth was Kurt was home but was high and
didn't want his father to see him in such a state. When they next spoke,
Kurt promised to call as soon as he got a break from his busy career.

That career—at least when it came to Nirvana—was essentially over
by the second week of March. Kurt's decision to cancel the tour, turn
down Lollapalooza, and refuse to practice had finally confirmed what
Novoselic and Grohl had suspected was looming for some time. "The
band was broken up," Krist recalled. The only musical project Kurt
planned was with R.E.M.'s Michael Stipe. Stipe had gone so far as to
send Kurt plane tickets to Atlanta for a session they had scheduled in
mid-March. At the last minute, Kurt cancelled.

On March 12 Seattle police were dispatched to the Lake Washington
house after someone called 911 but hung up. Courtney answered the
door, apologized for the call, and explained there had been a fight but
it was now under control. Kurt told the officer, "There was a lot of
stress" in his marriage. He said they should "go to therapy."

On March 18 Kurt threatened suicide once again, locking himself
in the bedroom. Courtney kicked the door, but was unable to break it
down. He eventually opened it willingly, and she saw several guns on
the floor. She grabbed a .38 revolver and put it to her head. "I'm going
to pull this [trigger] right now," she threatened. "I cannot see you die
again." It was the same game of Russian Roulette they had played in
Cedars-Sinai Hospital in 1992. Kurt screamed, "There's no safety! You
don't understand, there's no safety on that. It's going to go off!" He
grabbed the gun from her. But a few minutes later, he locked her out
again, and was back threatening suicide. Courtney called 911, and two
police officers arrived within minutes.

Officer Edwards wrote in his police report that Kurt claimed he was "not suicidal and doesn't want to hurt himself. . . . He stated that he had locked himself in the room to keep away from Courtney." Once police arrived, Courtney tried to downplay the episode so Kurt might avoid arrest. Just to be safe, she pointed out his guns, and police seized three pistols and the Colt AR-15 semi-automatic assault rifle from the incident the previous summer—these weapons had been returned to Kurt a month after the original domestic violence arrest. The police also impounded 25 boxes of ammunition and a bottle of "white pills"— these later turned out to be Klonopin, a benzodiazepine used primarily for seizure control. Kurt was taking massive quantities of this tranquilizer, thinking it would help him with withdrawal. Klonopin made him paranoid, manic, and delusional. It had not been prescribed; he was instead buying the drug on the street. The officers took Kurt downtown but didn't formally book him.

Ian Dickson was walking on Pine Street that night and ran into Kurt on a street corner. When Dickson asked what his old friend was up to, Kurt said, "Courtney had me arrested. I just got out of jail." He described the fight, downplaying the guns. "He said it was a lovers' spat," Dickson remembered, "and that he was bummed because he really loved Courtney." They walked to Piccora's Pizza, where Kurt complained of being broke. "He asked to borrow $100, and if he could stay at my place," Dickson recalled. "He was talking about how he was going to get his mom to wire him some money." Kurt suddenly left, announcing he had to make a phone call.

Four days later, Kurt and Courtney were quarrelling when they took a cab to the American Dream car lot. Courtney urged Kurt to consider another Lexus, but Kurt had other ideas: He bought a 1965 sky blue Dodge Dart for $2,500. He put a "for sale" sign on his trusty Valiant.

He didn't really need the car because he spent most of that March too messed up to drive. As his overuse spiraled, he found his usual dealers refused to sell to him: No one wanted the trouble of a famous junkie dying in their stairwell. He found a new dealer named Caitlin Moore, who lived at the intersection of 11th and Denny Way and would sell him "speedballs," a mixture of heroin and cocaine. This was not Kurt's preferred high, but Moore would allow rock-star clients to fix in her apartment, which was essential because Kurt no longer felt welcome at home.

When he wasn't at Moore's or at the Taco Time on Madison—his favorite place to buy a burrito—he could frequently be found at the Granada Apartments, home of Cali's girlfriend Jennifer Adamson. Jennifer found herself in awe, watching the most famous rock star in the world sitting on her sofa, many times doing drugs, but on other occasions just killing time. "He'd sit in my living room with the hat with the ear coverings, and read magazines," she said. "People came and went; there was always a lot of activity going on. Nobody knew he was there or recognized him." In the world of junkie culture, Kurt found some of the anonymity he lacked elsewhere. Yet as Jennifer grew to know Kurt better, she was bewildered at how lonely he seemed. He told Jennifer and Cali, "You guys are my only friends."

Courtney was unsure what to do to rein him in, and most discussions turned into arguments. "They started to fight a lot," Jennifer observed. "Clearly he wasn't reaching out to her at his most desperate time of need, or to anybody else for that matter." As Kurt moved away from Courtney, he favored Dylan, if only because Dylan never lectured him to clean up his act. One night that spring the two men cemented their relationship by hot-wiring a car and ditching it on Kurt's Carnation property. "I've got this millionaire husband," Courtney recalled, "and he's out stealing cars."

After Rome, even Kurt's drug buddies observed an increasing desperation to his usage. "When most people are doing a shot of heroin, they pay attention to how much," Jennifer observed. "They think, 'let's make sure this isn't too much.' Kurt never thought about that; there was never any hesitation with him. He really didn't care if it killed him; things would be taken care of that way." Jennifer began to fear Kurt would OD in her apartment: "It amazed me for such a small person, and such a slight guy, how much he could do. You couldn't fit enough in the syringe for him." The third week in March, she chastised Kurt on how he was putting his life in danger, but his reply frightened her even more: "He told me he was going to shoot himself in the head. He said, half jokingly, '*That's* how I'm going to die.'"

. . .

By the third week of March, like his beloved Hamlet in the fifth act, Kurt was a changed man and in a frenzy that showed no signs of abating. The drugs, combined with what many around him described as a life-long undiagnosed depression, shrouded him in madness. Even heroin had betrayed him; he reported it wasn't as effective a painkiller anymore; his stomach was still hurting. Courtney and Kurt's managers decided to force him into treatment. In Kurt's case, everyone knew this was a last-ditch effort at best, with little chance of changing him— he had previously gone through several interventions, and he wasn't likely to be surprised. He had already been in a half dozen drug treatment facilities, and none had worked for more than a few weeks. But as Courtney saw it, at least an intervention was *something* they could do, a physical action. As with many families around an active addict, those around Kurt felt increasingly hopeless themselves.

Danny Goldberg contacted Steven Chatoff, of Steps recovery center. "I started having telephone conversations with Kurt where he was very, very loaded," Chatoff recalled. "He was using quite a bit of heroin, or some other painkillers. But we also discussed, during some of his more coherent times when he wasn't gravely impaired, about some of his childhood issues and some of his unresolved family of origin issues, and the pain he was in. He had a lot of stomach pain, which he was med-icating with these opiates." Chatoff felt underneath Kurt's addiction was "a form of post-traumatic stress disorder, or some form of depressive disorder." He recommended an inpatient treatment program. Chatoff described Kurt's earlier rehabs as "detox, buff, and shine," suggesting that they were designed to get Kurt sober, but not deal with the un-derlying problems.

Chatoff found Kurt surprisingly cooperative, at least at first: "He agreed that he needed [inpatient treatment]; that he needed to work on his 'psychic pain,' as he put it." But one thing Kurt didn't admit to— and Chatoff at the time wasn't told by management—was that Rome was a suicide attempt: Chatoff believed what he'd read in the paper, that it had been an accidental overdose.

Kurt expressed grave doubts to Dylan whether rehab would help. Having tried treatment on a half dozen previous occasions, Kurt knew the odds were against repeat patients. Though there were brief moments when he would claim to be willing to go through the pain of withdrawal, most of the time he simply didn't want to stop: Jackie Farry recalled picking up Kurt from a $2,000-a-day rehab, only to have him direct her to a house she suspected was his dealer's. His other trips to rehab had all been the result of ultimatums from his managers, wife, or the court, and all had the ultimate same result: He'd gone back to using again.

Chatoff planned his intervention for Tuesday, March 21, but before those involved could even be assembled, Kurt was tipped off, and it was cancelled. Novoselic admitted he had tipped Kurt off, feeling the idea would backfire and that Kurt would flee. "I just felt so bad for him," Krist recalled. "He looked so fucked up. I knew he wouldn't listen to it." Krist saw Kurt for the first time since Rome that week at the Marco Polo Motel on Aurora Avenue. "He was camped out there. He was delusional. It was so weird. He was like, 'Krist, where can I buy a motorcycle?' I was like, 'Fuck, what are you talking about? You don't want to buy a motorcycle. You've got to get the fuck out of here.' " Krist invited Kurt to go away on vacation, just the two of them, to talk things out, but Kurt refused. "He was really quiet. He was just estranged from all his relationships. He wasn't connecting with anybody."

Kurt complained of being hungry, so Krist offered to buy him dinner at a fancy restaurant; Kurt insisted he wanted a Jack in the Box hamburger. As Novoselic drove toward Jack in the Box in the nearby U-District, Kurt protested: "Those hamburgers are too greasy. Let's go to the one on Capitol Hill—the food is better there." Only when they arrived on Capitol Hill did Novoselic realize Kurt didn't want hamburgers at all: He was simply using his old friend to get a ride to score drugs. "His dealer was right by there. He just wanted to get fucked up into oblivion. There was no talking to him. He just wanted to escape. He wanted to die, that was what he wanted to do." The two men began screaming at each other and Kurt bolted from the car.

· · ·

A new counselor named David Burr was hired, and another intervention was scheduled for later that week. Danny Goldberg remembered Courtney pleading on the phone, "You've got to come. I'm afraid he's going to kill himself or hurt someone." Burr's intervention occurred on Friday, March 25. Just to make sure Kurt didn't flee, Courtney slashed the tires on the Volvo and the Dart; the Valiant's tires were so bald she thought Kurt wouldn't risk driving it.

This intervention did surprise Kurt, though the timing ultimately was unfortunate: Kurt and Dylan had just gotten high. "Me and Kurt had been up all night partying," Dylan explained. "And both me and him had just woken up and done a wake-up shot, and walked downstairs, and this sea of people were there to confront him." Kurt was furious, showing the anger of a newly caged beast. His first reaction was to grab a recycling bin and throw it at Dylan, who he thought had lured him. Dylan told Kurt he wasn't in on it, and urged Kurt to leave. But Kurt stayed and faced a room full of his managers, friends, and bandmates. It was as if he were on trial, and like a remorseful criminal in a capital case, he kept his eyes focused on the floor during the entire proceeding.

In the room were Courtney; Danny Goldberg, John Silva, and Janet Billig from Gold Mountain; Mark Kates and Gary Gersh from his label; Pat Smear from the band; Cali, the nanny; and the counselor David Burr. Kurt's mother wasn't there because she was in Aberdeen caring for Frances. Many of the participants had flown on red-eye flights to arrive in Seattle on short notice. One by one, each person recounted a list of reasons Kurt should go into treatment. Each speaker ended with a threat, the consequence Kurt could expect if he didn't acquiesce. Danny, John, and Janet said they'd no longer work with him; Gary Gersh said Geffen would drop Nirvana; Smear said Nirvana would break up; and Courtney said she would divorce him. Kurt was silent during these warnings: He had already anticipated these endings, and in every instance he had already hazarded to sever these unions himself.

Though Burr told everyone they "had to confront Kurt," few present were capable of that. "Everyone was so scared of Kurt," Goldberg observed. "He had this aura around him, where even I would feel like I was walking on eggshells, and I didn't want to say the wrong thing.

He was so powerful an energy, the other people, with all respect, literally didn't talk to him at all. They just kind of hung around, and lurked around in the background." The person who said the most was Burr, who was attempting to professionally run an intervention, but in this case the patient was Kurt Cobain, who wasn't listening: His addiction was too strong and ingrained a shield for these blows to break it.

The real drama began when Courtney spoke. She was by far the most direct of those in the room, but then she had the most to lose. She begged Kurt to go to treatment, imploring, "This has got to end! . . . You have to be a good daddy!" And then she threw down the threat she knew would hurt the most: If they divorced, and he continued with his addiction, his access to Frances would be limited.

After everyone other than Kurt had spoken, there was a brief moment of silence, like that which precedes a major battle in a John Wayne movie. Kurt's eyes slowly rose and malevolently went from person to person, until he won every stare-down contest. When he finally spoke, he spat out words in anger. "Who the *fuck* are all of you to tell me this?" he bellowed. He took his own inventory of everyone in the room, describing, in explicit detail, instances he had witnessed of their drug usage. Danny Goldberg responded by telling Kurt it was his health they were all concerned with, not anyone else's. "How are we going to even have a conversation if you are fucked up?" Goldberg implored. "So you get a little clean, and then at least you can have a conversation about it." Kurt got angrier and angrier, and being a skilled verbal tactician he began to dissect everyone in the room, hitting each with an assault he knew would strike to their core weakness. He called Janet Billig "a fat pig," and he called everyone in the room a hypocrite. He frantically grabbed the Yellow Pages and turned to the section for psychiatrists. "I don't trust anybody here," he declared. "I'm going to get a psychiatrist out of the Yellow Pages I can trust."

His greatest rage was reserved for Courtney. "His big thing was that Courtney was more fucked up than he was," Goldberg recalled. Kurt's attack on Courtney was deflated when he was told she was flying to Los Angeles for rehab. He was urged to accompany her. He refused and continued to dial psychiatrists, getting only answering services. Courtney was a mess herself—the intervention and the last three weeks, where every day she expected to hear news of his overdose, had taken their toll. She had to be helped to a car, and Kurt was offered one more chance to accompany her. He refused, and as her car left, he was frenetically flipping through the Yellow Pages. "I did not even kiss or get to say good-bye to my husband," Love later told David Fricke.

Kurt insisted no one in the room had any right to judge him. He retired to the basement with Smear, saying that all he wanted to do was play guitar for a while. Those present slowly began to leave; most had to catch flights back to Los Angeles or New York. By evening, even Burr and Smear were gone, and Kurt was left with the same emptiness he felt most days. He spent the rest of the evening at his dealer's complaining about the intervention. The dealer later told a newspaper that Kurt had asked her, "Where are my friends when I need them? Why are my friends against me?"

The next day Jackie Farry came back to work for the Cobains and took Frances to Los Angeles to be near Courtney. Kurt's mother and sister drove to Seattle, urged by Courtney, to try to talk to him. Their confrontation went no better than the intervention, and it left all parties with a greater sense of heartache and loss. Kurt was obviously high, and it anguished Wendy and Kim to see him in so much emotional pain. He wouldn't listen: It had come to a point where nothing could be talked through anymore. As mother and sister were leaving—both in tears—Kim, being the most direct of the family, asked her brother one more question as she stood in the door: "Do you really hate us this much?" As she said this she was weeping, which must have appeared extraordinary to Kurt: Kim was always the tough one, the one that never cried. And here she was at the door of his house, and it was he who was making her cry. "Oh yeah," he replied, sounding as sarcastic as she had ever heard him. "Oh, yeah," he said. "I *really* hate you guys. I *hate* you guys." Kim couldn't say anything else—she had to leave.

In Los Angeles Courtney checked into the Peninsula Hotel to begin a controversial treatment plan called "hotel detox." She was to be seen several times a day by a drug counselor in a hotel suite, avoiding the glare of a more public treatment center. She tried calling the Seattle house but got no answer.

Kurt, as she suspected, was out doing drugs. He was now alone in the house with Cali. Kurt showed up at a local dealer's house later that day, but had bought and used so much heroin that the dealer refused to sell him any more: They did this both out of feigned concern for his health and fear that if he overdosed on their dope, it might bring the police upon them. "He was on a binge," reported Rob Morfitt, who knew several people who encountered Kurt that weekend. "He was going around and getting extremely screwed up." Kurt's normal carelessness was replaced by a death wish that frightened even the most seasoned, cynical junkies. The last few months of his drug use, he had wantonly shared needles with other users, ignoring public health warnings about HIV and hepatitis. Black tar heroin frequently caused abscesses from the impurities used to cut it. By March, Kurt's arms had scabs and abscesses, which themselves were a potential health danger.

Later that day he bribed other users to score heroin for him, promising them drugs in return. When the drugs were split up in their apartment and cooked, Kurt prepared a syringe that was as black as coal—he had failed to use enough water to dilute it. His compatriots looked on in horror as upon injecting himself, he immediately began to suffer the consequences of an OD. A panic went through the apartment, as Kurt began to gasp for air: If he died there, the police would inevitably be involved. The apartment residents ordered Kurt to leave, and when he was incapable of moving, they dragged him outside. His Valiant was parked on the street and they planted him in the back seat. One person offered to call 911, but Kurt was conscious enough to hear this and shook his head. They left him alone, figuring that if he wanted to die, he was going to do it on his own watch.

This is what it all had come to: The most famous rock star of his generation was lying in the backseat of a car, unable to talk, unable to move, and one more time coming just inches away from dying. He had spent many nights in this car—it was as reliable and cozy a home as he ever had—and it was as good a place to die as any. The "for sale" sign on the back window, written on a piece of a cardboard, had his home phone number on it.

Kurt didn't die that weekend. In yet one more feat that defied science, his constitution survived another dose of heroin that would have killed most people. When he woke up in the car the next day, his emotional and physical pain were back: What he wanted more than anything was to be free from all hurts. Even heroin wasn't helping now.

When he returned home, there were numerous messages from Courtney, and also messages from a new psychiatrist named Dr. Steven Scappa, who Buddy Arnold had recommended. Kurt called Scappa back and began to have long conversations with him. He seemed to be softening and connecting with Scappa in a way that he hadn't with some of the other doctors. That Monday, he also took a call from Rosemary Carroll, who tried to talk him into treatment. "You are making it easy," she told him, "for a lot of these people that you want to stop controlling your life to paint a completely negative picture of you; for them to essentially maintain control, because of the drug issue. If you go do the treatment thing, you give them one less arrow in their quiver, you radically diminish their ammunition. It may not make any sense, and it may not be based in logic, but that's the way it is. So you go, and deal with this. It will make solving these problems easier when you get out. It will give us a basis to stand on." Kurt's response was, "I know." He told Carroll he would try treatment one more time.

That Tuesday, reservations were made for Kurt to fly to Los Angeles, and Krist was enlisted to take him to the airport. When Kurt arrived at Krist's house, it was obvious he did not want to go. As they took the 25-minute drive, Kurt sobbed and yelled and screamed. On Interstate 5, near the Tukwila exit, Kurt tried to open the door and jump from the moving car. Krist couldn't believe this was happening, yet with his long arms he managed to hold on to Kurt as he drove, even as his car swerved. They made it to the airport a few minutes later, but Kurt hadn't improved: Krist had to drag him by the collar, the way a school-master might escort a ruffian to the principal's office. In the main terminal, Kurt punched Krist in the face and attempted to flee. Krist tackled him, and a wrestling match ensued. The two old friends brawled on the floor of the crowded airport terminal, cursing and punching each other like two drunks in an Aberdeen bar brawl. Kurt freed himself from his friend's grasp and ran through the building screaming, "Fuck you!" as shocked passengers looked on. The last Krist saw of Kurt was his blond mop turning the corner.

Krist drove back to Seattle alone, sobbing. "Krist had such a huge, huge amount of love for Kurt," Shelli recalled. "We both did. He was family to us. I'd known him for almost half his life." As a teenager, Shelli had slipped Kurt free Big Macs from behind the counter at the Aberdeen McDonald's. For a couple of weeks back in 1989, Kurt, Tracy, Krist, and Shelli had all shared the same double bed, sleeping in shifts. Kurt had once lived in a van behind their house, and Shelli would bring him blankets to make sure he didn't freeze to death. Krist and Kurt had driven what seemed like a million miles together, and they had told each other things they had never told another soul. But that Tuesday night, Krist told Shelli he knew in his heart he would never see Kurt alive again, and he was right.

Later that night, Kurt talked on the phone with Scappa several times, and also had what Courtney remembered as a pleasant conversation with her. He nodded out during it, but despite his actions earlier with Krist, he again was agreeing to treatment. Arrangements were made for him to fly out the next day.

Having resignedly agreed to go, Kurt did what most active addicts do before heading into treatment: He tried to do so much heroin that some would remain in his system during those first horrible days of withdrawal. The next afternoon, Kurt drove to Dylan's with a favor to ask: He wanted to buy a gun "for protection and because of prowlers," since the police had taken away all his other weapons, and he wondered if Dylan would purchase it for him. Dylan accepted this logic, even though there was no registration in Washington for rifles. They drove to Stan Baker's Sports at 10000 Lake City Way. "If Kurt was suicidal," Dylan later recalled, "he sure hid it from me." Inside, Kurt pointed to a Remington M–11 twenty-gauge shotgun. Dylan bought it and a box of shells, paying $308.37 in cash, which Kurt handed him. Having purchased the shotgun, Kurt went home.

That night Harvey Ottinger, a driver for Washington Limousine Service, arrived in his town car as scheduled at the Lake Washington house. He waited an hour, and Kurt finally came down carrying a small satchel. On the way to the airport, Kurt realized he had left the box of shotgun cartridges in his bag, and asked Ottinger if he'd dispose of them. The driver said yes, and as they pulled up to Sea-Tac, Kurt exited the car and hurried for his flight to Los Angeles.

24 | ANGEL'S HAIR

LOS ANGELES, CALIFORNIA-
SEATTLE, WASHINGTON
MARCH 30-APRIL 6, 1994

Cut myself on angel's hair and baby's breath.
—From "Heart-Shaped Box."

Pat Smear and Gold Mountain's Michael Meisel met Kurt at LAX on Wednesday evening and drove him to Exodus Recovery Center, part of the Daniel Freeman Marina Hospital in Marina Del Rey. This was the same facility Kurt had attended in September 1992. It was a rehab favored by rock stars—Joe Walsh of the Eagles had left the day before, and Gibby Haynes of the Butthole Surfers was there when Kurt arrived. Kurt checked in for what was scheduled to be a 28-day program.

He was assigned room 206 in the twenty-bed facility. That first night he went through a 40-minute intake interview with a nurse. Afterwards, he came down to the common room and sat next to Haynes, who had been one of his idols as a teenager. "Everyone was going to a Cocaine Anonymous meeting, but Kurt said he was going to stay at Exodus, because he'd just gotten there," Haynes recalled. "He looked sick and tired of being sick and tired."

Thursday morning, Kurt began his course of treatment, which consisted of group therapy, meetings, and individual therapy with his substance abuse counselor, Nial Stimson. "He was totally in denial that he had a heroin problem," Stimson said. "I asked him if he understood the seriousness of his Italy thing: 'Man, you almost died! You have to take this seriously. Your drug abuse has gotten you to where you almost lost your life. Do you get how serious this is?' " Kurt's response was, "I understand. I just want to get cleaned up and out of here." Stimson had not been informed that Rome was a suicide attempt. As a result, Kurt was in a regular room at Exodus, though just a short distance away was the locked-down psychiatric unit of the hospital.

Courtney called Exodus several times that day and she argued with the staff when she was told Kurt was unavailable. In his sessions with Stimson, Kurt rarely mentioned his battles with Courtney. Instead, he said the worry of potentially losing a lawsuit with original "Heart-Shaped Box" video director Kevin Kerslake was what scared him the most. Kerslake had filed a suit on March 9, claiming he, not Kurt, had come up with many of the ideas in the video. Kurt told his counselor he had thought about almost nothing else since Kerslake's suit had been filed and he worried the case would wipe him out financially. "He told me his biggest fear was that if he lost that suit, he would lose his house," Stimson said.

During Thursday afternoon, Kurt was visited by Jackie Farry and Frances—Courtney did not visit because her physician had advised against it in the early stages of Kurt's sobriety. Frances was nineteen months old at the time; Kurt played with her but Farry noticed that he seemed out of it, and she assumed it was because of drugs the center had given him to help with withdrawal. When talking with Farry, Kurt didn't mention the Kerslake suit, but did bring up the battle with Court-ney over Lollapalooza. Jackie and Frances only stayed a short while but promised to return the next day.

They came back on Friday morning at eleven and Jackie found Kurt looking surprisingly rested. "He was in this incredibly happy mood, which I just didn't get," Farry recalled. "I was thinking, 'God, for one second, maybe he really is for real this time.' He was laying it on thick, saying all these incredibly complimentary things to me and being really positive. And that wasn't his deal—sitting around and trying to make the world look great. Usually he was kind of grumpy. But I just took it as a sign that it was a positive 24-hour turnaround." Farry told Kurt about her plans for a television show and Kurt was uncharacteristically encouraging, telling her that she'd make a "great famous person" be-cause she "wasn't all screwed up."

Kurt's change in mood wasn't enough to alarm Farry—she just assumed he was on pills provided by the rehab. Compared to the first visit, he was more physical with Frances, and threw her in the air to make her giggle. Farry went down the hall for a moment, thinking she would give the two of them time alone together. When she returned, Kurt was holding Frances over his shoulder, patting her on the back, and sweetly talking in her ear. Farry gathered Frances and told Kurt they'd see him the next day. He walked them to the door, looked his daughter in the eyes, and said, "Good-bye."

In the early afternoon Kurt sat in the smoking area behind Exodus, chatting with Gibby. Most repeat-rehab patients—which both Kurt and Gibby were—approached treatment with a gallows humor, and the two of them gossiped about others with problems worse than their own. One drummer had developed such severe abscesses that his arm had been amputated. Gibby joked he was glad he was just the singer, and Kurt had a long laugh at this. They chuckled over a mutual acquaintance who had escaped Exodus by jumping over the back wall: This was completely unnecessary, since the front doors were unlocked. "Me and Kurt were laughing about what a dumb-ass he was for escaping over the wall," Haynes recalled.

That afternoon, Kurt was visited by Pat Smear and Joe "Mama" Nitzburg. Mama was an artist friend of Courtney's who had been through drug treatment before himself. The previous year, in an act of altruism never publicized, Kurt paid for Mama's art school tuition when Mama's financial aid was denied. Courtney had sent Mama to Exodus with a letter for Kurt, along with some candy and a fanzine she thought he'd like. Mama was surprised at how lucid Kurt was with just a day of sobriety. "You look good; how do you feel?" he asked. "I don't feel that bad," was Kurt's deadpan response.

The three of them went to the back patio so Kurt could smoke. Gibby was still out there, and making the same jokes about jumping the wall. They chatted for almost an hour, but it was mostly small talk. Kurt had always wanted to go to art school and told Mama he was envious. Mama was left with the impression that Kurt was serene: "Whatever had troubled him, he seemed to have already made peace with it." Pat and Joe left about five in the evening, and as they parted,

Mama told Kurt they'd visit again. "He gave the impression that you want a drug addict in recovery to give you," observed Mama, "the 'I-can't-do-this-anymore-I-give-up' impression."

That Friday afternoon, Courtney repeatedly tried to reach Kurt on the patients' pay phone. She finally called when he was near it, and they had a short conversation. "No matter what happens," he told her, "I want you to know that you made a really good album." She found it odd he would mention this, since her record wouldn't be released for another week. "What do you mean?" she asked, confused at the melodrama in his voice. "Just remember, no matter what, I love you." With that, he hung up.

At 7:23 that evening Michael Meisel's roommate answered the phone. It was Kurt. "Michael's out for the evening," the roommate announced, "should I have him call you?" Kurt said he wasn't going to be near a phone. Two minutes later, he walked out the back door of Exodus and climbed the six-foot wall he and Gibby had joked about earlier in the day.

He departed Exodus with only the clothes on his back. In his room, he left a couple of shirts and a recently started journal containing four embryonic songs. Over his 27 years he had filled two dozen different spiral notebooks that served as his journals, but by 1994 he was rarely writing down his thoughts. Yet sometime during Kurt's stay at Exodus, he completed a Rorschach-like assignment that asked him to illustrate a dozen words; the results read like something from his diaries. It was the type of drill Kurt had excelled at his entire life, ever since his grandfather challenged him to draw Mickey Mouse.

When asked to illustrate "resentment," he drew two angry eyes with red flames next to them. For "jealousy," he drew a Nazi sign with legs. To express "lonely," he sketched a narrow street with two giant skyscrapers dwarfing the sides. For "hurt," he drew a spinal cord with a brain and heart attached to it: It looked a bit like the back of *In Utero*. For "safe," he depicted a circle of friends. For "surrender," he drew a man with a bright light emanating from him. For "depressed," he showed an umbrella surrounded by ties. For "determined," he drew a foot stepping on a syringe. And for the final page of the exercise, to show "abandon," he drew a tiny stick figure the size of an ant on an immense landscape.

Two hours after he jumped the fence, Kurt used his credit card to buy a first-class ticket to Seattle on Delta Flight 788. Before boarding, he called Seattle Limousine and arranged to be picked up at the airport—he specifically requested they not send a limo. He made an attempt to call Courtney; she wasn't in, so he left a message that he had called.

Courtney was already searching L.A. for him, convinced as soon as she heard word he'd left Exodus that he was going to score drugs and potentially overdose. "She was hysterical," Joe Mama remembered. Courtney began phoning drug dealers and inquiring whether Kurt was there; she didn't trust their word, so she visited. She also decided to spread the rumor that she had overdosed, assuming this deception would get to Kurt and he'd contact her. As a distraught Courtney—with three days of sobriety—found herself back in familiar dealers' haunts, she fell off the wagon.

Meanwhile, Kurt was on the plane. He found himself sitting next to Duff McKagan of Guns N' Roses. McKagan had begun his career in several Northwest punk bands, and despite all the bad blood between Nirvana and Guns, Kurt seemed happy to see Duff. Kurt admitted he had left rehab; Duff said he understood, as he was in recovery from heroin himself. McKagan could tell things were amiss. "I knew from all my instincts something was wrong." The two talked about mutual friends, but there was also a wistfulness to their conversation—both were leaving Los Angeles and returning to the Northwest. "We were talking about what it feels like to be going back home," McKagan recalled. "That's what he said he was doing, 'going home.' " Kurt announced this like someone who had been away for years, not three days. When the plane arrived in Seattle, McKagan went to ask if Kurt needed a ride, but when he turned around he was gone.

Kurt arrived home at 1:45 in the morning on Saturday, April 2. If he did sleep, it wasn't for long: At around 6 a.m., as dawn broke, he appeared in Cali's room on the first floor of the house. Cali was there with girlfriend Jessica Hopper, on spring break from her Minneapolis boarding school. Cali was simultaneously dating Jessica and Jennifer Adamson (he previously had been involved with Academy Award–nominated actress Juliette Lewis). Though Jessica was younger than Cali, and straight-edge (did no drugs or alcohol), she adored him.

Cali had passed out Saturday morning from cocaine. The previous night, in an attempt to warm the giant house after the heating oil had run out, a stoned Cali lit a Presto Log outside before attempting to carry it into his room; he dropped it on the living room floor. As his drug problems had increased and his nanny duties had been curtailed, Cali had become the Kato Kaelin of the Cobain household. "By that point, Cali wasn't in charge of anything," Jessica observed, "other than helping get drugs or making sure Kurt didn't die."

That morning Kurt walked into Cali's room and sat on the end of the bed. Jessica woke, but not Cali. "Hey skinhead girl," Kurt sang to Jessica, mimicking the lyrics to a punk song. Jessica implored Kurt, "Call Courtney! You've got to call Courtney; she's freaking out." She grabbed a number off a table, handed it to him, and watched as Kurt dialed the Peninsula. The hotel operator announced Courtney wasn't taking any calls. "This is her husband. Let me through," Kurt demanded. Kurt had forgotten the code name that was needed to reach his wife. He kept repeating, "this is her husband," but the hotel operator wouldn't let him through. Frustrated, he hung up. Cali momentarily woke up and, seeing Kurt, told him to call Courtney.

As Cali fell back asleep, Jessica and Kurt sat silently for a few minutes, watching MTV. Kurt smiled when a video by the Meat Puppets came on. Five minutes later, he called the hotel again, but they still wouldn't let him through. Jessica fell asleep watching Kurt leafing through a copy of *Puncture* magazine.

Twenty minutes later, Kurt called Graytop Cab. He told the driver that he had "recently been burgled and needed bullets." They drove downtown, but seeing as it was 7:30 a.m. on a Saturday morning, sporting goods stores were closed. Kurt asked the driver to take him to 145th and Aurora, saying he was hungry. Most likely Kurt checked into either the Crest or Quest Motel, places he had stayed before—they were near one of his dealers. That day he also went to Seattle Guns and bought a box of twenty-gauge shotgun shells.

Back at the Cobain house, the main phone rang every ten minutes but Cali was afraid to answer it, thinking it was Courtney. When he finally answered, he told her he hadn't seen Kurt. Still fried from drugs, Cali thought Kurt's bedside visit was simply a dream. Cali and Jessica were fighting about his drug use, and in a fit of rage he suggested she take an early flight home. He tried to use the $100,000-limit Mastercard Kurt had given him to buy her an airline ticket but the charge was denied. He called Courtney to complain and she told him she'd cancelled Kurt's cards, thinking this would help determine his whereabouts. Feeling ill, Jessica went to bed and spent much of the next two days sleeping and trying to ignore the house phone, which rang endlessly.

Over the next two days there were scattered sightings of Kurt. On Sunday evening he was seen at the Cactus Restaurant having dinner with a thin woman, possibly his dealer Caitlin Moore, and an unidentified man. After Kurt finished his meal, he licked his plate, which attracted the attention of other patrons. When the bill was presented, his credit card wouldn't go through. "He seemed traumatized by hearing that his card was denied," recalled Ginny Heller, who was in the restaurant. "He was standing at the counter, trying to write a check, but it looked like a painful process for him." Kurt made up a story about his credit card being stolen.

That Sunday, Courtney phoned private investigators in the Los Angeles Yellow Pages until she found one working on a weekend. Tom Grant and his assistant Ben Klugman visited her at the Peninsula that afternoon. She said her husband had skipped rehab; she worried for his health; and she asked Grant to watch dealer Caitlin Moore's apartment, where she figured Kurt might be. Grant subcontracted with a Seattle investigator, giving directives to observe Dylan Carlson's house and Caitlin Moore's apartment. Surveillance was set up late Sunday night. However, private detectives did not immediately set up at the Lake Washington house or the home the Cobains owned in Carnation, where Kurt's sister Kim was living at the time. Courtney assumed that Cali would let her know if Kurt showed up at their house.

Early Monday, Cali and Jessica were in the middle of yet another argument when the phone rang, and Cali barked, "Don't answer it. It's just Courtney and we don't know anything about Kurt." Jessica asked Cali if he'd talked to Kurt since they saw him. "What do you mean, 'since I saw him?' " Cali inquired, his eyes widening. Jessica recited the events from Saturday. Cali finally told Courtney Kurt had in fact been at the house on Saturday.

In Los Angeles, Courtney was attempting to do press, despite the fact that she was again going through a hotel detox. On Monday, she met with Robert Hilburn of the *Los Angeles Times* to talk about Hole's new album, *Live Through This*. She kept sobbing during the interview, and a Narcotics Anonymous handbook sat on her coffee table. Hilburn's story began with the subhead: "Just when Courtney Love should be focusing on Hole and her career, she can't help worrying about her husband." "I know this should be the happiest time of my life," Love said, "and there have been moments where I felt that happiness. But not now. I thought I went through a lot of hard times over the years, but this has been the hardest."

It got harder that very day. After her interview, Courtney phoned Dylan, who reported he hadn't heard from Kurt. Courtney thought Dylan was lying, and she kept challenging him. But her attitude didn't seem to change his demeanor and he flatly said, "The last time I saw him was when he was going to L.A. and we bought the shotgun." It was the first Courtney had heard of a shotgun, and she became hysterical. She phoned Seattle Police and filed a missing persons report, claiming she was Kurt's mother. The report read: "Mr. Cobain ran away from a California facility and flew back to Seattle. He also bought a shotgun and may be suicidal. Mr. Cobain may be at [Caitlin Moore's address] location for narcotics." It described Kurt as "not dangerous" but "armed with shotgun." Courtney asked the police to check the Lake Washington home, and officers drove by several times, but saw no activity. Courtney met with Tom Grant again on Monday, and told him to search some of the motels Kurt frequented. Seattle investigators checked these locations, but didn't locate Kurt.

On Monday night Cali left the house for the evening, leaving Jessica alone in his room. Around midnight she heard noises. "I heard footsteps upstairs and in the hall," she recalled. "They were walking with a purpose, you know, not tip-toeing about, so I assumed it was Kurt." She called out "hello" into the darkness of the hallway, but heard no answer and returned to Cali's bedroom. Jessica and Cali had been lectured by Courtney that as "staff" they should stick to Cali's room. Cali didn't return until after 3 a.m., and he and Jessica slept late the next morning.

On Tuesday afternoon Courtney sent Hole's Eric Erlandson to the Lake Washington home to look for Kurt. "He burst in the house, like this big lightning bolt, and he was furious at Cali," Jessica remembered. "You guys have got to help me look," he ordered. Erlandson told them to search every nook and cranny, because Kurt had stashed a shotgun: He specifically insisted they look in a secret compartment in the back of the master bedroom closet, which Courtney had told him Kurt used. They found the compartment but no guns. They also searched a mattress for a hole Kurt had cut in it to store drugs—it was empty. No one thought to search the garage or greenhouse, and Erlandson rushed off, headed to the Carnation home.

Courtney had been scheduled to do a phone interview with *The Rocket* on Tuesday morning. Erlandson phoned the magazine and said it would have to be postponed, as would all of Courtney's interviews the rest of the week. She certainly didn't have time: She was on the phone every moment trying to find someone who had seen Kurt after Saturday. She hounded Dylan, still convinced he was hiding something, but he seemed as puzzled to Kurt's whereabouts as she was.

On Wednesday morning, April 6, Jessica Hopper called a cab to take her to the airport. She still felt ill: During her visit there had been no food in the Cobain house except bananas and soft drinks, and it had been so cold she had rarely left Cali's bed. As she walked out the long driveway to the car, she threw up.

Courtney continued to phone home, but her calls went unanswered. On Wednesday morning she told Grant she thought Cali might be hiding Kurt. Grant flew to Seattle that night, picked up Dylan, and together they checked Caitlin Moore's apartment, the Marco Polo, the Seattle Inn, and the Crest, but found no sign of Kurt. At 2:15 a.m. Thursday they searched the Lake Washington house, entering through a kitchen window. The temperature outside had dropped to 45 degrees, but it seemed colder inside than outdoors. They went from room to room and found the bed unmade in the master bedroom, but cold to the touch. MTV was on the television with the sound off. Not seeing any sign of Kurt, they left at 3 a.m., without searching the grounds or garage.

On Thursday afternoon Courtney reached Cali at Jennifer Adamson's apartment—he had been staying there because he was afraid to be in the Cobain house. Courtney was incensed and demanded he return to look for Kurt. Cali and Jennifer drove together, bringing a friend, Bonnie Dillard, who wanted to see where such famous rock stars lived. It was dusk when they arrived, and Cali complained about how spooky the dark house was. He told Jennifer he didn't want to go back in, but he knew that if he didn't, Courtney would be enraged.

They entered and began searching once again, turning on lights as they went. Cali and Jennifer held hands as they entered each room. "Frankly," Jennifer recalled, "we were expecting to find him dead at any minute." Though the house was ostensibly Cali's place of residence at the time, he jumped at every floor creak, the way a character in a Vincent Price movie would leap as a bat flew from a belfry. They searched all levels including the third-floor attic.

Jennifer and Dillard urged Cali to leave the instant they had surveyed every room. Night was falling and the old, gabled house—which was eerie on a sunny day—was filled with long shadows in the twilight. Cali hesitated to jot a note: "Kurt I can't believe you managed to be in this house without me noticing. You're a fuckin' asshole for not calling Courtney and at least letting her know that you're okay. She's in a lot of pain, Kurt, and this morning she had another 'accident' and now she's in the hospital again. She's your wife and she loves you and you have a child together. Get it together to at least tell her you're okay or she is going to *die*. It's not fair man. Do something now!" He left the message on the main staircase.

It was with a great sigh of relief that the trio entered the car and began to head down the long driveway, Cali and Jennifer in the front, and Dillard in the back. As they pulled onto Lake Washington Boulevard and sped toward town, Dillard meekly voiced: "You know, uh, I hate to say this, but as we were going down the driveway, I thought I saw something above the garage." Jennifer exchanged a glance of abject terror with Cali. "I don't know," Dillard continued. "I just saw a shadow up there." "Why didn't you say something?" Jennifer snapped. "Well, I don't know," Dillard explained. "I didn't think it was real." Jennifer knew how superstitious Dillard was, and she kept the car headed toward town. "Well, I've had enough," Jennifer announced. "I'm not going back."

Two days earlier, in the predawn hours of Tuesday, April 5, Kurt Cobain had awoken in his own bed, the pillows still smelling of Courtney's perfume. He had first taken in this fragrance when she sent the silk-and-lace heart-shaped box to him three short years before: He had sniffed the box for hours, imagining she had touched it with intimate parts of her body. In the bedroom that Tuesday, her aroma mixed with the slightly acrid smell of cooked heroin; this too was a smell that aroused him.

It was cold in the house, so he'd slept in his clothes, including his brown corduroy coat. Compared to the nights he'd spent sleeping outside in cardboard boxes, it wasn't so bad. He had on his comfy "Half Japanese" T-shirt (advertising a Baltimore punk band), his favorite pair of Levi's, and, as he sat on the edge of the bed, he laced up the only pair of shoes he owned—they were Converse sneakers.

The television was on, tuned to MTV, but the sound was off. He walked over to the stereo and put on R.E.M.'s *Automatic for the People*, turning the volume down so that Stipe's voice sounded like a friendly whisper in the background—Courtney would later find the stereo still on and this CD in the changer. He lit a Camel Light and fell back on the bed with a legal-sized notepad propped on his chest and a fine-point red pen. The blank piece of paper briefly entranced him, but not because of writer's block: He had imagined these words for weeks, months, years, decades. He paused only because even a legal-sized sheet seemed so small, so finite.

He had already written a long personal letter to his wife and daughter that he'd jotted down while in Exodus; he'd brought this letter all the way back to Seattle and had stuck it under one of those perfume-infused pillows. "You know, I love you," he wrote in that letter. "I love

Frances. I'm so sorry. Please don't follow me. I'm sorry, sorry, sorry."
He had repeatedly lettered "I'm sorry," filling an entire page with this
plea. "I'll be there," he continued. "I'll protect you. I don't know where
I'm going. I just can't be here anymore."

That note had been hard enough to write, but he knew this second
missive would be equally important, and he needed to be careful with
these words. He addressed it "To Boddah," the name of his imaginary
childhood friend. He used tiny, deliberate characters, and wrote in a
straight line without the benefit of rules. He composed the words very
methodically, making sure each was clear and easy to read. As he wrote,
the illumination from MTV provided most of the light, since the sun
was still rising.

Speaking from the tongue of an experienced simpleton who obviously would rather be an emasculated, infantile complainee. This
note should be pretty easy to understand. All the warnings from the
punk rock 101 courses over the years. Since my first introduction
to the, shall we say, ethics involved with independence and the
embracement of your community has proven to be very true. I
haven't felt the excitement of listening to as well as creating music
along with reading and writing for too many years now. I feel guilty
beyond words about these things. For example, when we're backstage and the lights go out and the manic roar of the crowd begins
it doesn't affect me the way in which it did for Freddie Mercury
who seemed to love, relish in the love and adoration from the
crowd. Which is something I totally admire and envy. The fact is I
can't fool you. Any one of you. It simply isn't fair to you or me.
The worst crime I can think of would be to rip people off by faking
it and pretending as if I'm having 100 percent fun. Sometimes I feel
as if I should have a punch in time clock before I walk out on stage.
I've tried everything within my power to appreciate it, and I do,
God believe me I do, but it's not enough. I appreciate the fact that
I and we have affected and entertained a lot of people. I must be
one of those narcissists who only appreciate things when they're
gone. I'm too sensitive. I need to be slightly numb in order to regain
the enthusiasm I once had as a child. On our last three tours I've

had a much better appreciation for all the people I've known personally and as fans of our music, but I still can't get over the frustration, the guilt and empathy I have for everyone. There's good in all of us and I think I simply love people too much. So much that it makes me feel too fucking sad. The sad little, sensitive, unappreciative, Pisces, Jesus man! Why don't you just enjoy it? I don't know. I have a goddess of a wife who sweats ambition and empathy and a daughter who reminds me too much of what I used to be. Full of love and joy, kissing every person she meets because everyone is good and will do her no harm. And that terrifies me to the point where I can barely function. I can't stand the thought of Frances becoming the miserable self-destructive, death rocker that I've become. I have it good, very good, and I'm grateful, but since the age of seven I've become hateful towards all humans in general. Only because it seems so easy for people to get along, and have empathy. Empathy! Only because I love and feel for people too much I guess. Thank you all from the pit of my burning nauseous stomach for your letters and concern during the past years. I'm too much of an erratic, moody baby! I don't have the passion anymore and so remember, it's better to burn out than to fade away.

When he put the pen down, he had filled all but two inches of the page. It had taken three cigarettes to draft the note. The words hadn't come easy, and there were misspellings and half-completed sentences. He didn't have the time to rewrite this letter twenty times like he had many of the letters in his journals: It was getting brighter outside and he needed to act before the rest of the world woke. He signed it "peace, love, empathy. Kurt Cobain," printing his name out rather than using a signature. He underlined "empathy" twice; he had used this one word five times. He wrote one more line—"Frances and Courtney, I'll be at your altar"—and stuck the paper and pen into his left coat pocket. On the stereo Stipe was singing about the "Man on the Moon." Kurt had always loved Andy Kaufman—his friends used to crack up back in junior high school in Montesano when Kurt would do his Latka imitation from "Taxi."

He rose from the bed and entered the closet, where he removed a board from the wall. In this secret cubbyhole sat a beige nylon gun case, a box of shotgun shells, and a Tom Moore cigar box. He replaced the board, put the shells in his pocket, grabbed the cigar box, and cradled the heavy shotgun over his left forearm. In a hallway closet, he grabbed two towels; he didn't need these, but someone would. Empathy. He quietly walked down the nineteen steps of the wide staircase. He was within a few feet of Cali's room and he didn't want anyone catching sight of him. He had thought this all through, mapped it out with the same forethought he put into his album covers and videos. There would be blood, lots of blood, and a mess, which he didn't want in his house. Mostly, he didn't want to haunt this home, to leave his daughter with the kind of nightmares he had suffered.

As he headed into the kitchen he passed the doorjamb where he and Courtney had begun keeping track of how tall Frances had grown. Only one line was there now, a little pencil mark with her name 31 inches from the floor. Kurt would never see any higher marks on that wall, but he was convinced his daughter's life would be better without him.

In the kitchen he opened the door of his $10,000 Traulson stainless-steel refrigerator and grabbed a can of Barq's root beer, making sure not to lose grip of the shotgun. Carrying his unthinkable load—root beer, towels, a box of heroin, and a shotgun, all of which would later be found in a bizarre grouping—he opened the door to the backyard and walked across the small patio. Dawn was breaking and mist hung close to the ground. Most mornings in Aberdeen felt just like this: wet, moist, dank. He would never see Aberdeen again; never actually climb to the top of the water tower on "Think of Me Hill"; never buy the farm he had dreamed about in Grays Harbor County; never again wake up in a hospital waiting room having pretended to be a bereaved visitor just to find a warm place to sleep; never again see his mother, or sister, or father, or wife, or daughter. He strolled the twenty paces to the green-house, climbed the wooden steps, and opened the rear set of French doors. The floor was linoleum: It would be easy to clean. Empathy.

He sat on the floor of the one-room structure, looking out the front doors. No one could see him here, not unless they were climbing the trees behind his property, and that wasn't likely. The last thing he wanted was the kind of fuck-up that might leave him a vegetable, and leave him with even more pain. His two uncles and great-grandfather had taken this same grisly walk, and if they had managed to pull it off, he knew he could too. He had the "suicide genes," as he used to joke with his friends back in Grays Harbor. He never wanted to see the inside of a hospital again, never wanted a doctor in the white lab coat poking him, never wanted to have an endoscope in his painful stomach. He was finished with all that, finished with his stomach; he couldn't be more finished. Like a great movie director, he had planned this moment to the smallest detail, rehearsing this scene as both director and actor. There had been many dress rehearsals over the years, close brushes that almost went this way, either by accident or sometimes with intent, like Rome. This had always been the thing he kept in the back of his mind, like a precious salve, as the only cure for a pain that would not go away. He didn't care about freedom from want: He wanted freedom from pain.

He sat thinking about these things for many minutes. He smoked five Camel Lights. He drank several sips of his root beer.

He grabbed the note from his pocket. There was still a little room on it. He laid it on the linoleum floor. He had to write in larger letters, which weren't as straight, because of the surface he was on. He managed to scratch out a few more words: "Please keep going Courtney, for Frances, for her life which will be so much happier without me. I love you. I love you." Those last words, written larger than anything else, had completed the sheet. He laid the note on top of a pile of potting soil, and stabbed the pen through the middle, so that like a stake it held the paper aloft over the soil.

He took the shotgun out of its soft nylon case. He carefully folded the case, like a little boy putting away his best Sunday clothes after church. He took off his jacket, laid it on top of the case, and put the two towels on top of this pile. Ah, empathy, a sweet gift. He went to the sink and drew a small amount of water for his drug cooker and sat down again. He pulled the box of 25 shotgun shells open and took three out, sticking them in the magazine of the gun. He moved the action on the Remington so that one shell was in the chamber. He took off the gun's safety.

He smoked his last Camel Light. He took another sip of the Barq's.

Outside an overcast day was beginning—it was a day like the one in which he had first come into this world, 27 years, one month, and sixteen days earlier. Once, in his journal he had attempted to tell the story of that very first moment of his life: "My first memory was a light aqua green tile floor and a very strong hand holding me by my ankles. This force made it clear to me that I'm no longer in water and I cannot go back. I tried to kick and squirm, back to the hole, but he just held me there, suspended in my mother's vagina. It was like he was teasing me, and I could feel the liquid and blood evaporating and tightening my skin. Reality was oxygen consuming me, and the sterile smell of never going back into the hole, a terror that could never be repeated again. Knowing this was comforting, and so I began my first ritual of dealing with things. I did not cry."

He grabbed his cigar box and pulled out a small plastic bag that held $100 worth of Mexican black tar heroin—it was a lot of heroin. He took half, a swab the size of a pencil eraser, and stuck it on his spoon. Methodically and expertly he prepared the heroin and his syringe, injecting it just above his elbow, not far from his "K" tattoo. He put the works back into the box and felt himself drift, rapidly floating away from this place. Jainism preached that there were thirty heavens and seven hells, all layered throughout our lives; if he had any luck, this would be his seventh and final hell. He put his works away, floating faster and faster, feeling his breathing slow. He had to hurry now: Everything was becoming hazy, and an aqua green hue framed every object. He grabbed the heavy shotgun, put it against the roof of his mouth. It would be loud; he was certain of that. And then he was gone.

A LEONARD COHEN
AFTERWORLD

SEATTLE, WASHINGTON
APRIL 1994–MAY 1999

Give me a Leonard Cohen afterworld, so I can sigh eternally.
—From "Pennyroyal Tea."

Early Friday, April 8, electrician Gary Smith arrived at 171 Lake Washington Boulevard. Smith and several other workers had been at the house since Thursday, installing a new security system. Police stopped by twice and told workers to alert them if Kurt arrived. At 8:40 Friday, Smith was near the greenhouse and glanced inside. "I saw this body laying there on the floor," he later told a newspaper. "I thought it was a mannequin. Then I noticed it had blood in the right ear. I saw a shotgun laying across his chest, pointing up at his chin." Smith called police, and then his company. A friend of his firm's dispatcher took it upon himself to tip off radio station KXRX. "Hey, you guys are going to owe me some pretty good Pink Floyd tickets for this," he told DJ Marty Riemer. Police confirmed that a body of a young male had been found at Cobain's house and KXRX aired the story. Though police were not identifying the deceased, initial news reports speculated it was Kurt. Within twenty minutes, KXRX received a tearful phone call from Kim Cobain, who identified herself as Kurt's sister, and angrily asked why they were broadcasting such a fallacious rumor. They told her to call the police.

Kim did, and after hearing the news, she phoned her mother. An *Aberdeen Daily World* reporter showed up on Wendy's doorstep soon after. Her quote would go on the Associated Press wire and be reprinted around the world: "Now he's gone and joined that stupid club. I told him not to join that stupid club." She was referring to the coincidence that Jimi Hendrix, Janis Joplin, Jim Morrison, and Kurt had all died at age 27. But something else his mother said wasn't reported in any other newspaper—though every parent who heard the news of Kurt's death didn't need to read it to know the loss she felt. At the end of her interview Wendy said of her only son, "I'll never hold him again. I don't know what to do. I don't know where to go."

Don heard about his son's death from the radio—he was too broken up to talk to any reporters. Leland and Iris learned from watching television. Iris had to lie down after the news—she wasn't sure if her weakened heart could take it.

Meanwhile, in Los Angeles, Courtney had become a patient in Exodus, having checked in on Thursday evening. On Thursday she had been arrested at the Peninsula after police had arrived at her "vomit-and blood-spattered room" and found a syringe, a blank prescription pad, and a small packet they believed to be heroin (the substance turned out to be Hindu good-luck ashes). After being released on $10,000 bail, she checked into inpatient treatment, giving up on her hotel detox.

Friday morning Rosemary Carroll arrived at Exodus. When Courtney saw the expression on Rosemary's face, she knew the news without having to even hear it. The two women looked at each other for several moments in complete silence until Courtney finally uttered a one-word question: "How?"

Courtney left Los Angeles in a Learjet with Frances, Rosemary, Eric Erlandson, and nanny Jackie Farry. When they arrived at the Lake Washington house, it was surrounded by television news crews. Love promptly hired private security guards, who placed tarps over the greenhouse so media couldn't peer in. Prior to the coverings going up, *Seattle Times* photographer Tom Reese shot a few frames of the greenhouse through a hole in the fence. "I thought it might not be him," Reese remembered, "that it could be anyone. But when I saw that sneaker there, I knew." Reese's photograph, which ran on the front page of Saturday's *Seattle Times*, showed the view through the French doors, including half of Kurt's body, his straight leg, his sneaker, and his clenched fist next to a cigar box.

By afternoon, the King County Medical Examiner's office had issued a statement confirming what everyone already knew: "The autopsy has shown that Cobain died of a shotgun wound to the head and at this time the wound appears to be self-inflicted." Dr. Nikolas Hartshorne performed the autopsy—the task was particularly emotional because Hartshorne had once promoted a Nirvana gig in college. "We put 'apparent' self-inflicted gunshot wound to the head in the report at the time because we still wanted to cross all our *t*'s and dot all our *i*'s," Hartshorne recalled. "There was absolutely nothing that indicated it was anything other than a suicide." Still, because of the media attention and Kurt's celebrity, Seattle Police didn't complete their full investigation for 40 days, and spent over 200 hours interviewing Kurt's friends and family.

Despite rumors to the contrary, the corpse was recognizable as Kurt, though the scene was ghastly: The hundreds of pellets from the shotgun shell had expanded his head and disfigured him. Police fingerprinted the body, and the prints matched those already on file from the domestic violence arrest. Though a later analysis of the shotgun concluded "four cards of lifted latent prints contain no legible prints," Hartshorne said the prints on the gun were not legible because the weapon had to be pried from Kurt's hand after rigor mortis had set in. "I know his fingerprints are on there, because he had it in his hand," Hartshorne explained. The date of death was determined to be April 5, though it could have been 24 hours before or after. In all likelihood, Kurt had been dead in the greenhouse while several searches of the main house occurred.

The autopsy found evidence of benzodiazepines (tranquilizers) and heroin in Kurt's blood. The level of heroin found was so high that even Kurt—notorious for his enormous habit—may not have survived much longer than it took to fire the gun. He had pulled off a feat that was quite remarkable, though it bore similarities to his Uncle Burle's actions (gunshots to both the head and abdomen) and those of his great-grandfather James Irving (knife to abdomen, and later ripping the wound apart): Kurt had managed to kill himself twice, using two methods that were equally fatal.

Courtney was inconsolable. She insisted police give her Kurt's blood-speckled corduroy coat, which she wore. When the cops finally left the grounds, and with only a security guard as a witness, she retraced Kurt's last steps, entered the greenhouse—which had yet to be cleaned—and immersed her hands in his blood. On her knees on the floor, she prayed, howled, and wailed, held her blood-covered hands up to the sky, and screamed "Why?" She found a small remnant of Kurt's skull with hair attached. She washed and shampooed this gruesome souvenir. And then she began blotting out her pain with drugs.

That night she wore layers of Kurt's clothes because they still smelled of him. Wendy arrived at the house, and mother and daughter-in-law slept in the same bed, clutching each other during the night.

On Saturday, April 9, Jeff Mason was employed to take Courtney to the funeral home to view Kurt's body before it was cremated—she had already requested that plaster casts be made of his hands. Grohl was also invited, and declined, but Krist came, arriving before Courtney. He spent a few private moments with his old friend and broke down crying. As he left, Courtney and Mason were brought into the viewing room. Kurt was on a table, dressed in his nicest clothes, but his eyes had been sewn shut. It was the first time Courtney had been with her husband for ten days, and it was the last time their physical bodies would be together. She stroked his face, spoke to him, and clipped a lock of his hair. Then she pulled his pants down and cut a small lock of his pubic hair—his beloved pubes, the hair he had waited so long for as an adolescent, somehow these needed to be preserved. Finally, she climbed on top of his body, straddling him with her legs, and put her head on his chest and wailed: "Why? Why? Why?"

That day friends had begun to arrive to comfort Courtney, and many brought drugs, which she indiscriminately ingested. Between the drugs and her grief, she was a catastrophe. Reporters phoned every five minutes, and though she wasn't in much shape to talk, she occasionally took the calls but to ask questions, not answer them: "*Why* had Kurt done this? *Where* had he been that last week?" As with many grief-stricken lovers, she focused on the tiny details so as to avoid her loss. She spent two hours on the phone with the *Post-Intelligencer*'s Gene Stout pondering such musings and announcing, "I'm tough and I can take anything. But I can't take this." Kurt's death made the front page of the *New York Times*, and dozens of television and newspaper reporters descended on Seattle, trying to cover a story where few sources would talk to the media. Most filed think-pieces about what Kurt meant to a generation. What else could be said?

A funeral needed to be arranged. Soundgarden's Susan Silver stepped forward and scheduled a private service in a church, and a simultaneous public candlelight vigil at Seattle Center. That weekend, a slow procession of friends arrived at the Lake Washington house—everyone seemed shell-shocked, trying to make sense of the unexplainable. Added to their grief was physical discomfort: When Jeff Mason arrived Friday, he found the oil tank completely dry. To heat the huge house, he began to send limos out to buy kindling from Safeway. "I was breaking up chairs because the fireplace was the only way to heat the house," he recalled. Courtney was upstairs in their bedroom, wrapped in layers of Kurt's clothes, recording a message to be played at the public memorial.

On Sunday afternoon the public candlelight vigil was held at Seattle Center's Flag Pavilion, and 7,000 attended, carrying candles, flowers, homemade signs, and a few burning flannel shirts. A suicide counselor spoke and urged struggling teens to ask for help, while local DJs shared memories. A short message from Krist was played:

We remember Kurt for what he was: caring, generous, and sweet. Let's keep the music with us. We'll always have it forever. Kurt had an ethic towards his fans that was rooted in the punk rock way of thinking: No band is special; no player royalty. If you've got a guitar, and a lot of soul, just bang something out and mean it—you are the superstar. Plug in the tones and rhythms that are universally human. Music. Heck, use your guitar as a drum. Just catch a groove and let it flow out of your heart. That's the level that Kurt spoke to us on: in our hearts. And that's where the music will always be, forever.

Courtney's tape was played next. She had recorded it late the night before in their bed. She began:

I don't know what to say. I feel the same way you guys do. If you guys don't think that to sit in this room, where he played guitar and sang, and feel so honored to be near him, you're crazy. Anyway, he left a note. It's more like a letter to the fucking editor. I don't know what happened. I mean, it was gonna happen, but it could've happened when he was 40. He always said he was gonna outlive everybody and be 120. I'm not gonna read you all the note, because it's none of the rest of your fucking business. But some of it is to you. I don't really think it takes away his dignity to read this, considering that it's addressed to most of you. He's such an asshole. I want you all to say "asshole" really loud.

The crowd shouted "asshole." And then Courtney read the suicide note. Over the course of the next ten minutes, she mixed Kurt's final words with her own comments on them. When she read the section where Kurt mentioned Freddie Mercury, she yelled: "Well, Kurt, so fucking what! Then don't be a rock star, you asshole." Where he wrote of having "too much love," she asked, "So, why didn't you just fucking *stay*?" And when she quoted his line about being a "sensitive, unappreciative, Pisces, Jesus man," she wailed: "Shut up! Bastard. Why didn't you just enjoy it?" Though she was reading the note to the crowd— and the media—she spoke as if Kurt were her only audience. Toward the end, before reading the Neil Young line Kurt quoted, she warned: "And *don't* remember this because this a *fucking* lie: 'It's better to burn out, than fade away.' God, you *asshole*!" She finished the note, and then added:

Just remember, this is all bullshit! But I want you to know one thing: That eighties "tough love" bullshit, it doesn't work. It's not real. It doesn't work. I should have let him, we all should have let him, have his numbness. We should have let him have the thing that made him feel better, that made his stomach feel better, we should have let him have it instead of trying to strip away his skin. You go home, and you tell your parents, "Don't you ever try that tough love bullshit on me, because it doesn't fucking work." That's what I think. I'm laying in our bed, and I'm really sorry, and I feel the same way you do. I'm really sorry, you guys. I don't know what I could have done. I wish I'd have been here. I wish I hadn't listened to other people. But I did. Every night I've been sleeping with his mother, and I wake up in the morning and I think it's him because their bodies are sort of the same. I have to go now. Just tell him, he's a fucker, okay? Just say, "*Fucker*, you're a *fucker*." And that you love him.

As Courtney's extraordinary tape was being played at the Seattle Center, across town 70 people gathered at the Unity Church of Truth for the private memorial. "There was no time for a program or invitations," remembered Reverend Stephen Towles, who presided. Most attendees had been invited by phone the previous night. Several of Kurt's closest friends—including Jesse Reed—were overlooked or couldn't make it on such short notice. The crowd included a contingent from Gold Mountain and several carloads of friends from Olympia. Bob Hunter, Kurt's old art teacher, was one of the few from Aberdeen. Even Kurt's ex-girlfriend Mary Lou Lord came and sat in the back. Courtney and Frances were in the front flanked by Wendy and Kim; the Cobain women seemed to be the only thing stopping Courtney from collapse. Don and Jenny and Leland came; Iris was too ill. Tracy Marander was there and was as distraught as the family—she had been as close to Kurt as his blood kin.

Inside the church, mourners found pictures of Kurt as a six-year-old laid out on the pews. Towles began with the 23rd Psalm, and then said: "Like a wind crying through the universe, time carries with it the names and deeds of conquerors and commoners alike. And all that we were, and all that remains, is in the memories of those who cared we came this way but for a brief moment. We are here to remember and release Kurt Cobain, who lived a short life that was long in accomplishment." Towles recited the story of the Golden Buddha who spent years hidden under a coating of clay before his true worth was known, and followed that with a poem titled "The Traveler." He then asked the crowd to consider a series of questions, designed to make them ponder the deceased. He asked: "Was there unfinished business between you?" If

Towles had called for a show of hands in response, the room would have been filled with raised arms.

Towles then urged others to step forward and share their memories. Bruce Pavitt of Sub Pop spoke first and said, "I love you, I respect you. Of course, I'm a few days late in expressing it." Dylan Carlson read from a Buddhist text. Krist read from prepared notes, similar to his taped message.

Danny Goldberg told of the contradictions in Kurt, how he said he hated fame, yet complained when his videos weren't played. Goldberg said Kurt's love for Courtney "was one of the things that kept him going," despite his ongoing depression. And Goldberg spoke of Aberdeen, albeit with a New Yorker's perspective: "Kurt came from a town that no one had ever heard of, and he went on to change the world."

And then Courtney stood, and read with the actual suicide note in her hands. She yelled, cried, wept, and mixed Kurt's note with selections from the Bible's Book of Job. She ended by talking about Boddah, and how much this imaginary friend meant to Kurt. Almost no one in the hall knew who she was speaking of, but the mention of Kurt's childhood imaginary friend was enough to make Wendy, Don, Kim, Jenny, and Leland quietly sob. Reverend Towles ended the ceremony with a reading from Matthew 5:43.

As the service ended the old feuds returned. Mary Lou Lord exited, afraid for her life. Don and Wendy barely spoke. And one of Kurt's Olympia friends was so offended by Danny Goldberg's comments that he circulated a parody the next day by fax. But nowhere was the divisiveness more apparent than in the scheduling of two competing wakes after the service. One was held by Krist and Shelli and the other by Courtney, and only a handful of mourners visited both. Courtney was late to the wake at her house since after the ceremony she had ventured to the candlelight vigil. There she handed out some of Kurt's clothing to fans who were astounded to see her clutching the suicide note. "It was unbelievable," recalled security guard James Kirk. "It wasn't in a plastic bag or anything. She would show it to the kids, and say, 'I'm so sorry.' " On her way back home, Courtney stopped by radio station KNDD, and demanded air time. "I want to go on the air and make them stop playing Billy Corgan and just play Kurt," she announced. The station politely turned her away.

A week later, Courtney received the urn of Kurt's ashes. She took a handful and buried them under a willow tree in front of the house. In May, she took the rest in a teddy-bear backpack and traveled to the Namgyal Buddhist monastery near Ithaca, New York, where she sought consecration for the ashes and absolution for herself. The monks blessed the remains and used a handful to make a *tsatsa* memorial sculpture.

The bulk of Kurt's remains sat in an urn in 171 Lake Washington Boulevard until 1997, when Courtney sold the home. She moved to Beverly Hills with Frances and Kurt's urn. Before selling the house, she insisted on a covenant allowing her to return one day and remove the willow tree.

Five years after Kurt's suicide, on May 31, 1999, Memorial Day, Wendy organized a final service for her son. The plan was for Frances to scatter Kurt's ashes in a creek behind Wendy's house while a Buddhist monk recited a prayer. Courtney and Frances were already in the Northwest that week vacationing. Since Kurt's death, Courtney had become close to Wendy, and had purchased her a $400,000 house on acreage just outside of Olympia. It was behind this house that the service was planned, and a handful of family and friends were invited. Though Wendy wouldn't call Don herself, Courtney's managers invited him, and he came. But some of the internal family feuds continued: Leland, who was only 30 minutes away—and spent most of his days alone in his trailer since Iris died, in 1997—wasn't called. Courtney did invite Tracy Marander, and she came, wanting to say a final good-bye to Kurt. When Tracy arrived and saw Frances, she was taken aback by the girl's beauty—barefoot, wearing a purple dress, her eyes looking remarkably like those of a boy Tracy had once loved. It was a thought Courtney has every day of her life.

Over the years since Kurt's death, many had suggested a memorial be erected in Aberdeen, and his birthplace might have also served as an appropriate location to scatter his ashes. Scattering Kurt under his myth-making bridge would have been a kind of rough justice and literal irony; for the first time, he would sleep there.

But instead, as the monk chanted, six-year-old Frances Bean Cobain scattered her father's ashes into McLane Creek, and they dissolved and floated downstream. In many ways, this too was a fitting resting place. Kurt had found his true artistic muse in Olympia, and less than five miles away he sat in a shitty little apartment that smelled of rabbit pee and wrote songs all day. Those songs would outlive Kurt and even his darkest demons. As his one-time foster father Dave Reed once remarked, in as good a summation of Kurt's life as was ever offered: "He had the desperation, not the courage, to be himself. Once you do that, you can't go wrong, because you can't make any mistakes when people love you for being yourself. But for Kurt, it didn't matter that other people loved him; he simply didn't love himself enough."

There was another larger piece of fate, and a nugget of ancient history that bonded this particular plot of water and earth and air with these mortal remains; just over the hill, less than ten miles away, the source of McLane Creek and all the streams in the area, was the small range of Washington mountains known as the Black Hills. It was here, years ago, where a young family would go sledding after the first cold snap. They would drive their Camaro down the two-lane road, past the tiny logging town of Porter, up a funny little hill called Fuzzy Top Mountain. In the car was a mom, a dad, a baby daughter, and a little six-year-old boy with the same ethereal blue eyes as Frances Cobain. The boy loved nothing in the world more than sledding with his family, and during the drive from Aberdeen he would implore his father to drive faster because he couldn't stand to wait. When the Camaro would come to a stop near the summit of Fuzzy Top, the boy would dash out, grab his Flexible Flyer sled, take a running start down the mountain, and race as if his flight alone could somehow stop time. At the bottom of the hill, he would wave his mitten-covered hand at his family, and a wide, warm smile would come over his face, his blue eyes sparkling in the winter sun.

SOURCE NOTES

Writing this book entailed conducting more than 400 interviews over the course of four years. Most interview sessions were done in person and tape-recorded, though a few were conducted over the phone, or through e-mail, and a handful were even done through jailhouse protective glass. To avoid 50 pages of source notes reading "from an interview with the author," each chapter begins with a list of my interview subjects in order of citation in the text for that particular section. Most of my subjects are quoted in the text: Many other sources provided background and their names do not appear in the manuscript, but their help and memories were nonetheless essential in piecing together this history. The first time a subject is listed, the year of my interview is noted. In addition to the numerous people listed here, many colleagues assisted by providing resources or support. I hope I have included them all in the Acknowledgments that follow.

Prologue

Page 2   "I woke up at 7 a.m.": An e-mail from Courtney Love to
          Charles R. Cross, 1999.
Page 4   "It wasn't that he OD'd": Ibid.

Chapter 1: Yelling Loudly at First

Author interviews with Don Cobain, 1999; Mari (Fradenburg) Earl, 1998, 1999, 2000; Rod and Dres Herling, 1999; Brandon Ford, 2000; Tony Hirschman, 1999; Leland Cobain, 1998, 1999, 2000; Shirley DeRenzo, 1999; Colleen Vekich, 1999; Dorothy Vekich, 1999; Michael Vilt, 1999; James Ultican, 1999; Norma Ultican, 1999; Kendall Williams, 1999; and Kim Cobain, 2000. Hilary Richrod of the Aberdeen Timberland Library and Leland Cobain provided essential background on the history of Grays Harbor County and I am grateful to them both for their extensive assistance.

Chapter 2: I Hate Mom, I Hate Dad

Author interviews with Don Cobain; Leland Cobain; Kim Cobain; Gary Cobain, 1999; Mari Earl; Stan Targus, 1999; Steve Shillinger, 1999; Jenny Cobain, 1999; Lisa Rock, 1999; Darrin Neathery, 1999; Courtney Love, 1998, 1999, 2000, 2001; John Fields, 1999; Roni Toyra, 1998; John Briskow, 1999; Lois Stopsen, 2000; Rod Marsh, 2001; Miro Jungum, 1998; and James Westby, 2000.

Page 16   "I had a really good childhood": "Family Values," Jonathan
           Poneman, *Spin*, December 1992.
Page 23   Iris Cobain once described 1976: Christopher Sandford, *Kurt
           Cobain* (Carroll & Graf, 1996), page 30.

Chapter 3: Meatball of the Month

Author interviews with Don Cobain; Tim Nelson, 1999; Bill Burghardt, 1999; Leland Cobain; Rod Marsh; Roni Toyra; Jenny Cobain; Kim Cobain; John Fields; James Westby; Mike Bartlett, 1999; Scott Cokely, 1999; Teri Zillyett, 1999; Beverly Cobain, 1999; Trevor Briggs, 1999; Mari Earl; and Jim Cobain, 1998.

Page 30   The article ran under the heading: *Puppy Press* courtesy of
           Scott Cokely.
Page 31   Kurt's artwork was "always very good": Interview with Nikki
           Clark by Hilary Richrod, 1998.

Page 34   Fields was not the only friend of Kurt's: Bill Burghardt, Mike
          Bartlett, Rod Marsh, Trevor Briggs, Darrin Neathery and
          others have similar stories.
Page 37   As Kurt later described it: Michael Azerrad, *Come As You Are:
          The Story of Nirvana* (Doubleday, 1993), page 21.

Chapter 4: Prairie Belt Sausage Boy

Author interviews with Don Cobain; Leland Cobain; Jim Cobain;
Warren Mason, 1999; Dan McKinstry, 1999; Rick Gates, 1999; Bob
Hunter, 1999; Theresa Van Camp, 1999; Mike Medak, 1999; John
Fields; Kathy Utter, 2000; Shayne Lester, 2000; Mike Bartlett; Tre-
vor Briggs; Mari Earl; Darrin Neathery; Brendan McCarroll, 1999;
Kevin Hottinger, 1999; Evan Archie, 2000; Buzz Osborne, 1999;
Bill Burghardt; Steve Shillinger; Andrea Vance, 1999; Jackie Hagara,
1999; Jesse Reed, 1999, 2000; Kurt Vanderhoof, 1998; Greg Hok-
anson, 1999; and Kim Cobain.

Chapter 5: The Will of Instinct

Author interviews with Jackie Hagara; Buzz Osborne; Krist Novoselic, 1997, 1998, 1999; Kim Cobain; Greg Hokanson; Paul White,
1999; Justine Howland, 1999; Jenny Cobain; James Westby; Beverly
Cobain; Don Cobain; Jesse Reed; Dave Reed, 1999; Ethel Reed,
1999; Det. John Green, 2000; Det. Mike Haymon, 2000; Shee-la
Wieland, 2000; Bob Hunter; Theresa Ziniewicz, 1999; Mike Poitras, 1999; Stan Forman, 1999; Kevin Shillinger, 1999; Det. Michael Bens, 2000; Trevor Briggs; Lamont Shillinger, 1999; Steve
Shillinger; Mari Earl; Shelli Novoselic, 2000; and Hilary Richrod,
1998, 1999, 2000.

Chapter 6: Didn't Love Him Enough

Author interviews with Kim Cobain; Matt Lukin, 1998; Jesse Reed;
Shelli Novoselic; Tracy Marander, 1998, 1999, 2000; Steve Shillinger; Kurt Flansburg, 1999; Mark Eckert, 1999; Krist Novoselic;

Ryan Aigner, 1999; Aaron Burckhard, 1999; and Dylan Carlson, 1996, 1998, 1999, 2000.

Chapter 7: *Soupy Sales in My Fly*

Author interviews with Kim Cobain; Krist Novoselic; Shelli Novoselic; Aaron Burckhard; Tracy Marander; Jeff Franks, 1999; Michelle Franks, 1999; Vail Stephens, 1999; Kim Maden, 1999; and Tony Poukkula, 1999. Special thanks to Jeff Franks for his research assistance.

Chapter 8: *In High School Again*

Author interviews with Tracy Marander; Steve Lemons, 2000; Slim Moon, 1998, 1999; Jim May, 1999; John Purkey, 1999; Krist Novoselic; Ryan Aigner; Krissy Proctor, 1999; Buzz Osborne; Jack Endino, 1997, 1999; Chris Hanszek, 1998; Dave Foster, 2000; Kim Cobain; Bob Whittaker, 1999; Bradley Sweek, 1999; Argon Steel, 1999; Win Vidor, 1998; Costos Delyanis, 1999; Dawn Anderson, 1999; Shirley Carlson, 1998; Veronika Kalmar, 1999; Greg Ginn, 1998; Jason Finn, 1998; Scott Giampino, 1998; Kurt Danielson, 1999; and Rich Hansen, 1999.
Page 97   "SERIOUS DRUMMER WANTED": *The Rocket,* October 1987.
Page 103   "The Seattle Scene is gearing up": Bruce Pavitt, *The Rocket,* December 1987.

Chapter 9: *Too Many Humans*

Author interviews with Tracy Marander; Steve Shillinger; Krist Novoselic; Dave Foster; Chad Channing, 1997; Gilly Hanner, 1998; Ryan Aigner; Jan Gregor, 2000; Debbie Letterman, 1997; Chris Knab, 1998; Jack Endino; Alice Wheeler, 1997, 1999, 2000; Dawn Anderson; King Coffey, 2000; Slim Moon; John Purkey; Daniel House, 1997; Tam Orhmund, 1999; Damon Romero, 1998; Hilary Richrod; and Kim Cobain.

Page 114   "I've seen hundreds of Melvins' ": "It May Be the Devil,"
Dawn Anderson, *Backlash*, September 1988.

Page 119   "Nirvana sit sort of at the edge": Grant Alden, *The Rocket*,
December 1988.

Chapter 10: Illegal to Rock 'N' Roll

Author interviews with Tracy Marander; Amy Moon, 1999; Krist
Novoselic; Dylan Carlson; Joe Preston, 1999; Jason Everman, 1999;
Rob Kader, 1998; Chad Channing; John Robinson, 1998; J. J.
Gonson, 1998; Sluggo, 1999; Michelle Vlasimsky, 1999; Slim Moon;
Steve Fisk, 1999; Mark Pickerel, 1999; and Kelly Canary, 1997.

Page 131   "the last wave of rock music": "Hair Swinging Neander-
thals," Phil West, *The Daily*, May 5, 1989.

Page 133   "You're talking about four guys": "Sub Pop," Everett True,
Melody Maker, March 18, 1989.

Page 133   "Nirvana careens from one end": Gillian Gaar, *The Rocket*,
July 1989.

Page 135   "I kinda reach my end of things to do": "Nirvana," Al the
Big Cheese, *Flipside*, June 1989.

Page 141   "Bob Dylan picked 'Polly' ": Chuck Crisafulli, *Teen Spirit*
(Fireside, 1996), page 45.

Chapter 11: Candy, Puppies, Love

Author interviews with Tracy Marander; Kurt Danielson; Chad
Channing; Alex MacLeod, 1999; Nikki McClure, 1999; Garth
Reeves, 1998; Mark Arm, 1998; Carrie Montgomery, 2000; Steve
Turner, 1998; Matt Lukin; Krist Novoselic; Pleasant Gehman, 1997;
Jennifer Finch, 1999; Jesse Reed; Slim Moon; Damon Romero;
Stuart Hallerman, 2000; Jon Snyder, 1998; Alex Kostelnik, 1998;
Maria Braganza, 1998; Greg Babior, 1998; Sluggo; and J. J. Gonson.

Page 146   "I feel like we've been tagged": "Berlin Is Just a State of
Mind," Nils Bernstein, *The Rocket*, December 1989.

Page 151   "had even come up with the term 'grunge' ": Mark Arm,
            Desperate Times.
Page 154   "they cut eight songs": Charles R. Cross and Jim Berken-
            stadt, *Nevermind: Nirvana* (Schirmer Books, 1998), page 32.

Chapter 12: Love You So Much

Author interviews with Tracy Marander; Dylan Carlson; Slim Moon;
Alice Wheeler; John Goodmanson, 1998; Tam Orhmund; George
Smith, 1999; Krist Novoselic; Susan Silver, 2000; Don Muller, 1998;
Alan Mintz, 2000; Brett Hartman, 1998; Kim Cobain; Sally Barry,
1999; Paul Atkinson, 1998; Kevin Kennedy, 2000; Bettina Richards,
1999; Alex Kostelnik; Gordon Raphael, 1999; Ken Goes, 1998; Angee Jenkins, 1999; Nikki McClure; Jennifer Finch; Ian Dickson,
1999; and Mikey Nelson, 1998.

Page 162   "It's probably the most straightforward": "Heaven Can't
            Wait," Everett True, *Melody Maker*, December 15, 1990.
Page 169   "some of my personal experiences": "The Year's Hottest
            New Band Can't Stand Still," Chris Morris, *Musician*, Janu-
            ary 1992.

Chapter 13: The Richard Nixon Library

Author interviews with Jesse Reed; Krist Novoselic; Dylan Carlson;
Tracy Marander; Kaz Utsunomiya, 1999; Mikey Nelson; Joe Preston;
Nikki McClure; Lisa Fancher, 1997; Damon Stewart, 1997; Susan
Silver; Kim Thayil, 1997; Jeff Fenster, 1997; Alan Mintz; Dave
Downey, 1999; John Purkey; Kathy Hughes, 1999; Craig Mont-
gomery, 1999; Don Cobain; Michael Vilt; Lou Ziniewicz-Fisher,
2000; Susie Tennant, 1997; Bob Whittaker; Shivaun O'Brien, 1996;
and Barrett Jones, 2000.

Page 181   "There was graffiti": Cross and Berkenstadt, *Nevermind: Nir-
            vana*, page 58.

Chapter 14: Burn American Flags

Author interviews with Krist Novoselic; Ian Dickson; Danny Goldberg, 2000; Michael Lavine, 1997; Carrie Montgomery; Courtney Love; Dylan Carlson; Slim Moon; John Troutman, 1997; John Rosenfelder, 2000; Mark Kates, 1999; John Gannon, 1999; Dave Markey, 1999; and Alex MacLeod.

Page 186 "I thought she looked like Nancy Spungen": Azerrad, *Come As You Are*, page 169.

Page 189 "Uniformly," Wallace recalled: Cross and Berkenstadt, *Nevermind: Nirvana*, page 97.

Page 196 "The most exciting time for a band": Azerrad, *Come As You Are*, page 187.

Chapter 15: Every Time I Swallowed

Author interviews with Krist Novoselic; Lisa Glatfelter-Bell, 1997; Patrick MacDonald, 1997; Susie Tennant; Jeff Ross, 1997; Bill Reid, 1997; Robert Roth, 1998; Jeff Gilbert, 1998; Kim Warnick, 1998; Jamie Brown, 1997; Scott Cokely; Mary Lou Lord, 1998; Mark Kates; Courtney Love; Marco Collins, 1997; Amy Finnerty, 1999; Peter Davis, 1999; Lori Weinstein, 1998; Rai Sandow, 1998; Tim Devon, 1998; Ashleigh Rafflower, 1999; Craig Montgomery; Carrie Montgomery; Danny Goldberg; Alison Hamamura, 1999; Jim Fouratt, 2000; Jeff Liles, 1999; Gigi Lee, 2000; Darrell Westmoreland, 1997; Kim Cobain; and Steve Shillinger.

Page 212 *The Rocket* review noted: Charles R. Cross, *The Rocket*, November 1991.

Chapter 16: Brush Your Teeth

Author interviews with Courtney Love; Krist Novoselic; Mary Lou Lord; Alex MacLeod; Carolyn Rue, 1988; Carrie Montgomery; Ian Dickson; Nikki McClure; Jerry McCully, 1997; Bill Holdship, 1997; Jeremy Wilson, 1998; Rob Kader; Amy Finnerty; Danny Goldberg;

Bob Zimmerman, 1998; Michael Lavine; Mark Kates; and Kurt St. Thomas, 1999.

Page 214   "That's when we started really": Azerrad, *Come As You Are*, page 205.

Page 219   "This letter is directed more": *Aberdeen Daily World*, November 11, 1991.

Page 221   "They were like clones, glued": "The Power of Love," Dana Kennedy, *Entertainment Weekly*, August 12, 1994.

Page 222   "nodding off occasionally in mid-sentence": "Spontaneous Combustion," Jerry McCully, *BAM*, January 10, 1992.

Page 222   "I'm getting married": Ibid.

Page 228   "My attitude has changed drastically": "Ain't Love Grand," Christina Kelly, *Sassy*, April 1992.

Page 229   "I just want to be situated and secure": Ibid.

Chapter 17: Little Monster Inside

Author interviews with Rosemary Carroll, 2000; Courtney Love; Danny Goldberg; John Gannon; Kim Cobain; Kaz Utsunomiya; Naoko Yamano, 1998; Michie Nakatani, 1998; Atsuko Yamano, 1998; Dylan Carlson; Krist Novoselic; Shelli Novoselic; Barrett Jones; Craig Montgomery; Jennifer Finch; Carolyn Rue; Bob Timmins, 2000; Buddy Arnold, 2000; Sean Tessier, 1998; Tim Appelo, 1998; Mari Earl; Michael Azerrad, 2000; Jackie Farry, 2001; Robert Cruger, 2000; Alan Mintz; Jesse Reed; Alex MacLeod; and Anton Brookes, 2000.

Page 231   "We knew it really wasn't the best": Azerrad, *Come As You Are*, page 245.

Page 233   "My fame. Ha ha. It's a weapon": Poppy Z. Brite, *Courtney Love, the Real Story* (Simon & Schuster, 1997), page 131.

Page 234   "wasn't very high. I just did a little": Azerrad, *Come As You Are*, page 251.

Page 235   "if I quit then, I'd end up doing it again": Ibid., page 255.

Page 240   "I don't even drink anymore": "Inside the Heart and Mind of Kurt Cobain," Michael Azerrad, *Rolling Stone*, April 16, 1992.

Page 241   "[Nirvana's] low profile has renewed": Steve Hochman, *Los Angeles Times*, May 17, 1992.

Page 244   "from nobodies to superstars to fuck-ups": "Love Will Tear Us Apart," Keith Cameron, *NME*, August 29, 1992.

Chapter 18: Rosewater, Diaper Smell

Author interviews with Rosemary Carroll; Courtney Love; Danny Goldberg; Kim Cobain; Neal Hersh, 2000; Anton Brookes; J. J. Gonson; Jackie Farry; Krist Novoselic; Alex MacLeod; Craig Montgomery; Buddy Arnold; Marc Fremont; Amy Finnerty; and Duff McKagan, 2000.

Page 246   "You get out of this bed": Azerrad, *Come As You Are*, page 269.

Page 247   "I'm having the baby": Ibid.

Page 247   "I was so fucking scared": Ibid.

Page 247   "I held this thing in my hand": "Life After Death," David Fricke, *Rolling Stone*, December 15, 1994.

Page 247   "He almost died": Ibid.

Page 260   "I don't want my daughter": "Nirvana's Kurt Cobain," Robert Hilburn, *Los Angeles Times*, September 21, 1992.

Page 260   "We might not go on any more long tours": Ibid.

Chapter 19: That Legendary Divorce

Author interviews with Alex MacLeod; Kim Cobain; Anthony Rhodes, 1999; Mikey Nelson; Don Cobain; Courtney Love; Jeff Mason, 2000; Krist Novoselic; Jim Crotty, 1998; Michael Lane, 1998; Victoria Clarke, 1998; Jackie Farry; Danny Goldberg; Mari Earl; Neal Hersh; Rosemary Carroll; Jesse Reed; Karen

Mason–Blair, 1998; Inger Lorre, 1999; Buddy Arnold; Jack Endino; Michael Azerrad; Charlie Hoselton, 1998; Greg Sage, 1999; Jeff Holmes, 1997; Tim Silbaugh, 1998; Jamie Crunchbird, 1999; Earnie Bailey, 1998; Danny Mangold, and Barrett Jones.

Page 265   "They chased me up to the Castle": Jim Crotty, *Monk #14*, January 1993.

Page 266   "If I ever find myself destitute": Azerrad, *Come As You Are*, page 268.

Page 268   "This whole concept of the man": "Love in the Afternoon," Gillian Gaar, *The Rocket*, November 1992.

Page 268   "We knew we could give": Poneman, *Spin*, December 1992.

Page 270   "It's just amazing that at this point": "The Dark Side of Kurt Cobain," Kevin Allman, *The Advocate*, February 9, 1993.

Page 274   "of which $380,000 went to taxes": Ibid.

Chapter 20: Heart-Shaped Coffin

Author interviews with Krist Novoselic; Alex MacLeod; Courtney Love; Pat Whalen, 1999; Neal Hersh; Jackie Farry; Rosemary Carroll; Ingrid Bernstein, 1998; Kim Cobain; Dylan Carlson; Jessica Hopper, 1998, 1999; Nils Bernstein, 1999; Pare Bernstein, 1999; Neal Karlen, 1998; and Michelle Underwood, 1997.

Page 283   "Geffen and Nirvana's management": Greg Kot, *Chicago Tribune*, April 1993.

Page 284   "symptoms associated with an overdose": This and all police notes that follow are from official Seattle Police Department reports.

Page 288   "a whirling dervish of emotion": "Heaven Can Wait," Gavin Edwards, *Details*, November 1993.

Page 290   "If Freud could hear it, he'd wet his": "Domicile on Cobain St.," Brian Willis, *NME*, July, 24, 1993.

Chapter 21: A Reason to Smile

Author interviews with Courtney Love; Krist Novoselic; Alex MacLeod; Dylan Carlson; Anton Brookes; Craig Montgomery; Jackie Farry; David Yow, 1998; Lori Goldston, 1998; Bob Timmins; Mark Kates; Danny Goldberg; Rosemary Carroll; Sean Slade, 1999; Paul Kolderie, 1999; Robert Roth; Mark Pickerel; Kristie Gamer, 1999; Jim Merlis, 2000; Kim Neely, 1998; Thor Lindsey, 1998; Curt Kirkwood, 1999; Derrick Bostrom, 1999; Amy Finnerty; Jeff Mason; and Janet Billig, 2000.

Page 295   Fremont's son Marc asserted it was suicide: Marc Fremont, *The Doctor Is Out*, unpublished manuscript.

Page 295   "I desperately wanted to have": "Howl," Jon Savage, *The Guardian*, July, 22, 1993.

Page 297   "Cobain ricochets between opposites": "The Band That Hates to Be Loved," Jon Pareles, *New York Times*, November 14, 1993.

Page 301   "I'm glad you could make it": "Kurt Cobain," David Fricke, *Rolling Stone*, January 27, 1994.

Chapter 22: Cobain's Disease

Author interviews with Courtney Love; Krist Novoselic; Jackie Farry; Alex MacLeod; Jim Barber, 2000; Dylan Carlson; Alan Mintz; Danny Goldberg; Amy Finnerty; Alice Wheeler; John Robinson; Dave Markey; Larry Reid, 1998; Rosemary Carroll; Leland Cobain; Don Cobain; Jennifer Adamson, 1999; Jenny Cobain; Shelli Novoselic; Danny Sugerman, 2000; Lexi Robbins, 1999; Bill Baillargeon, 1998; Don Muller; and Buzz Osborne.

Page 312   "It was a fruitful year. Nirvana finished": Letter to *The Advocate*, January 25, 1994.

Page 319   "He hated everything, everybody": Fricke, *Rolling Stone*, December 15, 1994.

Page 321   "He was getting really fed up,": "Kurt Cobain," Steve Dougherty, *People*, April 25, 1994.

Page 323   "I know this is a controlled substance": "Love and Death,"
            Andrew Harrison, *Select*, April 1994.
Page 323   "Even if I wasn't in the mood": Fricke, *Rolling Stone*, De-
            cember 15, 1994.

Chapter 23: Like Hamlet

Author interviews with Courtney Love; Jackie Farry; Krist Novo-
selic; Alex MacLeod; Kim Cobain; Shelli Novoselic; Leland Cobain;
Travis Myers, 2000; Dylan Carlson; Rosemary Carroll; Marc
Geiger, 1998; Ian Dickson; Jennifer Adamson; Danny Goldberg;
Steven Chatoff, 2000; Dr. Louis Cox, 2000; Rob Morfitt, 1999;
Karen Mason-Blair; Buddy Arnold; Mark Kates; and Anton
Brookes.
Page 325   "He *was* dead, legally dead": "The Trials of Love," Robert
            Hilburn, *Los Angeles Times*, April 10, 1994.
Page 326   "in a profession he doesn't have": Claude Iosso, *Aberdeen
            Daily World*, April 11, 1994.
Page 327   "I flipped out": Fricke, *Rolling Stone*, December 15, 1994.
Page 327   "I wish I'd just been the way": Ibid.
Page 335   "I did not even kiss or get to say good-bye": Ibid.

Chapter 24: Angel's Hair

Author interviews with Courtney Love; Krist Novoselic; Dylan
Carlson; Jackie Farry; Alex MacLeod; Michael Meisel, 1999; Gibby
Haynes, 2000; Bob Timmins; Harold Owens, 2000; Buddy Arnold;
Nial Stimson, 2000; Harold Owens, 1999; Joe "Mama" Nitzburg,
2000; Duff McKagan; Jessica Hopper; Ginny Heller, 1999; Bret
Chatalas, 1999; Jennifer Adamson; Rosemary Carroll; and Danny
Goldberg. The events of Kurt's final hours are pieced together from
police reports, forensic evidence reports, and pictures of the scene.
Page 347   "I know this should be the happiest": Hilburn, *Los Angeles
            Times*, April 10, 1994.

Epilogue: A Leonard Cohen Afterworld

Author interviews with Courtney Love; Marty Riemer, 1998; Mike
West, 1998; Kim Cobain; Don Cobain; Leland Cobain; Jenny Co-
bain; Jackie Farry; Rosemary Carroll; Tom Reese, 1998; Nikolas
Hartshorne, 1999; Dave Sterling, 1998; Sharon Seldon, 1999; James
Kirk, 1994; Jeff Mason; Alan Mitchel, 1999; Gene Stout, 1998; Dan
Raley, 1998; Cynthia Land, 1998; Krist Novoselic; Susan Silver;
Rev. Stephen Towles, 2000; Bob Hunter; Alice Wheeler; Tracy
Marander; Dylan Carlson; Danny Goldberg; Janet Billig; and Leland
Cobain.

Page 356   "I saw this body laying there on the floor": *The Seattle Post-
Intelligencer*, April 9, 1994.

ACKNOWLEDGMENTS

Writing a book of this length is a task that by its nature is a solitary endeavor, yet one that can't be accomplished without the help and assistance of interview subjects, friends, and family. My greatest thanks goes to Kurt Cobain's friends and family, who took time out of their lives to sit for multiple interviews, which on many occasions took up entire days. A book of this scope would not have been possible without their trust and commitment to this story and this author. Additionally, there were dozens of people who provided me with documents, recordings, photographs, permissions, research assistance, and advice, and whose names do not appear in the text. The following are some of the many people who gave me assistance in this process and without whose help this book would not have been possible: Joe Adkins, Shannon Aldrich, Joel Amsterdam, Joris Baas, Stephanie Ballasiotes, Paula Balzer, Jim Barber, Jennifer Barth, Ryan Teague Beckwith, Jenny Bendel, Jim Berkenstadt, Peter Blecha, Janet Billig, Jeff Burlingame, Rose Burnett, Tom Butterworth, Blaine Cartwright, John Chandler, Maura Cronin, Bettie Cross, Cathy Cross, Herb Cross, Nick Cua, Dennee Dekay, Adam DeLoach, David Desantis, Don Desantis, Dwayne DeWitt, Gail Fine, Rick Friel, Deborah Frost, Gillian Gaar, Cam Garrett, Kennedy Grey, Fred Goodman, Nancy Guppy, Joe Hadlock, Manny Hadlock,

Heather Hansen, Daniel Harris, Teresa Heacock, Louise Helton, Angela Herlihy, Bill Holdship, Rasmus Holmen, Pete Howard, Josh Jacobson, Larry Jacobson, Miro Jungum, John Keister, Sharon Knolle, John Kohl, Mary Kohl, Ed Kosinski, Thirza Krohn, Robin Laananen, Michael Lavine, Lauren Lazin, Brandon Lieberman, James Lindley, Amy Lombardi, Ben London, Courtney Love, Alison Lowenstein, Cathy Maesk, Tracy Marander, Benoit Martigny, Cindy May, Jeannie McGuire, Carmen Medal, Michael Meisel, Lauren Mills, Richard Milne, Sandy Milne, Curtis Minato, Teresa Parks, Nina Pearlman, Peter Philbin, Marietta Phillips, Rebecca Polinsky, Jonathan Pont, Holly Cara Price, Bernie Ranellone, Rozz Rezabek-Wright, Patrick Robinson, the staff of *The Rocket* magazine (1979–2000), Phil Rose, Melissa Rossi, Rex Rystedt, Gihan Salem, Robert Santelli, Kristin Schroter, Mary Schuh, Arlen Schumer, Jill Seipel, Deborah Semer, Clint Shinkle, Eric Shinkle, Martha Shinkle, Neal Shinkle, Neal Skok, Matt Smith, Kurt St. Thomas, Denise Sullivan, Sharrin Summers, Carrie Svingen, Susie Tennant, Alison Thorne, Brad Tolinski, Mitch Tuefel, Jaan Uhelszki, Andrew Uhlemann, Josh Van Camp, Alice Wheeler, Drew Whittemore, David Wilkins, Kendall Williams, Mike Ziegler, and Bob Zimmerman.

There were also dozens of Nirvana fans who generously loaned me materials and recordings that weren't already in my collection. My e-mail contact for any sources with additional information is charlesrcross@aol.com and any addendum to this manuscript will be posted on www.charlesrcross.com.

I wish to thank Pam Wilson-Ehrbar for her help in transcribing many of my interviews conducted for this book. Sarah Lazin was essential in seeing this book through, over the course of several years, from conception to completion. Peternelle van Arsdale went beyond the call of her duty in working on this project and being an advocate for me. Several colleagues took the time to read or listen to the manuscript in progress, and for that I owe special thanks to Carla Desantis, Joe Ehrbar, Erik Flannigan, Joe Guppy, John Keister, Carl Miller, Chris Phillips, Christina Shinkle, Adem Tepedelen, and my son Ashland.

I particularly wish to acknowledge the musicians who made the records

I listened to as a teenager—especially those who allowed the Columbia Record and Tape Club to license their albums—and those who create the music that continues to make me feel that teen spirit once again.

—*Charles R. Cross*
April 2001

INDEX

NATIONAL BESTSELLER

"Funny, poignant, provocative and sometimes disturbing."

—Seattle Post-Intelligencer

"A revelation…an excellent portrait, probably unbeatable both for its moving depiction of his youth and thrilling rise to fame and for its myth-busting finality."

—Los Angeles Times Book Review

"The perfect nostalgia item…Mr. Cross's detailed, engrossing book makes the memory of Hendrix even stronger."

—The New York Times